History of Structuralism
Volume 1

History of Structuralism

Volume 1: The Rising Sign, 1945–1966

François Dosse

Translated by Deborah Glassman

University of Minnesota Press
Minneapolis
London

The University of Minnesota Press gratefully acknowledges financial assistance provided by the French Ministry of Culture for the translation of this book.

Originally published as *Histoire du structuralisme*, I. *Le champ du signe, 1945–1966*. Copyright Éditions La Découverte, Paris, 1991.

Published by the University of Minnesota Press
111 Third Avenue South, Suite 290, Minneapolis, MN 55401–2520
Printed in the United States of America on acid-free paper

Library of Congress Cataloging-in-Publication Data

Dosse, François, 1950–
    [Histoire du structuralisme. English]
    History of structuralism / François Dosse ; translated by Deborah Glassman.
      p. cm.
    Includes bibliographical references and index.
    Contents: v. 1. The rising sign, 1945–1966—v. 2. The sign sets, 1967–present.
    ISBN 0-8166-2239-6 (v. 1 : hc : alk. paper).—ISBN 0-8166-2241-8 (v. 1 : pbk. : alk. paper).—ISBN 0-8166-2370-8 (v. 2 : hc : alk. paper).—ISBN 0-8166-2371-6 (v. 2 : pbk. : alk. paper).—ISBN 0-8166-2240-X (set : hc : alk. paper).—ISBN 0-8166-2254-X (set : pbk. : alk. paper)
    1. Structuralism—History. I. Title.
B841.4.D6713   1997
149'.96'09—dc21
                                   96-51477

The University of Minnesota is an equal-opportunity educator and employer.

To Florence, Antoine, Chloé, and Aurélien

Structuralism is not a new method, it is the awakened and troubled consciousness of modern thought.

Michel Foucault

Contents

Translator's Preface

François Dosse's *History of Structuralism* has created quite a stir since its publication in 1991. This book, written by a historian, weaves together a rich range of materials—interviews, books, journals, newspaper articles and television programs, disciplinary histories and contemporary contexts—to produce a densely saturated and highly readable account of a productive, prolific, and energetic moment in French intellectual life when the social sciences exploded and a new paradigm arose.

Because the question of whether such a history is possible, and indeed whether structuralism was itself a movement whose history can be written, Dosse rightly claims the Frenchness of the phenomenon and lays out, with varying intensity, the roles played by the major contributors to the phenomenon, the pioneers present at the "structuralist banquet," and their students or other participants. He looks at their works, strategies, institutions, and instruments invested in the effort to establish institutional legitimation in an academic setting governed by the venerable Sorbonne and the classical humanities, which were more than reticent about any theoretical reinvigoration.

If Dosse is right to insist on the Frenchness of structuralism, our interest in this history is even greater on this side of the Atlantic, where structuralism left an indelible mark on American universities, particularly in French departments. Minor mirror struggles were waged between the ancients and the moderns, between purveyors of literary history and philology and those more textually bound readers attuned to the subtle nuances of language and more readily at home in this new, semiological, adventure. And much to the consternation of more traditional humanists, history and context were largely left to other disciplines as the enthusiasm of a new perspective caught the imagination of a younger generation. Other humanities have been invigorated by the energies of the structural approach—art history, comparative literature, literature, cinema studies—as have been, if to a lesser degree, the social sciences, which were already better anchored in American universities than they were in parallel French institutions during the fifties, sixties, and seventies.

More than an approach to reading has changed. Structuralism has brought with it—or is already a piece of that larger movement of which we are now struggling to take the measure—a shift in perspective that listens to many whose voices have long been stifled, assigned to what Foucault calls the underbelly of reason, the place to which reason consigns its nether side. The repressed of history in their singular manifestations and in the major manifestations of social life attracted all the pioneers of structuralism—Saussure, Foucault, Althusser, Lévi-Strauss, Lacan, Barthes. Even as they looked to scientific knowledge as an ideal in their polemical engagement with the institutions that resisted the presence of these new disciplines, these early structuralists sought out the unconscious structures and logics apparent in language, madness, social relations, neurosis, and myth. Structuralism was therefore a movement that in large measure reversed the eighteenth-century celebration of Reason, the credo of the Lumières, a movement whose multiple threads and echoes in the works, work, and lives of the major players and on the disciplines shaped our vision of a world. A vision that can never be the same after structuralism, argues François Dosse.

Volume 1, *The Rising Sign*, covers the first years of the structuralist phenomenon, ending in 1966, a crowning year for structuralism. Volume 2 chronicles the waning years of the phenomenon.

François Dosse is a lively writer whose verve drives his verb. I have tried to let this energy inform the translation, even if it is generally impossible to reproduce the puns, alliterations, and rhythms of his writing. Many longer sentences were shortened; but if clarity has often sobered style, the consolation might be that English readers can fully appreciate the immense efforts involved in bringing together so many pieces of the paradigm.

The question of citations and bibliography has been a vexing one. All titles mentioned in the text have been rendered into English; the original French title is given in a note. Where well-known titles are mentioned in passing without any reference to specific citations or bibliographical adumbration (Sartre's *Being and Nothingness*, for example), there is no accompanying note.

The case of citations is somewhat more complicated. I have quoted extant translations of those authors for whom something resembling standard translations exist—Nietzsche, Foucault, Lacan, Lévi-Strauss. In the case of ambiguities or variations (where the English translation varies from the French original, is incomplete, or realigns volumes, for example), I have indicated the original source and given my own translation. For works where no standard translation exists or where I had no access to one, I have provided my own translations and given the original source in the note. In the Appendix, the reader will find a list of interviewees and their institutional affiliations.

Acknowledgments

I would like to thank all those who were kind enough to agree to be interviewed. These interviews were entirely transcribed and their contribution was absolutely fundamental to the project of writing this history of French intellectual life. The specifics of the area and current affiliation of each of the interviewees are to be found in the Appendix.

Marc Abélès, Alfred Adler, Michel Aglietta, Jean Allouch, Pierre Ansart, Michel Arrivé, Marc Augé, Sylvain Auroux, Kostas Axelos, Georges Balandier, Étienne Balibar, Henri Bartoli, Michel Beaud, Daniel Becquemont, Jean-Marie Benoist, Alain Boissinot, Raymond Boudon, Jacques Bouveresse, Claude Brémond, Hubert Brochier, Louis-Jean Calvet, Jean-Claude Chevalier, Jean Clavreul, Claude Conté, Jean-Claude Coquet, Maria Daraki, Jean-Toussaint Desanti, Philippe Descola, Vincent Descombes, Jean-Marie Dolmenach, Joël Dor, Daniel Dory, Roger-Pol Droit, Jean Dubois, Georges Duby, Oswald Ducrot, Claude Dumézil, Jean Duvignaud, Roger Establet, François Ewald, Arlette Farge, Jean-Pierre Faye, Pierre Fougeyrollas, Françoise Gadet, Marcel Gauchet, Gérard Genette, Jean-Christophe Goddard, Maurice Godelier, Gilles Gaston-Granger, Wladimir Granoff, André Green, Algirdas Julien Greimas, Marc Guillaume, Claude Hagège, Philippe Hamon, André-Georges Haudricourt, Louis Hay, Paul Henry, Françoise Héritier-Augé, Jacques Hoarau, Michel Izard, Jean-Luc Jamard, Jean Jamin, Julia Kristeva, Bernard Laks, Jérôme Lallement, Jean Laplanche, Francine Le Bret, Serge Leclaire, Dominique Lecourt, Henri

Lefebvre, Pierre Legendre, Gennie Lemoine, Claude Lévi-Strauss, Jacques Lévy, Alain Lipietz, René Lourau, Pierre Macherey, René Major, Serge Martin, André Martinet, Claude Meillassoux, Charles Melman, Gérard Mendel, Henri Mitterand, Juan-David Nasio, André Nicolaï, Pierra Nora, Claudine Normand, Bertrand Ogilvie, Michelle Perrot, Marcelin Pleynet, Jean Pouillon, Joëlle Proust, Jacques Rancière, Alain Renaut, Olivier Revault d'Allonnes, Élisabeth Roudinesco, Nicolas Ruwet, Moustafa Safouan, Georges-Elia Sarfati, Bernard Sichère, Dan Sperber, Joseph Sumpf, Emmanuel Terray, Tzvetan Todorov, Alain Touraine, Paul Valadier, Jean-Pierre Vernant, Marc Vernet, Serge Viderman, Pierre Vilar, François Wall, Marina Yaguello.

Others were contacted but were not interviewed: Didier Anzieu, Alain Badiou, Christian Baudelot, Jean Baudrillard, Pierre Bourdieu, Georges Canguilhem, Cornelius Castoriadis, Hélène Cixous, Serge Cotte, Antoine Culioli, Gilles Deleuze, Jacques Derrida, Louis Dumont, Julien Freund, Luce Irigaray, Francis Jacques, Christian Jambet, Catherine Kerbrat-Oreccioni, Victor Karady, Serge-Christophe Kolm, Claude Lefort, Philippe Lejeune, Emmanuel Levinas, Jean-François Lyotard, Gérard Miller, Jacques-Alain Miller, Jean-Claude Milner, Edgar Morin, Thérèse Parisot, Jean-Claude Passeron, Jean-Bertrand Pontalis, Paul Ricoeur, Jacqueline de Romilly, François Roustang, Michel Serres, Louis-Vincent Thomas.

I would also like to thank all of those whose difficult task it was to read this manuscript in its early stages and whose comments and suggestions made it possible for me to carry out this undertaking: Daniel and Trudi Becquemont, Alain Boissont, René Gelly, François Gèze, and Thierry Paquot.

Lastly, for having given me the print runs of a certain number of works of the period, I would like to thank Monique Lulin at Éditions du Seuil, Pierre Nora at Éditions Gallimard, and Christine Silva at Éditions La Découverte.

Introduction

Structuralism's success in France during the 1950s and 1960s is without precedent in the history of the intellectual life of this country. There was such widespread support for structuralism among most of the intelligentsia that the resistance and minor objections put forth during what we can call the structuralist moment were simply moot. We can better understand how so many intellectuals could be at home in the same program if we understand the context. There were two fundamental reasons for this spectacular success. First, structuralism promised a rigorous method and some hope for making decisive progress toward scientificity. But even more fundamentally, it was a particular moment in the history of thought, which we can characterize as a key moment of critical consciousness; for the structuralist program attracted a particularly broad range of enthusiasts, including the trainer of the national football team who, in the sixties, announced a "structuralist" reorganization of his team in order to win more games.

The triumph of the structuralist paradigm is therefore first of all the product of a particular historical context, characterized since the end of the nineteenth century, and particularly since 1945, by the West's progressive slide toward what Lévi-Strauss called a cooler temporality. But it is also the product of the remarkable growth in the social sciences, which ran up against the hegemony of the aged Sorbonne, bearer of scholarly legitimacy and dispenser of the classical humanities. The structuralist program was a veritable unconscious strategy to move beyond the academicism in power, and it served the twofold purposes of contestation and counterculture. In the academic realm, the structural paradigm successfully cleared the ground for proscribed knowledge that had long been kept at bay, in the margins of the canonical institutions.

Structuralism was contestatory and corresponded to a particular moment in Western history. It expressed a certain degree of self-hatred, of the rejection of traditional Western culture, and of a desire for modernism in search of new models. Antique values were no longer glorified; structuralism demonstrated an extreme sensitivity to everything that had been repressed in Western history. Indeed, it is no accident that the two leading sciences of the period—anthropology and psychoanalysis—privilege the unconscious, the nether side of manifest meaning, the inaccessible repressed of Western history.

The structuralist period was also a time when linguistics was a pilot science guiding the steps of the social sciences as a whole toward scientificity. In this respect, structuralism was the banner of the moderns in their struggle against the ancients. As the disillusionment of the second half of the twentieth century grew, structuralism also became an instrument of de-ideologization for many politically committed intellectuals. A specific political moment characterized by disenchantment and a particular configuration of knowledge requiring a revolution in order to successfully carry through a reform made it possible for structuralism to become the rallying point for an entire generation. This generation discovered the world behind the structural grid.

The important quest for a solution to existential confusion produced a tendency to ontologize structure that, in the name of Science and Theory, became an alternative to traditional Western metaphysics. Ambitions were boundless during this period in which boundaries were being redefined and the limits of imposed figures extended. Many struck out along the newest paths opened up by the flowering of the social sciences.

Suddenly, however, everything changed. Tragedy struck structuralism at the beginning of the eighties. In the same fell swoop, most of the French heroes of this international epic left the stage of the living, as if the theoreticians of the end of humanity had all allowed themselves to be carried off simultaneously in a spectacular death. Nicos Poulantzas killed himself by leaping from his window on October 3, 1979, just after having justified his refusal to betray Pierre

Goldmann; his suicide was concrete punishment for a purely imaginary crime. After lunching with Jacques Berques and François Mitterrand, then chairman of the Socialist Party, Roland Barthes was run down by a dry cleaner's truck on the rue des Écoles. Barthes suffered only a slight cranial trauma, but, according to the witnesses who visited him at the Pitié-Salpêtrière Hospital, he let himself decline, and died on March 26, 1980. During the night of November 16, 1980, Louis Althusser strangled his faithful wife, Helen. The eminent representative of the most rigorous rationalism was judged not to be responsible for his act, and was hospitalized at Sainte-Anne, a Parisian psychiatric hospital, before being admitted to a private clinic in the Paris area, thanks to the help of his former philosophy teacher, Jean Guitton. The man of words, the great shaman of modern times, Jacques Lacan, died on September 9, 1981, aphasic. Barely a few years went by before the ill wind of death carried off Michel Foucault. At the height of his popularity and completely immersed in his work on a history of sexuality, Foucault was struck with the new scourge of the century, AIDS. He died on June 25, 1984.

So many dramatic and proximate deaths reinforced the impression of the end of an era. Some went so far as to theorize the coincidence of these tragedies as the revelation of the impasse of a common way of thinking popularly called structuralism. In this view, the break between speculative thinking and the real world leads to self-destruction. Such a juxtaposition is even more artificial than the mediatized glorification of the sixties, when the structuralist banquet rose to the heights of its glory, and along with it, the four musketeers, who were five at the time: Michel Foucault, Louis Althusser, Roland Barthes, Jacques Lacan, and their common father, Claude Lévi-Strauss.

This collective shipwreck nonetheless remains a milestone on the French intellectual landscape. The disappearance of the master thinkers, and Jean-Paul Sartre must be counted among them, opened up a new period of doubt. Nostalgia was already in the air at the beginning of the 1980s, when it was fashionable to evoke these figures with an ambivalent mixture of awe and fascination heightened by their unusual fates, which had transformed them into something resembling heroes. While some took pleasure in signing the death certificate of structuralism, the body was still alive and kicking hard, according to the survey published in *Lire* in April 1981. When hundreds of writers, journalists, professors, students, and politicians were asked,

"Who are the three living intellectuals of the French language whose work seems to you to have the greatest and most profound influence on philosophy, letters, arts, and sciences, etc.?" they answered: Claude Lévi-Strauss (101), Raymond Aron (84), Michel Foucault (83), and Jacques Lacan (51).

The concept of structuralism has stirred as much enthusiasm as opprobrium. From the Latin *struere*, derived from *structura*, the term "structure" initially had an architectural meaning. Structure designated "the manner in which a building is constructed" (*Trévoux Dictionary* [1771]). In the seventeenth and eighteenth centuries, the meaning was modified and broadened by analogy to include living creatures. Fontenelle saw the human body as a construction; Vaugelas and Bernot saw language as a construction. The term came to describe the way in which the parts of a concrete being are structured into a whole, and it could apply to a variety of structures—anatomical, psychological, geological, mathematical. It was only later that the structural approach appropriated the social sciences. For Spencer, Morgan, and Marx, the term described an enduring phenomenon linking the parts of a whole together, in a complex manner, and in a more abstract way. The term "structure"—nowhere to be found in Hegel and only infrequently in Marx, with the exception of the preface to the *Critique of Political Economy* (1859)—was established in 1895 by Durkheim, in *The Rules of Sociological Method*. Between 1900 and 1926, structure gave birth to *structuralism*, which André Lalande, in his *Vocabulaire*, calls a neologism. For psychologists, structuralism is born at the beginning of the century, by opposition to functional psychology. But the true origins of the practice, in its modern sense, and on the scale of all the human sciences, comes from developments in the field of linguistics. Saussure used the term "structure" only three times in his *Course on General Linguistics*. Later, the Prague school (Trubetzkoy and Jakobson) generalized the use of the terms "structure" and "structuralism." The Danish linguist Hjelmslev claimed to make reference to the term "structuralism" as a founding program, a tendency made explicit by his activity. In 1939, he founded the review *Acta linguistica,* and its first article addressed "structural linguistics." From this linguistic kernel, the term produced a veritable revolution in all the social sciences that were at the core of the twentieth century, and each in its turn believed that it received a scientific baptism.

Miracle or mirage? The history of science is nothing more, after all, than the history of the graveyard of its theories. This is not at all to say that each of the stages left behind is no longer effective, but simply that any program loses its productivity and necessarily undergoes methodological renewal. With structuralism, however, the changes risked falling into the same traps that the previous method had avoided. Whence the necessity of illuminating the richness and productivity of structuralism before seizing upon its limits. This is the adventure that we will undertake here. Notwithstanding the dead ends into which structuralism has run on occasion, it has changed the way we consider human society so much that it is no longer even possible to think without taking the structuralist revolution into account.

The structuralist moment is a piece of our intellectual history that opened up a particularly fertile period of research in the social sciences. Reconstructing its history is complicated because the contours of the "structuralist" reference are particularly vague. In order to understand the principal positions of the period, we have to reconstruct its many methods and personalities, while at the same time, and without being reductionist about it, seeking some coherent centers. Beyond the multiplicity of objects and disciplines, these centers reveal the matrix of a procedure. Different levels are to be sorted out and the many structuralisms underlying the term "structuralist" differentiated. We can clarify the fundamental intellectual issues, which are as theoretical as they are disciplinary, and explore the wealth of individual trajectories, which cannot be summed up in a group history. As it presents the contingencies of fortuitous but essential meetings, this history proposes to amalgamate bodies and bring many explanatory factors to bear without in any way reducing them to any single causality.

The social sciences appropriated structuralism in a number of ways. But beyond the interplay of borrowed ideas, analogies, and a contiguity that we will be obliged to sketch out, as Barthes counseled the future historians of structuralism to do, we can make a distinction that does not coincide with disciplinary boundaries. Scientistic structuralism is represented in particular by Claude Lévi-Strauss, Algirdas Julien Greimas, and Jacques Lacan, and simultaneously involved anthropology, semiotics, and psychoanalysis. Contiguous with this search for the Law was a more supple, undulating, and shimmering structuralism to be found particularly in the work of Roland Barthes, Gérard Genette, Tzvetan Todorov, and Michel Serres, and which we might call semiological structuralism. There is also, finally, a historicized or epistemic structuralism. The work of Louis Althusser, Pierre Bourdieu, Michel Foucault, Jacques Derrida, Jean-Pierre Vernant, and, more broadly, the third generation of the *Annales* falls into this group. Beyond these distinctions, however, we can identify a community of language and goals that sometimes gives the impression that we are reading the same book despite the variations in style and discipline that distinguish a Barthes from a Foucault, a Derrida, or a Lacan. Structuralism was the *koine* of an entire intellectual generation, even if there is no doctrinal solidarity and even less a school or a battle among its various representatives.

It is no less difficult to reconstruct the history of this moment than it is to periodize the structuralist moment. The fifties clearly saw an irresistible increase in structural phenomena that in the sixties became a veritable structuralist mode that most intellectuals adopted. Until 1966, structuralism was in an ascending phase and its growth seemed unstoppable. The year 1966 is a central point of reference. This was the year structuralist activity beamed forth most forcefully in intellectual life and the intensity of the mixture of a universe of signs shone forth beyond all established disciplinary frontiers. Nineteen sixty-seven, however, saw the beginning of the ebb, of criticisms, of distantiation from the structuralist phenomenon, which was everywhere showered with praise by the press. If the ebb was latent in 1967, it began before 1968, when the four musketeers endlessly took their distance from the structuralist phenomenon.

There was another temporality, however, that was less affected by changes in intellectual fashion. University research continued to thrive even as the body was about to be buried. This research was like so many wellsprings of a program that had lost in media glamour what it had gained in pedagogical effectiveness. Not that there was a single academic temporality, for there are always numerous lag times among the humanistic disciplines. For linguistics, sociology, anthropology, or psychoanalysis, for example, structuralism offered an adaptable scientific model. Other disciplines, which were better rooted in the university and better sheltered from epistemological turbulences, such as history, would only be transformed later, and adopt the structuralist program at the moment when its wane was becoming general. Temporal lags and disciplinary uncertainties in these intellectual exchange games notwithstanding, structuralism made many conversations possible, multiplied the numbers of fruitful colloquia, generated much research, and sparked an interest in the work and progress of related disciplines. This was an intense period enlivened by thinkers who were seeking, in the main, to harmonize their research and their lives. Our vision of the world is still shaped by this veritable revolution.

Some call ours the *era of emptiness* and others call it *postmodern*; in either case it invites an approach to man in which a binary opposition, every bit as illusory, is played out between the human dissolution proferred by structuralism, and in reaction, the divinization of man. Man the creator, beyond the constraints of his time, is a mirror image of the death of man. Humanity, the lost paradigm of the structural approach, burst forth again in its narcissistic image of the era of the pre-social sciences. The great structural wave carried the social sciences toward shores on which historicity was a stranger. But we are at an important turning point, expressed as a return to an ancient form of writing in the name of a decline in thinking, a loss of values, and a reliance upon our heritage. The old sawhorses are back: the discreet charms of a Vidalian landscape, the heroes of Lavissian history, the masterpieces of the national literary patrimony in Lagarde and Michard. Beyond this return to a very particular nineteenth century is a particular eighteenth-century vision of man perceived as an abstraction, free from temporal constraints and master of the legal-political system bodying forth his rationalism.

Can we, however, reflect upon man as if the Copernican-Galilean revolution, the Freudian and Marxist fractures, and the progress of the social sciences had not taken place? Pointing out the shortcomings of structuralism does not imply returning to the golden age of the Enlightenment. To the contrary, it means moving forward toward a future in which a historical humanism can be established. It is important that the false convictions and the true dogmatisms as well as the reductionist and mechanistic procedures be clearly pointed out, and the validity of transversal concepts used across disciplines by the social sciences questioned. Not in order to establish a catchall procedure or a shapeless flow, but to wrest from the Brownian motion the prolegomena of a science of man wrought from a certain number of concepts and operational structuring levels.

We call upon the advances made in the social sciences to answer to the emergence of a humanism of the possible, perhaps around the transitory figure of a dialogic man. Moving beyond structuralism requires returning to it in order to examine the method that was broadly adopted by all the social sciences, sketching out the stages of its hegemonic conquest, valorizing the processes that made it possible for a single method to be adopted by the many humanistic disciplines, and understanding the limits and impasses in which the vitality of this attempted renewal waned.

In order to give an account of this French intellectual chapter of the fifties and sixties, we have asked authors and disciples to comment upon the major works of the period; members of other schools and supporters of other trends have also been asked to cast a critical eye upon these works. A great many interviews with philosophers, linguists, sociologists, historians, anthropologists, psychoanalysts, and economists have been incorporated into these pages, and they raise the question of structuralism's importance for their own work and research, and the ways of moving beyond it. This two-volume inquiry reveals the centrality of the structuralist phenomenon, despite and beyond the diversity of viewpoints, and makes it possible to periodize.*

That form of criticism that tries to go ever further in deconstructing Western metaphysics and penetrating the fissure in the foundations of semiology, to empty out every signified and all meaning so that the pure Signifer can circulate more effectively, belongs to a moment in the Western history of self-hate that we have left behind, thanks to a progressive reconciliation between the intelligentsia and democratic values. But it is not possible, in moving beyond a period denominated by the critical paradigm, to simply return to what preceded. A return is nonetheless necessary in order to better understand this period whose contributions have irrevocably changed our understanding of humankind.

---

*This inquiry is organized in two volumes, corresponding to the two major phases of the structuralist adventure: the ascension (vol. 1, *The Rising Sign, 1945–1966*), and the decline (vol. 2, *The Sign Sets, 1967–Present*).

Part I

The Fifties: The Epic Epoch

One

The Eclipse of a Star: Jean-Paul Sartre

The law of tragedy requires a death before a new hero can come on-stage. The reign of structuralism required a death, therefore, and the death was that of the postwar intellectual tutelary figure, Jean-Paul Sartre. Since Liberation, Sartre had had an exceptional following as he brought philosophy to the streets. But from the streets, slowly, began to echo the persistent rumor of new themes. The rising generation would slowly but surely cast Sartre to the sidelines.

Sartre experienced a series of interpersonal breaks during the decisive decade of what was later called the structuralist phenomenon, and these were as painful as they were dramatic for him. With the years, Sartre was increasingly isolated despite his undiminished popularity with the public. He was partly responsible for his painful eclipse because of his own desire to erase the years of his apoliticism and blindness. During the thirties and despite the rising horrors of Nazism, Sartre had remained true to the long-standing *khâgne*[1] tradition of remaining closed off from the world outside, of remaining deaf and dumb, inattentive and indifferent to the social struggles going on around him. His own personal history came back to poison him after the war, and he tried to compensate by closely allying himself with the French Communist Party (PCF) in 1952, at the height of the Cold War, a time when an entire generation of intellectuals was beginning to leave the party because of the ongoing revelations about Stalinism in the Soviet Union. The grand unity that had reigned at the time of the Democratic Revolutionary Union and that, on December 13, 1948, saw André Breton, Albert Camus, David Rousset, Jean-Paul Sartre, and many other intellectuals[2] come together in the same concert hall (Salle Pleyel) around the theme "Internationalism of the Mind" fell apart.

This was the beginning of a number of breaks for Sartre. Cold War disturbances were to affect the team of *Les Temps modernes* and Sartre would pay dearly for "Don't let Billancourt despair!"[3] In 1953, in a bitter polemic, he let Claude Lefort, a linchpin in his editorial team, leave the review.[4] Two other important breaks followed. The first was with Camus and then Etiemble, and the second with Maurice Merleau-Ponty, one of Sartre's closest friends and one of the founding members of the editorial board of *Les Temps modernes*. The Sartre-Merleau-Ponty relationship had been so harmonious until that point that the two men "were even, briefly, practically interchangeable."[5] But in the summer of 1952, Merleau-Ponty left *Les Temps modernes* and shortly thereafter, in 1955, he published *The Adventures of the Dialectic* in which he denounced Sartre's ultra-Bolshevist tendencies.

Other adventures were to unfold without Sartre, but the younger generation continued to be fascinated with him. Régis Debray writes that "for many of us in my high school in the fifties, *Being and Nothingness* quickened our pulse."[6] Yet Existentialism came under fire. The oratory joust pitting Sartre against Althusser at the École Normale Supérieure (ENS) on the rue d'Ulm[7] in 1960, at which Jean Hyppolite, Georges Canguilhem, and Maurice Merleau-Ponty were in attendance, ended, according to Debray, who was preparing his philosophy *agrégation*[8] at the time, in favor of Louis Althusser. Despite his glory, Sartre came to represent outmoded values and to incarnate the disappointed hopes of the Liberation. This unshakable image would cling to him and he would be its first victim.

The Sartrean star was eclipsed because of political issues, but it was also affected by what was beginning to take shape in the intellectual world. The rise of social sciences was forcing the issue of an institutional existence, so there needed to be a middle ground between the traditional humanities, primarily literature, and the hard sciences. As a result, questions were being asked differently and Sartre, faithful to his position as a philosopher and absorbed in making up for his political past, was left behind. His status as philosopher had warranted thanks and recognition, but he remained a foreigner to the changes taking place. If Sartre asked *What Is Literature?* in 1948, it was in order to dwell on the relationship between an author, the reasons for writing, and the public. The existence of literature and its singularity were givens for him. But by the end of the fifties, this assumption came under question and was contested.

The collapse of the tutelary figure that Sartre incarnated created a moment of uncertainty and doubt regarding philosophers who turned to the ascending social sciences to sharpen their critical questioning. Sartrean man exists only by virtue of the intentionality of his conscious mind; he is condemned to freedom because "existence precedes essence," and only alienation and bad faith clutter the paths of freedom. Roland Barthes, for example, who defined himself as a Sartrean immediately following the war, progressively abandoned this philosophy in order to fully embark upon the structuralist adventure. Existentialism, as a philosophy of subjectivity and of the subject, came under attack and the subject and conscience gave way to rules, codes, and structure.

Jean Pouillon: The Man of the Middle Ground

One figure symbolized both this evolution and an attempt to reconcile apparent contradictions: Jean Pouillon. He was Sartre's intimate friend and became the sole link between *Les Temps modernes* and *L'Homme*, which is to say between Sartre and Claude Lévi-Strauss. Jean Pouillon had met Sartre very early on, in 1937, and the two men were to enjoy an untroubled friendship to the end, despite their different intellectual paths. Pouillon's career was unusual, to say the least.

> I had been a philosophy professor during the war and then, in 1945, Sartre asked me: Do you like doing philosophy? I answered that I enjoyed clowning in front of a class but the problem was the homework, which had to be corrected, and the low salary. So he told me to go and see a friend of his from Normale Supérieure who had discovered something that still exists, the analytic report of the National Assembly. Given the separation of powers, the legislature was particularly generous in approving the budget of its own administration, which was better paid than were teachers and usually had six months' vacation a year. I took the test and at the same time I was doing what I wanted to be doing, writing for *Les Temps modernes*. It was doubtless because of that that Claude Lévi-Strauss asked me to join the team at *L'Homme* in 1960; I was not on a career path, I threatened no one, and no one was jealous of me.[9]

At that point, Jean Pouillon knew nothing at all about ethnology. But when *Tristes Tropiques* was published in 1955, Sartre liked the book and asked Pouillon, as a member of the editorial board of *Les Temps modernes*, to review it. "Why not you?" But rather than simply writing up a review acclaiming the book, Pouillon decided to take things a step further and undertook an in-depth study of the evolution of Claude Lévi-Strauss's thinking, and not just of its culmination in *Tristes Tropiques*. He therefore read everything that Lévi-Strauss had published, including *The Elementary Structures of Kinship* and the articles that were to be published in 1958 as *Structural Anthropology*. More than a simple inventory, Pouillon tried to evaluate Lévi-Strauss's work and, in 1956, he published his article in *Les Temps modernes* entitled "L'œuvre de Claude Lévi-Strauss."[10]

What had at first seemed to be a gratuitous detour or exotic adventure in foreign climes became, for Pouillon and for an entire generation, a lifelong engagement, an existence turned toward new and more anthropological questions, and an abandonment of classical philosophy. Pouillon discovered the investigation of alterity: "It is as essentially other that the other must be seen."[11] He joined in the structuralist enterprise, which goes beyond empiricism, description, and lived experience. For Pouillon, Claude Lévi-Strauss provided a rigorous model allowing the logical construction of "mathematizable relationships."[12] Pouillon completely supported Lévi-Strauss's priority of the linguistic model in order to move beyond the scoria of the narrow relationship between observer and observed: "Durkheim used to say that social facts had to be treated like things. . . . To paraphrase Durkheim, therefore, we must treat them like words."[13]

In the mid-fifties, then, we witness a veritable conversion, with this small reservation that Jean Pouillon adopted Claude Lefort's arguments regarding Lévi-Strauss's relegation of historicity to a secondary position. Here he remained faithful to Sartre's positions on the historical dialectic, opposing the diachronic logic of a bridge game to the synchronic logic of a chess game. But his double allegiance to structuralism and to anthropology was absolute, and from this point on Jean Pouillon attended Claude Lévi-Strauss's seminars at the Fifth Section of the École Pratique des Hautes Études.[14] A book review led to a choice about existence and Jean Pouillon could not resist the call of the tropics. He obtained some funding and, on the advice of Robert

Jaulin, who described Chad as an as yet unexplored territory for the ethnologist, he left in 1958.

Was Sartre aware that he was undermining himself? Absolutely not, according to Pouillon. Sartre was wrong about the import of *Tristes Tropiques*, which he had liked because it valorized the observer's presence in the observation and the communication established with members of the indigenous population.[15] Pouillon's greater sensitivity to an ethnology that was more encompassing than explanatory led to his conversion. As he himself put it so well, this was an example of the "fecundity of misunderstandings." In Chad, Pouillon studied seven or eight groups of a maximum of ten thousand members each, identifying an ever-varying organization of political and religious roles. By contrast, however, "the vocabulary, the lexicon was always the same, identical."[16] In order to understand these differences, it was necessary to have recourse to a structure not as it was concretized in the daily life of this or that group, but as it offered the possibility of permutations, like the logic of a grammar that lets us fathom different possible expressions.

In 1960, when the first volume of *Critique of Dialectical Reason* was published, Claude Lévi-Strauss invited Jean Pouillon to give a presentation in his seminar. Pouillon was the best specialist on Sartre's thinking, and he devoted three two-hour-long lectures to a reading of this work. Typically, these lectures attracted no more than about thirty people, but on this occasion they were transformed into a "dense crowd invading the lecture hall, and among whom I saw people like Lucien Goldmann,"[17] which gives some idea of how much interest Sartre continued to exert. If Jean Pouillon tried to reconcile Sartre and Lévi-Strauss, he was undoubtedly disappointed by the publication, at the end of 1962, of Lévi-Strauss's response to *Critique of Dialectical Reason*. His attack at the end of *The Savage Mind*, and to which we will come back, was violent, but Pouillon was not discouraged and in 1966 he compared the two books in *L'Arc*, arguing that they were complementary but incommensurable. He still maintains this position today. "It is pleasant to read one or the other of these works without any visual interference: when one is present, the other one is not."[18]

If Jean Pouillon was converted to the promising human science of anthropology, Sartre remained quite distant from the many challenges of the different social sciences. As a philosopher of consciousness, of the subject, he considered linguistics to be a minor science and avoided it practically systematically. Psychoanalysis does not square well with Sartre's theory of bad faith and of individual freedom, and in *Being and Nothingness* he considered Freud to be the instigator of a mechanistic doctrine. But Sartre was forced to enter the Freudian labyrinth altogether by accident. In 1958, John Huston asked him to write a screenplay on Freud. This order from Hollywood meant that Sartre had to read all of Freud's work, as well as his correspondence. On December 15, 1958, Sartre sent Huston a ninety-five-page synopsis, and a year later he finished the screenplay. But the two men argued; Huston found the screenplay long and boring and wanted Sartre to trim it. Sartre lengthened it instead, and ended up withdrawing his name from the film credits of *Freud, passion secrète*. Sartre therefore knew Freud's work by the end of the fifties, but if psychoanalysis came to interest him little by little, he remained closed to its central tenet of the unconscious. Sartre continued to support the idea that humans can be entirely understood through their praxis, as he tried to demonstrate in his unfinished work on Flaubert. It was clearly not possible to bring together "these two cannibals"[19]—Sartre and Claude Lévi-Strauss—without running the risk that one would devour the other. For want of a place, history allowed a man, Jean Pouillon, to thwart any effort at anthropophagia.

The Crisis of the Militant Intellectual

Sartre was challenged on a third front as well for his notion of the engaged intellectual, which belongs to a French tradition going back to the Dreyfus Affair. Sartre embodied the tradition quite magnificently until such time as the intellectual was no longer allowed to give an opinion in every realm and was forced to limit remarks to his or her area of expertise. The intellectual's critical enterprise became increasingly limited and confined to specific events, but it gained in pertinence what it lost in freedom of intervention. This retreat in the name of rationality also corresponded to a disinvestment, and even a refusal, of history in the large sense. "Structuralism appeared ten years after the end of the war, but the war had left us in a frozen world. Nineteen forty-eight threatened another outbreak, the two blocs faced off, the one crying Liberty and the other crying Equality. All of this contributed to a denegation of history."[20]

Two important structuralist figures clearly expressed this withdrawal from Sartrean engagement: Georges Dumézil and Claude Lévi-Strauss. When asked if he ever felt any sympathy for the tradition of the committed intellectual, Georges Dumézil answered, "No, I even felt a sort of revulsion for those who played this role, and for Sartre in particular."[21] This disengagement comes from a fundamentally reactionary approach that no longer holds out any hope for the future and considers the world with incurable nostalgia for the most distant past. "It seemed, and continues to seem, to me preferable that not just a monarchic principle but a dynastic principle preserve the country's highest position from caprice and ambition, rather than to live with general elections, as we have done since the Revolution and Bonaparte."[22] We see this same hesitation in Claude Lévi-Strauss before he takes any position on current events or takes sides. To the same question regarding commitment, Lévi-Strauss answered, "No, I consider that my intellectual authority, insofar as I am considered to have any, rests on my work, on my scruples of rigor and precision."[23] And he contrasts a Victor Hugo, who could imagine himself able to solve his epoch's problems, to our own period with problems that are too complex and diverse for any single man to be able to find his bearings and be committed. The figure of the philosopher as the questioning subject who problematizes the world in its diversity faded, and Sartre along with it. The classifying and often determinist social sciences had free range.

Two

The Birth of a Hero: Claude Lévi-Strauss

Structuralism quickly became identified with one man: Claude Lévi-Strauss. In an era in which the division of intellectual labor limited a researcher to increasingly fragmented knowledge, Lévi-Strauss sought to balance the material and the intelligible. Torn between a desire to restore the internal logic of material reality and a poetic sensibility that strongly tied him to the natural world, Lévi-Strauss forged important intellectual syntheses in much the same way as one writes musical scores.

Born in 1908, Lévi-Strauss was constantly exposed to artistic creation in his family milieu: a violinist great-grandfather, a father and uncles who were painters. As an adolescent living in the city, he spent all his free time in antique stores and only discovered the intense pleasure of exotic nature when his parents bought a house in the mountains in the Cévennes, in southeast France. There, he regularly wandered the countryside for ten to fifteen hours a day. Art and nature were his two passions and they marked him as he straddled two worlds: his thinking broke with precedents, yet his work remained fundamentally aesthetic in its ambitions. Lévi-Strauss rejected the spell of his own sensibility, and, without renouncing it, sought to contain it by constructing broad logical systems. His unwavering attachment to his initial structural program is apparent here, despite the changes in style.

From the time he was quite young, Lévi-Strauss was also interested in social issues. As soon as he was in high school, he joined the socialist movement. At seventeen, thanks to Arthur Wanters, a young Belgian socialist who had been invited to the family home one summer, Lévi-Strauss read Marx. "Marx immediately fascinated me. . . . I very soon read *Capital*."[1] But it was especially in *khâgne*, in the socialist studies group and under Georges Lefranc's influence, that Lévi-Strauss acquired a solid basis for his political involvement. He was increasingly vocal, giving lectures and speaking publicly so often that in 1928 he was elected secretary-general of the Federation of Socialist Students. During the same period, he became secretary to Georges Monnet, a socialist deputy, but had to give up these time-consuming responsibilities two years later in order to prepare his *agrégation* in philosophy, about which he was lackluster. His professors— Léon Brunschvicg, Albert Rivaud, Jean Laporte, Louis Bréhier—were fundamentally unsatisfying. "I went through that period a bit like a zombie."[2] He nonetheless passed his exams brilliantly in 1930, third in his class.

Lévi-Strauss's socialist engagement quickly came to an end because of a minor accident, and a much-awaited letter that never arrived. Although he was a pacifist, the trauma of the French defeat at the beginning of the "drôle de guerre," as Marc Bloch called it, quickly ended his political involvement. He concluded that it was dangerous "to enclose political realities within the framework of formal ideas."[3] Lévi-Strauss never recovered from this disappointment and never again became politically involved in any way, even if, beyond what he espoused, his position as an ethnologist had a political dimension to it. But this turning point was important: rather than looking ahead to the world to come, Lévi-Strauss turned, nostalgically, to the past at the risk of appearing anachronistic and out of step like his childhood idol, Don Quixote.

The Call of the Sea

Lévi-Strauss's career as an ethnologist began, he tells his reader in *Tristes Tropiques*, one autumn Sunday in 1934 when Célestin Bouglé, director of the École Normale Supérieure called him up to propose that he apply for the sociology professorship at the University of São Paulo. Célestin Bouglé naively thought that the outskirts of São Paulo were filled with Indians and suggested that Lévi-Strauss spend his weekends there. So Lévi-Strauss left for Brazil, not in search of exoticism ("I hate traveling and explorers")[4] but to abandon speculative philosophy and be definitively converted to this new and as yet very marginal discipline, anthropology. He had already seen one example of such a conversion in Jacques Soustelle. When he returned, Lévi-Strauss organized an exhibit in Paris of what he had been able to collect during his two years there and was granted enough money to organize an expedition to the Nambikwara. His work began to be noticed by a small circle of specialists, particularly Robert Lowie and Alfred Métraux. He was forced to leave France in 1939 and seek refuge from the German occupation. Invited to New York by the New School for Social Research as part of an immense plan to save European scholars organized by the Rockefeller Foundation, Lévi-Strauss crossed the Atlantic on the *Captain Paul-Lemerle*, a ship of hope on which he was accompanied by what the police considered rabble: André Breton, Victor Serge, Anna Seghers.

At the New School in New York, he discovered that he had to change his name so as not to be confused with the blue jeans, Levi's. Henceforth he would be known as Claude L. Strauss: "Never a year goes by without an order for Levi's, usually from Africa."[5] Beyond these amusing problems, New York became the definitive site for working out a structural anthropology, thanks to a decisive meeting at the New School with a colleague in linguistics, Roman Jakobson. Jakobson, like Lévi-Strauss, was exiled, and taught courses in French on structural phonology. Their meeting proved to be particularly rich, intellectually as well as affectively, and the amicable collaboration that took hold from the beginning never faltered. Jakobson came to Lévi-Strauss's lectures on kinship and Lévi-Strauss attended Jakobson's courses on sound and meaning: "His classes were dazzling."[6] The symbiosis of their respective research gave birth to structural anthropology. Moreover, it was Jakobson who, in 1943, advised Lévi-Strauss to begin writing the thesis that would became *The Elementary Structures of Kinship*.

Back in France again in 1948, Lévi-Strauss took on some temporary assignments as a researcher at the Centre National de la Recherche Scientifique (CNRS), and then as assistant director of the Musée de l'Homme. He was finally elected, thanks to Georges Dumézil's influence, to the chair of "Religions of Primitive Peoples" in the Fifth Section of the École Pratique des Hautes Études. He quickly changed the name of the chair after some discussions with black students to the chair for

"Religions of Peoples without Writing Systems." "People coming to talk with you at the Sorbonne could not be called uncivilized!"[7]

Scientific Ambitions

Structural anthropology did not, however, burst forth spontaneously from an erudite mind. It was the product of the specific situation of a nascent anthropology, and, more broadly, of the rise of the concept of science in the realm of the study of societies. In this respect, and even if Lévi-Strauss did take his distance and innovate, structuralism followed on the positivist tradition of Auguste Comte and his scientism. Which is not to say that structuralism shared Comte's optimistic view of a history of humanity progressing by stages toward a positive age. But Comte's idea that knowledge is only interesting if it borrows from a scientific model or manages to transform itself into a science or a theory had made some headway: "In this respect, traditional philosophy is avoided,"[8] which was characterististic of Lévi-Strauss's development. The other aspect of Comte's influence is his aspiration toward "holism,"[9] his desire to totalize. Comte condemned psychology just as Lévi-Strauss would later. In sociology as it was taking shape at the beginning of the twentieth century, Durkheim inherited Comte's aspiration to totalize, limiting his object to the social sciences. Even if Lévi-Strauss was converted to ethnology and left for Brazil in revolt against Durkheim, who did no fieldwork, he could not have escaped Durkheim's influence in the thirties. Raymond Boudon is right to say that "anthropologists took in a bit of holism along with their mother's milk."[10]

For Durkheim, just as for Auguste Comte, society is a whole that cannot be reduced to the sum of its parts. This would be the basis on which sociology would be constructed. The increasingly popular notions of system and then of structure came to be tied to an ensemble of scientific changes in linguistics, economics, and biology at the turn of the century, particularly insofar as these disciplines could explain the interdependence of elements constituting their specific objects. Lévi-Strauss, therefore, could not avoid setting himself in Durkheim's lineage. Did he not explicitly reiterate François Simiand's 1903 challenge to historians in 1949? And yet, Lévi-Strauss and Durkheim took completely different paths. When he was writing *The Rules of Method*, Durkheim favored written sources, which are the historian's tools, and mistrusted information gathered by ethnographers. At the time, historical positivism was in full force and it was only later, around 1912, that Durkheim placed history and ethnography on the same plane, a change in orientation hastened by the founding of *L'Année sociologique*. Conversely, for Lévi-Strauss, who had begun his painstaking fieldwork in Brazil, observation preceded any logical construction or conceptualization. Ethnology is first and foremost an ethnography. "Anthropology is above all an empirical science. . . . Empirical study determines access to the structure."[11] Observation is not an end in itself, certainly—and Lévi-Strauss crossed swords with empiricism—but it is a first, and indispensable stage.

Against Functionalism and Empiricism

Lévi-Strauss's first important object of study, the incest taboo, gave him the opportunity to distance himself from Durkheim's position on the same topic.[12] Given an explanation relegating the incest taboo to an archaic mentality, to a fear of menstrual blood, to outmoded beliefs, and therefore to a heterogeneous relationship to our modernity, Lévi-Strauss, who refused a definition limited to a single geographical area and temporal era, sought the atemporal, universal roots of this interdiction that would shed some light on its permanence. Lévi-Strauss's intellectual forebears were Auguste Comte, Émile Durkheim, and Marcel Mauss, but Marx's influence must not be forgotten. And, as we have already seen, his early and profound knowledge of Marx influenced his entire militant period; Marx was one of his "three mistresses,"[13] along with Freud and geology. From Marx, Lévi-Strauss retained the principle that manifest realities are not the most significant but that the researcher must construct models allowing to reach beyond material appearances and accede to the bases of reality: "Marx established that social science is no more founded on the basis of events than physics is founded on sense-data."[14]

Loyal to Marx, and strictly orthodox in his Marxism, Lévi-Strauss made it clear that he refused to occult the determining role of infrastructures, even if his intention was to construct a theory of superstructures. "We in no way intend to insinuate that ideological transformations engender social transformations. Only the reverse is true."[15] Of course, over the years this Marxist influence, along with the underlying dialogue with Engels, was to disappear completely. But at the beginning in Brazil, Lévi-Strauss clearly seemed to present himself first of all as a Marxist. Apropos of this, he remarked to Didier Éribon that the Brazilians were disappointed to see a non-Durkheimian sociologist. What could anyone be at the time but a Durkheimian? "My bet is that he was a Marxist. He was on the road to becoming the official philosopher for the Section Française de l'Internationale Ouvrière.[16]. . . Clearly, something happened in Brazil that meant that what he was when he got there was not what he was later; it must have been his encounter with the field, but not only that."[17]

Confronted with anthropological terrain, Lévi-Strauss refused the only two possible directions for research in this domain: evolutionism or diffusionism, and functionalism. Of course he admired the quality of Malinowski's fieldwork, his studies of sexual life in Melanasia and on the Argonauts, but he denounced his cult of empiricism as well as his functionalism: "But the idea that empirical observation of a single society will make it possible to understand universal motivations appears continually in his writings, weakening the significance of data whose vividness and richness are well known."[18] In Lévi-Strauss's eyes, Malinowski's functionalism fell into the trap of discontinuity, of singularity. Social structures and visible social relations were confused and the analysis therefore remained superficial, missing what is essential in social phenomena. With respect to the incest taboo, Malinowski never got beyond biological considerations of the incompatibility of parental feelings and love relationships. Slightly closer to a structuralist approach, Radcliffe-Brown had already used the idea of social structure in his study of Australian kinship systems, seeking a systematic way of classifying each system, and then of making valid generalizations for all human societies. "The analysis seeks to reduce diversity (from two or three hundred kinship systems) to a single order, whatever it might be."[19] But Lévi-Strauss considered Radcliffe-Brown's methodology too descriptive and empirical, and it shared with Malinowski a functionalist interpretation that goes no deeper than the surface of social systems.

Leaving Anglo-Saxon empiricism behind, Lévi-Strauss found his masters in anthropology among those descendants of the German historical school who had left history, proponents of cultural relativism: Lowie, Kroeber, and Boas, "authors to whom I willingly proclaim my debt."[20] In Robert H. Lowie he saw the initiator who, as early as 1915, opened the promising path to the study of kinship systems. "The very substance of social life can sometimes be rigorously analyzed as a function of the mode of classification of parents and allies."[21] After arriving in New York, Lévi-Strauss immediately sought out Franz Boas, who at the time dominated American anthropology and whose range of interests and study was limitless. Lévi-Strauss was even present at the death of the great master during a lunch given by Boas in honor of Rivet's visit to Columbia University. "Boas was very gay. In the middle of the conversation, he violently pushed himself away from the table and fell backward. I was sitting next to him and rushed over to lift him up. Boas was dead."[22] Boas's major contribution and his influence on Lévi-Strauss were to underscore the unconscious nature of cultural phenomena and to have considered that the laws of language were central for understanding this unconscious structure. Here was the linguistic thrust coming from anthropology as of 1911, and it was auspicious for the fruitful meeting between Lévi-Strauss and Jakobson.

Importing the Linguistic Model

Lévi-Strauss innovated in the true sense of the word here, by importing the linguistic model into anthropology, which had been linked in France until then with the natural sciences: physical anthropology had dominated during the entire nineteenth century. Lévi-Strauss had easy access to these models of natural science. Back in France again in 1948, he became associate director of the Musée de l'Homme. But this was not the approach that he took. He looked, rather, for a model of scientificity in the social sciences, and in particular in linguistics. Why this detour, which proved to be fundamental? "I have my own little answer, which I will give you. Biological, physical anthropology had been so compromised by all kinds of racism that it was difficult to borrow from this discipline in order to establish the mirage of a kind of general science, a general anthropology integrating the physical as well as the cultural. The historical liquidation of physical anthropology had made theoretical debate unnecessary. Claude Lévi-Strauss arrived on the spot that history had prepared for him."[23]

The break that Lévi-Strauss represented was all the more spectacular given the general prevalence of the naturalist and biologist relationship in French anthropology. Anthropology designated the search for man's natural foundations, and it was based on an essentially biological determinism. The war had swept things clean, however, and Lévi-Strauss could reappropriate the term "anthropology" without any ideological risk. He therefore raised French anthropology to the rank of a semantic field of Anglo-Saxon anthroplogy by establishing it on the pilot discipline of linguistics.[24]

Three

Where Nature and Culture Meet: Incest

Back in France in 1948, Claude Lévi-Strauss defended his thesis, *The Elementary Structures of Kinship* and his complementary thesis, *The Social and Family Life of the Nambikwara*, before a jury composed of Georges Davy, Marcel Griaule, Émile Benveniste, Albert Bayet, and Jean Escarra. The publication of his thesis the following year was one of the major events of postwar intellectual history and a touchstone for the founding of the structuralist program.[1] Forty years later, anthropologists continue to consider this event as an advent. "What seems most important and most fundamental to me is *The Elementary Structures of Kinship*, by the will to scientificity it introduced in the analysis of social multiplicity, by its quest for the most encompassing model to account for phenomena that do not appear, initially, to be part of the same categories of analysis, and by the transition from the question of filiation to one of alliance."[2]

The French school of anthropology experienced a veritable episte-mological revolution with the publication of Lévi-Strauss's thesis; other groups, including, of course, philosophers, were also dazzled. Olivier Revault d'Allonnes, a young *agrégé* in philosophy, was one of these: "This was an important, decisive moment. I had just been as-signed to the high school in Lille after my *agrégation* in philosophy in 1948, and it was fundamentally enlightening. At the time, I saw a con-firmation of Marx in *The Elementary Structures of Kinship*."[3] The shock waves extended beyond the small circle of anthropologists and continued to have their effect. Ten years after its publication, a young *normalien* discovered *The Elementary Structures of Kinship* with equal dazzlement as soon as he got to the École Normale Supérieure in 1957. Emmanuel Terray was a philosopher who was already attracted to anthropology and who needed to leave a France fully embroiled in a colonial war that he condemned and against which he militated. At the time, his friend Alain Badiou lent him *The Elementary Structures of Kinship* because it was difficult to find. "Alain lent me the book and I copied one hundred pages from it by hand, which I still have. And when I finished copying the pages, given the effort it had taken, Alain could not but give me the book. That is how I have the first edition. For me, at the time, and I still hold this opinion, the progress this book represented was comparable, in its field, to Marx's *Capital* or to Freud's *Interpretation of Dreams*."[4] Once again, our young philosopher was seduced by giving some order to an area where apparently total incoherence and total empiricism reigned. His admiration confirmed his choice of career and a way of life in anthropology.

The Universal Constant

In search of constants that would take into account the universals of social practices, Lévi-Strauss found the incest taboo, which remains unchanged beyond the diversity of human societies. He made a fundamental shift in the traditional approach, which usually considered incest in terms of moral interdictions without taking its social positivity into account. Lewis Henry Morgan, for example, saw the incest taboo as the species' means of protecting itself against the baneful effects of intermarriage. For Edward Westermarck, the incest taboo could be explained by the wearing effects of daily routine on sexual desire, a thesis completely refuted by Freud's oedipal theory. The Lévi-Straussian revolution consisted in debiologizing the phenomenon and removing it from the simple structure of consanguinity and from ethnocentric moral considerations. The structuralist hypothesis effected a shift here thanks to which the taboo's character of transaction, or communication established by matrimonial alliances, was reasserted. Lévi-Strauss considered kinship to be the principal basis for social reproduction.

In order not to get lost in the labyrinth of the multitude of matrimonial practices, Lévi-Strauss made a reduction, in the mathematical sense of the term, by defining a limited number of possibilities as elementary kinship structures: "Elementary structures of kinship are . . .

those systems which prescribe marriage with a certain type of relative or, alternatively, those systems which, while defining all members of the society as relatives, divide them into two categories, *viz.* possible spouses and prohibited spouses."[5] Based on a nomenclature, these elementary structures allow the circle of relatives and that of relations by marriage, to be determined. Thus, in this type of structure, marriages between sisters, brothers, and first cousins are proscribed whereas marriages between cousins by marriage, and sometimes more specifically between crossed matrilinear cousins, are prescribed. Societies are therefore divided into two groups: the group of possible spouses and that of prohibited spouses. This same system is found among the Australians in the *kariera* system and the *aranda* system studied by Lévi-Strauss. In the *kariera* system, the tribe is divided into two local groups, each of which is subdivided into two sections; membership in local groups is transmitted patrilineally, but the son belongs to the other section. There is, therefore, first a generational alternation and a marriage system established by the female bilateral crossed cousin (the cousin is bilateral because she is both the daughter of the father's sister and of the mother's brother). The *aranda* system is similar, but in matrilineal groups. Here Lévi-Strauss groups symmetrical marriages together as restricted exchanges as opposed to other systems, which are also elementary but have an indefinite number of groups and unilateral marriages, in which case there are generalized exchanges: "Whereas a bilateral marriage system can function with two lines of descendants, at least three are necessary for a system of unilateral alliance to operate. If A takes his wives from B, he must give his wives to a third line, C, which can later give its wives to B, closing the circle."[6] Unlike those elementary kinship systems that try to keep the marriage within the family framework, other, semicomplex structures, such as the Crow-Omaha systems, seek to make marriage and family links incompatible. In this case, one cannot marry into a clan that has, for as long as can be remembered, already given a spouse to one's own clan.

Lévi-Strauss abandoned an analysis made in terms of filiation or blood ties in order to demonstrate that the joining of the sexes is the object of a socially regulated transaction: the transaction is a social and cultural fact. Prohibition is no longer therefore perceived as a purely negative fact, but, on the contrary, as a positive fact engendering social links. The kinship system can be analyzed as part of an arbitrary system of representation, much like Saussure's arbitrary sign.

By breaking with the naturalism surrounding the notion of the incest taboo, and by making it the reference for the passage from nature to culture, Lévi-Strauss brought about a major shift. The social order is born of the organization of an exchange around the incest taboo, which therefore becomes a founding element: "Considered from the most general viewpoint, the prohibition of incest expresses the transition from the natural fact of consanguinity to the cultural fact of alliance."[7] The incest taboo is the decisive intervention in the birth of the social order. Because of its centrality and its aspect as a basic principle, it cannot be considered to be only a part of the natural order, even if it shares a universal and spontaneous quality, nor only a part of the cultural order, characterized by norms, specific laws, and a restrictive quality. The incest taboo belongs to both realms at once; it is the meeting point between nature and culture, the indispensable arbitrary rule that man substitutes for the natural order. There are specific rules in the incest taboo, as well as a normative code (culture) and a universal character (nature). "The incest prohibition is at once on the threshold of culture, in culture and, in one sense, as we shall try to show, culture itself."[8] Fundamental structures resulting from this interdiction are not to be considered as natural facts that can be observed, but as "a grid for deciphering or, in Kantian terms, a design in which all the terms or all the aspects need not be present for it to operate smoothly."[9] With this exemplary study, Lévi-Strauss freed anthropology from the natural sciences and placed it immediately and exclusively on cultural grounds.

Meeting Jakobson

The model making this shift possible for Lévi-Strauss was drawn from structural linguistics. In this respect, the birth and developments in phonology created an upheaval in the thinking in the social sciences. For Lévi-Strauss himself, borrowing the model represented a veritable Copernican-Galilean revolution. "Phonology cannot help but play the same renovative role with respect to the social sciences that nuclear physics, for example, has played for all of the hard sciences."[10] The growing successes of the phonological method proved the existence of an effective system from which anthropology should draw some basic principles in order to apply them to the complex social domain. Lévi-Strauss therefore adopted its founding paradigms, virtually on a term for term basis. Phonology sought to go beyond the stages of conscious linguistic phenomena. Considering the specificity of terms was not enough; the goal was to understand them in their interrelationships, and phonology therefore introduces the notion of system in an effort to construct general laws. The entire structuralist method is embodied in this project.

Lévi-Strauss's exchanges in New York with Roman Jakobson were clearly the source of this contribution. "At that time, I was a kind of naive structuralist. I was doing structuralism without even knowing it. Jakobson showed me the corpus of a doctrine that had already been constituted in linguistics, and that I had never studied. It was an illumination for me."[11] Lévi-Strauss did not limit himself to adding a new realm of knowledge to his expertise, however, but incorporated it into his method and, as a result, his general perspective was fundamentally changed. "Like phonemes, kinship terms are elements of meaning; like phonemes, they acquire meaning only if they are integrated into systems."[12] Lévi-Strauss attended Jakobson's classes in New York, and wrote a preface for their publication in 1976.[13]

The two important lessons Lévi-Strauss retained for anthropology were, on the one hand, the search for constants beyond the multitude of identifiable variations, and, on the other, avoiding all recourse to the consciousness of a speaking subject, whence the prevalence of the structure's unconscious phenomena. For him, these two principles held as much for phonetics as for anthropology. The two disciplines, however, do not for all that lose touch with concrete reality by favoring a systematic formalism. Invoking the Russian phonologist Nicolai Trubetzkoy, Lévi-Strauss remarks: "Current phonology does not limit itself to declaring that phonemes are always elements of a system, it shows concrete phonological systems and brings their structure to the fore."[14] The structural anthropologist must therefore follow the linguist along a path established by structural linguistics, which has rejected a diachronic explanation of linguistic evolution in favor of identifying the differential variations between languages. Breaking down the complex materials of a language into a limited number of phonemes is supposed to help the anthropologist in his approach to the systems at work in primitive societies; he must deconstruct in the same fashion, reduce observable reality by being attentive to a number of variables, which are also limited. This would be the case for matrimonial systems organized around the relationship between the law of filiation and that of residence, a relationship every bit as arbitrary as the Saussurean sign. By taking Jakobson as his inspiration, Lévi-Strauss made the Saussurean break his own.

While Lévi-Strauss reiterated Saussure's most famous distinction between signifier and signified, he adapted it to his own field. Saussure opposed sound and meaning, but for Lévi-Strauss structure became the signifier and meaning the signified. While the model was modified in this respect, when it came to the linguistic perspective on the relationship between synchrony and diachrony, Lévi-Strauss adhered to Saussure's priority of synchrony. This move bore within it the future polemics against history. Having adopted the phonological model, "Claude Lévi-Strauss began the critique of the efficacy of a historical approach, or of consciousness, for a scientific explanation of social phenomena."[15]

Fascinated by the success of their model, Lévi-Strauss joined the linguists:

> We should like to learn from the linguists how they succeeded in doing it, how we may ourselves in our own field, which is a complex one—in the field of kinship, in the field of social organization, in the field of religion, folklore, art, and the like—use the same kind of rigorous approach which has proved to be so successful for linguistics.[16]

But to imagine that the anthropologist would simply give up, once he found his master in the linguist, is to not know Lévi-Strauss. On the contrary, his gesture must be seen in a comprehensive perspective integrating linguistics into a more general scheme in which the anthropologist would be the prime mover. Interpreting social structures would be the product of a three-tiered "theory of communication":[17] the communication of women between groups, thanks to kinship rules, the communication of goods and services, thanks to economic rules, and the communication of messages, thanks to linguistic rules. These three levels were incorporated into Lévi-Strauss's comprehensive anthropological project in which the analogy between the two methods remained a constant. "The kinship system is a language."[18] "If a substantial identity were assumed to exist between language structure and kinship systems, one should find, in the following regions of the world, languages whose structures would be of a type comparable to kinship systems."[19] Lévi-Strauss thereby elevated linguistics to the rank of a pilot science, of an initial model, basing anthropology on the cultural and social, rather than on the physical. Thanks to Jakobson,

Lévi-Strauss understood this strategic role very early on, and we must therefore disagree with Jean Pouillon's reductive evaluation of the importance of linguistics for Lévi-Strauss as the simple idea that "meaning is always positional meaning."[20] The two major thrusts of the structuralist paradigm are present as early as *The Elementary Structures of Kinship*, and come from linguistics and mathematics, the formalized language by definition. Lévi-Strauss benefited from the services of structural mathematics of the Bourbaki group thanks to a meeting with Simone Weil's brother, André Weil, who wrote the mathematical appendix to the book. In this mathematical transcription of his discoveries, Lévi-Strauss found the continuation of a displacement that was analogous to a shift made by Jakobson: from an attention to the terms of a relationship to the importance of the relationships themselves between these terms, independent of their content.

This double fecundity, rigor, and scientificity, brought to the soft belly of a social science still in its infancy, could only nourish the dream of having at last reached the final stage of a scientificity equal to that of the hard sciences. "We give the impression that the social sciences will become full-fledged sciences like Newtonian physics. There is that in Claude Lévi-Strauss. . . . Scientism becomes credible because linguistics seems like something scientific in the sense of the natural sciences. . . . This is basically the key to success."[21] A fertile path, certainly, but also the key to the dreams and illusions that, for twenty years, hung over the community of researchers in the social sciences.

A Resounding Event

The publication of *The Elementary Structures of Kinship* had an immediate resounding effect. Simone de Beauvoir took up her pen to review it in *Les Temps modernes*, whose wide readership of intellectuals, in the broadest sense, could immediately make the voluminous thesis well known beyond the limited circle of anthropologists without anyone having to read it. Jean Pouillon, for example, only read Lévi-Strauss when *Tristes Tropiques* was published. It was paradoxical that this highly structuralist work be first noticed by a review that was the organ of expression of Sartrean existentialism. Simone de Beauvoir, who was the same age as Lévi-Strauss and had known him since just before the war from their *agrégation* teacher-training class, was in the process of finishing *The Second Sex*.

Simone de Beauvoir had heard from Michel Leiris that Lévi-Strauss was going to publish his thesis on kinship systems. Interested in the anthropological point of view on the question, de Beauvoir asked Leiris to contact Lévi-Strauss on her behalf and ask him to send her the proofs, before finishing her own book. "To thank Claude Lévi-Strauss, she therefore wrote a long review in *Les Temps modernes.*"[22] The article was particularly positive about the value of Lévi-Strauss's theses. "French sociology had been dormant for quite some time, until now."[23] De Beauvoir agreed with Lévi-Strauss's methods and conclusions, and encouraged readers to read him, but at the same time she drew his work into the Sartrean purview by giving it an existentialist thrust; clearly she had misread or was trying to co-opt Lévi-Strauss. Remarking that Lévi-Strauss did not say where the structures whose logic he described come from, she gave her own, Sartrean answer: "Lévi-Strauss did not allow himself to venture onto philosophical grounds, and he never gives up his rigorous scientific objectivity; but his thinking is clearly inscribed within a broad humanism according to which human existence brings its own justification with it."[24]

In early 1951, and once again in *Les Temps modernes*, which contributed considerably to the renown of Lévi-Strauss's work, Claude Lefort wrote an article in which he criticized Lévi-Strauss for setting the meaning of experience outside experience itself and giving priority to a mathematical model presented as more real than reality. "We would reproach Mr. Lévi-Strauss for perceiving rules rather than behavior in society."[25] In 1956, Jean Pouillon answered Lefort's criticism, which he considered unfounded, when he was preparing an article on Lévi-Strauss's work. For Pouillon, Lévi-Strauss neither confused reality with its mathematical expression nor differentiated between them in order to give priority to the second. The model was not ontologized since "this mathematical expression of reality is never confused with reality."[26] In the mid-fifties, there was broad support for the structuralist method, but it soon drew criticism from the Anglo-Saxon and French sides when the paradigm became vulnerable, particularly in May 1968.

Four

Ask for the Program: The Mauss

Where Lévi-Strauss focused on kinship, a specifically anthropological concern, in *The Elementary Structures of Kinship*, his *Introduction to the Work of Marcel Mauss* (1950) was different.[1] Rather than simply presenting the work of one of the Durkheimian masters of French anthropology, he used the preface to define his own structuralist program, and to present a rigorous methodology. Oddly enough, what initially appeared as a modest and ritual preface became something of moment: the first definition of a unified program proposed for all the social sciences since the beginning of the nineteenth century, when Destutt de Tracy and the ideologues had attempted to define a vast science of ideas, a project left unfinished. Another surprising fact was that Georges Gurvitch, a sociologist who later became quite hostile toward Lévi-Strauss's theses, had asked him to write this introduction for a collection that he had launched at the Presses Universitaires de France.

Georges Gurvitch immediately understood the differences separating him from Lévi-Strauss and he added a postscript to express his reservations, qualifying Lévi-Strauss's interpretation as a very particular reading of Mauss's work. "Things began to sour at that point."[2] Algirdas Julien Greimas was right about the importance of this text. In Alexandria at the time, and hungry for intellectual nourishment, he had come upon the *Introduction to the Work of Marcel Mauss*, which, along with other works, encouraged him in his project of forging a comprehensive methodology for the social sciences. "Perhaps it was at that point, if books count, that one was going to play the most important role. Structuralism, after all, is the encounter between linguistics and anthropology."[3] Lévi-Strauss relied, therefore, on Marcel Mauss's authority to ground anthropology theoretically and thus open theory up to a model able to account for the meaning of facts observed in the field. Whence the use made of linguistics, presented as the best means to make the concept adequate to its object. Lévi-Strauss initially had a position similar to that of modern linguistics: there are only constructed facts in anthroplogy and the natural sciences. Linguistics therefore became a tool that could lead anthropology toward culture, and the symbolic, by eliminating its old naturalist or energist models. Here again, Lévi-Strauss drew attention to himself with this methodological program with respect to the French ethnological context, by distancing anthropology from technology, and from museums, and by orienting it toward a concept and toward theory. "Everything begins with the museum and everything returns to it. However, Lévi-Strauss leaves the museum in order to invent anthropology theoretically."[4]

Lévi-Strauss saw Marcel Mauss as the spiritual father of structuralism. But, as with all choices, this one had an arbitrary and unfair quality about it, which Jean Jamin emphasized when he exhumed Robert Hertz from forgotten memory. Jamin considered that when it came to the archaeology of structuralism, Hertz more than Mauss was the founder of the structuralist paradigm. Robert Hertz died in 1915, during the First World War, and left some texts that are, "to my mind, the founders of structuralism, so much so that the British ethnologist Needham devotes an entire book, *Right and Left*, to pay homage to Robert Hertz's memory."[5] In one of these texts, we do indeed find structural binarity. "Right-handed preeminence"[6] is the discovery of the religious polarity between a sacred right and a sacred left. Robert Hertz demonstrated how lateralization, which may have a biological basis, has above all a symbolic basis opposing the pure and auspicious right to the impure and evil left. "This discovery became even more important than is generally thought, since Michel Leiris, Georges Bataille, and Roger Caillois would take up this polarization of the sacred again in the Collège de Sociologie."[7]

The Unconscious

Lévi-Strauss, however, based himself on Mauss, emphasizing his "modernity."[8] Mauss had understood and opened up anthropological inquiry to the other human sciences, and in doing so, had laid out a prolegomena for future rapprochements. Ethnology and psychoanalysis, for example, discovered a common object of analysis in the symbolic field, which included economic as well as kinship or religious systems. Here again, Lévi-Strauss referred to Mauss who, in 1924, defined social life as "a world of symbolic relationships."[9] Lévi-Strauss carried on in the same vein, citing his own work in which he compared the shaman in a trance with a neurotic.[10] Lévi-Strauss clearly aspired to what Mauss had expressed in *The Gift* [11]—to study the total social fact. Totality only exists, however, once things have moved beyond social atomism and it has become possible to incorporate all the facts into "an anthropology, that is, a system of interpretation accounting for the aspects of all modes of behavior simultaneously, physical, physiological, psychical, and sociological."[12] The human body is at the center of this totality, an apparent sign of nature but entirely cultural, in fact. However, Mauss introduced "an archaeology of body positions,"[13] a program that Michel Foucault adopted and developed further.

Lévi-Strauss stressed the overarching importance of the unconscious at the heart of the body; this position would become a principal characteristic of the structuralist paradigm. He understood Mauss's intention of giving it a fundamental importance. "So it is not surprising that Mauss . . . referred constantly to the unconscious as providing the common and specific character of social facts."[14] However, it is only through the mediation of language that we can reach the unconscious. For this, Lévi-Strauss mobilized modern, Saussurean linguistics, which situates the facts of speech at the level of unconscious thought; "it is the same kind of operation which in psychoanalysis allows us to win back our most estranged self, and in ethnological inquiry gives us access to the most foreign others as to another self."[15] Lévi-Strauss established the fundamental alliance between two guiding sciences of the structuralist period, anthropology and psychoanalysis, both of which were based on linguistics, that other pilot science offering a veritable heuristic model.

Another characteristic of this period, which Lévi-Strauss had already expressed in this text-manifesto and which Jacques Lacan in particular developed, was to take up the Saussurean sign once again, but pushing it toward an emptying of the signified, or in any case diminishing its importance with respect to the signifier. "Like language, the social *is* an autonomous reality (the same one, moreover); symbols are more real than what they symbolise, the signifier precedes and determines the signified."[16] The totalizing project was defined for all the social sciences, which are summoned to create a vast semiological program whose driving force would come from anthropology as the only discipline able to synthesize the work of the others. Beyond Lévi-Strauss's definition of the prospect of interdisciplinarity, structuralism's canonical thesis that the code precedes and is independent from the message, and that the subject is subjected to the signifier's law, was clear at this point. Indeed, it was the heart of the structural undertaking. "The definition of a code is to be translatable into another code. This property defines it and is called structure."[17]

The Debt to Marcel Mauss

If Lévi-Strauss was a bit forced when he credited Marcel Mauss with being at the origin of his structuralist program, he nonetheless paid his debt this way, since Mauss was his principal source of inspiration for the central thesis of *The Elementary Structures of Kinship*. Mauss's *The Gift* was a model, in this respect, along with his theory of reciprocity, which Lévi-Strauss extended and systematized in his work on kinship. The rule of reciprocity, and its triple obligation of giving, receiving, and returning, establish the economy of matrimonial exchanges. The gift and countergift made it possible to see the network of connections, equivalences, and alliances extending beyond the material gift by virtue of the universality of its rules. The incest taboo became intelligible at this level, as did its universality, which made it a fundamental key for understanding all societies. "The incest taboo, like exogamy, which is its extended social expansion, is a rule of reciprocity. The sole function of the incest taboo is not to forbid; it is set in place to ensure and found an exchange, directly or indirectly, immediately or not."[18]

Exchange, therefore, plays a central role in the phenomenon of the circulation of women in matrimonial alliances and constitutes a veritable structure of communication that enables groups to establish their relationship of reciprocity. It is not moral reprobation that makes incest illicit, nor a murmur of the heart, but the exchange value establishing a social relationship. Marrying one's sister made no sense to Margaret Mead's informants, the Arapesh, because it would mean depriving oneself of a brother-in-law, with whom one would go hunting or fishing. "The question of incest is socially absurd before it is morally culpable."[19] A new era began with the *The Gift*, which Lévi-Strauss, who absorbed all of its lessons, compared to the discovery of combinatory analysis in modern mathematical thought. "The prohibition of incest is less a rule prohibiting marriage with the mother, sister or daughter than a rule obliging the mother, sister or daughter to be given to others. It is the supreme rule of the gift."[20] The *Introduction to the Work of Marcel Mauss* brilliantly restored an obvious fecundity and filiation. In addition to the Maussian point of view, Lévi-Strauss's program included phonology's decisive contributions—the work of Trubetzkoy and Jakobson, whose notions of secondary and combinatory variations, group names, and neutralization made possible the necessary condensations of empirical material. Lévi-Strauss clearly defined the structuralist program here. "For me, structuralism is the theory of the symbolic in *Introduction to the Work of Marcel Mauss*: the independence of language and of kinship rules shows that the symbolic, the signifier, are autonomous."[21]

A Form of Kantianism

Lévi-Strauss left the philosopher's territory for other continents of knowledge, but Kantian philosophy has nonetheless left its mark, albeit inexplicit, on the substructure of the structuralist program in its determination to tie all social systems to constituent categories that operate like noumenal categories. For Kant, thinking is controlled by these a priori categories, which are brought appropriately to bear in different societies. The spirit, however, remains present in each case. Lévi-Strauss borrowed this Kantianism more from phonology than from philosophy; in his definition of the symbolic value zero, he adopted Jakobson's definition of the zero phoneme term for term. For Jakobson, the zero phoneme resembles no other phoneme because it has no differential character and no constant phonetic value whose specific function is to allow the presence of a phoneme. For Lévi-Strauss, the system of symbols defines any given cosmology. "It would simply be a symbolic value zero, a sign indicating that a symbolic content, in addition to the one which the signifier already bears, is needed, but which can be any value."[22]

Like Gurvitch, who considered that Lévi-Strauss's appropriation of Mauss's work deformed its truth, Claude Lefort, in his 1951 article in *Les Temps modernes*, attacked *The Elementary Structures of Kin-*

ship and the *Introduction to the Work of Marcel Mauss*. He denounced the program's will to mathematize social relationships and the consequent loss of meaning implied by it. For Lefort, reducing social phenomena to symbolic systems "seems foreign to his inspiration: Mauss aims at meaning, not at symbols; he wants to understand the immanent intention of behavior without leaving the realm of experience, not to establish a logical order in which concrete reality is seen simply as appearances."[23] Lefort criticized the scientism underlying Lévi-Strauss's program, his belief in a deeper reality lying beneath mathematical reality. Underlying the term "unconscious," he also discerned traces of Kantian idealism that basically meant transcendental consciousness in Kant's sense; expressions such as "unconscious category" or "category of collective thinking"[24] reveal this. Lefort reversed Lévi-Strauss's idealism by asserting that the empirical behavior of subjects cannot be deduced from a transcendental consciousness but, to the contrary, is established through experience. Both the proclamation of a program and Claude Lefort's critiques provided the rational kernel for all the debates and polemics that developed in the fifties and sixties around the structuralist banquet.

Five

Georges Dumézil: An Independent

On June 13, 1979, Georges Dumézil was received into the ranks of the Académie Française.[1] Welcomed into the Academy, he was invited to give an overview of his work by none other than Claude Lévi-Strauss. The choice was no accident, and resulted from their similar, if obviously distinctive, projects. Dumézil, of course, had always been mistrustful of any assimilation of his work to a model with which he did not agree. He would not, for example, have accepted being included in a history of structuralism, which was foreign to him. "I am not, I do not have to be or not to be, a structuralist."[2] His position was unequivocal and he went so far as to refuse any reference to the word "structure" in order to avoid any form of co-optation. Burned by his youthful enthusiasm for abstract systems, Dumézil kept himself safely removed from the tumult and confined his work to philology.

Dumézil obviously had a special place. The different influences that had given rise to his work, like his legacy, took a course that is difficult to define. Unlike Lévi-Strauss, he was not the master of any school, nor did he carry a programmatic banner for any particular discipline. He was removed from traditional disciplinary fields that he ignored and that ignored him. Georges Dumézil was like an ingenious and independent innovator, the veritable herald of comparative mythology, which he alone shaped. He renewed and inspired much research without any concern for either appropriating it or seeking institutional legitimation. Given this, can we go against his will and evoke some of the innovations of this adventurer in Indo-European mythology in the context of the development of the structuralist paradigm? Yes, and as he received him in the Academy, Lévi-Strauss was right in saying that the word "structure," or "structural," would have come immediately to mind had Dumézil not refused it in 1973.

The intellectual complicity between these two men dated back to well before Dumézil's membership in the French Academy. They had met in 1946 and Dumézil had played a decisive role, first in Lévi-Strauss's election to the École Pratique des Hautes Études and then in his election to the Collège de France in 1959. Their relationship was not, however, based only on career moves. Lévi-Strauss had discovered Dumézil's work while preparing his *agrégation*, but this was only a fortuitous initial contact. Later, after the war and as an ethnologist, lengthy meditation upon his discoveries convinced Lévi-Strauss that Dumézil "was the pioneer of the structural method."[3] The two men had, moreover, two common masters: Marcel Mauss, whose importance we saw for Lévi-Strauss and whose courses Dumézil took, and Marcel Granet, who, as Lévi-Strauss recalled, was instrumental in his decision to study kinship relationships. He had come across Marcel Granet's work *Matrimonial Categories and Proximate Relationships in Ancient China* at his high school in Montpellier. Dumézil was even more influenced by Granet's work because he had taken his courses at the École des Langues Orientales from 1933 to 1935. "Listening and watching Granet at work provoked a kind of indefinable metamorphosis or maturation in me."[4]

Looking at the structuralist sphere of influence, Dumézil has a place apart that explains his reluctance to be assimilated into the current: Ferdinand de Saussure, the obligatory reference for every structuralist work, is absent from his. Dumézil always considered himself a philologist and as such his work is part of a legacy that precedes the Saussurean "break"; he is in the tradition of nineteenth-century comparative philology, especially the work of the Schlegel brothers, Friedrich and August Wilhem, of August Schleicher, and particularly of Franz Bopp, who brought to light the lexical and syntactic relationships between Sanskrit, Greek, Latin, and Slavic.[5] Dumézil belonged therefore, more to this historical linguistic current that, as early as the beginning of the nineteenth century, held that different languages with a common root shared a mother language, Indo-European. Dumézil also drew his fundamental notion of transformation from this branch of historical philology, which was essential for the birth of a science of language. The idea met with a ringing success and quickly became the center of most structuralist works. Here again, Lévi-Strauss considered Dumézil to be a pioneer. "With the idea of transformation, which you were the first among us to use, you have provided them [the social sciences] with their best tool."[6]

Dumézil, of course, did not remain aloof from modern linguistics. If he was basically unaware of Saussure's work, he was nonetheless familiar with that of one of his disciples, Antoine Meillet, and especially that of Émile Benveniste, who strenuously supported him in a difficult battle for election to the Collège de France in 1948. All the proponents of tradition opposed this bothersome pioneer: Edmond Faral, the medievalist, André Piganiol, the specialist on Rome, and the Slavist André Mazon. But the fight led by Émile Benveniste, together with the support of Jules Bloch, Lucien Febvre, Louis Massignon, Alfred Ernout, and Jean Pommier, succeeded and he was elected. Dumézil embodied at one and the same time both the Durkheimian will, expressed by Marcel Mauss, for a total social fact, and the idea that society, mythology, and religion are to be thought of as a whole; this naturally led him to use the idea of structure. He also shared with the other structuralists a view of language as the essential vector for comprehensibility, for transmitting tradition, for incarnating the invariable, making the perception of the permanence of ideas underlying words possible. In order to understand the variations of the model, Dumézil used the notions of difference, of resemblance, and of value opposition, so many instruments of a method that can be called comparative or structuralist.

Trifunctionalism

The real bomb with which Georges Dumézil shook up traditional certainties dated from 1938, although it exploded only after the war. If an epistemological break existed in his many publications that began in 1924, it occurred then. After having groped around in a comparison between a group of Indian and Roman artifacts, he found an explanation for the three principal Roman priests serving Jupiter, Mars, and Quirinus in their parallel with the three social classes of Vedic India: priests, warriors, and workers. Dumézil's hypothesis that all Indo-Europeans have a common tripartite and trifunctional ideology dates from this discovery and he continued to work on it until his

death. He thus became the archaeologist of the Indo-European imagination and, despite what he said about it, this discovery in fact placed
him among the pioneers of structuralism because his entire reading
of Western history was organized around this plan, which he first
called a cycle, then a system, and finally a structure, and which was
trifunctional. For Dumézil, this plan was common to the mental representations of Indo-Europeans, and took root during a very broad
cultural area and era stretching between the Baltic and the Black Seas
and between the Carpathian and Ural Mountains at the end of the
third millennium B.C. Dumézil disagreed with Lévi-Strauss; for him,
the phenomenon was indeed unique, but could not be tied to the universal laws of the human mind. His method resembled a structuralist
method insofar as he did not believe that the trifunctional invariant
resulted from successive borrowings from an original kernel. On the
contrary, he favored a method of genetic comparison that eliminated
the thesis of borrowed elements. In an approach that he termed
"ultrahistorical" because it took myths as its object, Dumézil systematically compared the elements of the Veda and then of the *Mahab-
harata* with those of the Scythians, the Romans, and the Irish. For
him, all of these societies and periods could be cast into a common
structure differentiating between the functions of sovereignty and of
the sacred (Zeus, Jupiter, Mitra, Odin), of the warrior (Mars, Indra,
Tyr), and, finally, of the (re)productive and nourishing (Quirinus,
Nasatya, Njördr).

Dumézil's relative isolation can also be attributed to the difficulties he encountered in adapting his model, which is not to say that his
work had no impact. But having restricted his organizational model to
a specific era made it immediately less available for the generalizing
extrapolations that blossomed during the structuralist heyday. Moreover—and in this way he also set himself apart from the structuralist
phenomenon—Dumézil placed his method midway between a quest
for explanatory elements that are exogenous to myths, and a quest for
an independent internal structure to which myths refer. Dumézil was
between the nineteenth-century comparatist philologists and the
structuralist method by his integration of both the articulation of concepts between themselves in their own structure and the aspects of the
universe dealt with in myths. His hybrid nature and his concern for
history ("I would like to define myself as a historian")[7] inspired enormous amounts of work by historians of the third generation of the

Annales who continued along the same lines of his discoveries. Even if the trifunctional plan was unimportant for the Hellenist world, specialists of ancient Greece—Pierre Vidal-Naquet, Jean-Pierre Vernant, and Marcel Détienne—changed their approach to the Pantheon on the basis of Dumézil's work, and medievalists like Jacques Le Goff and Georges Duby, when considering a society divided into three orders, could not help but wonder about the bases of its tripartite division. But these consequences came in the 1970s, and we will come back to them when we address that period.

Dumézil's lessons did not disappear with him, therefore, when he died at the Val-de-Grâce hospital in Paris on October 11, 1986, at the age of eighty-eight. He was honored in *Le Monde* by the linguist Claude Hagège, whose article was entitled "La clé des civilisations": "After Dumézil, the science of religions can no longer be what it was before him. Reason gave order to chaos. In place of the charms of a vague notion of religiosity, he substituted the illuminating clarity of structures of thought. This is one of his important lessons."[8] The word "structure" clearly stuck to Dumézil despite his wishes, even after his death, but the meaning of a work does not necessarily conform to the wishes of its author. Georges Dumézil was an initiator, a herald of a structuralist epic.

Six

The Phenomenological Bridge

French philosophy was dominated by phenomenological concerns in the 1950s. Consonant with and in the tradition of Husserl's work, the issue was a return to "things themselves," with its corollary of intentional consciousness oriented always toward things. Phenomenology is very attentive to experience, therefore, to description, and to the concrete, and subjectivity clearly receives priority. Husserl's ambition was to see philosophy evolve from an ideology to a science. The phenomenological undertaking was not based on facts, however, but on the essences that constituted the original basis of the meaning of the possibilities of consciousness, correlatively with its object.

At the time of Liberation, French phenomenology was above all Sartrean, and it emphasized a consciousness able to know itself. Maurice Merleau-Ponty, for his part, resumed Husserl's project but oriented it more toward the dialectic played out between proffered meaning and the meaning revealed in things. This led him to a dialogue that was increasingly close to the social sciences, which were rapidly expanding at the time. Merleau-Ponty took up Husserl's idea of purging the givens of experience available to the phenomenologist of all the elements inherited from scientific thinking, to which philosophy had capitulated. Whence the formula, "Phenomenology is first of all the disavowal of science." But he was far from repudiating science, and clearly hoped to reappropriate it into philosophical thinking. As early as the war, Merleau-Ponty had began to carry out this work with respect to biology, and above all with respect to psychology, by criticizing their reifying and mechanistic character.[1] He was equally critical of the idealism of a pure consciousness and therefore increasingly interested in the structures of signification that the new social sciences offered him. These were so many centers of regional ontologies that the philosopher could reappropriate by assembling their overlapping perspectives and renewing their meaning. His ability to do so resulted from the philosopher's position as a subject conceived as transcendence toward the world in its entirety. "Merleau-Ponty had the very ambitious project of entertaining a kind of complementarity between philosophy and the social sciences. He therefore tried to keep up with all the disciplines."[2]

The Phenomenological Program

Signs was published in 1960 by Gallimard. In a text that was fundamental for an entire generation, Merleau-Ponty introduced philosophers to modern linguistics and to the progress of anthropology, coming back to a lecture that he had given in 1951 in which he had shown how important Saussure's work was for inaugurating modern linguistics.[3] "Saussure taught us that individually, signs do not signify anything; it is not so much that each sign expresses a meaning but that each one marks a difference in meaning between itself and other signs."[4] In the same work, he also dealt with the relationship between philosophy and sociology, deploring the barriers separating them, and calling for a common enterprise. "The separation which we are fighting against is no less harmful to philosophy than to the development of knowledge."[5] Merleau-Ponty considered it the philosopher's responsibility to define the range of possibilities and to interpret the empirical work done by the social sciences; through his hermeneutic efforts, the question of meaning is brought to the work of each one. Moreover, the philosopher needs the positive sciences because his thinking must be based on what is known and validated by scientific procedures.

The other link that Merleau-Ponty built in this area was aimed at Lévi-Strauss's anthropology. Merleau-Ponty had drawn closer to Lévi-Strauss after his break with Sartre. Elected to the Collège de France in 1952, Merleau-Ponty suggested to Lévi-Strauss two years later that he seek election, which meant sacrificing "three months of a life whose thread was so soon going to break."[6] Merleau-Ponty devoted the fourth chapter of his book to anthropology—"De Marcel Mauss à Claude Lévi-Strauss"—and ardently defended the program established in 1950 by Lévi-Strauss in his *Introduction to the Work of Marcel Mauss*. "Social facts are neither things nor ideas; they are structures. . . . Structure takes nothing away from a society's depth or breadth. It is itself the structure of structures."[7] A true friendship was born of this intellectual association and Merleau-Ponty's photograph always sat on Lévi-Strauss's desk.

But what was Merleau-Ponty seeking in these many dialogues? Did he think that he had to surrender the philosopher's arms to the social sciences? Certainly not, but he believed that the phenomenological philosopher should appropriate the works of Mauss, Lévi-Strauss, Saussure, and Freud, not so much in order to provide epistemological bases for each of these disciplines as to subject them to a thoroughgoing phenomenological renewal, which would redefine them philosophically, assuming of course that the philosopher accepted the validity of the specialists' information, which he could not verify. The phenomenologist was like an orchestra leader drawing together all the objective results produced by the social sciences and assigning them a meaning, a value in terms of subjective experience and of total meaning. "I remember his class on Lévi-Strauss, where he presented him as the algebra of kinship in need of completion by the meaning of the familial for humans: paternity, filiation."[8]

Reversing the Paradigm

The rapprochement Merleau-Ponty attempted to create in the fifties between philosophy and the social sciences was a forerunner of the paradigm's later reversal. It was no longer anthropology that was trying to situate itself with respect to philosophy, as when Marcel Mauss borrowed the notion of a total social fact from his philosophy professor, Alfred Espinas. On the contrary, it was philosophy, and Merleau-Ponty in this case, that was positioning itself in relationship to anthropology, linguistics, and psychoanalysis while the work of Michel Leiris and Claude Lévi-Strauss was being published in *Les Temps modernes*. Merleau-Ponty therefore opened up some very promising horizons when he wrote, "The task is therefore to broaden our reason in order to make it capable of understanding what it is in us and in others that precedes and exceeds reason."[9] He opened philosophy up to the irrational through the twin figures of the madman and the savage. Anthropology and psychoanalysis would thus hold positions of major importance, and indeed they held them in the sixties.

But why did philosophy lose its footing here? Why did the phenomenological project come up short so quickly? The first answer would be biographical: phenomenology's failure would be the result of Merleau-Ponty's premature death on May 4, 1961, at the age of fifty-four. The man who incarnated the phenomenological enterprise left behind him a construction site where the work had barely been begun, as well as numerous orphans. But a more fundamental reason exists, and Vincent Descombes's answer is edifying: "This philosophical project was bound to fail for a very simple reason. The scholarly disciplines were already active in their own conceptual development and did not need Merleau-Ponty or any other philosopher to interpret their discoveries. They were all already at work on both levels."[10] Recuperating the social sciences became a trap for philosophy in the grips of its own doubts, and soon left behind in favor of the promising, young social sciences.

Merleau-Ponty played an important role for an entire generation of philosophers whom he awakened to new problems, and they abandoned philosophy well armed to become either anthropologists, linguists, or psychoanalysts. This paradigmatic reversal dominated the entire structuralist period of the sixties. The anthropological landscape was substantially changed and, with few exceptions, such as Lucien Lévy-Bruhl, Marcel Mauss, Jacques Soustelle, and Claude Lévi-Strauss, who came from philosophy, ethnologists came from very different backgrounds, an effect of fusion rather than of filiation:[11] Paul Rivet came from medicine, as did most of the other researchers; Marcel Griaule, who was an aviator first, came from Langues Orientales;[12] Michel Leiris came from poetry and surrealism, Alfred Métraux from the École des Chartes,[13] where he was a student with Georges Bataille. It was not a uniform milieu; ethnologists "do not embrace a tribal logic."[14]

It was above all thanks to Merleau-Ponty that an entire generation of young philosophers flocked toward these modern sciences. While studying philosophy at the Sorbonne in 1952–53, Alfred Adler discovered Merleau-Ponty's work. "Through Merleau-Ponty, we became interested in psychoanalysis, in child psychology, and in the theoretical problems of language."[15] This awakening and the evolution of the political situation complemented each other and by the beginning of the sixties, Adler had become an ethnologist. In linguistics, Michel Arrivé reconfirmed Merleau-Ponty's important role. "Merleau-Ponty was an eminent mediator; it is very certainly thanks to him that Lacan read Saussure."[16] That Jacques Lacan discovered Saussure thanks to Merleau-Ponty is an entirely plausible hypothesis, because they often saw each other privately at the beginning of the fifties along with Michel Leiris and Claude Lévi-Strauss. Merleau-Ponty's text on Saussure dates from 1951 and Lacan's Rome Report from 1953. Algirdas Julien Greimas accords him the same importance.

> The real send-off came from Merleau-Ponty's inaugural lecture at the Collège de France (1952) when he said that we would see that Saussure and not Marx invented the philosophy of history. It was a paradox that made me think of the fact that, before doing the history of events, it would be necessary to construct the history of systems of thought and of economic systems and only afterward to try and understand how they evolve.[17]

The philosopher Jean-Marie Benoist, a close friend of Lévi-Strauss and author of *The Structural Revolution* (1975), also confirmed that he had come to read Lévi-Strauss through Merleau-Ponty, whom he read during his *khâgne*, in 1962. "Merleau-Ponty acted like a precursor phase conditioning the reception of the richness of the structuralist labor."[18]

These conversions provoked a veritable hemorrhage from which philosophy would have some difficulty recovering and which was only the beginning. One of philosophy's own prodigal children, Michel Foucault, dealt a final blow to the phenomenological project and to the pretensions of a philosophy sitting somewhere above the tussle of the empirical sciences. Foucault's critique came only during the sixties, but it developed above all out of his dissatisfaction with the phenomenological program dominating philosophy while he was writing his *Madness and Civilization: A History of Insanity* between 1955 and 1960. He blamed philosophy for being too strictly academic, and for systematically avoiding Kant's question of knowing what our current reality is. Foucault opened his inquiry up to new objects and displaced the phenomenological perspective of an interiorized description of lived experience, to which he preferred bringing problematized social practices and institutions to light. "Everything that happened around the sixties clearly sprang from this dissatisfaction with the phenomenological theory of the subject."[19] Foucault changed directions as much with respect to the phenomenological problematic as to Marxism. However, phenomenology had been responsible for broadening philosophical inquiry by emphasizing that man is not known, but the knower, and that it is therefore impossible for the knower to accede to self-knowledge without a play of reflections making quite apparent the invisible split between the face and its representation.

Jacques Lacan broadened this point of view before the war in "Le stade du miroir," seeking to bypass biological reductionism, and hoping the phenomenologists would help him. Foucault himself began *The Order of Things* by discussing the famous painting *Las Meninas*, in which the subject-king is in the painting only thanks to his reflection in the mirror.[20] But phenomenology could not, or was not able to, rip itself from the anthropological circle and Michel Foucault, in proposing to go further, was therefore proposing a fundamental shift:

> It is probably impossible to give empirical contents transcendental value or to displace them in the direction of a constituent subjectivity without giving rise, at least silently, to an anthropology—that is, to a mode of thought in which the rightful limitations of acquired knowledge (and consequently of all empirical knowledge) are at the same time the concrete forms of existence, precisely as they are given in that same empirical knowledge.[21]

The phenomenological investigation, with its internal tension between the empirical and the transcendental, kept apart but equally targeted in the notion of experience, had to be shifted in order to ask whether man really exists or if he is not the site of the lack of being that Western humanism ignored with utter impunity. Notwithstanding the ambition of declaring itself able to stand within and outside of its own perceptual and cultural field, phenomenology ended up in a dead end because of its will to found the unthought within man himself, whereas for Foucault, it lies in his shadow, in the Other, in an irrevocable alterity and dualism. The lining must be rent in order to make way for that which escapes the primacy of the "Ego" in the living, speaking, and working subject and, beyond the empiricism of lived experience, that which allows the sciences of language and of psychoanalysis to blossom. Foucault's goal was to explore the palpable consistency of that which speaks in man, more than of what he means to say. The phenomenological subject is quite clearly eliminated from such a project, which soon thereafter would become one of the most important and most highly debated aspects of structuralist philosophy.

Seven

The Saussurean Break

The term "structuralism" applies to a very diversified phenomenon, which is more than a method and less than a philosophy. But its central core, its unifying center, is the model of modern linguistics and the figure of Ferdinand de Saussure, presented as its founder. Whence the period's prevailing theme of returning to Saussure as part of a more general movement of "returns," and including Marx and Freud. The program that sought to incarnate modernity and the rationality that had finally been discovered in the human sciences needed to mobilize the past. Between the two moments of the initial break and of a rediscovery, it would seem that something had been lost.

Saussure appeared as the founding father figure, even if many researchers knew his work only secondhand. Saussure offered his solution to the ancient question raised in Plato's *Cratylus* in which Hermogenes and Cratylus debate two opposing views of the nature-culture relationship. Hermogenes argues that culture arbitrarily assigns words to things, while Cratylus considers that words copy nature in a fundamentally natural relationship. Saussure's position in this ancient and recurrent debate was to agree with Hermogenes' notion of the arbitrary nature of the sign. Vincent Descombes humorously evokes the "revolutionary" nature of this discovery and cites Molière's philosophy master in *Le Bourgeois gentilhomme* (act 2, scene 5) as the originator of the structuralist method.[1] The plot is familiar: Monsieur Jourdan writes prose without realizing it, and wants to write a letter to a Marquise to tell her, "Lovely Marquise, I am dying for love of your beautiful eyes." This simple declaration gives rise to five successive alternatives that are broken down into 120 possible permutations and that allow for as many connotations of the same denotation.

But the birth of modern linguistics had to wait for the publication of the *Course on General Linguistics* (*CGL*),[2] which, as we know, was the transcription of students' notes of Saussure's lectures between 1907 and 1911, collected, analyzed, and organized along with the rare written documents left by the master. Charles Bally and Albert Séchehaye, two professors from Geneva, published the *CGL* after Saussure's death in 1915. The heart of his demonstration is to establish the arbitrariness of the sign, showing that language is a system of values established neither by content nor by experience, but by pure difference. Saussure's interpretation of language firmly places it in abstract terms in order to better remove it from empiricism and from psychologizing. Saussure established linguistics as a new discipline that claimed autonomy from the other human sciences. Once its own rules were established, linguistics was to rally all the other disciplines by virtue of its rigor and high degree of formalization, and make them adopt its program and methods.

The *CGL*'s destiny is rather paradoxical. Françoise Gadet traced its history, showing that when it first came out the *CGL* had relatively little effect compared to that of the last thirty years.[3] The number of translations and reprints increased as a function of the rising wave of generalized structuralism: five translations between 1916 and 1960 compared with twelve during the twenty years between 1960 and 1980. Two events were decisive for this success making the *CGL* the little red book for hard-core structuralists. After the First World War, the Russians and the Swiss came to dominate linguistics, wresting the discipline from the Germans who had dominated it until then but who had essentially defined it as comparative philology. As of the First International Congress of Linguists at The Hague in 1928, an important alliance was established that was to have a brilliant future. "The propositions presented by the Russians (Jakobson, Karcevski and Trubetzkoy), on the one hand, and by the Genevans (Bally and Séchehaye), on the other, made common reference to Saussure in their description of language as a system."[4] Geneva and Moscow were therefore at the beginnings of the definition of the structuralist program. Moreover, this was the first time that the term "structuralism" was actually employed. And it was Jakobson who used it, whereas Saussure had only used the term "system," which he repeated 138 times in the three hundred pages of the CGL.

The second event that determined the future of the CGL occurred in France. This was the publication in 1956 of Greimas's article, "L'actualité du saussurisme" in Le Français moderne (no. 3, 1956). "In this paper, I showed that while linguistics was invoked everywhere—by Merleau-Ponty in philosophy, by Lévi-Strauss in anthropology, by Barthes in literature, by Lacan in psychoanalysis—nothing was going on in linguistics itself, and it was high time that Ferdinand de Saussure be put in his right place."[5] Greimas's article was not the only one on Saussure, and it is clear that during the fifties and sixties, the evolving definition of a total semiological program reaching beyond linguistics and encompassing all the human sciences in a common project, which was the great ambition of the period, was justified and encouraged by Saussure's definition of semiology as the "science that studies the life of signs at the heart of social life."

The Theme of Rupture

In order to understand the structuralist paradigm, therefore, we have to begin with the Saussurean break, since an entire generation read and considered the CGL to be the founding moment. This alone makes the hypothesis of a break plausible, even if, according to some, it was basically a myth. Nonetheless, and in order to better understand its influence, we can ask whether or not there really was a break between pre- and post-Saussurean linguistics. Answers vary with the linguist, and nobody is naive enough to believe that linguistic thinking could spring full-blown from a single individual's mind, but some insist more on the discontinuity of Saussure's thinking, whereas others emphasize a more progressive shift.

Françoise Gadet argued in favor of a very clear break between "the ideas of the pre-Saussurean period" and those of the period that opens with Saussure.[6] The descriptive approach, the prevalence of the idea of system, the concern for going from constructed and explicit procedures back to elementary units, Saussure's new orientation offered all of this and would become the lowest common denominator for the entire structuralist movement. Saussure represented the veritable birth of modern linguistics for Roland Barthes as well. "There is an epistemological change with Saussure: analogy replaces evolutionism, imitation replaces derivation."[7] Barthes, in his enthusiasm, even presented Saussure as the harbinger of a democratic model thanks to a homology between the social contract and the linguistic contract. An entire lineage here refers to structuralism's enduring rootedness. Poetry, according to the Schlegel brothers, was supposed to be a Republican discourse,[8] and there is indeed a debt to German Romanticism, which had argued for a notion of art as a structure freed of mimesis.

Claudine Normand, a linguistics professor at Paris X who came to linguistics starting from the idea of the Saussurean break, saw a break, but not where it was usually situated. "It is difficult to place: the Saussurean discourse is very unclear because it is part of the positivist discourse of the period."[9] Saussure's essential contribution was not to discover the arbitrary nature of the sign; all linguists were already convinced of this by the end of the nineteenth century, and all the comparative work had already adopted the conventionalist argument and rejected the naturalist model. However, "he did something else with it; he attached it to the semiological principle, which is to say, to the theory of value, which allowed him to say that in language there are only differences without any oppositional sign."[10] The break would therefore essentially be at the level of the definition of a theory of value, in the principles allowing a generalization of the description, and in the project's abstraction. Saussure's idea of system expressed the construction of an abstract, conceptual procedure because a system cannot be observed, even though each linguistic element depends on it. For Claudine Normand, the diachrony/synchrony distinction was already in the making prior to Saussure, especially in the work being done in dialectology, where synchrony would quite naturally receive precedence in the collection of dialects, for want of written traces. On this matter, Saussure would have only "systematized things that were already being said and done."[11]

Jean-Claude Coquet, on the other hand, takes things back to the nineteenth century and even to the end of the eighteenth century, to the important movements that established contemporary linguistics. The idea of system predated Saussure. "It is first of all a taxonomic idea and we therefore see the first successful efforts among biologists. This is the period of Goethe and Geoffroy Saint-Hilaire."[12] Saussure only consolidated the idea of system, thereby reducing its field of study to the synchronic system in order to give it the greatest possible impact, but abandoning the historical and panchronic aspects. Like Michel Foucault, Jean-Claude Milner sees in Bopp's work the basic foundation for a grammar that leaves the world of the classical age and of representation behind. Saussure would have simply cleaned up the fundamental principles needed by the linguistics of his period, which is to say, historical linguistics. But historical linguists had needed general linguistics since the end of the nineteenth century, and needed to renew its links with a time when general linguistics existed before being repressed by the historicism of philological research. "There is therefore no reason to prefer the argument of discontinuity," since general linguistics is a term that we begin to find as of the 1880s.[13] André Martinet, who contributed considerably to Saussure's being read and known, nonetheless considers that Saussure yielded to pressure from sociology by distinguishing between language and speech, and "failed in his plan to study the linguistic phenomenon in itself and for itself."[14] For Martinet, a program truly establishing structuralism was defined only with the advent of the Prague Circle and phonology. "I am a Saussurean, and I say this with the greatest admiration for Saussure: he is not the founder of structuralism."[15]

Synchrony Prevails

André Martinet criticized above all the fact that the important problem of the regularity of phonetic changes, raised during Saussure's time, went unanswered in the *CGL*. In order to account for this phenomenon, structure needed to remain diachronic rather than being limited to synchrony, which is static: "A structure is something that moves."[16] Saussurean categories served, however, as epistemic tools for generalized structuralism even if different works took some liberty with Saussure's text in order to adapt it to the specificity of their field. The principal inflection gave priority to synchrony and Saussure illustrated this and its corollary, the insignificance of historicity, with the metaphor of a chess game that is well played when the situation and possible combinations of the pieces on the board are visible. "It is altogether unimportant that one get there by one path or another."[17] Studying the reciprocal combination of discrete units reveals the internal laws regulating a language. That the synchronic investigation be independent in order to gain access to the system breaks with the methods of both comparatists and classical philosophers, who sought the successive borrowings in the different layers of languages as they were taking shape.

In this radical change of perspective, diachrony becomes a simple derivative and linguistic evolution is seen as the passage from one synchrony to another. Foucault's epistemes come to mind even if the reference to Saussure is not really explicit. Linguistics was freed from the historian's tutelage through this power play, which encouraged its scientific autonomy, but at the high price of ahistoricity, resulting in an amputation that may have been necessary to break with the evolutionism of the time, but that led to aporias because the links between diachrony and synchrony were not set in any dialectical relationship. Saussure made it possible to show that the laws of change for a language and a society differ, and that language is not therefore the simple expression of a racial particularity, as nineteenth-century linguists believed as they reconstructed the history of Indo-European societies through known and recognized languages.

Linguistic Closure

The other fundamental aspect of the Saussurean approach was to see language as hermetic. The linguistic sign does not join a thing with its name, but a concept with an acoustic image whose link is arbitrary; reality, or the referent, is therefore placed outside the field of study in order to define the linguist's perspective, which is limited, by definition. The Saussurean sign only concerns the relationship between the signified (the concept) and the signifier (the acoustic image), and excludes the referent. Signs differ from symbols, which retain a natural link in the signified/signifier relationship. "Language is a system that knows only its own order." "Language is form and not substance."[18] Therefore, the linguistic unit, by virtue of its phonic and semantic character, always points to all the other units in a purely endogenous combinatory activity.

The referential function, otherwise known as denotation, is repressed. Referentiality is located in the relationship between sign and referent. Saussure gave no priority to the signifier over the signified, since both were, for him, as indissociable as the two sides of a piece of paper, but he defined the signifier by its material presence, whereas the signified is characterized by its absence: "The sign is both a mark and a lack: dual from the beginning."[19] Jacques Lacan, in particular, addressed this unequal relationship in signification, and reduced the signified in favor of the signifier in a twist that further accentuated the immanent quality of this approach to language. By his immanent orientation, Saussure limited his project and escaped any correlation between two of his propositions, "the proposition according to which language is a system of signs and the proposition according to which language is a social fact."[20] He enclosed his linguistics within a restrictive study of the code and thereby cut language off from the conditions of its appearance and signification.

Saussure chose the sign rather than meaning, which he banished to the metaphysical past, a choice that came to characterize the structuralist paradigm. Such a formalization made it possible to go quite far in describing languages, but rather than a means, formalization became an end; as such, it often served to occult, if not to mystify. Two ways of dividing the internal combinatory of language made it comprehensible: the linear relationships of contiguity, called syntagmatic, and the relationships that are in absentia, and which Saussure called associational and later encompassed in the notion of paradigm.

Saussure was restrictive by definition, but his project of constructing a general semiology integrating all those disciplines concerned with the life of the signs at the core of social life was very ambitious: "Linguistics is only one part of this general science."[21] But by its impetus, linguistics became the pilot science at the heart of the structuralist project, which clearly participates in the realization of this ambitious program wherein all the sciences of the sign converge around the same paradigm. Buttressed by a method that had already yielded results, it was the melting pot of all the human sciences.

The exceptional and innovative character of this configuration on the French intellectual landscape should be nuanced when compared with a similar situation prevailing in Germany in the nineteenth century, at a time when philology and comparative grammar were the first disciplines to become institutionalized as modern sciences. The number of university chairs, of research money, and of reviews confirms their anteriority. "I think that comparative grammar had a larger budget than physics in nineteenth-century Germany."[22] Saussure's descendants therefore basically equated Saussure with the *CGL*, but it was only one aspect of his personality; his systematicity and formalism were developed like a program even if he lectured in unwritten improvisations, or as a bit of paper folded in fours, according to his students.

Two Saussures?

Saussure's binarism is apparent in his personal interests and even in his personality. He frequently traveled to Marseilles from his native Geneva, taking with him small notebooks that he filled with meditations on Vedic and Saturnine texts of Indian and Roman sacred poetry. Two hundred such notebooks were filled up on anagrams and in a cabalistic search for hidden proper names that would reveal both for whom the texts were intended and their ultimate meaning.

Disturbed by his discoveries, Saussure even became interested in spiritist séances between 1895 and 1898. In 1898, he was called in by Fleury, a psychology professor in Geneva, to consult on a case of glossolalia. Miss Smith, under hypnosis, announced that she spoke Sanskrit, and Saussure, professor of Sanskrit, deduced that "it was not Sanskrit, but there was nothing that went against Sanskrit."[23] Not that Saussure was the only scientist with a spiritual dimension. We need only recall Newton, who wrote thousands of pages on alchemy while writing his *Principia*; the founder of classical mechanics and of Western rationality was also seeking the philosophers' stone. The second Saussure, as Louis-Jean Calvet called him,[24] thought that a language existed beneath language, that a conscious or unconscious encoding of words existed beneath words. However, no trace of his search for latent structures appears in the official Saussure of the *CGL*.

Saussure's notebooks were all carefully kept secret by his family and it was only in 1964 that Jean Starobinski was able to partially publish the anagrams.[25] The discovery opened up an entirely new and different line of research, in the mid-sixties, especially with Julia Kristeva's work. We can, together with Jakobson, speak about a long-repressed "second Saussurean revolution."

The Absent Subject

This second filiation would allow a return of the subject, which had been explicitly reduced to insignificance, if not to silence, in the *CGL* with its critical distinction between language and speech. This opposition included the distinction between the social and the individual, between the concrete and the abstract, between the contingent and the necessary, and linguistic science as such had to limit itself to language, which was the only object that could be scientifically explained. Consequently, the speaking subject, the man of words, was eliminated:

"Language is not a function of the speaking subject, but the product that the individual passively records. . . . Language, distinct from speech, is an object that can be studied separately."[26] Linguistics only acquires the status of a science for Saussure on condition that its specific object—language—is clearly determined. The dross of speech, of the subject, and of psychology had to be eliminated. Banished from the Saussurean scientific perspective, the individual becomes the victim of a formalist reduction in which he no longer has his place.

This negation, which was already the blind spot on the Saussurean horizon, would also become an essential element of the structuralist paradigm elsewhere than in linguistics. It drives into paroxysms a formalism that, after having eliminated meaning, excludes the speaker so that "everything happens as if no one were speaking."[27] With its initial negations as well as their consequences, we can see that modern linguistics had to pay a heavy price in order to establish itself. But once again, Saussure's singularity has to be seen in relation to nineteenth-century Germany comparatists who sought out true linguistic structures, which they considered destroyed by the activity of speaking. According to this current of thought, the structure of language was independent of what was done with it and needed to be restored. So Saussure, once again, was only systematizing something that had predated him.

Behind this language/speech opposition, Oswald Ducrot sees Saussure as mixing two levels, "and it would be interesting to distinguish them clearly, which is what I tried to do."[28] The opposition between language and speech can be considered first like the distinction between what is given (speech) and what is constructed (language). This indispensable methodological or epistemological distinction remains valid; indeed, it is even the very condition of the scientific enterprise, although it does not presuppose Saussure's second, and arguable, opposition between an abstract linguistic system where the subject has been removed from speech activity, between an objective code and the use made of it by subjects. But the whole Saussurean current of the sixties revisited the confusion between these two levels, generating the themes of the death of man and of theoretical antihumanism. Scientific hopes were fanned to great heights as the speaking subject was finally eliminated.

Eight

Roman Jakobson:
The Man Who Could Do Everything

Among other things, the success of structuralism in France was the product of a particularly fruitful meeting in New York in 1942 between Claude Lévi-Strauss and Roman Jakobson. Their friendship, born of a misunderstanding—Jakobson thought he had found a drinking partner in Lévi-Strauss—never waned and, on the eve of his death, Roman Jakobson sent his friend an offprint of an article dedicated to "My brother Claude." This friendship culminated in the unity and reciprocal integration of their respective work: Lévi-Strauss borrowed the phonological model into which Jakobson initiated him and Jakobson opened linguistics up to anthropology. They shared methodology, ideas, and dynamism.

"The Common Language of Linguists and Anthropologists" is a programmatic chapter in *General Linguistics* in which Jakobson emphasized the important roles played by the mathematical theory of communication and information theory for advancing linguistics since Saussure and his contemporary, Peirce.[1] It was now time for linguistics to concern itself with meaning and for the game of hide-and-seek between sign and signification to come to an end. "We are facing the important task of incorporating linguistic signification into the science of language."[2] A vast and common research program opened up for linguists and anthropologists in which the codes of one language could be substituted for those of the other thanks to the isomorphism of internal structures. Jakobson, like Lévi-Strauss, sought universals:

"The moment has come to address the question of the universal laws of language."[3] He was clearly determined to anchor linguistics in the modernity of the hard sciences and compared recent developments in general linguistics—its transition from a genetic to a descriptive approach—to the transformation of classical mechanics into quantum mechanics: "Structural linguistics, like quantum mechanics, gains in morphic determinism what it loses in temporal determinism."[4]

Jakobson was already quite receptive to anthropology before meeting Lévi-Strauss, however, for he was in the double line of European linguistics and ethnolinguistics, a branch of American linguistics based on Sapir's and Boas's work on Amerindian languages. This tradition had explored paths different from those taken by Saussure, but it had also emphasized the description of languages and the fundamental importance of linguistic structure. Learning about the coherence of Amerindian languages was an urgent enterprise because they were rapidly disappearing.

Before coming to settle in America, Roman Jakobson had had an unusual past. A veritable globe-trotter of structuralism, his pivotal position and influence were the products of an itinerary that took him from Moscow to New York by way of Prague, Copenhagen, Oslo, Stockholm, and Uppsala—not to mention his very frequent trips to Paris. Retracing his steps amounts to following the international path of the nascent structuralist paradigm.

The Linguistic Circle of Moscow

Jakobson was particularly receptive to everything having to do with modernity, in the arts as well as in science. Born in Moscow on October 11, 1896, he became interested in folktales when he was quite young and, by the time he was six, was already a "voracious reader."[5] He learned French and German when he was very young and discovered the poetry of Pushkin and Verlaine and then Mallarmé when he was only twelve! In 1912, he joined the new and particularly creative futurists, and read the poetry of Velimir Khlebnikov and then that of Vladimir Mayakovski, with whom he became friends, as he did with the painter Cazimir Malevich. "I grew up in a milieu of painters."[6] Like Lévi-Strauss, Jakobson lived close to painting, which was for him the most intense aspect of creative culture.

In 1915, on Jakobson's initiative, the Linguistic Circle of Moscow came into being and assigned itself the task of promoting poetic linguistics. The first meeting was held in the dining room of Jakobson's parents' home but it was difficult to take charge of the Circle at the height of the war under the czarist regime, and Jakobson quickly joined the Dialectology Committee of the Academy of Sciences. The formalists and futurists therefore were essentially responsible for this push in the direction of linguistics; Saussure came only later, when Jakobson came upon the *CGL* in 1920, in Prague. As early as 1914–15, however, he made the acquaintance of Prince Nicolai Trubetzkoy, who spoke to him about the work being done in France under Meillet. Their encounter was decisive.

According to Antoine Meillet, Trubetzkoy was the mastermind of modern linguistics and responsible for its definitive renewal, through phonology. The friendship that took hold between Trubetzkoy and Jakobson, especially after 1920, and until Trubetzkoy's death in 1938, was so strong that Jakobson says that, given their very frequent and fruitful impassioned exchanges, he can no longer clearly distinguish between his own thinking and that of his friend. "It was a surprising collaboration; we needed one another."[7] He read Husserl, whose *Logical Quests* "had, perhaps, the greatest influence on my theoretical work."[8] In early 1917, Jakobson participated in the creation of *Opoyaz*, a Saint Petersburg society for the study of poetic language. He continued to develop the relationship between theory, poetics, and practice, while frequenting poets including Eikhenbaum, Polivanov, Yakoubinsky, and Chlovsky. "The linguistic aspect of poetry was deliberately emphasized in all of these enterprises."[9]

During that period, Jakobson argued for the immanence of the study of the literary texts and of an internal coherence making the whole greater than the sum of its parts. Jakobson hoped that linguistics would allow him to successfully bridge creation and science, and at the same time he wanted to see linguistics reach the level of a nomothetic science. Poetic language offered him a good starting point because, unlike daily language, which is shaped by elements external to its own logic and is heterotelic, poetic language is fundamentally autotelic. But this formalist enterprise did not square well with Stalinism, which was crashing down on Russia in the twenties and thirties.

The Prague Circle

Unlike his friend E. Polivanov, who stayed behind in Russia, Jakobson left. He went first to Czechoslovakia, where he worked as an interpreter for the Soviet Red Cross Mission in Prague. "It was an accident of history, which gave rise to the development of structuralism in the West."[10] In fact, structuralism could have developed in the Soviet Union and the Soviets could have been in the forefront of linguistic research. Linguists like Polivanov who remained in Russia were liquidated, along with their work, by the Soviet authorities. Ironically, this repression proved, *a contrario*, the formalist theses claiming that literature is its own end independent of any historical context and quite clearly showed that writing has political stakes. Jakobson became the Soviet cultural attaché to the Prague embassy, thanks to Ambassador Antonov, who had taken the Winter Palace in October 1917 under Trotsky, a crime for which he too was liquidated somewhat later. "Antonov was called back with the entire embassy. They were gunned down from A to Z, including the office boys and the cleaning woman."[11]

But Jakobson was bored in Prague. He began frequenting Czech poets and translating Russian poets into Czech at their meetings at a time when Russian culture was considered to be that of an enemy country. They improvised translated readings of Gorky and Mayakovski which provoked impassioned debates and led to an important realization for Jakobson, who

> suddenly discovered the difference in musicality between these two languages, the difference in tonality between Russian and Czech, two languages that are very close because of their roots and lexical bases, but that had made completely different phonological choices that were nonetheless similar enough that a listener could grasp the fact that only very slight changes would suffice for the pertinent difference to change.[12]

Structural phonology was born of this interaction between natural, cultural, and poetic languages. Jakobson also again met Prince Nicolai Trubetzkoy, whom he had known since 1915 and who had fled the Russian Revolution and taken refuge in Vienna. On October 16, 1926, at the initiative of the Czechs Wilém Mathesius, Makarovsky, and J. Vachek, and the Russians Nicolai Trubetzkoy, Roman Jakobson, and Serge Karcevsky, the Linguistic Circle of Prague was born. Its publications began appearing as of 1929, and they defined an explicitly structuralist program: "It [the Circle] took the name of structuralism because its fundamental concept was the structure, conceived as a dynamic ensemble."[13] The Prague Circle was in line with the thinking of Saussure, Russian formalism, Husserl, and of the Gestalt, and created ties with the Vienna Circle. Its "1929 theses" were the equivalent of a program for several generations of linguists. These theses strictly distinguished between internal and manifest language: "In its social role, language has to be defined according to the relationship that exists between it and extralinguistic reality. Either it has a communication function, which is to say that it is directed toward a signified, or a poetic, function, which is to say that it is directed toward the sign itself."[14] The Prague Circle intended to devote itself essentially to the study of poetic language, which had been neglected until then.

Jakobson was vice president of the Circle and professor at Brno University until 1939. He helped diffuse the Circle's structuralist program in the West. The first Congress of General Linguistics held at The Hague April 10–15, 1928, also helped. The Prague Circle came to this congress with its modernist theses carefully prepared beforehand. Given its influence, the first two days were devoted to theoretical questions: "For the first time, we have used the term 'structural and functional linguistics.' We have posed the question of structure as central, for without it nothing in linguistics can be considered."[15] Jakobson also had an excellent relationship with the Copenhagen Circle, which had been created in 1939 by Louis Hjelmslev and Viggo Brondal, both of whom were invited to present their work to the Prague Circle. In fact, Jakobson was published in *Acta linguistica*, the Copenhagen Circle's journal, despite disagreements particularly with Hjelmslev, who, in Jakobson's view, wanted to go too far in eliminating all phonic and semantic material from the study of language.

But the collaboration between the Prague and Copenhagen Circles was aborted for historical reasons. Following the 1939 Nazi invasion of Czechoslovakia, Jakobson fled first to Denmark and then to Norway and Sweden. But with Nazi troops advancing farther and farther West, he had to leave Europe in 1941 to seek refuge. He came to the New School for Social Research in New York. A Linguistics Circle of New York had been established in 1934 and Jakobson therefore landed on receptive ground. He joined the editorial board of *Word*, the review founded by the Circle in 1945. *Word*'s first issue gave a condensed version of the structuralist program, dealing with the applications of structural analysis in linguistics and anthropology. And since the review sought to consolidate "cooperation between American and European linguistics of different schools,"[16] it is clear that Jakobson was once again in an excellent position.

The 1920s and 1930s in Prague were the most productive and foundational years. Even if the 1929 theses of the Prague Circle had a Saussurean bent, the Circle had at the same time put some distance between itself and Saussure on a number of fundamental issues. It defined its conception of language as a functional system; however, "the adjective functional introduces a teleology that is foreign to him [Saussure], since it is inspired by Bühler's functions."[17] In addition, the theses were less radical with respect to Saussure's break between diachrony and synchrony, which was not considered to be an unbreachable barrier. Jakobson refused this line of division on several occasions, preferring the notion of dynamic synchrony. "Synchronic does not equal static."[18] The rational kernel of structuralism was to come less from a linguistic model than from structural phonology, the model of models.

In Prague, Nicolai Trubetzkoy was the best specialist in phonology. His 1939 *Principles of Phonology* became a classic. In it, he defined the phoneme by its place in the phonological system. His method consisted of locating phonic oppositions by taking account of four distinctive traits: nasality, the point of articulation, labialization, and aperture. The Saussurean principle of pertinent difference is clear here, as is the search for minimal pertinent units: in this case, the phoneme. Trubetzkoy adopted both Saussure's position of keeping the referent at a distance and his search for the internal laws of the linguistic code. Phonology is removed from all extralinguistic reality, and attempts to describe sonorous material. This culminated in Jakobson's table of all pertinent traits, organized using twelve oppositional pairs, which were supposed to account for all the oppositions in all the languages in the world. The structuralists' dream of universality would thus be realized.[19] The phonologist's central quest remained that of the invariable underlying the variable.

Jakobson considered that from the outset, as far back as early childhood, the phonematic code was binary, like formal, mathematical language. Binarism is at the heart of the phonological system, where once again we find Ferdinand de Saussure's dichotomous thinking. The sign's dualism between signifier and signified, between the sensible and the intelligible, finds its echo in the binarity of the phonological system.

Receptivity to Psychoanalysis

Thanks to Jakobson's studies on aphasia, the application of the phonological model was broadened, particularly to psychoanalysis. His distinction between two types of aphasia made it possible to examine the
mechanisms of language acquisition and its specific laws, and to draw
some clinical conclusions about two types of dysfunction. Jakobson
differentiated between the combination of signs among themselves
and their selection, or the possibility of substituting one sign for another. In so doing, he adopted the Saussurean opposition between syn-
tagma and association, which made it possible for him to distinguish
two types of aphasia. "For aphasics of the first type (selection deficiency), the context is the indispensable and decisive factor. . . . The
more his utterances are dependent on the context, the better he copes
with his verbal task. . . . Thus, only the framework, the connecting
links of the communication, is spared by this type of aphasia at its
critical stage."[20] This type of aphasia is contrasted with another in
which, rather than suffering from a deficiency with respect to the context, the patient has a problem of contiguity, which produces an
agrammatism, or a heap of words. Jakobson linked the two phenomena to two important rhetorical figures—metaphor and metonymy.
Metaphor is impossible in the first type of aphasia, where there is a
problem of similarity, and metonymy is impossible where there are
difficulties of contiguity.

Jacques Lacan met Jakobson in 1950 and became his close friend.
He adopted this distinction and shifted it onto Freud's ideas of condensation and displacement in order to explain how the unconscious
operates. "Phonology became a model for disciplines having some
relationship with language; so many disciplines had rather weak formalization. Phonology offered them a system of formalization by
pairs of oppositions that were both simple and seductive, because they
were exportable; it was structuralism's central element."[21] The phonological model was perfected at the end of the twenties, but it only enjoyed a veritable expansion as of the Second World War and had to
wait for the end of the sixties in France before becoming institutionalized. In order to understand this lag time, we have to take a look at
the situation of linguistics in France in the fifties.

Nine

A Pilot Science without a Plane: Linguistics

The same linguistic effervescence that arose in Europe in the thirties spread to France relatively quickly, but there was a particular distortion. Institutional sluggishness braked the integration of modern linguistics into the university; the discipline laid siege to the fortress of the Sorbonne, but it lost. A veritable strategy of encirclement was necessary but the undertaking was all the more difficult because the mandarins were well established.

Antoine Meillet was the grand master of French linguistics, which had its Society for Linguistics and a *Bulletin*, and kept itself abreast of the ongoing revolution. But although the information may have gotten through, it remained somewhat removed from the concerns of researchers who were profoundly influenced by their classical training and trapped in the sluggishness of the classical Greco-Latin tradition. It was therefore rather difficult for the modern structural methods to make any significant headway. And at the same time, the discipline was receptive and counted such disciples of Saussure as Antoine Meillet, Grammont, and Vendryès, although they were more deeply influenced by the comparatist Saussure of the end of the nineteenth century than by the Saussure of the *CGL*.

The university, by contrast, was completely cut off from these concerns, and its slumber would continue uninterrupted for quite some time, despite the repeated assaults. Linguistics in France in the thirties was already heavily centralized, a characteristic that would

bring the structure crashing down in 1968. Antoine Meillet's authority appears to have gone unchallenged at the time and, with few exceptions, the training and therefore the orientation of scholars was
classical. Linguists were for the most part grammar *agrégés* who held
a very traditional view of linguistics. There were atypical cases, of
course, such as Guillaume, who attracted many disciples from that
enclave of modernity, the École des Hautes Études: "Guillaume's case
is interesting. He worked in a bank. He had thought about linguistic problems on his own. Meillet had him named as a lecturer in
1919–20 at the École des Hautes Études."[1] There was also Georges
Gougenheim's very innovative 1939 work, *Système grammatical de la
langue française*. But those who took the traditional path leading to
the *agrégation* generally sidestepped the structuralist phenomenon
that was being born in linguistics.

If modernity had some difficulty establishing itself in the prewar
period, what was the situation in the fifties? France lagged increasingly behind and the Sorbonne remained completely removed from
the few places where linguistic research was being carried on. André
Martinet, who could have dynamized the situation, was in the United
States, and he only returned to France in 1955. Moreover, Meillet's
death in 1936 and that of Édouard Pichon in 1940 further accentuated the difference between France and the rest of Europe and the
United States. Robert-Léon Wagner's nomination to the Sorbonne
might have provided some hope for renewal if he hadn't been given a
chair in Old French. Wagner deplored the situation: "It is obviously
abnormal that France be the country in Europe where students of
French linguistics are the least well considered by those whose function was or will be to teach French."[2] There were a few scholars here
and there whose work indicated signs of renewal, but they were still
quite isolated. Marcel Cohen, for example, taught Ethiopian at
Langues Orientales and at the École des Hautes Études: "As early as
before 1950, [Marcel Cohen] was the linguist who showed the most
interest in what was new. . . . Cohen was a very important guide, and
one who considerably encouraged me."[3]

Most of those who were to impose a change at the end of the sixties were in the middle of their studies at the time, and, for the most
part, in very classical disciplines. They were French students in the
main, including grammar *agrégés* like Jean-Claude Chevalier, Jean
Dubois, and Michel Arrivé who discovered modern linguistics late

because their courses had completely ignored it. Jean Dubois, for example, had passed the grammar *agrégation* in 1945, but he only heard of Saussure in 1958! His courses in philology had been totally cut off from general linguistics: "Classical students, like me, who took courses leading to the grammar *agrégation*, could very easily not know what linguistics was."[4]

By contrast, the non-French students, who were further removed from a very traditional curriculum, could more easily discover modern linguistics at the Collège de France, the École des Hautes Études, or the Institut de Linguistique, as was the case for Bernard Pottier and Antoine Culioli. These enclaves were marginalized with respect to university structures, but they laid the foundations of the future revolution. "I wanted to be a linguist from the outset. . . . I began with Fouché in experimental phonetics at the Sorbonne, but it was above all at the École des Hautes Études that I got my training: I started there in 1944 and was there on and off until 1955."[5] Bernard Pottier was active in linguistic activities and publications rather early, and it was because he was a student in Spanish. Similarly, Antoine Culioli came to linguistics through his training as an Anglicist, like André Martinet.

In the mid-fifties, a young generation of linguists was beginning to take its place in the university, but it was still at the periphery, with the exception of Jean-Claude Chevalier, who in 1954 became the youngest assistant at the Sorbonne, thanks to Antoine Culioli. Bernard Pottier became a lecturer in Bordeaux in 1955, Jean Perrot was named *chargé d'enseignement* in Montpellier, and Antoine Culioli and Jean Dubois joined the Centre National de la Recherche Scientifique. André Martinet returned from the United States and replaced Michel Lejeune at the Sorbonne. But the certificate in general linguistics, for which he was responsible, was only offered as one of the options at the end of a bachelor's in foreign languages.

The Periphery Encircles the Center

Given the situation in Paris, the winds of change blew from the provinces, and the countryside progressively surrounded the Sorbonne, the linchpin of the French university structure. The administration provided a certain dynamism in this strategy of conquest, in the person of Gaston Berget, the director of the postsecondary educational sector, who in 1955–56 created the first center for linguistic research within the university.

Berger created the Center for Romance Philology in Strasbourg. It was here that Imbs and later Georges Straka organized numerous international colloquia, making it possible for French linguists to keep up with the most up-to-date research and to make their own research known through colloquia proceedings. As early as 1956 a veritable international community came together in Strasbourg around the researchers of the center on the theme "current tendencies in structural linguistics," and included Georges Gougenheim, Louis Hjelmslev, André Martinet, and Knud Togeby.

In the mid-fifties, director Gaston Berger created a lexicology center in Besançon, where the lexicologist Bernard Quémada had been in residence since 1950. Quémada made Besançon a particularly dynamic center, expanding beyond lexicology by creating a center for language learning, and then a center for applied linguistics at which "as many as 2,200 summer trainees, often for eight weeks," came together.[6] This training center made it possible not only to diffuse new methods, but also to obtain supplementary funding and therefore to increase the numbers of roundtables. Bernard Quémada invited the entire generation of young linguists to Besançon: Henri Mitterand became his assistant, Algirdas Julien Greimas, Jean Dubois, Henri Meschonnic, Guilbert, Wagner, Roland Barthes at the moment when *Mythologies* was published—all came. The Sorbonne, of course, knew nothing of this intense activity, but it was beginning to be well known through its publications. Quémada took over the *Cahiers de lexicologie* in Besançon in 1959, which addressed itself to a broad readership from the outset; fifteen hundred copies of its first issue were printed. "I was convinced that lexicology was a crossroads discipline that did not much interest linguists but did hold interest for many other disciplines—literature, history, philosophy, the military . . ."[7]

Bernard Quémada was a talented broker for structural linguistics. In 1960, he began the *Études de linguistique appliquée* based on his activities in Besançon. It too had a first printing of fifteen hundred copies, subsidized by Didier, a national editor. Berger's idea of circumventing the Sorbonne—which had refused to create these research centers—gained ground and made it possible for the young assistant, Jean-Claude Chevalier, to feel less isolated in the aged Sorbonne by participating in the many work groups that were forming. He met the linguists and Communist Party members Jean Dubois, Henri Mitterand, and Antoine Culioli at the CERM, and his trips to Besançon became more frequent: "We all met there during vacations—there was Barthes, Dubois, Greimas—and we also had news from our American cousins."[8]

While linguistics was rather effervescent, literature remained mistrustful. Structural methods did not easily penetrate the heart of the university organization of the classical humanities, where any mention of logic or science in the field of literature was profoundly incongruous. "Paradoxically, we might say that the systematic overvalorization of literature as a privileged subject in the high-school and university curriculum, taught only as literary history, made it impossible to truly renew theoretical thinking before 1955–60."[9]

Of course, we do find once again some isolated innovators in literary analysis, such as Pierre Guiraud, who, at the 1960 colloquium on modern literature in Liège, presented a paper entitled "For a Semiology of Poetic Expression." Leo Spitzer, who also participated in this colloquium, gave three reasons to explain why France lagged behind: first, the fact that the French university was closed in on itself and university professors were unfamiliar with the work of the Russian formalists, with Anglo-Saxon New Criticism, or with German research; second, the prevalence of studies of genesis, of traditional literary history; third, the French tradition of the scholarly, didactic practice of textual analysis. Philippe Hamon added a fourth reason: "A quasi-total misunderstanding of linguistics as an autonomous discipline."[10] A renewed approach to literature had to wait for the authority of linguistics to be accepted, which did not happen before 1960. There were some individual but important exceptions like Roland Barthes, who linked literature and linguistics and met with immediate and spectacular popularity. "I remember conversations with Roland Barthes in the fifties when he said that it was absolutely necessary to read Saussure."[11]

The French Breach: André Martinet

Even if he was in the United States until 1955, André Martinet nonetheless dominated linguistics in France. Martinet was a grammar *agrégé*, and, as early as 1928, he took advantage of an interesting proposal made by Vendryès to translate Jespersen's *Language*. The translation led Martinet to Denmark, where he met Jespersen and Hjelmslev. Martinet had published his first article in 1933 in the *Bulletin de la société de linguistique* and had already introduced innovations in phonology, which later became his specialty. He published in the *Work of the Linguistic Circle of Prague* in 1936, and worked with Trubetzkoy. Martinet actively participated in the renewal of European linguistics that was going on in the thirties, and in 1937 he was elected to a new chair in phonology created specifically for him at the École des Hautes Études.

The war, however, forced Martinet into exile, but not in 1941 like Jakobson. In 1946, the Liberation paradoxically forced Martinet to leave, not because of his own activities—he had even been a German prisoner—but because he had married a Swedish woman who had collaborated with the Germans. He was therefore forced to abandon his familial as well as his national roots. It was Jakobson who welcomed the exiled Martinet to New York, where he took on some particularly important duties as editorial director of *Word*, the periodical of the New York Linguistic Circle and the most important linguistics journal in the United States. Martinet was particularly lucky in having been in Europe when Europe was in the avant-garde and then, at Jakobson's side, where he could build bridges between European and Anglo-Saxon linguistics since he taught and directed the linguistics department at Columbia University in New York from 1947 to 1955. When he returned to France in 1955, his fame among linguists was worldwide and yet the reception he met with in France made clear just how marginal linguistics was at the time. "He was in a difficult situation when he arrived in France. I remember it quite well. I was an assistant at the Sorbonne at the time and he appeared to the literature professors and the historians as a fearful and scandalous reformer, an antihumanist who had to be pushed out."[12] Despite his notoriety, Martinet had to get angry and threaten to resign unless he was given a tenured professorship at the Sorbonne. In the same year, 1955, his major theoretical work, *Economy of Phonetic Changes*, appeared and was clearly in the line of the Prague Circle. In it, he argued for an approach to linguistics that appeared more dynamic than Saussure's and that took up the Prague Circle's emphasis on the communication function of language:

> That comes from Prague. The important idea is the notion of pertinence. Every science is based on pertinence. A science cannot develop independently of a metaphysics unless it concentrates on a single aspect of reality. . . . Yet, it is because linguistics is useful for communication that we can know what the linguist must seek. . . . It is senseless to do linguistic structuralism if it is not functional.[13]

Martinet therefore focused his study on the choices that language makes possible. His approach was first of all syntagmatic—inventory the possibilities to be established—before it was paradigmatic. Martinet introduced a social dimension into linguistic research by considering the communication function as having its own identity. However, Martinet defined the singularity of linguistic research—in studying language for and through itself—so restrictively that it cut him off from other social sciences and shut him up in the strict description of linguistic function. His goal was to determine the boundaries of distinctive basic units of language, which he called monemes (first articulation units) and phonemes (second articulation units). He codified these rules of description in what became the international best-seller of the sixties, *Elements of General Linguistics*.

An Untraditional Path: André-Georges Haudricourt

André-Georges Haudricourt was another great French linguist. Essentially an autodidact, his rather disconnected path and permanent marginalization bear witness to the difficulties linguistics had in establishing itself in France and the meanders it had to take in order to go forward. In 1939, the Prague Circle published an article on phonology by Haudricourt, who, in contrast to the classical grammarians, was a very curious personality. He first set foot in school only at the age of fourteen, and lived removed from urban life on a family farm in Picardy, in northern France. Haudricourt learned to write thanks to the teacher's widow in the neighboring town, and he passed the *baccalauréat* on his seventh try. He went on to study agronomy and became an agronomist in 1931, but he was revolted forever by agronomy. Three individuals counted considerably for him: Marcel Mauss, "who tamed me," Marc Bloch, who published his first article in 1936 in the *Annales*, and Marcel Cohen, his teacher become friend.[14] When Cohen joined the Resistance, he gave Haudricourt his library in order to save it from the Germans: "'Go get the books that interest you.' I went to Viroflay with wicker baskets, to get the books."[15] Our future linguist was going to get his supplies.

At that moment Haudricourt gave up botany for linguistics and changed his specialty within the Centre National de la Recherche Scientifique. Haudricourt is in Antoine Meillet's line: "Linguistics, I learned it with Meillet."[16] But he grants no scientific recognition either to Saussure—"that poor alcoholic Swiss who died of delirium tremens, it's grotesque!"—or to Jakobson, "that clown from Moscow, very pleasant but who spouted just about any nonsense."[17] Haudricourt remained a comparatist, by contrast; his historical approach was very close to that of Meillet.

Haudricourt, like André Martinet, had a functionalist and dia-chronic view of language. If Martinet supervised a great many theses on African languages, Haudricourt, for his part, made it possible to restore a number of Asian languages. From his interest in botany and linguistics, he adopted a concrete approach to language and rejected logico-mathematical formalism, which was cut off from the social realm. He was a very unusual personality; he considered himself to be the inventor of phonology: "Martinet would be furiously angry but, you see, I invented phonology myself."[18] Linguistics does not lack for pilots in France, but it nonetheless remained very marginal during the fifties for want of sufficiently solid scholarly and institutional legiti-mation. This lag explains the feverish activity that followed, as well as a certain ingenuity regarding the discovery of theories, which were presented as the expressions of the latest modernity when in fact they were often already in the process of being outmoded.

Ten

At Alexandria's Gates

The Sorbonne remained a fortress, like the Bastille, and was untakeable in the fifties. The paths of renewal were to be sinuous, therefore, and it was necessary to go to the Middle East, to Alexandria, to find one of the essential poles for defining the structuralist paradigm. We meet Algirdas Julien Greimas, an important linguist, in Alexandria. Born in 1917 in Lithuania, he had gone to Grenoble to study philosophy before the war with professors who upheld the standards of classical linguistics and were hostile to Saussurean theses. His professor, Duraffour, went so far as to compare Trubetzkoy to Tino Rossi in 1939, in order to explain to his audience, many of whom were Americans, the meaning of the adjective "idiot." Greimas remembers acquiring the methods of nineteenth-century linguistics with fondness, however. He was forced to return to his native Lithuania, where he spent the war years, first under Russian and then under German occupation, before finding his way back to France in 1945 to get his doctorate. He bitterly observed the lack of linguistic dynamism in Paris and turned away from most of the teaching that was going on in order to devote himself to his thesis on the vocabulary of style under the direction of Charles Bruneau. Immediately following the war, a small group was already forming in Paris that included Greimas, Georges Matoré, and Bernard Quémada and that discovered and worked on Saussure's work with the intention of creating a new discipline: lexicology.

In 1949, Greimas became a lecturer in Alexandria. "It was a big disappointment, I thought that we would find the Library, and there was nothing!"[1] But the Egyptian desert became the birthplace for a dynamic group around Greimas and Charles Singevin. For want of books, about ten European researchers met at least weekly from 1949 to 1958, around a bottle of whiskey.

> What can you talk about together when you have a philosopher, a sociologist, a historian, and a linguist? The only common theme was to think about epistemology. I remember having thrown out the word, because they made fun of me at first, not really knowing very well what it entailed. Phenomenology was in style and they were doing the phenomenology of whatever.[2]

Another decisive encounter took place in Alexandria and it too proved to be the beginning of a deep friendship and rich collaboration. Greimas and the man who would become the structuralist star, Roland Barthes, met in Alexandria, where Greimas suggested that Barthes, who had come to Egypt at the same time, read Saussure and Hjelmslev. For his part, Barthes had Greimas read the beginning of the manuscript that was to become his *Michelet by Himself*.[3] "'It's very good,' commented Greimas, 'but you could use Saussure.' 'Who is Saussure?' asked Barthes. 'But one cannot not know Saussure,' answered Greimas, peremptorily."[4] Barthes could not stay in Alexandria any longer because of pulmonary problems, but he had gotten a push, and when Greimas saw him in Paris, where he returned every summer, he maintained the valuable contact with his friend Barthes. In speaking of Greimas's considerable influence, Charles Singevin commented that "Barthes found the route to Greimas like Saint Paul found the route to Damascus."[5] Greimas, however, had already been converted to modern linguistics and he saw himself as heir to Saussure. This perspective made the work of the Linguistic Circle of Copenhagen particularly seductive, and especially the work of Hjelmslev, whom he presented as the only loyal heir to the teaching of the Genevan master: "The true and perhaps only successor of Saussure who has been able to make his intentions explicit and formulate them definitively."[6]

The Hjelmslevian Filiation

Greimas saw Hjelmslev as the veritable founder of modern linguistics for a number of reasons: his very restrictive conception of language reduced to an essence, his emphasis on the Saussurean break with an even more axiomatic method, and finally his desire to broaden a method into a vast semiotic field extending beyond strictly linguistic terrain. Hjelmslev defined a new discipline that he called glossematics, in keeping with the Saussurean tradition. He emphasized the marginalization of all extralinguistic reality and freed the linguist to concentrate on a search for an underlying structure to the internal linguistic order, independent of all reference to experience.

Hjelmslev defined his project in 1943 in the *Prolegomena to a Theory of Language*. The work was only translated in France in 1968, by Minuit. Between 1943 and 1968, then, it was essentially Barthes and Greimas who diffused Hjelmslev's work. Saussure's terms were slightly modified: signifier/signified was expressed as (signifier)/content (signified). These semantic slippages corresponded to a desire to dissociate the two levels of analysis so that the structure could be conceived as separate from what it structures, and therefore to force it to a purely formal level: "Only through typology does linguistics rise to quite general points of view and become a science."[7]

The mathematical model was even more central for Hjelmslev in his quest for scientificity than it was for Saussure. The structure subtending every linguistic sequence had to be found by abstraction based on a code combining associations and commutations. Glossematics took theories of logic as its model at the risk of making linguistics surreptitiously slip like a general epistemology, a particular case of a comprehensive logical approach, toward an ontologization of the subtending structures: "It is not altogether clear whether this algebra belongs to the hypothetico-deductive phase of research or whether it is part of the way in which language itself functions."[8] The principles of logical reduction perfected by Hjelmslev helped formalism succeed in Europe: in Germany with the discovery of the baroque; in France, Focillon's discovery of the Romanesque in art; in Russia with Vladimir Propp. The same episteme tied this formal research together. And Hjelmslev was also well known in France, where the "linguistic mirage" and the ambition of scientificity were particularly lively in the social sciences during the sixties. From its culminating conceptualization in the Vienna Circle with Rudolf Carnap and Ludwig Wittgenstein, a possible mathematization of the whole of the human sciences quickly seemed conceivable. Hjelmslev helped give form to this somewhat illusory hope by his increasingly mathematical reduction of linguistic givens. "The postulation of objects as something different from the terms of relationships is a superfluous axiom and consequently a mataphysical hypothesis from which linguistic science will have to be freed."[9] Hjelmslev took the logic of abstraction as far as he could, constructing a self-enclosed scholasticism. This was the orientation that clearly gained the upper hand.

There were other possibilities, however, in the Copenhagen Circle. At the same time, Hjelmslev's elder enemy brother, Viggo Brøndal, offered a slightly different linguistic orientation, which, although just as rigorous and as concerned with structure, was "at the same time, open to history and to movement: there was a dynamic aspect to Brøndal, who held that the facts of language should be understood as they developed and not within a closed system."[10] A language's system of internal relations was not enough, according to Brøndal, who agreed with Benveniste. However, "there are periods during which the most strict ideas carry the day, and that was the case for Hjelmslev and Brøndal."[11] If Greimas was undisputably Hjelmslev's successor by taking glossematics as his starting point, André Martinet also knew Hjelmslev as early as the beginning of the thirties, when he had gone to see Jespersen in Copenhagen. "We remained in touch until his death."[12] Initially their ties were rather close. At the 1935 Phonetics Congress in London, Martinet advised Hjelmslev, who was presenting his thesis as "phonematics," to change its name: "I told him, no, old boy, it can't be phonematics since we are not interested in substance. There can't be any 'phone.' . . . And the following year, he called it glossematics. . . . I read his work after the war and sweated blood trying to understand it."[13]

Martinet was the successor to the Prague school, whereas Hjelmslev, who hated Trubetzkoy, tried to create a different theory; but Martinet could not accept these antifunctionalist theses. He presented Hjelmslev's theses nevertheless at the Sorbonne, where they were unknown until their tardy translation. Paradoxically, Martinet also contributed significantly to making Hjelmslev's work known, even though he did not in the least accept it. "The *Prolegomena* were translated late. We only had access to a French version of them in 1968. I first encountered this book through Martinet's presentation of it,"[14] remarks Serge Martin, who applied Hjelmslevian principles to the semiotics of music.[15] Principles eliminated any transcendent element and constructed superposed hierarchies of classes, which constitute a comprehensive structure.[16]

Eleven

The Mother Figure of Structuralism: Roland Barthes

In 1953, a book received unanimous acclaim and quickly became the symptom of new literary demands, a break with tradition and the expression of a profound confusion nourished by Camus's *The Stranger*: Roland Barthes's *Writing Degree Zero*.[1] Since his meeting with Greimas in Alexandria, Barthes was no longer the Sartrean that he had been in the immediate postwar period, but he was not yet the linguist he would become at the end of the fifties. We can already discern those qualities that drew the largest numbers of followers to him, his mobility, his flexibility with regard to theories: quick to embrace them, Barthes was just as quick to disengage from them.

A mythic figure for structuralism, Roland Barthes was a subtle and supple incarnation of it wrought of moods rather than of rigor. He was structuralism's best barometer, just as able to sense the disturbances of the moment as those to come. Barthes's extreme sensitivity found the means of expressing itself within the framework of structures, however, although his was a shimmering structure, more a cosmogony incarnating the fusional universe of his relationship with a maternal image than the implacable mechanism of a binarized structure. Barthes was a weather vane for structuralism. Within him, through a subtle intertextuality, all the voices and paths of the paradigm came into play. A veritable magnet among the diverse structuralisms, Barthes was loved because he expressed more than a methodological program. He was a receptacle for the multiple variations of values of the period.

Indeed, we need only examine references to his works to discern his position at the intersection of voices and values. The empire of signs continued on in him as an empire of the senses, and it is useful to juxtapose the mother figure he incarnated with its binary other, structuralism's severe father figure: Jacques Lacan.

Degree Zero

Barthes joined in the formalist current with *Writing Degree Zero*, favoring an ethics of writing freed from all constraints: "What we hope to do here is to sketch out this connection and to affirm the existence of a formal reality independent of language and style."[2] Barthes adhered to the Sartrean theme of freedom conquered through the act of writing, but he innovated, no longer situating the commitment represented by writing in the content but rather in the form. Language became a finality identified with reconquered freedom. Literature, however, was at a zero point to be reconquered. It had degenerated through its dissolution in a daily language made up of habits and prescriptions, and through stylistics, which leads to an autarkic mode, to an ideology in which the author acts as if he were cut off from society and reduced to a splendid isolation.

Barthes recalls the theme that is specific to modern linguistics and to structural anthropology, of the fundamental importance of exchange, of the primitive relationship that must begin at a nodal or zero point and be defined not by its empirical content but by the fact that it allows content to establish itself relationally. We find the same search for a zero degree of familial relationships in Lévi-Strauss, for a zero degree of the linguistic unit in Jakobson, and for a zero degree of writing in Barthes: the search for a pact, an initial contract establishing the writer's relationship to society. In 1953, however, Barthes did not yet have a solid structuralist foundation. He was certainly receptive to Greimas's advice and already knew Brondal and Jakobson somewhat, but these remained for him curiosities among others. He was principally motivated by tracking down the ideological masks worn by literary expression, a concern that remained constant in his work.

Writing Degree Zero was successful because it participated in a new literary sensibility, which the New Novel would incarnate with a new stylistics beyond traditional novelistic norms. Barthes's remarks have a manifesto quality to them, but there was also a desperation to his quest for a new writing cut off from all language of value, apparently expressing the impasse of all forms of writing coming after the novel's high point, which was Marcel Proust. In fact, the work that Seuil published in 1953 was consecrated by the critics. Maurice Nadeau devoted eight pages to it in *Les Lettres nouvelles*, ending his article by celebrating the young author whom he had discovered in 1947: "An oeuvre whose beginnings must be saluted. They are remarkable. They announce an essayist who stands out from all the others today."[3] In *Les Temps modernes*, Jean-Bertrand Pontalis heralded above all the birth of a writer: "There is a great writer among us and he is more than period furniture, an economic organization, or even an ideology."[4]

Barthes examined all alienated forms of writing in his work: political discourse "can only confirm a police universe," intellectual writing is condemned to being a "paraliterature";[5] the novel, with its pretensions to universality, is the characteristic expression of bourgeois ideology, which collapsed in the middle of the nineteenth century, allowing a plurality of forms of writing by which the writer positions himself in relation to the bourgeois condition. But this plurality, this deconstruction of the universal, is never more than the expression of a period no longer carried forward by the historical dialectic: "What modernity shows us in the plurality of its writings, is the impasse of its own history."[6] Insofar as the creator must disrupt the established order and can no longer do so simply by adding his score to the orchestra already poised to receive him, he can only break, write from and around the lack, the silence: "To create white writing."[7] Barthes pursued and shifted Proust's quest for lost time, seeking instead a nowhere place in literature: "Literature becomes the utopia of language."[8] From this was born both a new aesthetic and, for Barthes, the realization of the impossibility of writing like a writer, as well as the beginnings of a theorization of the writing/writer as a writer of modernity.

Itinerary

While Roland Barthes was theoretically in search of a site that existed nowhere, he was quite deeply rooted in his own childhood, spent entirely with his mother in southwest France, in the Basque city of Bayonne. This very dense period unfolded around his absent father, who had died during the First World War, less than a year after Barthes was born. Barthes compensated for this absence by overinvesting in the maternal image: "We always simulate in the affective relationship, whether amicable or amorous, a certain maternal space that is a secure place, the space of a gift."[9] At the age of ten, Roland Barthes "came up" to Paris, to the Latin Quarter, where he went to Montaigne and Louis-le-Grand high schools and in 1935 began to study classical literature at the Sorbonne. At the same time, he was active in the theater, and together with Jacques Veille created the classical theater of the Sorbonne, which presented, among other things, Aeschylus's *Perseus* on May 3, 1936, the day of the Popular Front's victory. But Barthes spent the war in bed, in a sanitorium in Saint-Hilaire-du-Touvet, near Grenoble. By the war's end, he was both a Sartrean—"We discovered Sartre with a passion"[10]—and a Marxist. At the sanitorium, he had met a Trotskyist typographer, Georges Fournié, a friend of Maurice Nadeau, and Fournié initiated him into Marxism. Barthes's pulmonary illness and its treatment made it impossible for him to take the *agrégation* examination, but he lost the opportunity to pursue a traditional university career. He took up journalism, thanks once again to Maurice Nadeau, who asked him to write literary articles for *Combat*.

Barthes took a double detour. Since a traditional university career was not possible, he left France for Romania in 1948, then for Egypt in 1949. When he returned to Paris in 1950 he no longer had any traditional university affiliation and the consequences were significant. First of all, he had met Greimas in Alexandria, as we have seen, but he also developed a lifelong resentment toward the university. Barthes ceaselessly demonstrated his desire for university recognition, a desire made all the keener because he badly tolerated having only a *Licence*.[11] He only felt truly legitimated on the day in 1976 when he was elected to the Collège de France.[12] Until that point, he endlessly struggled with himself and confided to Louis-Jean Calvet, "You know, each time I publish a book, it's a thesis."[13] Here again, Barthes's enduringly tenuous institutional affiliation made his a full participation in the structuralist adventure. Like most of the structuralists, he had to circumvent the old Sorbonne in order to find a place.

Mythologies

Monthly from 1954 to 1956, Barthes sent Maurice Nadeau an article for *Les Lettres nouvelles*. He continued to strip contemporary myths and make an ideological critique of mass culture, which, thanks to the reconstruction of the postwar years (the "thirty glorious years,"

1946–76), began to become a part of French daily life. Barthes mocked petit-bourgeois ideology expressed in the tastes and values of the media, whose role was growing. For him, the ideology under attack masked an essentially ethical meaning, as Flaubert understood it, a concept that was at one and the same time social, ethical, and esthetic and included "everything that nauseates me in the average, the middle-road, the common, the mediocre, and most of all, the world of the stereotype."[14]

Against the passive acceptance of naturalized values that have become unquestioningly accepted stereotypes, Barthes systematically undertook to dismantle and demystify; his project was to demonstrate how a myth functions in contemporary society. Drawing concrete examples from daily life, he grouped together fifty-four short studies in what became one of the major works of the period: *Mythologies*, published by Seuil in 1957. The studies were theorized only in the second part of the book, in the final essay entitled "Myth Today." Here, Barthes defined a comprehensive semiological program, which clearly showed his recent linguistic training; he had just read Saussure and discovered Hjelmslev in 1956.

Formalization therefore followed the studies of myths of contemporary daily life in which the petite bourgeoisie was the designated adversary: "I have already demonstrated the petite bourgeoisie's predilection for tautological reasoning."[15] These were the false truths that Barthes wanted to upset by stripping them of their artifices. One by one, he took on a number of popular "cult" images, including wrestling, the advertisement for Astra margarine, Garbo's face, steak and french fries, Michelin's *Blue Guides*, the new Citroën, and literature according to Minou Drouet.

"Myth Today" owed a double debt. To Saussure (whom Barthes cites twice) for the notions of signifier/signified he uses, and to Hjelmslev (whom he does not cite) for the distinctions between denotation and connotation and between a language-object and a metalanguage. In his biography of Barthes, Louis-Jean Calvet points out that Barthes still hesitated about assimiliating Saussurean notions. In the preface to *Mythologies*, he writes that "myth is language," while at the end of the theoretical essay, the formula is "Myth is a kind of speech."[16] Barthes had not yet entirely adopted Saussure's fundamental distinction between language and speech, although by the time he wrote "Myth Today," his conversion to linguistics was complete, and that represents in 1957 an essential turning point in his work, and more generally: "He definitively entered linguistics the way one enters the orders."[17]

Fascinated by formalism, Barthes saw in semiology the means of elevating his work to a science. He could set content aside in favor of formal logic. He adopted Saussure's synchronic study as well, and as a result, all of his work took on a spatial rather than a temporal perspective: "The way in which a form is present is spatial."[18] *Writing Degree Zero* represented yet another break, therefore, for it offered a diachronic approach to the relationship to writing. A myth is a particularly suitable object for applying Saussurean principles: "A myth's function is to eliminate reality"; "A myth is constructed by the loss of the historical quality of things."[19] Barthes could therefore use Saussure's valorization of synchrony as well as the referent's marginalization.

Barthes's form of writing, his discrete use of a code within an accessible discourse, and his openness toward science and its critical corollary all contributed to his immense popularity and success and guaranteed him a favorably disposed reading public. *Mythologies* was so successful that it went well beyond a normal printing run in the social sciences: 29,650 copies were printed in the collection "Pierres vives" and, as of 1970, 350,000 copies in Points-Seuil. Even the most diverse intellectual milieus were affected, which furthered disciplinary rapprochements. The psychoanalyst André Green was very interested in *Mythologies* and reviewed it in *Critique*. He met Barthes on the occasion of his review in 1962, although they already knew each other through their mutual involvement in the theater in the classical theater group at the Sorbonne. Barthes was a director of studies at the École des Hautes Études[20] and asked Green to give a presentation on Jacques Lacan in his seminar.

> Which is what I did; it was my Lacanian period, and afterward we had a drink in a nearby café. Barthes leaned over toward me and said, "You see those two over there, they come to all my seminars, they torture me, they argue with me in a completely unpleasant way, they want to rip me apart." He was referring to Jacques-Alain Miller and Jean-Claude Milner.[21]

A New Aesthetic

During the fifties, Barthes was also actively involved in a drama review, *Théâtre populaire*. He frequently saw Jean Duvignaud, Guy Dumur,

Bernard Dort, and Morvan Lebesque and supported Jean Vilar's People's National Theater, helping Vilar to attract the widest possible public. It was within the context of this drama criticism that Barthes saw and was impressed by a Berliner Ensemble production of Brecht's *Mother Courage* at the Theater of Nations in 1955, and it was a shock. Barthes saw Brecht as the person who did in theater what he wanted to do with literature or with contemporary myths. Brechtian distantiation and Brecht's aestheticism completely won him over: "Brecht rejects . . . all the sticky or participatory theatrical styles that lead the spectator to completely identify with Mother Courage, to become lost in her."[22] Barthes saw in Brecht's theater the outline of a new ethics governing the relationship between playwright and public, a school of responsibility, a shift from psychological pathos to a real understanding of situations. Where the playwright showed in his revolutionary, avant-garde art that it was less a question of expressing than of implying reality, Barthes saw the very realization of the semiological and critical method.

The structuralist project took off with Barthes. His influence was unparalleled during this period, even if he took a fair bit of liberty with respect to strict Saussurean principles or linguistic canons. But he was more an "outsider to structuralism, fundamentally a rhetorician."[23] Georges Mounin considered Barthes's semiology to deviate from Saussure, who established the rules of a semiology of communication, whereas Barthes only made a semiology of signification: "What Barthes always wanted to do was make a symptomatology of the bourgeois world."[24] For Georges Mounin, Barthes confused signs, symbols, and indices. It is true that, at the time, Barthes gave the notion of sign a rather broad sense, which included everything that had any meaning. He sought the latent content of meaning, which is why Mounin considered it more legitimate to speak about a social psychology or a psychosociology than about semiology.

Even if professional linguists no longer recognized their object, Barthes's very extensive view of language would considerably contribute to the success of the linguistic model and to its role as a pilot science.

Twelve

An Epistemic Exigency

On December 4, 1951, Martial Guéroult, an important historian of philosophy, entered the Collège de France. His candidacy was given precedence over that of Alexandre Koyré, a preference that was symptomatic of the period. Koyré's philosophical project resembled that of the *Annales* historians and he kept up regular contact with Lucien Febvre. The project he submitted in his candidacy for the Collège de France emphasized the link between the history of science and the history of *mentalités*, embodied at that time by Lucien Febvre in his work on Martin Luther and François Rabelais, around the notion of mental equipment: "The history of scientific thought, as I understand and try to practice it, . . . makes it essential to resituate works in their intellectual and spiritual contexts, and to interpret them as a function of the mental habits, preferences, and aversions of their authors."[1] Guéroult, however, proceeded less by opening a philosophical text onto a comprehensive historical context than by limiting himself strictly to the mental realm. His success at being elected to the Collège de France therefore "clearly underscores how limited the recognition of a problematics of the historicization of truth was during the fifties."[2]

Martial Guéroult had been working since the thirties, removed from media lights and unknown to the general public. In 1951, he succeeded Étienne Gilson to the chair of the history and technology of philosophical systems. Beginning with his inaugural lecture (called a lesson), Guéroult argued in favor of the fundamental importance and legitimacy of a history of philosophy, despite the perceptible antinomy between history, presented as aleatory, and philosophy, which appears, by contrast, as eternal and atemporal. Fusing the historian's skepticism with the philosopher's dogmatism, however, made it possible for the historian of philosophy to move beyond this apparent heterogeneity.

Martial Guéroult proposed a solution that preserved the history of philosophy by absorbing it as a simple auxiliary science in psychology, sociology, and epistemology. He hoped that with the methodology of the historian he could reach and restore "the presence of a certain real substance in each philosophy. . . . While making systems worthy of a history, it is philosophy itself that lifts them out of historical time."[3] His historical project sought to negate temporality, diachrony, the search for relationships, and the genesis of systems. One of the characteristic aspects of the structuralist paradigm is apparent in the attention given essentially to synchrony, even if Guéroult owed nothing to Saussure. Guéroult justified his interest in monographs this way, arguing that they make it possible to grasp the singular structure of an author and of an opus in their internal coherence. Guéroult abandoned the search for a structure of structures, but worked at "finding out how each doctrine is constructed through and by means of the intricacies of its architectonic structures."[4]

Guéroult's Method

Take a specific philosophical work, imagine it cut off from its roots and from its polemical nature in order to better describe its internal logic, the links between its ideas, single out the lacunae and the contradictions. This was the method Guéroult applied to Fichte, Descartes, and Spinoza. "One of the ways of penetrating the notion of structure seems to me to come from Martial Guéroult."[5] He had only a limited number of followers and never established a school, but Guéroult could count several admirers, such as Gilles Gaston-Granger who was his friend, and a few disciples, such as Victor Goldschmidt.

His method, however, corresponded to the spirit of the times and came to constitute the very foundations of the philosophical training of many philosophers. This was true for the young generation at the end of the sixties. Marc Abélès took Guéroult's philosophy class at the École Normale Supérieure in Saint-Cloud: "Guéroult taught us to read texts in a perspective that could be called structural. However, one day someone was joking and called his viewpoint structuralist. He adamantly denied any similarity, considering himself to be a traditional professor, a true historian of philosophy."[6] His teaching was supposed to make students limber for significant intellectual gymnastics, and at Saint-Cloud they were subjected to "the little Guéroult exercise." Beginning with a philosophical proposition, the exercise consisted in demonstrating that the demonstration could have been done another way, and more expediently. "Guéroult's method was fascinating for the work done on the text, and consisted in always supposing that it was possible to virtually reconstruct it."[7] Guéroult's didactic contribution affected an entire period.

Another parameter of the structuralist paradigm that we see in Guéroult was his preference for immanence freed from causalities exogenous to the philosophical discourse, such as psychosociological causes. Guéroult therefore cut philosophical systems off from any representational function, just as Saussure had cut the sign off from the referent, granting these systems a fundamental autonomy from external reality. Their interest did not lie in what he called their "intellective mission," because "what is strictly philosophical is precisely the autonomous reality of the work's structures."[8] The historian understands philosophical discourses as so many "philosophical monuments insofar as they possess this intrinsic value making them independent of time."[9] The document becomes a monument and Michel Foucault would later address the question of implicit architectural analogy. Restoring a work's internal coherence requires an exhaustive, totalizing approach that is in harmony with and very sympathetic to the author's theses, the architectonics of his work, and his argumentation. Guéroult, in a word, defended "a holistic doctrine regarding a work."[10]

Defining a philosophical work as hermetic presupposes a view of the history of philosophy as discontinuous. Michel Foucault knew Guéroult's work well and pushed this notion in spectacular ways. Guéroult defined his methodological choices for establishing and legitimating an interest in the history of philosophy in his foreword to the work on Descartes.[11] Relativism and skepticism had to be avoided, despite the contradictions among the systems themselves. "The historians can dispose of two techniques for this purpose: criticism, strictly speaking, and the analysis of structures."[12]

Guéroult's Response to Modernity

Guéroult's viewpoint fully reflected a period that sought meaning in the depths of subtending structures. If critique is a necessary stage, its task was limited to preparing the discovery of the structure bearing the text's ultimate truth. Guéroult therefore responded to the challenges of the social sciences and the injunction of modernity when it shelved earlier philosophical systems based on outmoded scientific postulates. He refused to believe that philosophy had accomplished its task; philosophical structuralism, which defended the autonomous reality of philosophical systems, served as a breakwater against philosophy's dissolution in the social sciences. Later, others would be bolder and take their inspiration from the same method, but they came from the nascent human sciences and did not barricade themselves behind philosophical legitimation. This was the primary reason for the scarcity of Guéroult's direct disciples. Structuralism's ringing success had drawn his potential students to other shores; Guéroult's ambition had been strictly philosophical, echoing Fichte and Kant, "to realize, thanks to this methodological structuralism, the Copernican revolution that they had not been able to accomplish." [13] He criticized these two philosophers for having remained prisoners of realities and their representations, and he proposed, by contrast, philosophical self-sufficiency. His approach recalled the formalism of the period: "The philosophical objective applied to the objects of the history of philosophy . . . is a way of envisaging the material of this history, which is to say the systems as objects that have a value in themselves, a reality that belongs only to them and can be explained by them alone." [14] To the linguists' hermetically closed text, Guéroult answered with the closure of the philosophical system on itself.

The other link between Guéroult and the structuralist phenomenon is the insignificance of the philosophical personality behind the system: intentionality, intersubjectivity, the dialogue begun by the creation of an oeuvre are all eliminated in the same way that Saussure and Hjelmslev eliminated the consciousness of the speaking subject from their linguistics. In a certain sense, and even if Guéroult successively examined Fichte, Descartes, and Spinoza, "we no longer read philosophers, there is no longer any community or intersubjectivity with them." The relationship is one of discontinuity and of a maximum distantiation from a logic whose coherence—internal to the author and external to the reader—must be restored. Decentering the subject made it possible to undertake some particularly productive research that defines the manner in which concepts are constituted and validated. Here again, we can recall the importance of this philosophical orientation for Michel Foucault.

Epistemology Above All

This impetus gave epistemology a broader meaning. From a strict reflection on scientific procedures it came to consider the social realm and to establish a real dialectic with ideology. The structuralist period was also one of epistemological reflection. Disciplines questioned their objects and the validity of their concepts and scientific ambitions; scholars tended to abandon philosophy for the social sciences, as Lévi-Strauss had done, and he was not alone. One of the great epistemologists of the period, Jean Piaget, also abandoned philosophy: "The unity of science, our common goal, . . . can only take place at the expense of philosophy. . . . The sciences have all dissociated themselves from philosophy, from mathematics at the time of the Greeks to experimental psychology toward the end of the nineteenth century."[15] Some seemed to think that being freed of philosophy's tutelage was necessary to put the social sciences on an equal footing with the exact sciences. Piaget proposed to eliminate all questioning from the social sciences, beyond their specific objects, which would produce something like metaphysics. The sole criterion was to increase knowledge in a given realm. Piaget did, however, distinguish himself from the general paradigm by his interest in the historicity of ideas, and his structuralism can therefore be called genetic, as in his theory of the evolution of infantile perception, which, he argued, goes through several stages that he saw as so many systems of transformation allowing the child to assimilate new patterns and new perceptual structures.[16] Each of these stages included a moment of equilibrium.

Epistemological thinking in the social sciences depended on the changes occurring in the hard sciences, where the same formalist inflection was evident. The most striking example is the evolution in mathematics with the Bourbaki group's creation of the famous modern math of the fifties and sixties. Mathematics was applied to groups of elements of an unspecified nature, and was deduced from axioms of the mother structures. The prototype was algebraic structure, the group was the ordering structure, and finally, there was the topological structure. These structural models were just as present in Lévi-Strauss's work, through the mediation of André Weil, as in Jacques Lacan's work in the topology of Borromean knots and his graphs. But, in a more broadly metaphorical manner and as a scientific condition, the social sciences were nourished by a logico-mathematical discourse that made it possible to generalize and to explain processes of self-regulation beyond the examples in question. Other disciplines also contributed: biology, and experimental psychology with its Gestalt theory, and cybernetics, which permits the perfect regulation and therefore preservation of a structure.

But the most important intellectual epistemological phenomenon of the thirties occurred elsewhere. The connection between the formalism of the hard sciences and logical positivism was being elaborated, on the one hand, with the Vienna Circle, around Moritz Schlick and Rudolf Carnap, and on the other hand, at Cambridge, England, around Bertrand Russell, as well as with the work of Ludwig Wittgenstein, who was tied as much to the Vienna Circle as to Bertrand Russell, whom he joined in Cambridge in 1911. These logicians argued for a unified and coded science, based on formal logic, using a purely deductive method. They proposed a formalization that offered a common goal for all the sciences, integrating mathematics as one among other languages. Since logic has no particular content, it could provide a common framework to account for the universality of structures. The Vienna Circle favored language insofar as the first philosophical problem lies at the level of meaning: logic would become its tool and language its essential object. The legacy of this double logical and linguistic thrust was called analytic philosophy.

This renewal of logic together with an effervescent theorizing in Europe left France on the sidelines. "France was blocked by the combined actions of Poincaré and Brunschvicg."[17] Whence a lag in the teaching of logic, which was not included in schools of letters, nor in the teaching of philosophy, contrary to what was going on elsewhere. Bearing this in mind, semiotics in the sixties can be seen as an ersatz of this logic that escaped the French.

Cavaillès: Philosophy of the Concept

There was, however, a French philosopher, an epistemologist, whose object of predilection was mathematics and who was associated with the beginnings of the Vienna Circle: Jean Cavaillès. But history would interrupt the course of his work and his life very early and brutally. Cavaillès died a hero of the Resistance under Nazi fire in 1944 at age forty-one. Science was for him demonstration, which is to say logic, and he called this the philosophy of the concept. This notwithstanding, Cavaillès did not adhere to the Vienna Circle's extreme formalism and ambition of constructing a grand logic in which mathematics would find its problems resolved. His project was to understand the operation/object dichotomy, the gesture that created the linking of mental operations and that he called "the idea of the idea." The fate of his thought, however, would suffer the consequences of his brutal demise. Cavaillès's theses were dramatically resuscitated twenty years after his death by the success of the structuralist paradigm, and he can be credited with having laid the theoretical bases for the conceptual structuralism of the sixties.

In the work that he was writing while a German prisoner of war, and which came out after the war, Cavaillès introduced the concept of structure.[18] His idea of structure was already the same as the idea of structure that triumphed after the existentialist parenthesis. Cavaillès favored structure to radically contest philosophies of consciousness. Inspired by Spinoza, Cavaillès sought to construct a philosophy without a subject, and he already faulted Husserl's phenomenology for giving too much importance to the cogito. Here again we see the formalist orientation that allowed science, according to Cavaillès, to escape the reign of the ambient world and common experience. The structure's truth can only be given by the very rules governing it; there is no structure of structure, no metalanguage. If exogenous elements are to be eliminated from structural analysis, the autonomous and original movement of science unfolding its own laws must be found. And this closure, this strict autonomization of science, which considers only its discursive coherence, must be observed. Here again we see the parallel with Guéroult's approach to philosophical texts as well as to semiological formalism.

Bachelard and the Rupture

Despite Cavaillès's death, epistemological reflection continued in the immediate postwar period, thanks to Gaston Bachelard, who was profoundly influential for a very wide public. Bachelard explored the possibility of constituting a science of science by following the procedures and respecting the laws that constitute the sciences themselves.

An entire realm of reflection thus became available to epistemology, but some of its investment in the human subject, in experience, and in life must be relinquished. Here, closure is presented as an epistemological rupture that is necessary to make way for the very procedures of rigorous thought.

Bachelard attacked evolutionism and proposed relativism. Relativism made it possible to restore a view of scientific development as a long progression, full of inventions as well as mistakes and mistaken paths. In a postwar period that was essentially existentialist, Bachelard remained rather isolated, but his idea of an epistemological rupture had considerable impact later. Louis Althusser adopted and reinforced it in his reading of Marx, and Michel Foucault used it in his discontinuous notion of history.

Canguilhem's Seminal Role

The man who succeeded Bachelard at the Sorbonne in 1955 was less well known. Georges Canguilhem was, however, to play a major role in the epistemological thinking of the period. Bachelard's legacy of reflection on the sciences became his and he directed the Institut d'Histoire des Sciences at the University of Paris. The contrast between the two men was striking, however. "Bachelard was a wine-grower from Burgundy who overflowed with vitality, whereas Canguilhem was hard, a man of high interior tension, a Cathar by virtue of his rigor."[19] Admitted to the École Normale Supérieure in 1924, Georges Canguilhem was a student of Alain. From 1936 on, he taught at a high school in Toulouse where he was in charge of the *khâgne*. "When I got to Canguilhem's class in Toulouse, in 1940, I wanted to study classics. Canguilhem was giving a class on the Copernican revolution throughout history, starting with Kant. When I discovered this guy, I said to myself, I don't give a damn about literature, I want to study philosophy."[20] During that period, Canguilhem began to study medicine. He was a pacifist, first, and therefore a loyal disciple of Alain, but he understood the danger represented by Hitler in 1934–35, and had renounced his pacifism, with the "realization that Hitler could not be tolerated."[21] He immediately made an important choice in favor of the Resistance. In a France that was essentially pro-Pétain in 1940, Canguilhem refused all allegiance to the Vichy government. "I did not pass the philosophy *agrégation* to teach Work, Family, Country,"[22] he immediately told Robert Deltheil, the rector of the

Académie de Toulouse. He joined the Resistance and worked actively for the Liberation-South network. He was very much affected by the Second World War, but the battle he waged did not encourage his optimism and he maintained and transmitted a profound pessimism. His was a "tonic pessimism," however, which did not prevent him from taking action.[23]

The road toward proof was filled with trials and death stole doubly near. During the war and in the medical studies Canguilhem undertook, he was led to think about the proximity between health and illness, life and death, reason and madness. Defending his thesis, "An Essay on Problems concerning the Normal and the Pathological,"[24] in 1943, he became the epistemologist of medical knowledge: "The present work is an effort to integrate some medical methods and advances into philosophical speculation."[25]

He questioned the notion of the normal, and demonstrated the fragility of the limits between rational and irrational, arguing that it was useless to seek a founding moment for the norm, even in some Bachelardian break. Canguilhem took a Nietzschean perspective, rejecting all evolutionist views of the continual progress of science and reason. In place of the historicist discourse on the construction of medical knowledge, he proposed a search for the conceptual and institutional configurations that made it possible to delineate between normal and pathological. His project led him, therefore, to reject any dialectical, Hegelian vision. "Canguilhem could not stand Hegel."[26] The idea of historical progress was foreign to him, and was the basis of the pessimism in his philosophy. If the trauma of the Second World War lay at the root of his historical despair, Canguilhem had reason for this shaking up of the idea of progress, the consequences of the invention of the steam engine, the principles of energy loss, and therefore Carnot's principle: "Fire's motor force . . . has contributed to the decadence of the idea of progress by importing concepts developed by the founders of thermodynamics into philosophy. . . . One quickly saw death on the other side of energy loss."[27]

The same principle illustrated Canguilhem's method and led him to cross disciplinary boundaries and to seek out epistemic coherence within the same period. His transversal cuts established what Michel Foucault later called epistemes. Foucault was a direct heir to Canguilhem, who recognized him as such when he reviewed *The Order of Things* for *Critique*. At the end of his presentation of Foucault's work,

Canguilhem asked what Cavaillès meant when he called for a philosophy of the concept, and he wondered if structuralism might not be an answer. Although he referred to Lévi-Strauss and to Dumézil, Michel Foucault was, for him, the philosopher of the concept for the future.

Michel Foucault, for his part, emphasized the importance of Canguilhem's teaching for him and for all the philosophers of his period: "Take away Canguilhem and you will no longer understand much about a whole series of discussions that took place among the French Marxists, nor will you see the specificity of sociologists such as Bourdieu, Castel, Passeron . . . You will miss an entire aspect of the theoretical work being done in psychoanalysis, and particularly by the Lacanians."[28]

The Sites of Scientific Discourse

Canguilhem fundamentally changed the traditional inquiry about the question of origins, which became a way of asking about the site or the institutional setting of a discourse. He established a correlation between a discourse and the institutional setting that both made it possible and constituted its legitimacy. Canguilhem's research on determining the conditions making the enunciation of scientific knowledge possible oriented Michel Foucault's work on asylums, prisons, and madness.

Canguilhem also broke with the notion of cumulative scientific progress. He argued for a discontinuist approach within which the internal frontiers of scientific knowledge were constantly displaced, successively recast, and reorganized. The history of science was no longer the progressive elucidation or step-by-step unveiling of truth, but was rather marked by aporias and failures. "For Canguilhem, error is the permanent accident around which the history of man's life and his future are wound."[29] Through his search for the bases of the validity of concepts, Canguilhem opened up a vast field of study and brought to light the relationship between the ways in which different sciences constructed their knowledge and their institutional and social realities. As a result, there was a fruitful opening in philosophical to sociohistorical concerns. Canguilhem's influence was also very important for the Althusserian movement. Of course, the attempt to revivify Marxist concepts was rather removed from reflections on pathology, but in both fields of study the issue was the status of science and the validity of its ideas.

Pierre Macherey wrote the first in-depth study of Canguilhem's work in January 1964 and correctly evaluated its importance.[30] Louis Althusser himself introduced Macherey's article and welcomed this renewal of epistemological thought that broke not only with descriptive, scientific chronicles but also with the idealist approach to the history of scientific progress, whether mechanistic (d'Alembert, Diderot, Condorcet) or dialectical (Hegel, Husserl). Canguilhem represented a revolution in the history of science, which Pierre Macherey enthusiastically saluted: "With the work of G. Canguilhem, we possess, in the strong sense of the term, and not according to the specialized meaning that Freud gave it—which is to say, in its objective and rational meaning—the analysis of a history."[31]

Canguilhem's antipsychologist positions reinforced the Lacanian rupture in psychoanalysis as well. He essentially made war on psychology and attacked its positivism by deconstructing its disciplinary edifice to demonstrate that there were many psychologies.[32] He tried to destabilize psychology as a discipline by showing that its knowledge was not cumulative and that it brought incompatible paradigms together. Later, in the name of an archaeology and in an analogous way, Michel Foucault took on history itself. Georges Canguilhem also challenged the ethics of psychology by asking whether it was in the service of science or of the police. This mix of questioning, sociological as well as from the point of view of the history of science and moral consciousness, resulted in a productive French historical epistemology, but "you have to see that Canguilhem's reflections on psychology are not epistemological as epistemology is understood everywhere else in France."[33] Georges Canguilhem was an important initiator of a specifically French critical project and we see his influence in the work done during the structuralist period, even if he preferred to remain in the shadows of the paradigm to whose birth he greatly contributed.

Michel Serres's Loganalysis

This philosophy of the concept, as Cavaillès wished it to be named, underwent a spectacular renewal with Michel Serres's work. Cavaillès's and Canguilhem's thinking converged in Serres, who sought out the characteristic epistemic models of a period regardless of disciplinary boundaries. The history of science became a series of stages, of synchronic cuts: the paradigm of the fixed point and Leibniz's harmonics was followed by the modern age in which thermodynamics served as a model not only for all the sciences, but also for *mentalités*, for literature, and for all visions of the world that are completely permeated by the dominant models. Serres could therefore see the principles of thermodynamics in Zola's Rougon-Macquart. As a result, another division became possible. Rather than being divided, scientific knowledge and fiction could be joined by their support for the dominant paradigm of the period. Mythology encountered science just as the pathological intersected the normal for Canguilhem: "Myths are full of knowledge and knowledge full of dreams and illusions."[34] Error once again became consubstantial with truth.

Michel Serres was doubtless the first philosopher to have defined a comprehensive and explicitly structuralist program in philosophy, as early as 1961.[35] What he discerned in the critical use of a notion of structure imported from mathematics was the end of a second revolution in the twentieth century. For Serres, the symbolist nineteenth century culminated in Gaston Bachelard and the substitution of archetypal elements—fire, water, earth—for archetypal heroes. Structuralism opened a new era and Serres baptized its method "logoanalysis."[36]

Logoanalysis sought to purify structure of all meaningful content, cutting it off from any semantic content. "A structure is an operational group with an indefinite meaning, bringing together any number of elements with an unspecified content, and a finite number of relationships of an unspecified nature but whose function and certain results concerning the elements are defined."[37] Structural analysis would be located above meaning, contrary to a symbolic analysis, which would be crushed beneath it; whence a Kantian notion of structure to which Michel Serres adhered by distinguishing between structure and model, as Kant distinguished between noumenon and phenomenon. This 1961 text promised a very ambitious philosophical program, for although the method came from modern mathematics, it was exportable to all other problematic fields. A common paradigm, which Serres called loganalysis, based on cultural accumulation and dispersion, could therefore encompass all realms of knowledge, from myths to mathematics. For Serres, this conceptual advance also made it possible to once again renew ties with classicism's abstraction and to "understand suddenly the Greek miracle of mathematics and the delirious flowering of their mythology,"[38] thanks to the disappearance of the scholastic partition separating letters from science, thanks to the universality and the historic transversality of the project.

In 1960, Merleau-Ponty was defining his phenomenological program, and in 1961, Michel Serres was preparing to send the structuralist program into orbit. It would really take off in the sixties.

Thirteen

A Rebel Named Jacques Lacan

Where Roland Barthes evokes the shimmering image of structuralism, Jacques Lacan is the abrupt other face of the binary framework characterizing the structuralist paradigm, an incarnation of the severe father ever tending toward greater scientificity in order to defend analytic practice. Lacan's influence during the sixties was already spectacular even before the major part of his work was written, for the Jacques Lacan readers discovered in his *Écrits* of 1966 had already been engaged in a rupture begun in the early fifties.

The unconscious was at the center of the structuralist paradigm, but not only because of the spread of psychoanalytic therapy. It was present in Lévi-Strauss's anthropology as well as in Saussure's distinction between language and speech. The unconscious enjoyed an importance during this period that favored its expanding influence, and Lacan benefited from this situation.

Lacan was born into a Catholic family but renounced his faith rather early on. To symbolize the break, he dropped part of his first name: Jacques-Marie became known simply as Jacques. Later, it became clear that this change did not suffice for breaking with a Catholic tradition that suffused a good part of his rereading of Freud. This was the first of many ruptures for Lacan, however, as he moved through different areas of knowledge that nourished his chosen field of specialization—initially neuropsychiatry, and later psychoanalysis.

As early as the beginning of the thirties, Lacan embraced all forms of modernity, from dadaism in the arts to Hegelian thinking in political philosophy. He took Kojève's classes at the École des Hautes Études. "Kojève's teaching exerted an influence over Lacan in the literal sense of the word."[1] Lacan retained a number of Kojève's lessons on the Hegelian dialectic, particularly on the master/slave relationship, and above all his reading of Hegel, emphasizing man's decentering as well as that of consciousness, Hegel's critique of metaphysics, and the priority given to the notion of desire. This notion of desire was particularly clear at the heart of Lacanian theory, which reflected Kojève's reading of Hegel according to which "human history is the history of desired desires."[2] Thanks to Kojève, Lacan could claim that to desire is not to desire the other, but to desire the desire of the other. If Hegel's teaching informed Lacan's rereading of Freud, his altogether singular mode of writing resulted above all from his interest in and association with the surrealists. He was a friend of René Crevel, had met André Breton, saluted the surrealist renewal in Salvador Dalí, and, in 1939, he began to live with Georges Bataille's first wife, Sylvia, whom he married in 1953.

As early as 1930, Lacan was already quite attentive to the study of writing in his psychiatric practice. He describes the case of a certain Marcelle, a thirty-four-year-old erotomaniac and paranoid teacher who believed she was Joan of Arc and imagined that her mission was to reinvigorate the morals of her time. In order to describe the structure of her paranoia, Lacan began by examining the semantics and style of her letters.[3] Later, his analysis of Aimée established a decisive change because, as a student of Clérambault, he refused to integrate Freudian theory into psychiatry's organicism, and thus reversed the traditional relationship between psychiatry and psychoanalysis. He introduced "the primacy of the unconscious in clinical study."[4] The case of the psychotic Papin sisters again underscored the idea of the unconscious as the constituent structure of the Other, as a radical alterity of oneself.

In 1932, Lacan defended his doctoral thesis, "On Paranoia in its Relationship with Personality,"[5] which would have a resounding impact well beyond psychiatric circles. Georges Bataille and Boris Souvarine immediately noticed and discussed it in *La Critique Sociale*.[6] Lacan broke with all forms of organicism, and integrated paranoia, whose structure he defined, into Freudian categories. Structure, however, cannot be the product of a phenomenological approach to personality: "The specifically human meaning of human behavior is never as clear as when it is compared to animal behavior."[7] As early as his thesis, we can discuss Lacan's return to Freud. He did not return in order to repeat Freud's lessons, but rather to develop them, particularly concerning an area that Freud had given up: psychosis. Because for Lacan, psychoanalysis could only be useful if it could account for psychosis.

The Lacan of the thesis was not yet the author of the *Écrits*, however, in his geneticism. Influenced by Hegel, Lacan believed that a personality is constituted in successive stages until it reaches what he called the complete personality. This progressive construction resembles the transparency of the triumph of rationality at the end of history for Hegel. This moment was therefore still very much a "tributary of geneticism; . . . the first important Lacanian doctrine is an absolutely genetic doctrine."[8] In Marienbad in 1936, Lacan had the opportunity to express this genetic perspective at the Fourteenth International Psychoanalytic Congress, with his "The Mirror Stage."[9] At that point, Lacan was influenced by the psychologist Henri Wallon, with whom he would later part ways.

At the beginning of the thirties, Wallon held that a qualitative stage existed in the child's transition from the imaginary to the symbolic, a process Lacan also described, but which he shifted to the unconscious. This process entails a fundamental moment in which the child discovers the image of his own body, an identification making it possible for the ego to be structured and for the child to move beyond the prior stage of a fragmented body. Psychotics do not make this transition but remain mired in a state of subjective dispersion, forever disintegrated. Like the Hegelian dialectic, the child's mirror stage, which occurs between the age of six and eight months, has three moments. First, the child sees his image reflected in the mirror as that of another that he attempts to understand; here he remains in the imaginary. Second, "the child is suddenly led to discover that the other in the mirror is not a real being, but an image."[10] Finally, the child realizes his primordial identification in a third moment, when he realizes that this image he recognizes is his own. But this passage is premature for the child to come to know its own body: "This is nothing more than an imaginary recognition."[11] As a result, the subject will constitute his identity on the basis of an imaginary alienation, the victim of the traps of his spatial identification.

In 1936 this moment was presented as a stage, or step, in the Wallonian, genetic sense. Lacan addressed it again in his lecture at the International Congress of Psychoanalysis in Zurich, in 1949, but this time his reading was more structuralist than genetic. Indeed, if Lacan kept the term "stage" ("The Mirror Stage as Formative of the Function of the Ego as Revealed in Psychoanalytic Experience"),[12] he no longer saw it as a moment in a genetic process but as a founding matrix of identification, of the relationship established by the subject between exteriority and interiority resulting in a "configuration that cannot be superseded."[13] "Stage" therefore no longer corresponded to what Lacan described. Through this imaginary identification, the child was already structured for the future, trapped by what he believed to be his identity, which rendered any future attempt for the subject to gain access to itself impossible. The image of an ego refers to another self.

As of the postwar period, therefore, Lacan emphasized the split between the conscious and the unconscious, based on two registers with the one exterior to the other: one's own being inevitably eludes being, the world, and consciousness. This stage became the key making the split between imaginary and the symbolic possible, the first milestone along the path of the subject's alienation. "We can see in Jacques Lacan's 'Mirror Stage' a veritable structuralist crossroads."[14] There is a discernible double influence in this new approach. On the one hand, structural linguistics and Saussure, whom Lacan had discovered just after the war thanks to Lévi-Strauss, and, on the other, Heideggerian themes, which took up where Hegelian dialectics left off. The future post-Mirror Stage construction of the ego, always increasingly eluding the forever decentered subject, corresponded to Heidegger's essence of Being, lost a little bit more each day as Being is forgotten: "The progressive discordance between the ego and being will be emphasized throughout the psyche's history."[15]

As of 1949, therefore, Lacan was part of the structuralist paradigm even before his explicit reference to Saussure in 1953; the Mirror Stage, presented as an initial and irreversible structure that can no longer function other than by its own laws, eluded historicity. Progressing from one structure to another was impossible; it was possible only to live with the structure. As of this point, Lacan completely abandoned any Hegelian notion of a possible complete personality that knows itself, which he had articulated in his thesis. The initial structure can never be surpassed by any possible dialectic. The unconscious escapes historicity in the same way that it leaves the cogito and self-consciousness in the illusions of the imago. Lacan once more took his distance from the Hegelian dialectic of desire as desire for recognition, which for him belonged to the imaginary, and therefore to demand rather than to desire, which only finds its proper place in the unconscious. Lacan adopted Freud's notion of a divided subject, developing its implicit critique of the Hegelian notion of absolute knowledge, considered illusory. "I would even say that from beginning to end, Lacan makes a critique, and the most useful possible, of Hegelianism."[16]

In 1956, Lacan took issue with his master and the representative of Hegelianism, Jean Hyppolite, by presenting psychoanalysis as the possible successor not only of Hegelianism, but of philosophy. Hyppolite had given a presentation in Lacan's seminar at the beginning of the fifties, which was published with Lacan's answer.[17] At issue was the translation of the concept of denegation, or *Verneinung*. Hyppolite refused the underlying psychologism, which presupposes a judgment made in the internal tension between affirmation and denial. His reading aimed at integrating Freudianism as a constituent stage of logos, of the Spirit as Hegel saw it in history; he "wanted, finally, to show how Freud's work could be included in a phenomenology of the contemporary mind. He was ingeniously constructing a new figure of the mind, that of a denegating consciousness."[18] For Lacan, Freud was Hegel's future.

Scansion[19]

Lacan innovated theoretically and clinically. But the step he took made him a rebel, a psychoanalyst broken off from the official organization, the Société Psychanalytique de Paris (SPP). He spoke before the SPP on a number of occasions in the early fifties to justify his practice of varying the length of his sessions. The issue was to dialectize the transferential relationship by interrupting the session by a scansion, or pointed break, listening for the patient's meaningful word and using it to end the session, rather abruptly.

These sessions quickly came to scandalize, all the more so because, as the SPP pointed out, they varied in length but were more often short, and even very short. Lacan's practice became the golden apple of discord with the official psychoanalytic institution. In this respect, Lacan completely participated in the structuralist adventure of breaking with the academicisms in power. Of course, with these very short sessions he could earn a maximum amount of money in a minimal amount of time. Analysis became more lucrative than being a company president, which was one way among others of legitimating the profession socially and making it possible for analysts to earn a fortune. Lacan's taste for money became legendary: "If you went out to the movies with Lacan, you had to go to Fouquet's and have caviar. Why caviar? Because that was the most expensive thing on the menu," remarks Wladimir Granoff with a smile.[20] (As a Russian, he preferred whole caviar.) In a period of Taylorism, Lacan had a very highly developed sense of an hourly wage. Some, however, believed this to be a particularly revealing principle of Lacan's thinking, one of the master's most important contributions: "Scansion, punctuation, that's what allows an utterance to be structured. What is punctuation? It is the other's time. It is what makes the intervention fundamental, in that it is articulated with the other's time. Without punctuation, the patient talks all by himself."[21]

These short sessions also had the advantage of letting Lacan multiply the number of patients he saw. He wanted to gain a following outside of the school and train a generation of analysts, making them loyal disciples to his didactic teaching by involving them in a transferential relationship of total affective dependency on him. So short sessions had a market value and provided the means of consolidating the Lacanian rupture. This practice, moreover, goes back to the analytic cure as Freud himself understood it. Freud did not listen to patients in the same way that Lacan did; indeed, there is no mention of the idea of scansion, but "he let certain therapies last three or six months . . . , which amounts to the same idea, that of the head of a school who launches his theory on the market."[22] Lacan would later be excluded from the SPP because of this practice, and would thus find himself the head of a school. Freud and Lacan therefore shared the sense of a need for a certain proselytism. Long sessions for a short time or short sessions for a long time, the goal is more or less the same. Today, even outside the École de la Cause Freudienne (ECF), some grant the principle of scansion some legitimacy, considering that the unconscious is structured like a language. "We can altogether agree that a well-placed scansion intervenes in what the patient is saying, and points to something while at the same time momentarily stopping his speech in the analytic session," Joël Dor remarks, while regretting that this well-founded and fruitful idea of sessions of varying length was systematically transformed into extremely short sessions because of unacknowledged financial reasons.[23]

Others, like Wladimir Granoff, believed that the only thing responsible for the practice was Lacan's experience shortly after the war of being unable to resist the desire to put a patient out. Lacan later reproached himself for having yielded to his impatience and worried about whether or not his patient would return. At the appointed hour, the patient was on his couch. "On that day, the world changes. It changes in the same way each time an analyst does something that transgresses."[24] Lacan then began to shorten his sessions, seeing each time that nothing incited his patients to leave him at all. Beyond this personal experience, these short sessions as a therapeutic doctrine "were not at all interesting, they harmed no one, they never helped anyone, and are not a crime."[25]

Rereading Freud

The results were impressive. An entire generation of analysts was profoundly influenced by Lacan, not only by his seminars, but also, and even more so, by their time on his couch. Short sessions were indispensable if Lacan was to have such a wide influence and was to intensify the transferential relationship. In 1947, at a moment of great moral distress, Jean Clavreul began an analysis with Lacan. "He was the only one who could listen to me in the way I needed. He was someone who metaphorized problems."[26] Serge Leclaire met Françoise Dolto, who sent him to Lacan, and he began an analysis in 1949 that lasted until 1953. Leclaire thus became "the first Lacanian in history."[27] If some began a relationship with Lacan on the basis of a transferential relationship, others ended up on his couch after having gone to his seminars. Claude Conté is one such example. He was in training in psychiatry but was dissatisfied as much by psychiatry as by the way in which Freud was being read. He discovered Lacan in 1957 and took his seminars. From that point on, he reread Freud and, like a whole generation, returned to Freud in the way that Lacan was advocating. He then spent ten years on Lacan's couch, from 1959 to 1969. Reading/rereading Freud was one of Lacan's major contributions. Freudian thinking regained its notoriety and a second wind at a time in the fifties when "it was fashionable to consider Freud as a respectable ancestor, but he was no longer read."[28]

Lacan, therefore, made the return to Freud possible. He took the place of the Father who pronounces his Law thanks to his charisma, his distribution of sinecures, and his beknighting of vassals at the risk of transforming some of his loyal followers into simple mimetic reproductions of himself. But at the same time, Lacan ensured the uncontested success of psychoanalytic discipline in France, for at that point, it entered something of a golden age.

Fourteen

Rome Calls (1953):
The Return to Freud

If General de Gaulle became a politician thanks to his rallying cry of June 18, 1940, Lacan was consecrated by his Rome address of September 1953. But we too often forget that Lacan was initially a psychiatrist, and in this respect the positions he took need to be set in the discipline's epistemological context. In the thirties an important debate on cerebral topology in aphasia was being carried on between those who held that the area of the brain responsible for the language problem could be determined and those who disagreed, arguing that the brain had to be considered as a whole. Psychiatry was at stake.[1] Goldstein, using the theses of *Gestalttheorie*, rejected the reductionism of what for him amounted to functionally localizing a problem within the brain. He took a structural stance according to which neuronal changes affect all cerebral operations. The debate continued beyond the psychiatric world. In 1942, Merleau-Ponty published *The Structure of Behavior*,[2] in which he defended Goldstein's position. The idea of structure, though unlike the one used during the structuralist period, was thus already a central topic in the context where Lacan, a young psychiatrist, was working.

Psychiatry remained important for Lacan, not only because of his early training, but also because of his very strong friendship with Henri Ey, who became the pope of psychiatry. Ey worked in hospitals, and became the chief doctor responsible for psychiatric hospitals. He accepted a position near Chartres, in the old abbey of Bonneval, which he transformed into a forum for important theoretical encounters. Ey organized regular colloquia where psychiatrists and psychoanalysts met. He was, moreover, responsible for training an entire young generation of psychiatrists. "He had considerable moral weight as a result, and became the man behind the idea of structure in psychiatry. The rest of us, young psychiatrists at the time, therefore became completely familiar with structural thinking at a time when structuralism was taking off, only the structuralism that was attracting all the attention had nothing to do with that."[3]

Claude Dumézil, the son of Georges, is a symptomatic example of a conversion from psychiatry to psychoanalysis in the mid-fifties. A student both of Henri Ey and of Daniel Lagache, Dumézil was dissatisfied with psychiatry, which was caught between phenomenological concerns, a psychologizing discourse, and a pharmacological wing. Feeling that he was at an impasse, he discovered Lacan's seminars at Sainte-Anne in 1954: "His was really a discourse that stood out from the others."[4] As a result, he began reading Freud's complete works. Lacan's words had the effect of "a strong mental aphrodisiac; it got you working."[5] Not only was Lacan's discourse theoretically valuable, but it was also consistent with his clinical experience as a practitioner. For his audience, it played the role of free association and interpretation. This circularity also allowed Lacan to control the transferential relationship with his public. His words had an impact beyond their meaning, something that he could theorize. A neophyte at the time, Claude Dumézil remarks: "When I got to Lacan's seminar in 1954–55, he was already speaking about the name of the father and I heard the father's *no*.[6] I understand nothing about the issues, but even then I was completely on target."[7] So much so that he began an analysis with Lacan shortly thereafter, in 1958. But when Dumézil was on the couch, he discovered a different dimension of Lacan. "It was horrible; suddenly the brilliant character became as mute as a carp, the seductive man ripped off your dough. It was no longer theoretical; I was being bled."[8] Lacan's rejection of psychologism made his discourse seductive, but it was also responsible for the cross he had to bear and for his definitive conversion to psychoanalysis. The same was true for many psychiatrists of the period.

A Necessary Leap

But what was happening in psychoanalysis during the mid-fifties? Freudian thinking seemed to be going in a direction that imperiled its own identity. "The Freudianism we had in 1950 was a sort of medical biological mixture."[9] This tendency toward biologizing the psycho-analytic break was rooted in Freud's work itself, and could be based on his phylogeneticism, but Freud remained a prisoner of the positivism of his period in that respect. Nonetheless, the dominant reading of Freud in France in the fifties equated drive with instinct, desire with need. Freud was acknowledged as a good doctor who took care of neurotics with acknowledged skill. There was a double risk, therefore: psychoanalysis could lose its object, the unconscious, to a dynamic psychology, on the one hand, or, on the other hand, every kind of pathology could become a medical problem and psychoanalysis could be absorbed by psychiatry. Lacan's intervention, therefore, created a leap of almost Gaullian dimensions: "His arrival on the scene was without a doubt eminently salutary. He stopped a sort of tide of sludge, of illiterate imbecilities in which the official French school of analysis was slogging around."[10]

Wladimir Granoff illustrates the state of perdition of analytic thinking in the grips of mortal metastases, with an example of a post-war rule in analytic practice according to which missed sessions had to be paid for. The principles determining this practice were not at all secondary, however, but on the contrary, they had an axiomatic value.

> Just after the war, I began a supervisory analysis with someone in whom Parisian society had invested its greatest hopes, Maurice Bouvet. I was part of the first generation of his supervisees. During one group supervision, a colleague described the case of a patient who was sick at the moment and was therefore not coming to his sessions. What to do? Bouvet, this great theoretician, after having thought it over carefully, answered: we can make him pay up to a temperature of 101 degrees, but not beyond. Obviously, it was a probe, a thermometer in the discipline's ass. Bouvet was, however, a worthy representative of the discipline, convincing and eminent.[11]

Here, as elsewhere, Lacan's intervention was salutary because, in addition to his theoretical inspiration, he brought solid scientific guarantees to analytic practice, strict operational rules that allowed him to argue for the scientific autonomy of psychoanalysis with a procedural clarity that validated its degree of scientificity. Cleaning up psycho-analytic thinking and practice was significant for changing the social image of the psychoanalyst, who until that point had been seen a little bit as a dangerous wizard, and who was going to be considered from then on as a man of science:

> At the time, when a psychoanalyst went out at night and invited a woman to dance, he heard, "My God, you are psychoanalyzing me!" Analysts felt like that. Yet, they began at that time to feel as if they were part of a broader activity, the way scientists feel. This was a new identity that was opening up for them at that point.[12]

This scientific jolt happened at the right time. The world situation in fact favored it; it no longer offered any credible prospect of mobilizing for collective social change, and that encouraged an inward social attitude and a return to oneself. Psychoanalysis became the new "Eldorado"[13] at the end of the fifties.

The Break

The key moment of the Lacanian break came in 1953 during an internal rebellion of the Société Psychanalytique de Paris against Sacha Nacht, who intended to acknowledge only doctors as analysts in the new Institut de Psychanalyse. Sacha Nacht was ousted as director, and Lacan was elected as the new head. But Lacan did not seek the schism; on the contrary, he did everything he could to preserve the unity of the French school. He was very quickly obliged to resign as director and relinquish his place to Daniel Lagache; Lagache was responsible for the break. Lacan was in the minority and had to obey; he also resigned from the SPP. It was in this context of overt crisis that Lacan made his 1953 "Rome Report."

Lacan had to cut an attractive French path, therefore, toward the unconscious. In order to do so, he needed to find some institutional and theoretical backers. He sought solid supporters in the two popular organizations of the time, the French Communist Party (PCF) and the Catholic church. He gave a copy of his Rome speech to Lucien Bonnafé, a member of the PCF, so that the party leadership could pay attention to the theses he was developing,[14] and he sent a long missive to his brother Marc-François, who was a monk, and whom he asked to intercede on his behalf with Pope Pius XII, hoping that the pope would grant him a private audience. The pope refused, despite the trinitary order in which Lacan had just redefined Freudianism. These two failed attempts both demonstrate Lacan's concern for giving psychoanalysis a second wind, for putting an end to the crisis by an offensive and dynamic strategy of alliance.

All Roads Lead to Rome

The Rome Report is a return to Freud through Hegel, Heidegger, and Lévi-Strauss, and with a touch of Saussure. Lacan had already widened his sphere of influence by that date, since he was one of the most visible of the psychoanalytic figures in France, and he moved his lectures from his wife Sylvia's home to the lecture hall at Sainte-Anne Hospital. To define this new doctrine of a renovated Freudianism taking shape in the new Société Française de Psychanalyse (SFP), Lacan used the structuralist paradigm, this time explicitly, as the very expression of modernity in the social sciences. He asked that the meaning of the psychoanalytic cure be rediscovered, and aspired to see psychoanalysis attain the level of a science. "To this end, we can do no better than to return to the work of Freud."[15] This meant first of all putting some distance between French psychoanalysis and the fate of American psychoanalysis, which had gotten lost in pragmatism. Lacan denounced the behaviorism that had affected American psychoanalysis this way, and whose goal, as the work of Erich Fromm and Sullivan indicated, was to ensure that individuals adapt to social norms, and ensure as well that order and normalization be restored. For Lacan, the basis of the return to Freud lay in a particular attentiveness to language: "Psychoanalysis has only one medium: the patient's speech. That this is obvious is no excuse for our neglecting it."[16] Here, Lacan justified his practice of scansion in sessions; arguing that chronometric halts according to a stopwatch would be better replaced with the internal logic of the patient's speech. He quite clearly and strenuously asserted the overarching priority of language: "It is the world of words that creates the world of things."[17] Lacan again addressed the break he had established in his 1949 conference in Zurich on the Mirror Stage, between the imaginary and the symbolic. Far from a continuity between the two registers, the symbolic allows the subject to distance himself from his captive relationship with the other. In an analytic cure, symbolization occurs thanks to a transferential relationship toward the analyst, whom the patient invests doubly, attributing him the position of the imaginary other and the symbolic other, of the one who is supposed to know. Analysis therefore satisfies this symbolic function, and Lacan bases himself on Lévi-Strauss's *Elementary Structures of Kinship*: "The primordial Law is therefore that which, in regulating marriage ties, superimposes the kingdom of culture on that of a nature abandoned to the law of mating. The prohibition of incest is merely its subjective pivot. . . . This law, then is revealed clearly enough as identical with an order of language."[18]

In an approach that borrows from Heidegger, Lacan considered that the notion of science had been lost since the *Theaetetus*, that positivism had accentuated the slow degradation that had made the human sciences inferior to the experimental sciences. As early as 1953, Lacan considered that linguistics would make it possible to return to the source, and would thus clearly fulfill its role as pilot science: "Linguistics can serve us as a guide here, since that is the role it plays in the vanguard of contemporary anthropology and we cannot possibly remain indifferent to it."[19] The reference to Lévi-Strauss is explicit and in Lacan's eyes—and we will come back to this—Lévi-Strauss had made more headway, even regarding the Freudian unconscious, than had professional psychoanalysts. The key to his success lay in the implications of the structures of language, and especially phonological structures, for the laws of marriage.

Lacan rereads Freud through Saussure, giving priority to synchronicity: "Finally, the reference to linguistics will introduce us to the method which, by distinguishing synchronic and diachronic structurings in language, will enable us to understand better the different value that our language assumes in the interpretation of the resistances and the transference."[20] In this way, Lacan also fully participated in the structuralist paradigm and encouraged a new reading of Freud in which the theory of successive stages is no longer the core concern; he refers them to a basic oedipal structure that is characterized by its universality and made autonomous with respect to all temporal and spatial contingencies. This structure is already in place before any history begins. "What was very important about Lacan's contribution was that he introduced this synchronic perspective in place of a diachronic perspective."[21] Unlike Saussure, whose privileged object was language, Lacan privileges speech, a displacement made necessary by psychoanalytic practice. However, this does not mean that speech represents the expression of a conscious subject who is master of what he says. Quite to the contrary: "I identify myself in language, but only by losing myself in it like an object."[22] Speech is forever cut off from all access to reality and only uses signifiers that refer to each other. Man only exists by his symbolic function and it is through this function that he must be grasped. Lacan therefore radically reverses the idea of a subject conceived as the product or the effect of language; this is what gives rise to the famous formula according to which "the unconscious is structured like a language." There is no point in looking for a human essence elsewhere than in language. That is what Lacan meant when he asserted that "language is an organ"; or "the human being is characterized by the fact that his organs are outside of him." In his Rome Report, Lacan contrasted this symbolic function, which establishes man's identity, with the language of bees, which is valid only for the stability of the relationship with the reality it signifies. For Lacan, the Saussurean sign cut off from its referent is the quasi-ontological kernel of the human condition: "If we wanted to characterize this doctrine of language, we would have to say, finally, that it is overtly creationist. Language is a creator."[23] Human existence has no other site for Lacan than this symbolic level, and he therefore naturally concurs with Saussure and Lévi-Strauss in the precedence of language, culture, exchange, and the relationship to the other.

In Rome, Lacan therefore clad himself in and seized upon linguistic scientificity. "He was very happy to be able to ground himself in something that had a scientific basis. That was part of the plan of accounting for psychoanalysis in a scientific mode."[24] Thanks to Lacan, psychoanalysis could defy philosophy by coming to resemble it, by demedicalizing the approach to the unconscious, and by arguing for an approach to it as discourse. It was a renovated, revitalized psychoanalysis, claiming to be the continuation of philosophical discourse, that raised this new challenge to philosophy.[25]

The Return to Freud by Way of Saussure

In 1953, Lacan knew Saussure primarily through Lévi-Strauss. After 1953, he delved into Saussure directly by working on the *Course on General Linguistics*. This second reading provided Lacan with an entirely new vocabulary, which he appropriated and used brilliantly in 1957 in "The Agency of the Letter in the Unconscious." In this major text, Lacan based himself completely on structural linguistics, citing Saussure as fervently as he did his friend Jakobson, who came to see him regularly in Paris, where he stayed in Lacan's wife Sylvia's apartment. At that point, Lacan positioned himself within Saussurean concepts, which he accepted with some modification: "What the psychoanalytic experience discovers in the unconscious is the whole structure of language."[26] He took Saussure's algorithm, which, for him, established linguistic scientificity—"This sign should be attributed to Ferdinand de Saussure"[27]—although Lacan imposed a certain number of changes on the Saussurean algorithm that he considered very significant. He changed the symbolization, writing "Signifier" with a capital "S" and relegating "signified" to a lowercase "s." In the same spirit, the Signifier gets placed above the bar— $\frac{S}{s}$ —contrary to its position in Saussure's work.

Lacan removed the arrows that, in the *CGL*, indicated the inseparable reciprocity between the two sides of the sign, like the right and wrong sides of a piece of paper. Finally, while Saussure's bar remains, Lacan does not see it as establishing a relationship between Signifier and signified, but rather as "a barrier resisting signification."[28]

Linguists are justifiably perplexed when they see how Lacan uses Saussure, but we clearly understand his point of view, which once again fully belongs to the structuralist paradigm. Lacan eliminates the referent even more radically than Saussure had, and relegates the signified to a secondary position in which it is subjected to the signifying chain in a movement in which Lacan introduces "the notion of an incessant sliding of the signified under the signifier."[29] The subject is uncentered as a result and becomes the effect of the signifier referring to another signifier, the product of the language that speaks in him. The unconscious thus becomes an effect of language, of its rules and code: "It is nonetheless true that the philosophical *cogito* is at the center of the mirage that renders modern man so sure of being himself even in his uncertainties about himself. . . . I think where I am not, and therefore I am there where I do not think."[30]

This new vision of an uncentered and split subject is altogether consonant with the notion of the subject in other structuralist areas of the human sciences of the period. This subject is in a certain way a fiction that exists only through its symbolic dimension, through the signifier. Even if the signifier takes precedence over the signified, its elimination is not an issue. "The analytic phenomenon is incomprehensible with the essential duality of the signifier and the signified."[31] What remains is the interaction between these two different levels that Lacan attributes to Freud's discovery of the unconscious; for Lacan, Freud was the first structuralist. The signifier imposes a sort of passion on the signified. As we can see, Lacan twists a certain number of Saus-

surean concepts, and if Saussure would have found the idea of the signified's slippage beneath the signifier completely meaningless, the idea
of the unconscious similarly eluded him. Lacan adopted the two
major rhetorical figures of metaphor and metonymy, which Jakobson
had already used, to account for the way in which discourse unfolds,
and he assimilated these two procedures to the operations of the unconscious. Since the unconscious is structured like a language, it is
completely isologous with the rules of these procedures.

The Unconscious Structured like a Language

Freudian condensation can be assimilated to metaphor and displacement relates to metonymy. Metaphor functions like a significant substitution, thereby revealing the autonomy and supremacy of the signifier with respect to the signified. Joël Dor's enlightening example of
the metaphoric use of the term "plague" to describe psychoanalysis,
an adjective Freud used when he got to the United States, illustrates
the phenomenon:[32]

$$\frac{S1}{s1} \qquad \frac{\text{acoustic image: "psychoanalysis"}}{\text{idea of psychoanalysis}}$$

$$\frac{S2}{s2} \qquad \frac{\text{acoustic image: "plague"}}{\text{idea of a plague}}$$

The metaphoric figure will establish a significant substitution of S2 for
S1:

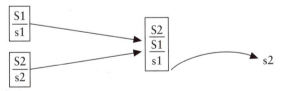

This substitution puts S1 under the bar of meaning, which becomes
the new signifier and in so doing expels the old signified: s2 (the idea
of illness, the concept of plague). With the figure of metaphor, Lacan
showed that the signifying chain determines the order of the signifieds,
and in 1956 in his seminar, he used Edgar Poe's novella *The Purloined
Letter* to demonstrate how the signifier takes precedence, "the realis-
tic imbecility," and the fact that "the signifier's displacement determines the subjects in their actions, in their destiny, in their refusal, and

in their blindnesses."[33] In Poe's novella, each of the authors—the King, the Queen, Dupin—is duped in turn and in their respective positions while the letter circulates unbeknownst to any of them. Each of the actors is acted upon by the signifier's (the letter) circulation without knowing the signified, its contents. Moreover, in this quest for the letter, the truth is always hidden and Lacan takes up the Heideggerian theme of truth as *alétheia*. The signifier, the letter, glitters in its absence.

Metonymy is another rhetorical procedure employed by the unconscious. Metonymic transfer can take a number of forms: substituting the container for the contained ("I drink a glass"), the part for the whole, the cause for the effect, or an abstract term for a concrete one. Let us again take Joël Dor's example, with the metonymic expression "to have a couch" to signify "to be in analysis."[34] The metonymy implies a relationship of contiguity with the previous signifier for which it is substituted:

$$\frac{S1}{s1} \qquad \frac{\text{acoustic image: "analysis"}}{\text{the idea of being in analysis}}$$

$$\frac{S2}{s2} \qquad \frac{\text{acoustic image: "couch"}}{\text{the idea of a couch}}$$

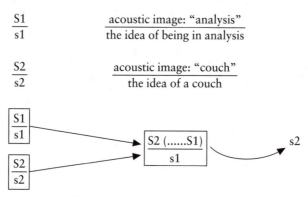

Here, unlike in metaphor, the signifier that has been displaced does not slip beneath the bar of signification, while the signified s2 (the idea of a couch) is eliminated: "The notions of metaphor and metonymy are, from Lacan's perspective, two of the fundamental pieces of the structural conception of unconscious processes."[35]

By their homology with condensation and displacement, these two tropes support Lacan's hypothesis of the unconscious being structured like a language. As a result, he counseled analysts to take patients literally; he is faithful in this to Freud's remarks about an analyst's floating attention to what the patient says. The literality of what is said reveals the signifying chain, the thread of the unconscious. We can understand how the formalist aspect of structuralism is effective in an analysis. And Lacan counsels analysts to familiarize themselves with linguistics: "If you want to know more, read Saussure, and since a clock tower can block even the sun, I would add that I am not referring to the signature to be found in psychoanalysis, but to Ferdinand, who can truly be said to be the founder of modern linguistics."[36] It is the very structure of language itself therefore that gives its status to Lacan's notion of the unconscious, and thereby makes its objectification possible, its operation accessible. Freud had already said that the dream was a rebus, and Lacan takes Freud literally. But the quest for the final meaning of the rebus is always deferred by the signifying chain, which forever veils the truth, beginning with *points de capiton*, those elements of a patient's discourse that stop the slip of the signifier, arrest the analyst's attention, and that can of course be observed in the relationships between signifiers and signifieds, but that radically miss the incommensurable and impossible dimension of the Real.

Lacan drew his vocabulary from another linguist as well, the grammarian Édouard Pichon, who had already emphasized the division between the ego and the "me." Lacan adopted this distinction by separating—and this time radically—the me, condemned to the imaginary, and the ego, the subject of the unconscious, which is itself split because of a double structuration forever cutting it off from any access to the subject of desire, just as Heidegger's Being is inaccessible to being. In 1928, Pichon had introduced the concept of forclusion, which was to become a key concept for Lacan. The issue was to name the failure of the original repression. While the process of repression lets the neurotic work on the return of repressed, "forclusion, on the contrary, never preserves anything that it rejects: forclusion simply and purely eliminates it, or draws a line through it."[37] The forclusion that results in psychosis has to do with confusing the signified and the signifier. Using the linguistic sign differently therefore establishes the pathology of the psychotic: "The schizophrenic lives as of that moment in a world of multiple symbols and what changes is the dimension of the imaginary, of concepts. For the person who raves, on the other hand, a single signifier can designate any signified. The signifier is not tied to any defined concept."[38]

When we observe how central the signifying order is for Lacan, we cannot agree with the linguist Georges Mounin when he sees a simple synonym for "meaning in the banal sense of the term"[39] in

Lacan's use of the notion of signifier. For Mounin, Lacan was a late-comer to linguistic contagion, the victim of "the typical enthusiasm of those who come to things late."[40] Lacan, who, in 1956, summing up the situation of psychoanalysis and evaluating the effects of the structuralist phenomenon, once again suggested that when listening to their patients analysts be particularly attentive to their phonemes, phrases, pronouncements, pauses, scansions, cuts, sentences, and parallels. What really makes Lacan a structuralist, therefore, are the structured linguistic underpinnings of analysis: "J. Lacan is a structuralist. He emphasized this in interviews. He even signed his name to the arrival of psychoanalysis into this current of thought."[41]

The role Lacan assigned to language allowed the issues of psychoanalysis to shift from what they had been in the mid-fifties—from medicalization to the fundamental importance of the analytic discipline at the center of the human sciences challenging philosophy and leading many philosophers astray because of their attraction to the conversion of psychoanalysis to structuralism, an attraction so powerful that they abandoned their own discipline to convert to psychoanalysis. But Lacan did not base himself only on Saussure and Jakobson. To consolidate the success of his enterprise of seduction and his goals of scientificity, he also used structural anthropology and therefore Lévi-Strauss.

Fifteen

The Unconscious:
A Symbolic Universe

In his *Introduction to the Work of Marcel Mauss* in 1950, Lévi-Strauss quoted Lacan to support his theses:

> For, strictly speaking, the person whom we call sane is the one who is capable of alienating himself, since he consents to an existence in a world definable only by the self-other relationship (note 13): The note reads: That seems to me to be the conclusion that emerges from Dr. J. Lacan's profound study, "Aggression in psychoanalysis," in the *Revue Française de Psychanalyse*, no. 3, July-September 1948.[1]

Lévi-Strauss used Lacan's work very early on, even before the Rome Report, but the influence was especially clear in the other direction.

Lacan broadly and quite explicitly borrowed from structural anthropology as inspiration for rereading Freud: "We use the term structure in a way that we believe Claude Lévi-Strauss's use of the term authorizes us to."[2] Lévi-Strauss's anthropological structuralism became the basis of Lacan's postwar rupture. Their convergence was such that Lacan constantly appealed to Lévi-Strauss (see the *Écrits* [1966]) and used him as the scientific guarantee for his approach to the unconscious.

Lévi-Strauss's success in effecting a shift from physical to cultural anthropology by valorizing the linguistic model resembled Lacan's goal of demedicalizing, or debiologizing, Freudian discourse. Lacan used the search for structural invariants in kinship links to extract the unconscious as a structure from psychologizing, behaviorist theories.

This intellectual symbiosis occurred against a backdrop of friendly complicity: "We were very close friends for several years. We lunched at the Merleau-Pontys' house in Guitrancourt."[3] We can be somewhat skeptical about Lévi-Strauss's frequent claims of not understanding Lacan's work, even though it is true that Lacan's baroque writing style quite clearly offended Lévi-Strauss's classicism. More fundamentally, it is certain that although Lévi-Strauss did not need Lacan's rather inflammatory guarantee, Lacan leaned very heavily on Lévi-Strauss in order to win currency for his theses and to broaden the intellectual range of psychoanalytic thinking.

Lévi-Strauss and Freudianism

What can we say about the relationship between Lévi-Strauss and psychoanalysis? Three levels need to be distinguished in order to understand a certain evolution. In the first place, with respect to his training, Lévi-Strauss discovered Freud's work quite early. The father of a classmate at Janson High School[4] was a psychiatrist who worked closely with Marie Bonaparte and was one of the first in France to introduce Freud. Thanks to this classmate, Lévi-Strauss became immediately aware of the existence of psychoanalysis. "Between 1925 and 1930 I read what had been translated of Freud until then, and this therefore played a very important role in shaping my thinking."[5]

The second level is the teaching of Freudian thinking for anthropology. Here Lévi-Strauss saw a broadening of the frameworks of the old rationalism, the possible understanding of phenomena that until then seemed to resist any logical interpretation, and the fact that the most obvious realities were neither the most profound nor the most edifying. At this level, Lévi-Strauss remained faithful to Freudian teaching.

But there is a third level in which the two disciplines of anthropology and psychoanalysis competed in their approach to the human. Yet their relationship was too close, and could only lead to a conflict, especially since Lévi-Strauss had some very serious doubts about the effectiveness of psychoanalytic therapy. With respect to the growing success of analysis, therefore, Lévi-Strauss tended to consider Freud's work to be the construction of a singular Western mythology whose logic he could decipher because he studied myths, and whose strength he could therefore evaluate. "What Freud really did was to construct grand myths."[6] The logic of disciplinary confrontation therefore led

Lévi-Strauss to "harden" (a term he used in 1962 in *Totemism Today*)[7] his judgment of psychoanalysis, whereas he had initially been fascinated by its approach to the unconscious and had been engaged in a constant dialogue with Freud's work. As early as *The Elementary Structures of Kinship* in 1949, Lévi-Strauss had criticized *Totem and Taboo*, considering that Freud had developed a myth. But, above all, he wrote two articles on the unconscious during the same year that had the greatest influence on psychoanalysts in general and on Lacan in particular: "The Sorcerer and His Magic" and "The Effectiveness of Symbols." These articles were later reprinted in *Structural Anthropology*.[8]

Lévi-Strauss described the healing activity of the shaman and the relationship he establishes with his audience. In order to describe the shaman's gesture, he used the psychoanalytic term of "abreaction," a process that resembles what happens in therapy when the analyst helps the patient to relive a traumatic situation that is at the origin of his or her neurosis. Lévi-Strauss borrowed a psychoanalytic structure as an interpretative tool in order to better understand primitive societies, but he nonetheless put some distance between himself and psychoanalysis as a discipline: "But the distressing trend which, for several years, has tended to transform the psychoanalytic system from a body of scientific hypotheses that are experimentally verifiable in certain specific and limited cases into a kind of diffuse mythology interpenetrating the consciousness of the group, could rapidly bring about a parallelism."[9] Lévi-Strauss compared the shamanistic cure to the psychoanalytic cure to show that the parallel between them does not mean that they are similar and that although the terms of the two types of practice are both present, their positions are reversed.

The Symbolic Unconscious

Lévi-Strauss deeply influenced Lacan with this comparative study; he gave his own definition of the unconscious as not being the refuge of the particularities of a purely singular, individual history, but by dehistoricizing the unconscious and affirming its link to the symbolic function: "[The unconscious] is reduced to a term by which we designate a function: the symbolic function."[10] Moreover, Lévi-Strauss called for a clearer distinction between the subconscious, the reservoir-site of specific memories, and the unconscious, which "is always empty, or more exactly, is as foreign to images as the stomach is to the food which transits through it. The organ of a specific function, it limits itself to imposing structural laws."[11] The Lévi-Straussian unconscious is therefore foreign to individual affects, to content, and to historicity. It is this empty site where the symbolic function takes place. We once again find the familiar hierarchies of the structural paradigm: precedence is given to an invariant over its variations, to form over content, to the signifier over the signified. As we will see, Lacan adopted this approach to the unconscious, allowing him to establish "the bases of a signifying algebra"[12] for psychoanalysis in the same way Lévi-Strauss had done for anthropology. In his *Introduction to the Work of Marcel Mauss*, Lévi-Strauss laid out his definition of the unconscious because he borrowed it at that time principally from Mauss. Defined by its exchange function, the unconscious was the mediating term between self and other rather than the subject's private garden. In this major text, Lévi-Strauss defined a path that Lacan would take, the path of symbolic autonomy: "Symbols are more real than what they symbolize, the signifier precedes and determines the signified."[13]

The Mind

There is cause for misunderstanding here, for the anthropologist's unconscious is very much removed from the Freudian unconscious, despite the analogies we can see between the semantic decoding of myths and psychoanalytic interpretative techniques. For Lévi-Strauss, "the unconscious is the site of structures,"[14] and is therefore defined as a system of logical constraints, a structuring whole, "the absent cause of these effects of structure that are kinship systems, rituals, forms of economic life, symbolic systems."[15] This purely formal, empty unconscious, this pure container, is a far cry from Freud's unconscious, which is defined by a certain number of privileged contents. In *Totemism Today*, Lévi-Strauss again cast aside contents and affects in his criticism of the psychoanalytic use of affectivity, emotions, and drives that correspond to the least clear level in humans and cannot lend themselves to scientific explanations. Lévi-Strauss justified the distinction between these two levels by explaining that the intellect can only account for something that is of a similar nature, and that this therefore excludes emotion. This notwithstanding, he claimed the unconscious as the specific object of anthropology: "Ethnology is first of all a psychology,"[16] whose goal, for him, is to restore the universal laws governing the operations of the human mind.

Of Freudian theory, which unfolds in two dimensions—the one topical in which different strata of the psychic apparatus are differentiated, and the other dynamic, of conflicts, reversals, and the evolution of forces set into play in the phenomena of repression, condensation, displacement, and censorship—Lévi-Strauss retained only the topical dimension. As a good structuralist, he held on to that dimension "that has to do with the system of sites defining the topology of the psychic apparatus."[17] The unconscious makes it possible to localize the symbolic function and, at the same time, the universality linking it to the mind. This function is therefore freed of spatiotemporal contingencies and becomes a purely autonomous, abstract, and formal entity. When asked why he avoided the dimension of desire in his notion of the unconscious, Lévi-Strauss answered: "Is this the fundamental dimension of the unconscious? I am not in the least convinced";[18] and he considered Freud's argument that dreams are the realization of a desire a singularly narrow view, a simple mask, a ridiculous smoke screen for hiding our ignorance of biological reality.

Rivalry: Psychoanalysis versus Anthropology

In *The Jealous Potter*, Lévi-Strauss returned to his uninterrupted dialogue with psychoanalysis, and clearly announced the stakes: the rivalry between two disciplines that are both working on the unconscious. The "jealousy" in the title refers to the anthropologist as he observes the psychoanalyst, who can examine a circumscribed object, an individual therapy, and enjoy his place in the social body. It was therefore Lévi-Strauss himself who set the tone of the discussion by placing himself in the realm of jealousy: "The myths that are analyzed in *The Jealous Potter*, especially those of the Jívaro, are particularly striking in that they prefigure psychoanalytic myths. Having psychoanalysts claim them for some legitimation had to be avoided."[19] He reiterated the criticism he had made of Freud—that he deciphered only according to a single code—and drew a parallel between the psychic life of savages and that of psychoanalysts. According to Lévi-Strauss, analysts have simply adopted the anal and oral traits that primitive societies had already discovered: "At almost every step we have encountered perfectly explicit notions and categories—such as the oral character and anal character—that psychoanalysts will no longer be able to claim they have discovered; they have only rediscovered them."[20]

According to Lévi-Strauss, Freud is therefore to be given a place alongside myths but does not even warrant being credited with inventing the idea since he only recycled it in a preexisting symbolic universe. The institutional stakes underlying this debate/fight for anteriority were even more clear: "Can we see in psychoanalysis anything other than a branch of comparative ethnology, applied to the study of the individual psyche?"[21] Lévi-Strauss even ended his book sarcastically by comparing Sophocles' *Oedipus Rex* with Labiche's *An Italian Straw Hat*, in order to grasp the same myth in two different registers. "It is a question of making psychoanalysts eat their hat,"[22] André Green quite correctly pointed out while addressing a group of anthropologists.

Lacan Appropriates the Unconscious according to Lévi-Strauss

Lacan would, in his own words, use Lévi-Strauss as his defense. He quoted him in "The Mirror Stage" in 1949, and later even more so, as his many references in the *Écrits* attest. However, Lacan did much more than simply use Lévi-Strauss as a scientific guarantee; we might even wonder how far he went in borrowing his anthropological approach to the unconscious and whether or not this influence represented a decisive turning point with respect to Freud.

Gérard Mendel sees in this appropriation a shift away from Freud's notion of the unconscious toward an intellectual reduction emptying the unconscious of all contents and naturalizing it. The Freudian unconscious is composed of primary processes where representations and fantasies are played out and momentarily activated or repressed, unlike Lévi-Strauss's notion, which Lacan adopted, of a contentless unconscious: "Believing that he is speaking about the unconscious, Lévi-Strauss never speaks about anything other than the preconscious. . . . What is negated here—as it was later in Lacan—is the very existence of a specific unconscious, Freud's decisive contribution."[23] In the name of the father Freud, Lacan, in the return of which he so often boasted, imperceptibly slid the unconscious beneath the signifying bar of the structuralist paradigm. Lacan paid a high price for his dialogue and anthropological guarantee: psychoanalysis's specific object, the basis of its scientific identity—the unconscious. "What I believe and have always believed is that Lacan thought he was work-ing on the unconscious, but he was working on the preconscious. . . . It is completely justifiable to say that the preconscious is structured like a language."[24]

Nearly ten years later, François Roustang, an ex-Lacanian, re-examined the same problem by arguing that Lacan's symbolic uncon-scious was only the transcription of Lévi-Strauss's idea transplanted to psychoanalysis.[25] Borrowing the symbolic was a decisive moment in Lacan's development for he had initially focused on the imaginary when studying specular images in "The Mirror Stage." He then used Lévi-Strauss to assert the irreducibility, the exteriority, of an uncon-scious that man cannot understand and whose internal logic would be his to explain. "This exteriority of the symbolic with respect to man is the very notion of the unconscious."[26] Any historical process becomes illusory because of this heteronomy. There is a chain that traps man from as early as before his birth and after his death making him some-thing "like the pawn in the signifier's game."[27] The symbolic order can no more be attributed to an individual than to the social order; it is empty, like Lévi-Strauss's idea of it, an exchange function.

François Roustang saw this borrowing as the need for a new dis-placement. Abandoning the underpinnings of the social, "Lacan is forced to substantiate speech and give it some power . . . in a word, to restore the theology of creation through the word."[28] Lacan was torn between metaphysical sirens, between Saint John the Evangelist, whom he cited in an exergue to his discourse, and the model of the hard sciences, including mathematics and physics: "How much should we approach the ideals of the natural sciences, by which I mean such as they have developed for us, in other words, physics? Well, it's with respect to these definitions of signifier and structure that the appropri-ate limits can be established."[29] Lévi-Strauss was therefore a model for psychoanalytic discourse in conquering scientificity, and Lacan en-vied him the symbiosis he was able to forge between ethnology, lin-guistics, mathematics, and psychoanalysis.

If Lacan undeniably borrowed the fundamental category of the symbolic from Lévi-Strauss and displaced it from anthropology to psychoanalysis, hypostasizing and radicalizing it with respect to Lévi-Strauss's use, analysts are not unanimous in arguing that Lacan oblit-erated Freud's notion of the unconscious. "It would be completely aberrant to say that Lacan could not reach the unconscious in a system that goes no farther than the first topic."[30] For Joël Dor, the unconscious as a signifying chain does not invalidate the two Freudian topics but, on the contrary, clarifies them and moves beyond them. Lacan was a student of Lévi-Strauss's rigor, but he displaced the instruments he borrowed. He adopted the idea of a structure, and of a circuit of exchange as a basis for the social dimension, but "he introduces the idea that Lévi-Strauss is mistaken in thinking that women are exchanged between tribes; it's the phallus that is exchanged."[31]

Despite these displacements, a common theme ran through Lévi-Strauss and Lacan in the fifties. Both strove for universality and scientificity, for antievolutionism, and for legitimation. Lacan said of history, for example, that it was "this thing he detests for the best of reasons."[32] His radical rejection of historicity, which also posed a significant problem for the analytic use of remembering, made it possible to participate in the structuralist paradigm because synchrony was given precedence. Even if we agree that Lacan reached the Freudian unconscious, we cannot hold that his reference to Lévi-Strauss is simply a "support rather than a key that would have allowed him to open this or that secret door."[33] Furthermore, Lacan was influenced not only by Lévi-Strauss but also by Monique Lévi-Strauss, a debt he publicly acknowledged. He in fact appropriated the formula she threw at him one day and that became a classic of his thinking: "the sender gets his message back, in reverse."

Through his symbiosis with Lévi-Strauss's work, Lacan also sought to include the progress of psychoanalysis within the general anthropological project of reflecting upon the dividing line between nature and culture. Whence the important theme of the Other for Lacan, his thinking about alterity, on what eludes reason, on the site of the lack, on the decentering of errant desire. Where Lévi-Strauss sought out these figures of alterity among the Nambikwara, Lacan developed the power of the forever inaccessible Other, of an eternal lack of being. Between Lévi-Strauss and Lacan there was more than a friendly encounter; the two intellectual projects of the fifties share a common kernel of understanding, a common theoretical policy, the same strategy despite the different objects of these two disciplines.

Sixteen

Real/Symbolic/Imaginary (RSI): The Heresy

Quite paradoxically, one of Lacan's important discoveries goes un-
mentioned in his Rome Report even though it preceded the lecture by
two months: the famous trilogy of the Real, the Symbolic, and the
Imaginary, which in July 1953 was announced as the Symbolic, the
Imaginary, and the Real. "To my mind this is Lacan's great find."[1]
Lacan called this his *theriac*, the name of the best-known medication
in antiquity, which long sustained the hope of finding a panacea. This
was also his ternary, and later, simply RSI, or his heresy with respect
to Freud. "I think that this idea is the fruit of his use of linguistics.
He was engaged at the time in a battle and he needed a policy on
theory."[2] The innovation therefore dates from 1953, a period during which Lévi-Strauss's influence was quite important. That the symbolic was at this time the first element in the tertiary order is therefore
noteworthy.

The structuralist influence was quite apparent in this dominant
and valorized third order, set between the Real and the Imaginary.
Linguistic binarism became a triadic order, consonant with the structure of Hegelian dialectics and with the Freudian topic separating the
id, the ego, and the superego, even if this subdivision had another
meaning for Lacan. Lacan reversed Freud; the symbolic governed the
structure whereas the id, which Lacan assigned to the Real, was at the
core of the drives for Freud. This was the major shift, both in language and in structure; the unconscious was no longer assigned to a

sort of interred Hell from which it had to be driven out, but could be grasped at the surface of words and in slips of the tongue.

Whence the precedence that Lacan attributed to linguistic methods in Rome in 1953, even if he did not announce his discovery. In his initial topology, the Symbolic was followed by the Real, which was not to be confused with reality for it was the hidden, inaccessible side of reality; the Lacanian Real is impossible. In the same way that Heideggerian Being was absent from being, the Lacanian Real was the lack of being of reality. The Imaginary was assigned to the dual relationship of the Mirror Stage and condemns the ego, beclouded by its affects, to that which is illusory. In the subject, this triad was articulated in an indefinite signifying chain around the initial lack of an inaccessible Real. Lacan's ternary order was radically opposed to any empirical perception of desire reduced to the expression of needs. Desire, for Lacan, was determined by the encounter with the desire of the Other, with the master signifier that once again pointed to the lack and clarified the demand.

In the early fifties, Moustafa Safouan, a young philosopher converted to psychoanalysis, was treating a hysterical patient abandoned by his father at the age of four. Safouan was losing hope of understanding why the image of the father continued to come up in analysis whereas the patient had never really known his father. Safouan was on the verge of giving up and returning to philosophy when Lacan invited him to participate in the seminar he was giving at his home on the rue de Lille, where he met Didier Anzieu, Pierre Aubry, Serge Leclaire, and Octave Mannoni and began to grasp Lacan's distinction between the Imaginary, Real, and Symbolic father. This in turn helped him better understand his patient and the disastrous effects of his superego, his self-punishing behavior, and his avoidances. "These distinctions changed the way I listened, as an analyst, and gave new life to the manner in which I responded to what was communicated."[3]

This new light definitively convinced Safouan that psychoanalysis could be effective and that Lacan's reading was well founded. He himself began a supervisory analysis with Lacan for fifteen years. The Lacanian trilogy begins with the postulate that the subject always signifies more than he is aware of, and that there are signifiers that are uttered without in any way illustrating the subject's mastery over meaning.

Is Lacan a Structuralist?

The year 1953 was important for two reasons: Lacan's important in-novation of the triple order and his use of the linguistic model in the Rome Report. Elsewhere he had acknowledged the existence of a be-fore and an after: "Y. G. W. O. I. A. B. L." which has to be read as "You got working on it a bit late."⁴ As of this point, Jacques-Alain Miller wondered, "Is Lacan a structuralist?"⁵ and his answer is full of contrasts. Lacan was part of the structuralist phenomenon since his notion of structure came from Jakobson through Lévi-Strauss, but he dissociated himself from structuralism since the structuralists' structure "is coherent and complete whereas the Lacanian structure is paradoxical and uncompleted."⁶ Unlike hermeneutics, in which the hidden place of structure was to be discovered and decoded, Lacan's structure was in the visible world by the way it undertook to seize the living body in which it speaks, unbeknownst to that body. Unlike Saussure's structure, which established itself by opposition and was defined by the completeness of the signifier and the signified, the sub-ject of the unconscious in Lacanian structure remained fundamentally inaccessible, forever split, always beyond any grasp on it, a lack of being, always elsewhere. "In this respect, it seems to me to be an alto-gether peculiar structuralism because it is a theory that, in the end, takes into account the fact that there is something that cannot be grasped, something that the theory leaves ungrasped."⁷

We can distinguish between a structuralism based on complete-ness and Lacan's structuralism, based on incompleteness, although both eliminate the subject from the field of investigation. Saussure and Lévi-Strauss reduced the subject to insignificance whereas Lacan overvalorized it, but because it was forever inaccessible, if not eradi-cated, the subject was avoided. Whether organic or social, the world of things remained at a distance.

There was no longer anything organic about the desire of Lacan's subject; it was disconnected from any physiological reality in the same way that the linguistic sign is cut off from any referent. Pierre Fougey-rollas, a Marxist sociologist, rejected this notion: "Freud knew that we desire sexually because we exist as human animals and he would have considered the idea that we exist because we desire a paranoid whim."⁸ From Fougeyrollas's point of view, Lacan reinforced Saus-sure's break between signifier/signified and proposed a personal version of linguistic structuralism, which François George humorously dubs "father-version."[9]

Lacan wanted to see psychoanalysis accepted as a science on a par with the hard sciences and, more precisely, a science modeled on the physical sciences. In 1953, he refused the factious opposition between the hard sciences and the social, or conjectural, sciences. Lacan recalled the problematic relationship between the experimental, formalized sciences, including physics, and nature, their anthropomorphism, and consequently the unfounded distinction between the hard sciences and the soft sciences. Having removed this separating wall, Lacan could aspire to scientificity in psychoanalysis based on the model of the more formal sciences: "We see how the mathematical formalization that inspired Boole's logic and even set theory, can bring to the science of human action this structure of intersubjective time, which psychoanalytic conjecture needs in order to assure its rigor."[10]

Bonneval: The Un-conscious

The schism within the École Psychanalytique Freudienne required that psychoanalysis have a solid base with scientific aspirations and that this be part of its theoretical position. In 1960, after the Rome Report, Henri Ey, a psychiatrist and friend of Lacan, decided to organize a colloquium on the unconscious at Bonneval. The colloquium made it possible not only to bring together the two camps in French psychoanalysis—the Société Psychanalytique de Paris (SPP), represented by Serge Lebovici, René Diatkine, André Green, and Conrad Stein, among others, and the Société Française de Psychanalyse, represented by Serge Leclaire, Jean Laplanche, François Perrier, and Jean-Bertrand Pontalis—but also philosophers, including Paul Ricoeur, Maurice Merleau-Ponty, Henri Lefebvre, Jean Hyppolite, and psychiatrists, the most frequent participants in Henri Ey's work groups.[11]

For Lacan, it was a question of demonstrating the scientificity of psychoanalysis to both the International Psychiatric Association (IPA) and phenomenologists by unsettling their convictions about the centrality of consciousness. Merleau-Ponty, while open to psychoanalytic thinking, as he demonstrated elsewhere in 1960, in *Signs*, disagreed with Lacan's conclusions: "I am rather uncomfortable when I see that the category of language occupies so much space."[12] At this colloquium devoted entirely to the unconscious, psychoanalysis's own object, many psychiatrists gave up psychiatry in favor of psychoanalysis, seduced by the Lacanian discourse, which proposed to be the most modern and the most rigorous, and for which linguistics and anthropology served as a double guarantee.

Two of Lacan's disciples, Jean Laplanche and Serge Leclaire, gave the most important talks at Bonneval. They coauthored a text in which the critical part was written by Laplanche and the more clinical part by Leclaire. Leclaire offered an extremely subtle analysis of the dream of a thirty-year-old Jewish patient (today we know that this was his own dream), intended to completely renovate the traditional treatment of dreams, limited to attempts at remembering and seeking the hidden meaning of what goes unsaid. The unicorn dream, as it was called, let him demonstrate the work and priority of the signifier. "Psychoanalysis proves therefore to be the practice of the letter. . . . the literal expression is what gives the representation its particular importance."[13] His dream illustrated Lacan's theory according to which the unconscious is structured like a language. There was a single point of divergence about which he had hoped for some discussion, which never occurred, regarding the notion of original repression: "At Bonneval, this discussion took place with Stein, but not with Lacan. Yet the view I put forward differed from Lacan's, but at the time, our divergence went unnoticed."[14]

Jean Laplanche, on the other hand, remained in the Lacanian camp, but was somewhat reserved about Lacan's essential formula. That Jean Laplanche, an ex-militant of the Socialisme ou Barbarie group, evoked a certain criticism of this structuralist orientation was not surprising for he reiterated Claude Lefort's criticism of Claude Lévi-Strauss at the beginning of the fifties, although in another context. Together with Cornelius Castoriadis and Claude Lefort, Laplanche had been a founding member of this postwar group and had begun to be interested by psychoanalysis in the United States in 1946. In New York, he had met Loewenstein, who suggested that he take classes in psychoanalysis at Harvard, and when he came back to France, Laplanche went to visit his ex-*khâgne* professor, Ferdinand Alquié, to ask him for the name of a psychoanalyst in order to begin an analysis. Alquié told him that there was a regular series of extremely interesting lectures given by a certain Jacques Lacan.

> He was speaking about the Mirror Stage at the time, of identification between doves, pigeons, and pilgrim crickets. I introduced myself

and began an analysis with him. I therefore knew Lacan as a psychoanalyst for years but during that time did not allow myself to go to
his seminar in order to avoid the confusion that he often made between his teaching and his analyses.[15]

Laplanche was therefore in an ambiguous and frustrating situation at Bonneval because he was Lacan's disciple with respect to the
SPP, but, on the other hand, he wanted to voice a certain number of
criticisms. Because they were not discussed, however, these reservations were sacrificed to the logic of the different camps. Laplanche
adopted the Freudian definition of the unconscious in its topical
meaning, as different from the conscious as the preconscious. He argued in favor of the idea of a second structure to account for Freud's
distinction between the representation of a thing and of a word, the
primary and secondary processes, thus giving a first nonverbal level of
language for the representations of things and a second verbalized
level for the representation of words. Laplanche deduced that "the unconscious is the condition of language,"[16] reversing Lacan's position
and giving metaphoric and metonymic operations a secondary position, without exhausting the reality of the unconscious: "What slips,
what is displaced, is the energy of the drive in its pure, unspecified
state."[17]

Laplanche therefore rejected Lacan's use of linguistics as a model
from the beginning. Later, he emphasized his disagreement by stating
that the unconscious is not structured as a language, as Lacan would
have it: "It is undeniable that there are elements of language in the
unconscious, but repression de-structures rather than structures these
elements."[18] Today, Laplanche distances himself even further from
Lacan's dictum that the unconscious is structured like a language, and
asserts even more radically than he did in 1960 first that language is
not as structured as it is said to be by reducing it to a binary structure,
and that in addition the unconscious is not made of words but of
traces of things, and that its operation is completely opposed to structure:[19] "The absence of negation, the coexistence of contraries, the absence of judgment, no retention or maintenance of investments."[20] To
Lacan's formulation he prefers "the unconscious is a like-a-language
but not structured."[21]

Lacan, in fact, rejected Laplanche's juncture between thought and
language and argued for a radical break in Saussure's algorithm. It
was doubtless strategically important for Lacan to anchor psycho-

analysis in the discoveries of modern linguistics and to consider that "the human is language."[22] Given his epistemological ambitions, Lacan saw in this idea the only possibility for having psychoanalysis be part of the general semiological adventure that was taking off at the beginning of the fifties. But he refused to discuss Laplanche's text at Bonneval because unity was supposed to reign under his aegis for tactical reasons. Lacan developed another idea, that the unconscious is an effect of language, of a cogito split between truth and knowledge, but only gave voice to his disagreement with his disciple in 1969 in a preface written for Anika Lemaire's thesis on him.[23]

Lacan also presented a paper at Bonneval, which he later reworked considerably for the *Écrits* in 1966 with the title "Position of the Unconscious." In it, he denounced the illusions of a Cartesian cogito and of classical philosophy and its reference to an absolute knowledge à la Hegel. Consciousness is entirely absorbed by the ego's specular reflection and therefore assigned to the "function of misunderstanding, which remains attached to it."[24] Lacan saw the Cartesian cogito as a first moment, a presupposition of the unconscious. The signifier has priority over the subject, which becomes a subject insofar as a signifier represents a subject for another signifier. The second moment is one of separation or of resplitting, and he illustrated this by the newborn's birth. A newborn is not separated from its mother, as is often and mistakenly said, but from a part of itself, for when the cord is cut, the newborn loses its anatomical complement: "Breaking an egg makes a man but also an omelet."[25] This initial break is ceaselessly reiterated in later life, and limits are necessary in order for this little man not to spread out in all directions and destroy everything in his path. This break makes the Real inaccessible and gives a deathlike dimension to the drive that refers back to the Real and is virtually a death drive.

The unconscious, on the other hand, refers to the symbolic, and is composed of phonemes and of groups of phonemes: language is its basis. This is what allowed Lacan to say in 1966: "Linguistics is surely the science on which the unconscious is based."[26] The Letter supplants Being:[27] this is the triumphant hour of the structural paradigm in psychoanalysis.

Seventeen

The Call of the Tropics

In the six years between the two conferences addressing the nonalignment of the emerging postcolonial countries, the New Delhi Conference of 1949 and the Afro-Asian Conference in Bandung of 1955, a new and increasingly clear set of demands was being articulated. The traditional East-West split was being redefined; nonalignment was being asserted as a third path. The South was demanding that people of color be recognized with a dignity equal to that enjoyed by Western civilization. It was during this period of decolonization that UNESCO asked Claude Lévi-Strauss to write an essay for a collection addressing the issues of race and modern science, published as "Race and History" in 1952.

This decisive text was a major contribution to the theorization of the phenomenon of emancipation that was under way. Lévi-Strauss attacked racial prejudices and his argument made it possible to bring anthropology to bear on debates on society as Paul Rivet had already done before the war, and to make the shift from physical to social anthropology quite palpable. Lévi-Strauss criticized a historical teleology based on the reproduction of the same, and proposed a different notion about the diversity of cultures and the irreducibility of difference. By attacking the foundations of a Eurocentrism that was already being significantly jolted by tricontinental revolts of peoples of the third world in the process of shaking off their colonial yoke, he fundamentally revolutionized the thinking on the subject. After him it was impossible to continue to think in terms of anteriority or inferiority; the hierarchical mold of a Western society that proposed to serve as a model to the rest of the world was broken; Western values were rejected and their underbelly was explored. By contesting evolutionism, Lévi-Strauss remained true to the Maussian tradition without falling into the trap of localism, in which every society was contained within the little universe of its own particularities. To the contrary, Lévi-Strauss believed that each society was the expression of a concrete universal. Not only was he a guide opening the West to an understanding of the Other, but he also made it clear that this Other could, in exchange, help the West learn something about itself, help transform it insofar as it was a meaningful piece of universal humanity.

The structuralist approach became a beginning for understanding the Other through the idea of the intercommunicability of codes. All systems can communicate between themselves at the level of the transition from one code to another, but "a direct dialogue cannot take place. Incomprehension comes from the inability to go beyond one's own system. If anyone contributed to this universal humanism, it was Lévi-Strauss."[1] Western-centered closure was opened up to a much larger universe based on cultural polymorphism, enriching the understanding of what is human.

Lévi-Strauss distinguished two kinds of relationship to historicity, contrasting the cumulative history of the major civilizations to the will to dissolve every innovation perceived as a threat to a primitive equilibrium. The West was not alone in this view of a cumulative history, which also operated in other climes. Moreover, Lévi-Strauss rejected any hierarchy that considered one civilization to be more advanced than another. All considerations of this order became relative by examining the criteria. Western civilization was clearly advanced if technology was the principal criterion, but if other criteria were brought to bear, those civilizations that seemed primitive or that Westerners considered to be the cradles of the world appeared in fact more ingenious than the West: "If we had used the criterion of how apt a civilization is at conquering hostile geography, there is no doubt that the Eskimos and the Bedouins would win hands down."[2]

The West lost on all but technological grounds in this game of variables. The same was true for spirituality, or for the relationship between the body and the mind, where the Orient is ahead "by many millennia"[3] in its practical exercise of spirituality. In this multiple-criteria list of honors, Australians won the prize for the complexity of kinship relationships, and Melanesians for aesthetic daring. Lévi-Strauss drew a double lesson: the evaluation of any given society is relative with respect to given criteria; human enrichment can only come from a process of coalescence of these diverse experiences, the source of new discoveries: "The only fatality, the single defect that can afflict a human group and prevent it from fully realizing its nature, is to be isolated."[4]

Lévi-Strauss spectacularly theorized the practice of rejecting colonial values. By the some token, he reappropriated those societies from the alterity in which the West had placed them, as much with respect to what we know about them as how we think about them. But difference was not only the expression of the Other's irreducibility; it was also an ideological concept that lent itself to analysis. In this respect, the structuralist paradigm weakened the bases of the West's philosophies of totality—Vico, Comte, Condorcet, Hegel, and Marx. We can see the return of a form of thinking born with the discovery of the New World in the sixteenth century. "Western thinking was being fissured; Montaigne had seen that its foundations were ruined by a completely heterogeneous element. This has been a constant in the West since the Greeks; power is never exercised without being based on a universal."[5] Montaigne had already said that we hastened the ruin of the nations of the New World, and he deplored the fact that the so-called civilizers had been unable to establish a fraternal and comprehensive relationship between themselves and the Indians. "Race and History" once again voiced this regret. This major essay quickly became the breviary for antiracist thinking.

The Polemic: Caillois versus Lévi-Strauss

Lévi-Strauss's article nevertheless provoked bitter criticism from Roger Caillois.[6] Paradoxically, it was Caillois who would accept Lévi-Strauss into the Académie Française in 1974, when he succeeded Montherlant. Caillois did not hide the virulence of the polemic: "The tone of your answer was so abundantly vehement, and your polemical approach so unusual in the debate of ideas, that I was speechless."[7] As Caillois suggested, Lévi-Strauss's answer was of an unequaled violence, such that he never reprinted "Diogène couché" in any other collections of articles.[8] What were the issues of the polemic?

Roger Caillois drew an extremely interesting parallel between the emergence of certain philosophies and their periods. What he observed was not that philosophy reflected its period but that it fulfilled something that was lacking. Until Hegel, Western philosophy had essentially conceived of history as linear and universal, whereas the relationship between the West and its empires was still incomplete and precarious. These philosophies saw a single causal link between human evolution and its effects, and exaggerated this view of singular causality, whereas human evolution included very different realities. With the First World War, history truly became global; scholarly research and collective sensibilities valorized plurality and the irreducibility of differences, while at the same time this plurality was evaporating. For Roger Caillois, "Race and History" was the scholarly substance of this second position giving value to plurality, and also expressed the premonition of Western decadence. He reproached Lévi-Strauss for having attributed exaggerated virtues to peoples who had been ignored in the past, and he generally criticized his relativism. Caillois pointed to Lévi-Strauss's own contradictions. On the one hand, he considered all cultures to be equivalent and incomparable ("Progress in one culture cannot be measured by the references of another. . . . This position can be justified"), while, on the other hand, he claimed that the East was thousands of years ahead of the West in terms of the mind-body relationship.[9] Lévi-Strauss's relativism took him too far afield, and Caillois contrasted the superiority of Western civilization, which for him lay in its constant curiosity about other cultures, whence ethnography, and which other cultures never felt the need to invent. "Contrary to what the proverb says, it is not that Lévi-Strauss's eye can't see his shortcomings. . . . The position is a noble one, but a researcher should spend his time seeing his own shortcomings and those of others where they really are."[10]

Lévi-Strauss's answer was not long in coming and it was brutal. Paradoxically, Sartre's *Les Temps modernes* again became the forum for developing his theses. The tone was clear from the outset: "Diogenes proved that movement existed by walking. Mr. Roger Caillois lies down in order to avoid seeing it."[11] Lévi-Strauss basically repeated the major points of his argument without in any way granting any points to Caillois's critique. In response to the allusion to cannibalism, Lévi-Strauss answered that morality was not to be located in the kitchen, and that in terms of the number of people killed, we outdo the Papuans. But it was the violence of the polemic that was surprising: "Mr. Caillois indulges in an exercise that begins with the antics of the head table, continues with the declarations of a preacher, and ends with the lamentation of a penitent. His style is that of the cynics and we can count him among their numbers."[12] "America had its McCarthy and we have our McCaillois."[13] Despite the polemical tone, this remained a major piece in the battle against racial prejudice in the early fifties. What's more, Caillois's intuition was right: pessimism was gaining ground in a Europe that was in the grips of an apparently inexorable decline.

A Book That Made Its Mark: *Tristes Tropiques*[14]

According to Léopold Sédar Senghor, one of the leaders of Afro-Asianism at the time, the 1955 Bandung Conference was like a global thunderclap. At the same time, civil aeronautics was taking Western tourists to the most distant cultures. A veritable frenzy of exoticism took hold of the Old World; travel agencies were offering a range of packages for exotic trips for every taste. The gurus of the tourist industry implanted themselves everywhere like so many extraterritorial, self-enclosed islands. Club Med was soon cutting up continents and offering the discovery of the Other for less, behind the fences of its camps, well hidden from the natives. It was during this period of shifting intellectual interests that *Tristes Tropiques*—the book event of 1955—appeared. Lévi-Strauss's triumph demonstrated how completely he satisfied the collective sensibilities of the period. He made the spectacular breakthrough he had hoped for in anthropology and for the structuralist agenda, by casting both fully into the glare of the French intellectual world. At the same time, he changed his own image from that of an inhuman scientist. "I was sick of seeing myself labeled in universities as a machine without a soul, good only for putting men into formulas."[15]

Curiously enough, *Tristes Tropiques* resulted from a double failure. Lévi-Strauss had wanted above all to write a novel using his ethnographer's experience, but he gave up after thirty pages; the only remaining traces include the title and a magnificent sunset. The other failure involved his first two attempts to be elected to the Collège de France; he was beaten in 1949 and again in 1950. At the time he was convinced that he would never be able to have a university career and so he began writing *Tristes Tropiques*, "which I never would have dared to publish if I had been applying for any university job whatso-

ever."[16] This episode was symptomatic of a time when the power and
the innovation of the structuralist program lay in the ability to cir-
cumscribe the university and to find other avenues of legitimation.
Thanks to this detour, Lévi-Strauss could intervene at a more oppor-
tune moment, as a travel philosopher. He looked at things with a mixture of scientificity, of literature, of nostalgia for lost origins, of guilt,
and of redemption that made it impossible to classify his work.

The subjectivity of his story demonstrated the link between the
search for identity and the discovery of the Other, by virtue of the notion that ethnography gives us access to the sources of humanity, and,
as Rousseau also believed, to a truth about man, who "never creates
anything truly great except at the beginning."[17] There is a nostalgia
for origins in this outlook that only sees human history as the pale
repetition of an authentic and forever lost moment of birth. "We will
accede to that nobility of thought that consists . . . in taking as the
starting point of our reflections the indefinable grandeur of man's beginnings."[18] In this celebration of beginnings, there is some measure
of expiation for the West and its genocides, of which ethnography was
clearly a part. Once a participant in missionary enterprises during the
glorious periods of colonization, the ethnographer pleaded his mea
culpa at the moment when Western values were being rejected; in ban-
daging some moral wounds, he became part of the ebb. The tropics
were so sad not only because of their acculturation, but also because
of the nature of ethnography, whose very object was undeniably becoming extinct, particularly in the area explored by Lévi-Strauss.
Moreover, these civilizations were in the process of being transformed, demanding their own identity as they cast off their colonial
identity, but also leaving their own traditions behind in order to become societies in ferment.

Decolonization paradoxically assured the triumph of *Tristes
Tropiques* and created a crisis for the book's orientation, which was
based on immobile societies caught up in the tension between conser-
vation and extinction: "The world began without man and will end
without him."[19] Third-world cultures, however, were not trapped in
this reductionism and could open up possible channels of change,
which clearly required that their identities be reforged. The social effectiveness of anthropology lay not in offering an additional opening
that could be inscribed in the program of package tours, but to participate in its era by bringing a scientific perspective to bear on the situa-

tion. This was what Lévi-Strauss meant when, after the French defeat at Dien Bien Phu, he said that "fifty years of modest and unprestigious research undertaken by adequate numbers of ethnologists could have found solutions in Vietnam and North Africa like the one England managed in India."[20]

If the anthropologist could counsel politicians, Lévi-Strauss defined a position as early as 1955 from which he never deviated: a scientist rejects all partisan struggles because he is committed to science. He withdrew from action and considered his withdrawal to be an intangible rule of professional ethics, something like a monk who takes orders and withdraws from society. The ethnographer's function "will be simply to understand these other societies,"[21] and in order to do so he had to accept a certain number of renunciations, of mutilations. "To understand or to act, one must choose"—such would seem to be the motto for this man who found ultimate comfort in "the meditation of the sage at the foot of the tree."[22] Lévi-Strauss invited us to a veritable dusk of humankind, and he even offered to convert anthropology into "entropology," a science that studies the processes of disintegration. His disengagement in no way excluded the ethnologist's expression of sensibilities as he describes the Other, of course. Lévi-Strauss's sensibility and his extreme receptivity received unanimous critical acclaim and contributed to the immense popularity of *Tristes Tropiques*.

Lévi-Strauss made it possible for us to participate in his enthusiasm at every step of his discoveries, but, above all, he went beyond the vogue for exoticism by restoring the underlying logic of the behavior he observed. The observer remained a man of science in search of the laws by which a society functions, requiring him to step outside of himself, despite his involvement in the field. This decentering fascinated the intellectual public and the human sciences embarked on the new adventure of structuralism. Rousseau was still the model here, and Lévi-Strauss vigorously praised him: "Rousseau, our master, Rousseau, our brother, whom we have shown such ingratitude."[23] According to Lévi-Strauss, Rousseau was a precursor for having answered the Cartesian cogito, "I think, therefore I am," with a question whose answer was unclear: "What am I?" And the ethnologist follows him in rejecting the evidences of the self in order to become receptive to the Other's discourse: "In truth, I am not myself, but the weakest, the most humble of others. This was the discovery of the *Confes-*

sions."[24] In his *Discourse on the Origins of Inequality*, Rousseau had already called for the discovery of societies that were unknown to the West, not for reasons of material wealth but in order to discover other customs that might shed light on our way of life: "Rousseau did not limit himself to foreseeing ethnography: he founded it."[25] When he wrote his confessions in *Tristes Tropiques*, Lévi-Strauss also placed the observer who reflects upon himself and his doubts and ambitions back into a context.

A Resounding Success

The reverberations of Lévi-Strauss's work were spectacular for a book in the human sciences. It was an unclassifiable hybrid accessible to an exceptionally broad public. Until then, only literary or philosophical works could hope to have such an effect by addressing some of the major philosophical questions. This had been the case with Sartrean Existentialism, especially in its literary and theatrical versions. Sartre's influence was still important, in fact, and Lévi-Strauss published some excerpts of his book in *Les Temps modernes*.[26] But the response to the book consecrated his emancipation and that of the structuralist program. Journalists, scholars from all disciplines, as well as intellectuals of all political persuasions took up their pens to salute the event.

In *Le Figaro*, Raymond Aron applauded this "supremely philosophical"[27] book, which resumes the tradition of the philosopher's journey as he confronts difficulties, following in the tradition of *The Persian Letters*. For *Combat*, Lévi-Strauss had "the stature of a Cervantes," while François-Régis Bastide saluted the birth of a poet and a new Chateaubriand.[28] In *L'Express*, Madeleine Chapsal spoke about the writings of a seer: "It has been some ten years since a book has come out that speaks to us so directly."[29] The philosophy columns of *Le Monde*, written by Jean Lacroix, were devoted to *Tristes Tropiques* and suggested the paradox in Lévi-Strauss's thinking: "He denounces progress yet no one does better justice to the progress of our culture than he."[30] Many commentators were seduced by his reflections on a researcher's involvement and investment in his object, in a quest that has nothing exotic about it: "He invites us first of all to find ourselves."[31] "The reader of this book, will find above all a man. Isn't that what he's looking for, after all?"[32] Claude Roy, the literary critic who wrote for *Libération*, made an exception to the rule of reviewing only literary works and wrote about *Tristes Tropiques*: "The most interesting book of the week is not a novel. It is the work of an ethnographer, M. Claude Lévi-Strauss."[33] *Le Canard enchaîné* (October 31, 1956) even spoke about the "refreshing tropics."

More substantial surveys were published in the *Annales* and the *Philosophical Review* written by Jean Cazeneuve. Lucien Febvre had planned to speak about the work himself because it had completely fascinated him, but he died before doing so. Georges Bataille, the director of *Critique*, wrote a long article entitled "A Human Book, a Great Book," in which he described the displacement of literature toward more specialized activities.[34] It was true that Lévi-Strauss's work, like that of Alfred Métraux,[35] was part of this new sensibility, this new relationship between writing and scientificity that goes beyond the traditional opposition between the work of art and scientific discovery: "From the beginning, *Tristes Tropiques* presents itself as a work of art, not as a work of science."[36] Its literariness came not only from the fact that it was first of all the expression of a man, his feelings, and his style, but also that its general spirit was guided more by what attracted and seduced its author than by the simple transcription of a logical order.

This shift of literature toward an ethnographic genre was so much an issue that the Goncourt brothers even published a communiqué saying that they regretted being unable to award their prize to *Tristes Tropiques*. In a long piece on Lévi-Strauss's work, René Etiemble saw in him a brother, a born heretic. *Tristes Tropiques* "is a book that you either take or leave. For my part, I take it and keep it in the treasury of my library, deeply within me."[37] Etiemble agreed with Lévi-Strauss's critical perspective on Western modernity, referring to Gilberto Freyre's work describing how the French, and after them the Portuguese, discovered what would later become Brazil and the physical and moral degradation of the native populations that followed. "They did not civilize, but there are indications that they syphilized Brazil rather well," recounted Freyre, himself a Brazilian.[38]

The enthusiasm was so widespread and so unanimous that certain misunderstandings were inevitable. Some were satisfied with a dose of exoticism, although that was what Lévi-Strauss repudiated, while others, who saw the book as the expression of an individual's sensibilities, were rather quickly unbalanced by the future celebration of the death of man, who is simply an ephemeral figure, "a passing efflorescence." The most famous quid pro quo was the prize given to Lévi-

Strauss on November 30, 1956, by the jury for the Golden Pen, which rewards travel and exploration books. *Tristes Tropiques* barely won (by a vote of 5 to 4 against Jean-Claude Berryer's *In the Land of the White Elephant*), although the book opens with the famous line "I hate traveling and explorers" and continues with "The first thing we see as we travel round the world is our own filth, thrown into the face of mankind."[39] Lévi-Strauss refused the prize, which earned him a flattering, new literary comparison: "The new Julien Gracq. An Indian specialist turns down the Golden Feather."[40]

In this concert of praises, the few discordant notes had a difficult time making themselves audible. Maxime Rodinson, for example, published a critique of *Tristes Tropiques*[41] in which he refused Lévi-Strauss's relativism and argued in favor of a historical dialectic: "According to this view of total relativism, nothing permits us to say that knowing Archimedes' principle is more important than knowing about our genealogy."[42] Etiemble's article, which basically praised Lévi-Strauss, made some criticisms. Lévi-Strauss went too far in seeing in the birth of writing the means of facilitating servility, a conclusion he drew from his observations of the Nambikwara. Etiemble replied that Hitler and Poujade began by speaking at meetings. As for turning anthropology into entropology, he observed: "Oh, no, not at all. . . . Lévi-Strauss gives a bit too much importance to cybernetics."[43]

Lévi-Strauss answered Rodinson, André-Georges Haudricourt, and Georges Granai in his seminar at the Musée de l'Homme on October 15, 1956. He accused them of falsely attributing intentions to him for he did not want to construct a model of models, but simply to come to some partial and limited conclusions.

> Is there anything here, as Rodinson claims, to reduce Billancourt to desperation? . . . Neither in "Race and History" nor in *Tristes Tropiques* did I intend to disparage the idea of progress; rather I should like to see progress transferred from the rank of a universal category of human development to that of a particular mode of existence, characteristic of our own society.[44]

Here, Lévi-Strauss took a defensive position, which he always adopted against any criticism of his ahistoricism. He claimed not to be the bearer of a general philosophy but only of a particular scientific method. This answer remained unsatisfactory, however, because it clearly veiled the undeniable philosophical postulate of the structuralist program. But the moment was not yet ripe in 1955 for the great philosophical debates that would take place in the sixties. Lévi-Strauss was, at the time, at the height of the triumph of a new discipline: anthropology.

The Conversion of the Philosophers

The response to Lévi-Strauss was not limited to the media. He generally shook up the intellectual world, but even more profoundly, he led a number of philosophers, historians, and economists who had broken with their original discipline to the tropics, to answer the call of foreign climes. The young generation was all the more attracted to this concern for reconciling one's own sensibility with a rational study of a living society with which one interacts in that the West no longer seemed to require the same kind of political commitments that it had in the past. *Tristes Tropiques* was something like the symptom of a new state of mind in this respect, a will to understand the vanishing points without abandoning the rigors of Reason, but by applying them to new objects.

Lévi-Strauss was the rallying point for many "converts." Luc de Heusch, an ethnologist already working in the Belgian Congo, today's Zaire, was one of these. A student of Marcel Griaule at the Sorbonne, he had been disappointed not to find his master's grand symbolic constructions. He returned to France in 1955 and discovered *Tristes Tropiques*. Although he had only cursorily glanced at *The Elementary Structures of Kinship* before leaving for Africa, he came back to Lévi-Straussland and adapted the methods used in Indian societies to the Bantus of Central Africa, comparing all the variations of myths in order to understand African symbolic thinking.

Lévi-Strauss's stunning success compensated for ethnology's weak incursion into the university system. The Institut d'Ethnologie had existed since 1925 at the Musée de l'Homme, but there was only one department, and a group of teachers whose sole audience was composed of students who had come to earn the only certificate that was both literary and scientific, without any intention of becoming ethnologists. It was above all an opportunity for philosophers needing a scientific certificate in order to earn their *Licence* degree to take courses directly linked to their interests. Michel Izard remembered his dissatisfaction. Of course there were clearly defined areas like cultural technology, physical anthropology, or prehistory, "but the rest seemed to us to be completely impoverished."[45] Teaching ethnology was divided either geographically into the large regions of the world or thematically, without any kind of organization. Therefore, the media's impact was essential for convincing the young generation that there was a viable alternative to a traditional career, that an anthropological breach could be made outside the citadel of the Sorbonne. The situation was very similar in linguistics at the same time, and this had a clear effect on their common destiny.

In the mid-fifties, *Tristes Tropiques* and Alejo Carpentier's *Le Partage des eaux* resonated for Michel Izard like "a call from elsewhere."[46] Lévi-Strauss was not proposing a journey to the promised land, however, but to disenchantment. It was the quest for a discovery that bore within it its own failure: "I was sensitive to the pessimism, to this end-of-the-road aspect."[47] Michel Izard therefore converted in the middle of the fifties from philosophy, at the Sorbonne, where he had already learned of Lévi-Strauss thanks to the prestige of *Les Temps modernes*, in which several of his major texts had already appeared. But ethnology was quite marginal in the training he received at the Sorbonne. His professors—Jean Hyppolite, who continued Hegel, Jean Wahl, Maurice de Gandillac, and Vladimir Jankélévitch— were not interested in this new field of study. Entire areas were being ignored in this way, including analytic philosophy, epistemology, and linguistics in general. Ethnology was practically nonexistent, with a few exceptions. "We had Mikel Dufrenne as our assistant. His complementary thesis had to do with basic personality and he gave a course on American cultural anthropology. Later, and late for me, there was Claude Lefort, a young assistant who had been writing about Lévi-Strauss's work since 1951–52."[48]

Michel Izard found epistemology more attractive. He read Georges Canguilhem and Gaston Bachelard and, on the advice of his friend Pierre Guattari, known as Félix, he took the exams for the certificate in ethnology during the year that he was working on his degree under Jean Wahl. At the Institut, he met Olivier Herrenschmidt, who had chosen history and was undergoing his conversion, thanks to a mix of anthropology, linguistics, and the history of religions. Michel Izard also met philosophers who were coming to anthropology, such as Michel Cartry. The year 1956 was supposed to be just a passing diversion for him, but what had started out as a detour suddenly took on an altogether different meaning: "By the end of the year, I had decided to give up philosophy in order to do anthropology."[49]

If *Tristes Tropiques* had a real effect on Michel Izard and led him to look toward ethnology for its research possibilities, *The Elementary Structures of Kinship* helped him to decide to break with philosophy. The book's modelization, the promises of scientificity held out by the structuralist program, together with his will to "turn my back on the West, to go elsewhere, beyond our history, the history that produced us,"[50] all contributed. Izard therefore took Lévi-Strauss's seminars in the Fifth Section of the École Pratique des Hautes Études (EPHE), as well as classes from Jacques Soustelle and Roger Bastide, with the intention of becoming a professional. At the end of 1957, Lévi-Strauss offered him two research options: he could either work in Khartoum, at the Sudan Museum of Antiquities, in order to create exhibits on the black animist south, although his dossier was not yet substantial enough, or work at the Institute for Applied Human Sciences, which was looking for an ethnologist and a geographer to do a study in Upper Volta. Our apprentice ethnologist was involved for a year's time in a study on African territory and his conversion became definitive.

The goal of the African expedition was to study a problem of population displacement created by a plan to construct a dam on one of the tributaries of the Volta. The mission was to discover why the area where the displaced population was to be sent had remained so unpopulated. "It was intelligent to ask ethnologists and geographers to study the question, because it was one of the first times that unauthorized displacements were being considered and that there was an attempt to understand people's reasons."[51] No geographer could be found to accompany Michel Izard, so Françoise Héritier, a historian, joined him. Héritier came from a discipline that was even more eccentric with respect to anthropology. As a history student at the Sorbonne between 1953 and 1957, she had considered studying ancient history but her contact with philosophy students, and particularly with Michel Izard, led her to anthropology. So, in 1957, she began to take Lévi-Strauss's courses in the Fifth Section of the EPHE. "It was clear that for someone who had studied history and geography and who was preparing to take the *agrégation*, these things were absolutely new."[52] Françoise Héritier experienced the triple shock of discovering societies whose very existence was unknown to her, of encountering unimagined rational practices, and an altogether new way of thinking. She was enthusiastic, and went on to take the ethnology certificate. She married Izard during their time in Africa.

The Indianist Pole

The year 1955 was clearly an important one for anthropology. Louis Dumont returned to France from Oxford and began his course at the EPHE; Fernand Braudel and Clemens Heller began the area studies program in the Sixth Section of the EPHE, which was supposed to bring many disciplines together, including anthropology, to focus on common objects. Dumont's return radically changed Olivier Herren-schmidt's plans. He had been at the Sorbonne and was specializing in the history of religions, and began his training not only in ethnology and linguistics, but with a speciality in Indian studies. André Martinet had just returned from America and Herrenschmidt took his courses at the Sorbonne, those of Lévi-Strauss's in the Fifth Section of the EPHE, and those given by Louis Dumont in the Sixth Section. This meeting between the study of Sanskrit, linguistics, and structural anthropology gave him a second wind and a different sense of Indian studies, which went beyond the stage of monographs based on field-work. A group took shape around Louis Dumont that included the philosopher and Brahman specialist Madeleine Biardeau, who was appointed to the EPHE in 1960, Daniel Thorner, an American economist, and Robert Lingat, a Sanskritist appointed in 1962 to a chair in Southeast Asian law and institutions. "It was a small, highly qualified, multidisciplinary team that was marginal to the French Indianist milieu."[53]

Of course this Indianist pole did not draw huge numbers because it was very demanding, and when Louis Dumont one day found him-self in front of twenty-five people, he immediately assumed that the students had made a mistake: "You are mistaken, I am not René Dumont, but Louis Dumont."[54] Indian studies remained a bit marginal in anthropology because, more than the other branches of research, they came under the authority of Sanskrit philologists. The breach that Dumont opened was contemporary with the one created by Lévi-Strauss and around the same programmatic axis, allowing the Indian-ists to get out of their ghetto and encouraging contacts with specialists in other cultural areas.

Leroi-Gourhan and the Technical Pole

A third pole contributed to anthropology's success in the mid-fifties. André Leroi-Gourhan was nominated in 1956 to the only chair of ethnology at the Sorbonne, following Marcel Griaule's death. A second chair was created in 1959 and held by Roger Bastide, and a certificate of prehistoric archaeology was created in 1960–61. André Leroi-Gourhan, who represented the archaeological and technical side of ethnology, was responsible for this program, and in this respect his contribution complemented Lévi-Strauss's cultural orientation. Indeed, in a colloquium in 1987, Lévi-Strauss recognized the similarity in the methodology of their undertakings.[55]

One of Leroi-Gourhan's important innovations was also to privilege synchrony, not as Lévi-Strauss did, based on Saussure's model, but in his method of excavation, which had to be horizontal. This led to an important controversy at the end of the forties between horizontalists and verticalists. Leroi-Gourhan had clear ideas about uncovering, and argued that it was necessary that "the earth be removed in order to let things speak horizontally."[56] The same totalizing ambition that was characteristic of the structuralist program was also present here. Leroi-Gouran's notion of ethnographic culture had as its object not so much singular cultural events as the relationships between their different branches. Coherence appeared once the pieces were assembled. Hélène Balfet, a student of André Leroi-Gourhan who gave courses on technology at the Musée de l'Homme when Leroi-Gourhan was named to the Sorbonne in 1956, clearly represented this bridge between the two poles of the anthropological universe since she was following Lévi-Strauss's work at the same time.

These two orientations in anthropological research were to remain separate, however, as they diverged according to their definition of the relationship between work and language. André Leroi-Gourhan explained both by the upright position, which freed the hands and allowed them to specialize in work and prehension, leaving the mouth free for speech. However, there is no work without language, as Marx showed in his famous text on the bee and the architect at the beginning of *Capital*. What characterized and distinguished the architect's activity is that he constructed his house mentally before building it in reality. But where was the break to be placed? Work or language? The answer differed according to Lévi-Strauss's viewpoint emphasizing language, or Leroi-Gourhan's viewpoint giving priority to praxis.

But despite their differences, these two poles dynamized and defined the directions of anthropological research for the next thirty years. The structuralist ambition seemed to bring together a community of researchers from a variety of disciplines and with a range of personalities. The context was that of a third-world pathos, against the backdrop of the beginning of the Algerian war, the end of the war in Indochina, and the Bandung Conference, in a France that had long refused to address the colonial question and that was suddenly discovering a critical reality that so profoundly affected consciousness that it created a fundamental bad conscience. All of this was more than an invitation to travel, a call of the tropics for a young generation uncomfortable in its own society. In the structuralist program, this generation was offered an ambitious and rigorous program that seemed to hold out the promise of reconciling a sensibility disenchanted with reason.

Eighteen

Reason Raves:
Michel Foucault's Work

While anthropology was addressing the question of the Other in the West by disinterring primitive societies from the ignorance to which Eurocentric thinking had long relegated them, a philosopher was writing a history of madness that looked at the unseemly side of Western reason. Beneath the triumph of reason, Michel Foucault hunted the repressed, placing himself from the outset at the edges of Western thinking and of its history.

The timing was striking. Michel Foucault began to write *Madness and Civilization: A History of Insanity in the Age of Reason* in 1956, shortly after *Tristes Tropiques* was published and the Bandung Conference had taken place. The book came out in 1961, shortly before the Évian Conference and Algerian independence. The coincidence of these political and cultural events is completely fortuitous since Michel Foucault was not a third-world militant at the time. And yet, *Madness and Civilization* quickly became the symptom of a break with a certain kind of history of the Western subject. Foucault presented a picture of madness, the forgotten and repressed double of reason, which he elevated from its position of exclusion.

Pierre Nora had just published *The French of Algeria*,[1] and he quickly understood the parallel between his own critique of French ethnocentricity in North Africa and Foucault's critique of the ethnocentricity of reason, for as Algerians were leaving the French political framework, they carried with them the mark of their own history of exclusion. Nora immediately wrote Foucault expressing his enthusiasm and later published him at Gallimard. The old war horses were tired and no longer heralded, the damned were no longer glorified. The dialectic was caught in its own entanglements in 1956 while Foucault emphasized the forgotten and repressed in the work of reason, and he sought a new historical sensibility, forging it by giving voice to that which history forgot, by following the tracks of reason's operation. He "opened up new horizons by transforming the prison and the madhouse into grounds for reflection . . . as so many theoretical and political issues."[2]

Just as Lévi-Strauss was making it possible to consider primitive societies as different by drawing them back into the purview of rational thought and reflecting upon them, Michel Foucault was on the heels of a similar adventure in which madness forces us to rethink reason, clearly exposing its strengths and weaknesses. Foucault thus hunted the work of repression in the fabrication of artificial rationalizations for the apparently unintelligible; he sought out the travesties of meaning and cut through the masks of power underlying knowledge, marvelously illustrating the spirit of his time. "The life that is missing in our lives is to be found at the geographic extremities (exoticism) or heroic horizons (the adventurous past or even the future of science fiction), or in the heights or depths of life."[3]

Michel Foucault offered the philosopher a new adventure, by pushing thinking to its limits and reflecting upon the boundaries, and for this he quickly came to have an important place in the nascent structuralist galaxy. His role was due in part to his prestige as a philosopher and to his capacity to historicize his object. Foucault made it possible to historicize structuralism in a way that Lévi-Strauss had not imagined when he set the primitive paradigm into place.

Georges Canguilhem saw in Michel Foucault the philosopher of the concept well positioned for drawing together the disciplines of structuralism even if in 1961 Foucault did not yet place himself in the structuralist lineage. This was a new, and at the time uncategorizable, exigency that seemed to disrupt disciplinary boundaries and end the phenomenological phase of the history of philosophy in France. Where did it come from? Michel Foucault, this exploder of prejudices and of consumer thinking, incessantly sought out truth even if it meant passing for a contrabandist of knowledge. His proposals were resolutely modest; far from presenting himself as the spokesman of the correct way of thinking, he simply tried to sketch the contours of the thinkable. In his journey to the nether side of reason, Foucault was also a travel philosopher of sorts, and, like Nietzsche, a "rummager of the gutters" of our civilization.

Foucault was a unique philosopher who clearly insisted on being seen as such, derisively rejecting all labels and vigilantly eschewing any attachments, much like a Gidean protagonist. Like Nathanael, this constantly shifting rebel can only be understood if each of the stages of a life that he constructed much like an artwork is examined in order to root his thinking as it evolved. Restoring what made Michel Foucault so unique lets us demonstrate both how he belonged to and how he diverged from the structuralist paradigm, not by reducing his thought to a common mold but by showing how it was articulated with it.

A Star Is Born

Michel Foucault often evoked the difficult relationship between writing and biography. He never revealed much about himself, for which Jean-Paul Aron reproached him shortly before he died of AIDS. He was born Paul-Michel Foucault on October 15, 1926, to a good, conservative Catholic bourgeois family of doctors who were well established on both his parents' sides, in Poitiers. His father was a well-known surgeon at the Hospitaliers clinic and his mother, Anne Malapert, came from the Vendeuvre-du-Poitou, about twenty kilometers from Poitiers, where she owned a magnificent house called "the château." Like Jacques-Marie Lacan, Foucault dropped half his name "because the initials read PMF, like Pierre Mendès-France, said Mme Foucault";[4] but, more seriously, it would seem that Foucault, who was given his father's first name, changed it out of opposition to the Name of the Father.

This biographical detail sheds some light on the philosopher-son's later positions and his "constant denial of the dimension of paternity, of the name, one of the keys to his subjective position."[5] Whence a complicated and conflictual history with psychoanalysis in general and with Lacan in particular, for Foucault did not agree that speech was one of the sites for the subject's truth. Foucault's fascination with crossing out, with the oxymoron as a rhetorical figure (amorous birds of prey often exemplifying this rhetorical figure), seems to compulsively repeat the paternal horizon that he wanted to destroy, without fully succeeding. He insisted constantly on the illusion that no one speaks behind his voice, and that no one authors his texts, and in this he fully adhered to the structuralist negation of the author as well as the attempt at literary renewal undertaken by Georges Bataille, Maurice Blanchot, and Pierre Klossowski. The name of the father was thus a burden with which Foucault broke quite quickly, "a break that was difficult in this milieu. He often said to me that if he did not become a doctor he had to at least be a professor at the Sorbonne."[6]

Foucault did not become a doctor, but the medical model became a prism through which to understand the human sciences, by using their visible traces and differences negatively, by looking at their underside, much like a doctor who tries, in healing the sick and restoring them to health, to understand pathology. In this respect, Michel Foucault created a veritable "medical paradigm in the human sciences."[7] Foucault had no problems in his high school, Henri IV, in Poitiers until he was about fifteen, at which point his parents put him in Saint-Stanislaus, a Catholic school, in order to finish secondary school and discipline his mind, which was increasingly critical, not to say caustic. "He was incredibly impressive, he was quite corrosive, and cast doubt on all our beliefs."[8]

This was another key moment in Foucault's biography, one that is essential for understanding how deeply his work was affected by the war. Foucault was given very little to confiding and never revealed his feelings in public, but later he spoke about this period in a very confidential context of a Canadian Indian review that preached silence and of which probably no more than ten copies were published. He confided what he remembered of his adolescence, in which the war and death were always present:

> What strikes me when I try to remember my impressions is that practically all my emotional memories are linked to the political situation. . . . I think that the childhood of girls and boys of my generation was shaped by these important historic events. The threat of war was always at our doorstep; it shaped our existence. And then the war came. . . . Perhaps this is why I am fascinated by history and by the relationship between personal experience and the events in which we are caught up. I think that that was the beginning of my desire for theory.[9]

Thinking about war was fundamental for Foucault; it was the basis for a central paradigm in his work involving notions of strategy, power tactics, breaks, and power relations. In his approach to governing and to every individual's ability to influence others' behavior at all levels of social and private activity, the problematization of war was something like an essential moment since it is where the confrontation with death was played out. This was the area on which he worked at the Collège de France at the end of the seventies and to which he had decided to devote himself after the *History of Sexuality.*[10] He alluded to this future research in the interview he gave when he was invited to the Catholic University at Louvain: "If God grants me life, after madness, crime, and sexuality, the final thing I would like to study would be the problem of war and the institution of war in what we might call the military dimension of society."[11]

The young Michel Foucault began his *hypokhâgne* in Poitiers, and began preparing for the entrance examinations for the École Normale Supérieure (ENS) on the rue d'Ulm in Paris. He was almost admitted the first time around and then decided to move to Paris to prepare for the exams there. In 1945 he found another Henri IV High School, in the heart of the city, and met André Wormser, François Bédarida, Robert Mausi, and François Furet, among others.

Thanks to Jean Hyppolite's introducing his *khâgne* students to Hegel, it became clear to Foucault that his field would be philosophy. Foucault found Hyppolite later at the ENS and even succeeded him at the Collège de France. "Those who were in *khâgne* after the war remember Mr. Hyppolite's classes on *Phenomenology of Mind*: in that voice that never stopped starting and stopping as if it were meditating within its own movement, we not only saw the voice of a professor but we heard something of the voice of Hegel."[12] Jean Hyppolite had translated *Phenomenology of Mind* and his courses gave Hegel's thinking the modernity that had been occulted behind his reputation as a Romantic philosopher. He had defended his thesis, "Genesis and Structure of the Phenomenology of Mind"[13] in 1947, and it was greeted in *Les Temps modernes* as a major event that restored Hegelianism's fundamental position in postwar philosophical thinking, in the legacy of the teaching of Jean Wahl and Alexandre Kojève. Even as late as 1975, Foucault sent Jean Hyppolite's wife a copy of *The Birth of the Clinic: An Archaeology of Medical Perception,*[14] and dedicated it "To Madame Hyppolite, in memory of him to whom I owe everything."[15] One of Foucault's major texts, "Nietzsche, Genealogy, and History,"[16] was written for a collective work in honor of

Jean Hyppolite. Contributors included Georges Canguilhem, Martial Guéroult, Jean Laplanche, Michel Serres, and Jean-Claude Pariente.[17]

Mental Illness

In 1946, Foucault entered the ENS on the rue d'Ulm with honors, fourth in his class. Success did not bring psychological stability, however, and in 1948 he attempted suicide. It was not easy to live one's homosexuality comfortably at the time and Foucault contacted a psychiatric institute. He had read Freud very early on thanks to a doctor correspondent of Freud in Poitiers, Dr. Beauchamp, and did not stop at taking courses at Ulm. But in addition to the courses at the ENS, he attended a number of Parisian institutes and took courses at Sainte-Anne. He was passionate about psychology and specialized in psychopathology. "Madness seemed to hold a certain fascination for him and he brought back innumerable anecdotes from his hospital visits about the world of the confined,"[18] recalls Jacques Proust.

Foucault's training extended beyond the normal curriculum and content of classical speculative philosophy, and brought him into contact with a specific field that was both theoretical and practical and that also prepared his later and rather rapid shifts, since his very first book, *Mental Health and Personality*,[19] dates from 1954 and is devoted to psychopathology, to psychoanalytic concepts, and to the reading of social representations of madness. He wrote this work at the request of Louis Althusser for the collection "Initiation philosophique" directed by his friend Jean Lacroix at Presses Universitaires de France (PUF). Michel Foucault also took courses at the Sorbonne with Daniel Lagache, Jean Hyppolite, named to the Sorbonne in 1949, Jean Beaufret, who dealt with Heidegger, Jean Wahl, and Jean-Toussaint Desanti, "but of course, it was Merleau-Ponty's courses that most strongly impressed the young students."[20]

In Search of the Mind's Limits

At the ENS itself, Michel Foucault was most influenced by Louis Althusser, the *caïman*[21] of philosophy there since 1948. At the beginning of the fifties, Marxism was the important thinking machine and Althusser introduced his audience, including Foucault, to Marx. He even introduced Foucault to the French Communist Party. "Impulse or adherence, then retreat, I no longer remember very well," remarked his party comrade Maurice Agulhon, while his colleague in Lille,

Olivier Revault d'Allonnes, remembers having seen Foucault crying upon learning of the death of the "little father of the people," Stalin, in 1953.[22] This was the period when the ENS was in fact divided between the "go-tos" (those who go to Mass) and the communists, many of whom were left-wing Christians who took the outstretched hand and joined the French Communist Party.

Everyone at the school expected Foucault to pass the *agrégation* in 1950 with flying colors, but he failed the oral exams after having passed the written exam. He had to prepare for the exams again the following year and his second attempt was something like a milestone righting his path on the road to his own destiny. The oral question he selected was unusual—sexuality—and Jean Hyppolite, who was on the committee, had to fight to get it through. The luck of the draw was inspired, for this would become Foucault's major area of work.

Having passed the exam, Foucault escaped the purgatory of teaching in a high school because, after a year at the Thiers Foundation, he was named a teaching assistant in psychology at the University of Lille. He continued to live in Paris and taught at Ulm thanks to Louis Althusser, and became the philosophy *caïman*. Foucault became friends with a group of communists who had been at the ENS—Gérard Genette, Jean-Claude Passeron, Paul Veyne, Maurice Pinguet, Jean Molino—who nicknamed him "le Fuchs" (German for fox) because Foucault was slyer than the others and because foxes dig more deeply than others. In 1953, "he went to Sainte-Anne every week for a new seminar of an unknown Dr. Lacan whom Foucault admired tremendously. He sometimes alluded to the specular image and to the Mirror Stage, which at the time was the ultimate subtlety."[23] His friend Maurice Pinguet recalls how important the discovery of Nietzsche was for Foucault in 1953:

> Hegel, Marx, Heidegger, Freud: in 1953, these were his points of reference until he met Nietzsche. . . . I see M. Foucault reading the *Considérations intempestives* in the sun on the beach at Civitavecchia. . . . From 1953 on, the general lines of a global project were beginning to take shape: an ethical decision inspired by Nietzsche's thinking crowned a genealogical critique of morality and science.[24]

In the early fifties, Foucault was also an avid reader of literature and was particularly fascinated by Maurice Blanchot's writing, which left his mark on Foucault's style, especially in his systematic use of the oxymoron. As Foucault confided to Paul Veyne, "At the time, I dreamed of being Blanchot."[25] His literary sensibility drew him to Samuel Beckett, Georges Bataille, Raymond Roussel, and René Char. A veritable fascination with reflecting upon the outside and upon limits also took hold then, and his literary influences translated his fundamental anxiety about death, which was no less calmed by his work in psychoanalysis, to which he always remained a stranger.

Foucault, who was quite precocious in his knowledge of Freud and Lacan, was counseled against hospitalization at Ulm by Louis Althusser, and Daniel Lagache later suggested to him that he begin analysis. He did, but he spent no more than three weeks. His relationship to psychoanalysis was always ambivalent, a mix of fascination and rejection. But it was thanks to Michel Foucault that a department of psychoanalysis was created in 1968 at Paris VIII-Vincennes, even though he ridiculed those who earned their living by "renting out their ears."[26]

Exile

The search for limits and for thinking the outside led Michel Foucault beyond France in 1955. He chose to leave for Uppsala in August, thanks to Georges Dumézil whom he did not yet know but who had to recommend someone to his Swedish friends for a position as a French reader, a position he himself had held in the thirties. Dumézil had lost touch with the ENS and turned to Raoul Curien for advice; Curien told him about Michel Foucault, whom he called "the smartest person I know."[27] Georges Dumézil offered the position to Foucault, who accepted it and spent three years in Sweden. When the two men met later, an intellectual complicity and a friendship were born "that never changed until his death."[28]

Foucault's participation in the structuralist adventure is due, certainly, to Georges Dumézil. Until then, Foucault had not really found direction in his constant search for an enterprise that would calm his existential anxiety. He was still uncertain as he stood at the crossroads of philosophy, literature, and psychology. Stalin's death in 1953 had been a shock, and the discovery of Nietzsche a substitute. But he was still without the base for the genealogy that he wanted to construct and his meeting with Dumézil—a meeting whose importance he would always reiterate—brought him an answer. In his preface to *Madness and Civilization*, he wrote, "I owe a debt to all those who helped me in this rather solitary task, and most of all to Mr. Georges Dumézil, without whom I would not have undertaken this work."[29] He told *Le Monde* that Georges Dumézil had been the most important of the influences on him, "thanks to the idea of structure. As Dumézil had done for myths, I have tried to discover the structured norms of experience whose shape can be found, with some modifications, at different levels."[30] Foucault wrote his thesis in the elsewhere of Sweden, seeking the manifestations of madness in the Carolina Rediviva library, where he found a very rich collection of seventeenth- and eighteenth-century medical works that a collector had left to the library. This collection served him well in giving voice to the world of silence.

The Thesis

On Saturday, May 20, 1961, a major event took place in the Louis-Liard Hall of the Sorbonne, the sanctuary where important theses are consecrated in an immutable ritual. Michel Foucault came to defend his thesis on madness, quite an incongruous object in this temple of the academy. Georges Canguilhem, his director, had told his students, "You must go."[31] Pierre Macherey was in attendance with many others in a room that was packed for the occasion. Foucault was completely unknown to Macherey when he walked into Louis-Liard, but he left it completely and permanently dazzled by this university ceremony. From then on, he bought each of Foucault's books the day they came out. "Something completely unheard of took place: the members of the jury were overwhelmed,"[32] a jury composed of august professors including its president, Henri Gouhier, a Sorbonne professor since 1948 and a well-known historian of philosophy, Georges Canguilhem, thesis director, and Daniel Lagache, Jean Hyppolite, and Maurice de Gandillac. "To speak about madness requires the talents of a poet," concluded Michel Foucault. "But you do possess those talents, sir," answered Canguilhem."[33]

Michel Foucault raised the problem of the claim to truth of a particular scientific discourse, namely, psychiatry. He studied the conditions of its validity and possibility, deliberately planting his probe in the heart of Western history in order to question triumphant reason. "In the case of a science as doubtful as psychiatry, couldn't we more clearly perceive the tangle between the effects of power and of knowledge?"[34] In order to displace traditional boundaries, Foucault began with the taboo object of madness, the repressed of Western reason, the image of its Other. He described where and how the pronouncements of nascent and uncertain psychiatric knowledge were validated, which led him to privilege the historicization of his object. For him, historical analysis was an "instrumental position"[35] within a political sphere, a means of not sacralizing science. The historicized discourse must ask what gives science its power, discerning everything in it that is not scientific, and look at "how, in our society, the truth effects of science are at the same time the effects of power."[36]

Madness, his research subject, was to be freed from the many discourses holding it captive. Scientific knowledge, whether legal, medical, or belonging to the police, was called to the witness stand to examine its contribution to the birth of this figure of the Other of reason. This quest for an object removed from the dredges of sedimented discourses corresponds completely to the structuralist theme, which at the time was taking the form of research into the different zero degrees—of writing, of language, of kinship, and of the unconscious. The Foucauldian project took its place in it by proposing to "find in history the zero degree of the history of madness, where it is an undifferentiated experience as yet undivided by division itself."[37] This work on the obscure limits of Reason aimed at restoring a life and voice to madness itself, behind the discourses with rationalist pretensions. "I did not want to make a history of this language, but rather an archaeology of this silence."[38]

Giving Voice to Silence: Madness

Michel Foucault constructed his history like a fiction based on some founding myths. "His histories are novels,"[39] in which positive affirmations, critical and even nihilistic critiques of canonical fields of knowledge confront the newly defined boundaries. He retraced a path leading us onto the medieval ship of fools, as much a mythical theme borrowed from the Argonauts as a reality of a medieval city that rids itself of its fools by placing them in the hands of boatmen, and up to the eighteenth-century world of asylums. The status of madness changes over time; first an object of exclusion, it later becomes an object of confinement.

Foucault discerned a reversal. During the Renaissance, the figure of the fool was inseparable from Reason. Erasmus discovered the immanent madness of Reason, and Pascal wrote that "men are so necessarily mad that not to be mad would amount to another form of madness."[40] In the eighteenth century, rationalism claimed an ability to choose its objects and, in the new rules of method as Descartes had defined them, excluded madness by relegating it to error, to the negative, to an illusory dream. Eliminated from the realm of the rational and born as a negative figure, apart, madness even became the decisive divide between the world of reason and unreason, picking up where the old division between Good and Evil had stopped. Madness was a world of non-sense that had to efface itself so that rational thought could prevail. Reduced to silence, immured in a carceral universe, the madman does not yet have his own place, for he is initially interned with paupers. The seventeenth century of Reason reacted by locking up the fear of madness that continued to haunt it. Madness became a menace and the madman's disappearance the condition for the reign of Reason. It thus found itself caught up in the important movement toward confinement whose beginnings Foucault placed with the royal edict of April 27, 1656, which created the Hôpital Général in which paupers were received and put to work. "The walls of confinement actually enclose the negative of that moral city of which the bourgeois conscience began to dream."[41] In this, he perceived a discontinuity in discursive practices that led to a new relationship to madness as well as to kinship. Whereas until that time, paupers had been included in a spiritual positivity as a possible object of redemption and as a condition of wealth, they were henceforth banished to negativity, as sources of disorder, the mark of divine punishment. The pauper became society's damned and therefore had to become invisible, like the madman.

Michel Foucault remained on the periphery of the social without ever engaging in a social history that would seek some general coherence in Western society. He was thus already on structuralism's terrain of predilection in which discourse enjoys a maximum degree of autonomy with respect to social contingencies. He refused to integrate the discursive reversal that he perceived into a general explanatory framework in which he might have established a relationship between the phenomenon of repression described and the historical change of a society in transition from the primarily religious to the ethical-economic, rooted in the mental structures and institutional practices of the modern era.

In the classical age, madness was a legal concern and was not yet a medical issue. Confinement was thus a legal act. The madman was located "at the meeting point between the social decree of confinement and the legal knowledge that determines the capacities of legal subjects.[42] Of course, the madman was not a prisoner like the others; he was not a beggar, but his bizarre behavior was considered to be a symptom of a profound animal nature (repressed in the man of reason), at the lower limits of humanity. Madmen were therefore chained by their jailers and even displayed in the loggias of Bicêtre Asylum.

The eighteenth century saw a decisive break in the perception of madness and the asylum was born as a specific institution reserved exclusively for those who were mad—a specific site of madness, a figure finally defined and removed from the shapeless heap it had been in the Hôpital Général. This institutional shift preceded the view of the madman as someone ill and in need of care: "A new dimension had to be established that would create a new space and something like another solitude so that in the middle of this second silence, madness could finally speak."[43] Mad speech was examined for signs of this or that clearly defined pathology and an entirely new field of knowledge was taken in hand by the medical world. "This was the apotheosis of the medical figure. . . . Since the end of the eighteenth century, a medical certificate had become almost obligatory for committing mad people. But within the asylum itself, the doctor's role was the most important insofar as he organized it as a medical space."[44] Its transition from an undifferentiated malady to madness, its situation within time, the consideration of a new perspective as well as of the new practices implied by the birth of madness as a specific figure, the dialectized relationship between knowledge and power, the substitution of medical for judicial power—all of these were the major lines of Foucault's approach, which went beyond a simple genealogy of madness to a more comprehensive view of the transition in a culture from power based on Law to a system relying on a norm that has become the criterion of division among individuals: this implies a completely different discursive economy.

The medicalization of the social body was one response to this process of normalization dividing normal and pathological. The new king was therefore the doctor at the center of the division whose limits he establishes. Problematizing such different perceptions of the boundaries between the normal and the pathological clearly echoed Georges Canguilhem's work, for he had already established the foundations of a structural history of science. Michel Foucault's theses remarkably and brilliantly demonstrate the fruitfulness of this method.

Madness and Unreason

In order to be defended at the time, a thesis had to be published, but in order to get it published, Foucault had to find an editor willing to accept a manuscript that was nearly one thousand pages long. He asked Brice Parain if he was willing to publish it at Gallimard and was rather hopeful since Parain had already published Georges Dumézil. However, we must remember that Claude Lévi-Strauss had had to take refuge at Plon after Brice Parain refused to publish *The Elementary Structures of Kinship*. Foucault met with the same categorical rejection. At that point, Jean Delay suggested his collection at PUF, but Foucault "had specifically wanted to avoid the thesis ghetto"[45] and do as Lévi-Strauss had done with *Tristes Tropiques*, getting beyond the circle of specialists in order to reach a broader intellectual readership.

Foucault therefore went to Plon, where he knew Jacques Bellefroid, who passed his thesis on to Philippe Ariès, the historian in charge of the collection "Civilisations d'hier et d'aujourd'hui." This was to be the first in a long series of contacts bringing philosophy and history together, yielding much fruitful collaboration, but also some misunderstandings and dead-end discussions. In 1961, however, the decisive meeting with Philippe Ariès was absolutely incongruous. Michel Foucault was a de-fuser of prejudices, a Nietzschean nihilist, whereas Philippe Ariès was an ultraconservative, royalist, ex-member of Action Française. What made a common ground possible was their shared sensitivity to the phenomena of *mentalités*. Ariès, the author of *The Family and the Child in the Ancien Régime*,[46] also valorized the premodern period, and had a certain nostalgia for the fetal world prior to the disciplinary partition in which madmen and reasonable men, young and old, would have cohabitated on the basic levels of sociability and conviviality.

Madness and Civilization was published therefore at Plon thanks to Ariès, to whom Foucault would later pay homage. "A thick manuscript came to my attention: a philosophy thesis on the relationship between madness and unreason in the classical age, written by an author whom I did not know. I was dazzled but I had to work extremely hard to get it published."[47]

When Michel Foucault was writing his thesis in the land of the midnight sun, he twice invited Roland Barthes to visit and enjoyed friendly visits with him on each of his trips to Paris. Barthes hailed this work as the first application of structuralism to history: "Michel Foucault describes a structural history that is doubly structural: its analysis is structural and the project itself is structural."[48] Roland Barthes quickly saw the link between Lévi-Strauss, Lacan, Foucault, and his own work, although none of them had collaborated in any way. For Barthes, Foucault's work illustrated the conquest of modern ethnology, and at the same time Foucault had successfully shifted nature to culture by studying what had been considered until then to be a purely medical concern. Just as Lévi-Strauss had analyzed kinship relations as marriage phenomena and Lacan had described the unconscious as being structured like a language, literary writing in the new literary critique became part of an apprenticeship or production of a form of writing that had nothing at all to do with any creative genius. Foucault "refused to consider madness as a nosographic reality."[49] Barthes read Foucault's work essentially as part of a general semiology constructing vast "sémantèmes" whose primary goal was to study forms, and in this respect, madness would never be more than an achronic form to be discerned but purified of all substance and transcendent content.

Maurice Blanchot similarly hailed Foucault's work, in which he saw his own experiment with a form of writing that explored limits and defined a new literary space: "To prepare, beyond culture, a relationship with what culture rejects: the voice of confinement, an outside of writing. Let us read and reread this book bearing this in mind."[50]

Michel Foucault finally met with a positive reception by the literary avant-garde, which counted a few historians[51] and epistemologists.[52] But for the most part, Foucault's work did not enjoy the popular success that had been expected and the book did not really get much response from philosophers (neither *Les Temps modernes* nor *Esprit* reviewed it), nor from psychiatrists, who considered it a simple exercise in literary style and metaphysics. *Madness and Civilization* had a fairly modest print run and it was not until *The Order of Things*[53] that Foucault's work elicited an excitement that never waned from that point on. Three thousand copies were initially printed in May 1961, followed by a modest second printing of twelve hundred copies in February 1964.[54] The book missed its intended mark the first time around since the psychiatric world in no way felt concerned by this philosopher. "It was thus only in a nonpractical way that Foucault's work had an impact."[55] According to Robert Castel, Foucault had a double impact: his work provoked an epistemological break, and it infused mental illness, which had become a positivist concept once again, with its alterity as the other of reason. Foucault's work was consecrated as an original but academic thesis in 1961, but it would have another fate thanks to two events: May 1968 and the lively interest it elicited among the Anglo-Saxon antipsychiatrists Ronald Laing and David Cooper. At the end of the sixties, the book finally found a receptive collective audience and a demand for a change in clinical practice; at that point, it became an inspiration to the movements protesting the practices of the asylum.

Exclusion or Integration?

Michel Foucault's structural method was founded on the loss of the substance of madness itself, a figure held prey to captive and fluctuating discourses. Madness loses all substance and consistency in this perspective and disappears within the folds of oppressive reason. Later, in 1980, Marcel Gauchet and Gladys Swain proposed a different thesis, thanks to an argument based on a very careful and detailed study of historical facts.[56] They looked at the chronology Foucault had proposed and argued that confinement did not really begin in the seventeenth century in France, but rather in the nineteenth century. But, above all, they saw the dynamic of modernity not as a logic excluding madness and alterity but rather as a logic of integration.

Foucault's diagnostic error gave rise to the illusion that the premodern period was a tolerant, undifferentiated society in which all difference was accepted. However, Marcel Gauchet and Gladys Swain showed that if the madman was accepted at the time, it was only insofar as he was considered to be the expression of a subhuman species: "In the cultural framework, defined by principles of inequality and natural hierarchy, absolute difference does not exclude proximity."[57] If madness creates a problem within the framework of modernity and is confined within the asylum, it is not because it is rejected but because the madman is considered an alter ego resembling Reason: "In the modern period, to the contrary, identity is a right and distance is only de facto.[58]

The history of madness in modern democratic society seems to be more a history of integration than a history of exclusion. Marcel

Gauchet also perceived a danger in the rising numbers of asylums, but, unlike Foucault, he considered this to be a problem of normalization, of an integrative utopia, more than a practice of exclusion. Foucault, in 1961, completely disagreed with a view of Reason as progressive. To the contrary, deconstructing Reason was supposed to enable a magnified image of the enigmatic figure of its Other to burst forth and fundamentally weaken the reign of the Lumières in order to better unveil its oppressive and disciplinary substructures.

The issue here is one of a radical critique of modernity and its categories. *Madness and Civilization* was above all the symptom of an era, the first step toward a new structural approach adapted to Western history, and a valorization of the repressed. The quest for truth took the form of examining the unspoken, ferreting around in the hiatuses and silences of a society that reveals itself in what it hides. Madness thus became an ideal object for both historical anthropology and psychoanalysis.

Nineteen

Marxism in Crisis:
A Thaw or the Deep Freeze Again?

In 1956, a good part of the French intelligentsia underwent some dramatic changes, which had some very real effects for the generation of a decade later. Structuralism was born as an intellectual phenomenon that, in a certain sense, took up where Marxism left off. Existentialism was the expression of postwar optimism, but the new relationship to history was more disenchanted. In early 1956, at the twentieth congress of the USSR's Communist Party, Nikita Khrushchev, the new secretary-general of the Communist Party, acknowledged Stalin's crimes; the year ended with the crushing of the Hungarian revolution by Soviet tanks.

The shock waves breached the sacrosanctity of the Soviet model, which came under criticism by the left. Communist ideology of hope for the future met historical reality to reveal the horrors of the logic of torture and totalitarianism. The seismic shock did not penetrate into the ranks of Billancourt, however, and the French Communist Party (PCF) remained the most powerful political machine outside of Moscow. Intellectuals whose work was based on the search for truth and on the critique of false appearances, however, could no longer unquestioningly accept that which till then had constituted their analytic framework. A period of mourning for lost hopes extended from 1956 until 1968, and yet the collective sensibility held to certain unshakable and unchanging ideas. What was it that was so well anchored that political voluntarism failed to triumph?

Postwar Europe was experiencing the most rapid economic changes since the end of the eighteenth century. "We were considerably behind in our perceptions and we could only measure how important the 'thirty glorious years' had been after they were over because while they were unfolding we said that nothing was happening."[1] Until then, the Russian Revolution had been seen as the continuation of the French Revolution; 1917 was the realization of the modern democratic ideal and was therefore an extension of 1789. Not only 1789, however, but the ideals and values of the Enlightenment themselves were beginning to be reevaluated in France. And indeed, many would make Bolshevism and its fatal destiny weigh heavily on those ideals.

Structuralism took root within the context of this critical rereading of Western democratic values. Independence, liberty, and responsibility were no longer the fundamental principles for the French intelligentsia. "The explanatory substitutes led to the primacy of totalities over that of subjects."[2] A critique of modernity and of the formal nature of democracy began to take shape, but it was no longer made in the name of a waning Marxism, but rather on the basis of Heidegger and Nietzsche, or by taking refuge in textual closure and internal architectonics.

This was also a time when French history was taken firmly in hand, in 1958, by General Charles de Gaulle, who put an end to the structural instability that afflicted political life since the end of World War II, and surrounded himself for the first time with technocratic ministers. His choices made it clear that the École Normale Supérieure was no longer the institutional mold for the country's future leaders; the École Nationale de l'Administration (ENA) came to play that role; whereas the École Normale had up to that point been the institutional incarnation of the reproduction of the humanities, the technocratic graduates of the ENA (énarques) now replaced the intellectuals. Ulm reacted. Indeed, it became the epicenter of a structural quake in 1966, and the voice of the most scientific of discourses, in an attempt to slow down the process that was relegating it to a secondary role in training the republic's elite. Since 1958, technical/technocratic thinking had been well established, however. "For me, structuralism was very successful because it was the basis of technocratic thinking and gave it a philosophical, logical daubing, a certain rationality, a kind of vigor. There was more than a single positive encounter between structuralism and these times, there was a marriage of reason."[3]

1956: A Time of Ruptures

The priests responsible for the cult questioned the "little father of the people" and brought the edifice of belief crumbling down. Structuralism provided a life raft for many at a time when institutional Marxism was in its agony: "A kind of ceremonious massacre. . . . This made possible a clean sweep, a big breath of fresh air, a hygienic act. We don't always choose the scent of our deodorant or detergent; they often stink, but they work."[4] A period of ruptures began for intellectuals who could no longer pretend and who subjected their own fetishes to attack.

Roger Vailland removed the portrait of Stalin from his office walls. Claude Roy was forced out of the French Communist Party for "having joined in the game of reaction by the enemies of the working class and the people."[5] Even Jean-Paul Sartre, who had borne his cross since the beginning of the fifties as an irreproachable fellow traveler of the French Communist Party, published an incendiary article about Hungary in *L'Express* on November 9, 1956, leading to an irreconcilable divorce between him and the party. The numbers of critical articles and remarks were increasing; it was clearly possible to be right even if it meant being subjected to a continuous flow of insults and calumny. But this form of intimidation culminated at this point since many who joined the anticolonial protest against the war in Algeria discovered the shattering proof of the lie of the accusation that they had joined the other side. In 1956, a good many of the postwar traumas were swept away for many intellectuals in the West, well before the cleanup was completed in the East in 1989. The question at the time was how to go on being a Marxist while keeping a historical consciousness.

History no longer held out hope of a better future, but was scrutinized for the failings that had borne the seeds of barbarism. The rift in 1956 "led us to stop being forced to hope for anything."[6] According to Michel Foucault, the intellectual should search out the range of possibilities and impossibilities in a given society rather than be buoyed up by the continuous flow of history or await the arrival of a messiah incarnated by the party as a guide to earthly salvation. But even before mapping out a site for research and identity, the party that considered itself to be the foyer of sociability, an adoptive family, and everything surrounding it, with its specific rites and habits, had to be abandoned.

Pierre Fougeyrollas quit the French Communist Party in 1956. "I was teaching at the Lycée Montaigne in Bordeaux at the time and was a member of the federal office of the PCF of the Gironde. I quit because of Hungary. When I came to Paris in 1958, I joined the group Arguments."[7] Gérard Genette also left the PCF in 1956. "At that point, I began a three-year detoxification with Socialisme ou Barbarie, where I often saw Claude Lefort, Cornelius Castoriadis, and Jean-François Lyotard. After having supported Stalin for eight years, I needed a centrifugal force to become a non-Marxist, and Socialisme ou Barbarie scraped things clean."[8] As Olivier Revault d'Allonnes put it, "We could have created an association of the class of 1956."[9] He had joined the PCF in Lille in 1953, where he found himself in the company of Michel Foucault when both were protesting the war in Indochina.

Through his support for Polish October, Jean-Pierre Faye was fascinated to discover the rigor of Lévi-Strauss's program in 1956. He had gone to an important and solemn UNESCO reception for Polish representatives in Louis-Liard Hall at the Sorbonne, presided by Fernand Braudel. The meeting ended on a spectacular note, with the arrival of Gomulka, the conqueror of the Polish revolt and an early victim of the Stalinist purges. At that point, Lévi-Strauss "harangued us from atop some kind of chair, explaining that structure reigned and that econometrics, structural linguistics, and anthropology, which was to become structural a few months later in another book, were the three sciences that would dominate."[10] Jean-Pierre Faye wondered how mythologies could function in the modern world, especially after the 1929 crash in the United States, but also after the depression that had affected Vienna in 1873. Taking a structural path seemed promising at the time because of the way, according to Lévi-Strauss, it explained the many, complex correlations between mythology and an economic situation, and between structure and the fluctuations of history.

Structuralism as the Outcome of the Crisis of Marxism

For others, recourse to Lévi-Strauss became the basis of a conversion to anthropology. This was true for the Communist philosophers whom we might call the club of four: Alfred Adler, Michel Cartry, Pierre Clastres, and Lucien Sebag. All four had quit the PCF in 1956, and had switched from philosophy to anthropology—a choice that cannot be dissociated from the changes in the political situation. "Nineteen fifty-six was a central date for us."[11]

Alfred Adler described the intellectual development that had led him from existentialism to structuralism.[12] He had joined the PCF in 1952 at the age of eighteen; his political militancy had led him to Marxism, but he had remained on the sidelines, and defined himself as a Communist in the sense of moral commitment rather than as a Marxist. While studying philosophy and taking courses with Jean Hyppolite, he discovered Hegel. "Hegelian Marxism gave us intellectual substance so long as political choices came first, and it also gave us a militant content."[13] When the events of 1956 unfolded, the PCF became an object of opprobrium, even if it took two years for the exclusion to fully take shape. "Nineteen fifty-six is the very condition of the choice of ethnology."[14] It was no longer possible to make ethico-political commitment adequate to Hegelian Marxist speculation, and Alfred Adler found himself in Claude Lefort's seminar on *The Elementary Structures of Kinship*. The discovery of Lévi-Strauss's work was a source of pleasure for the group of four for it had the merit of signifying a de-ideologization and of espousing an apolitical discourse: "We discovered *Tristes Tropiques*. I remember that Pierre Clastres was crazy about *Tristes Tropiques*, and had read it four or five times."[15]

This conversion led the group to become interested in everything having to do with the birth of the structural paradigm. They read all they could with great enthusiasm, an effective catharsis with respect to the past. They threw themselves into structural linguistics and began attending Jacques Lacan's seminar at Sainte-Anne Hospital in 1958. Between 1958 and 1963, their appetite for discovery led to a thorough theoretical introduction to ethnology, in relation to other disciplines, as well as to a number of trips to do fieldwork. At that point, the group split in two: Lucien Sebag and Pierre Clastres went to work on Amerindian cultures while Alfred Adler and Michel Cartry left for Africa. "They say jokingly that the only place to find true primitives is in Latin America."[16] They aspired to find something more profound than exoticism; for them, it was a matter of locating societies that had been sheltered from the unitary map of Hegelian Marxist thinking, societies that were not classified in Stalinist handbooks.

The spirit of discovery was also spurred by a disappointment in speculative philosophy and history, whose creative cycle seemed to have come to an end when Hegelian Marxist theory frayed. Unlike purely self-reflexive speculative discourses, Lévi-Strauss's work offered a veritable intellectual adventure: "In *Tristes Tropiques* Lévi-Strauss says that you have to lose a lot of time in order to find the name of a clan. Reading that, we realized that someone had introduced something new."[17] Setting off to do fieldwork, and the ensuing shift in personal and cultural history, were decisive aftereffects of the 1956 quake.

The Thaw

An ideological thaw shattered the vulgate, therefore, as of 1956. There had been some forerunners, of course, particularly among the members of Socialisme ou Barbarie, founded by Cornelius Castoriadis and Claude Lefort in 1949, to which a number of intellectuals turned in 1956. This group developed a radical critique of the left in order to analyze the Stalinist model of a bureaucratic and totalitarian system.

For Castoriadis and his group, structuralism was not an alternative to the vulgate, but a simple adaptation to the mode of domination of modern capitalism, which, in 1958, reigned. The discourse gave absolute priority to science; "whereas people were more and more oppressed in the name of science, they try to persuade them that they are nothing and that science is everything."[18] They denounced structuralism's elimination of living history and the way in which intellectual thought became infused with technocratic thinking.

In 1956, a new current was born and it fused around the journal *Arguments*. The group argued for a revision of Marxism, a rejection of the vulgate but also a clarification of the contradictions of modernization. Edgar Morin founded and directed the journal and his board included Kostas Axelos, Jean Duvignaud, Colette Audry, François Fejtö, Dionys Mascolo, Roland Barthes, and Pierre Fougeyrollas. The review was the very expression of the thaw that, in place of the previous dogmatism, offered a real questioning and multidimensionality. "Spring 1956 flowered. Gusts of hope came from Poland, Hungary, and Czechoslovakia. History hesitated between the ebb and the flow. . . . We realized that what we thought was the bedrock of our doctrine was little more than an ice floe without any real solidity."[19]

The review was born of a meeting between Edgar Morin and Franco Fortini, who was already publishing the review *Rugionamenti* in Italy. "During the years immediately prior to this, I had been a half-dead political corpse, I was a member of no party, and I had been

happy to meet some friends in Italy . . . with whom I could dialogue."[20] This was an open group that was intellectually vital from the
beginning and, unlike any political party organ, it established itself as
a simple laboratory or bulletin for ideas. *Arguments* measured political problems and offered reflections on our technical civilization and
on language in its search for a critical radicality beyond disciplinary
discoveries and party blinders. During its first two years, the review
focused on mourning its break with the French Communist Party, and
then its concerns grew less political, addressing such issues as love, the
universe, language. "During its six years of existence, *Arguments* enjoyed that rare, happy union between affect and thinking."[21]

This search for a new direction ended prematurely in 1962. "With
and without joy and sadness, *Arguments* was sabotaged by its cap-
tains."[22] This sabotage was due in part to the dispersion of the editorial board: Pierre Fougeyrollas left for Dakar and Jean Duvignaud was
in Tunisia. But, above all, one fact became clear, and this was that
times had changed and, at the beginning of the sixties, a new kind of
thinking was taking up where others had left off: structuralism.
"Within the university context, this way of thinking was taking over,
and it offered a scientific solution to all of our problems. So, it was
over. We had once again become deviants, but we were wise enough to
realize it."[23]

The Deep Freeze Again?

Edgar Morin saw structuralism's success as one more freeze after the
thaw. Structural epistemology replaced a totalizing Marxism, but it
was equally persuaded of its scientificity and adherence to the laws of
classical science. Determinism and objectification excluded the subject, which was too uncertain, as well as history, which was too contingent, to which it preferred a model as rigorous as the natural sciences: structural linguistics. Another form of deep freeze was also
evident, for there was a clear tendency to swap Moscow for Peking,
Hanoi, and Havana. And yet this need to scientize the approach of the
social sciences was easy to understand in terms of the errors accumu-
lated under Stalin, in the same way that there had been a need to hold
on to some certitudes. On the one hand, conferring the primary value
on structure made it possible to explain the persistent difference in the
relationship between determinism and freedom, and between the historical task of transformation and the inability to convince people of

its necessity. "Thanks to Saussure and Jakobson, the notion of an unconscious structure allowed us to better understand something that evolved not as a function of class or of social change, but outside of conscious will."[24] On the other hand, with anthropology, as with structural linguistics, other visions of the world and other systems of representation could be considered: "It became possible for us to renew the dialectical vision, which we had tended to regard as a form of getting beyond oppositions, since the notion of multiplying ever more subtle mediations seemed to us to renew dialectical thinking."[25]

Structuralism was the real beneficiary of the crisis in 1956. The bases of its programs had already been well established by the time it took root at the beginning of the century. Structuralism made it possible to confer a certain level of scientificity and operationality in a particular area of thought by preserving the goal of universality that prior forms of commitment had held to, without making this one part of the desire to transform the world. The enterprise was a limited one: an attempt to better understand the world by integrating alterity and the unconscious into it.

Twenty

The French School of Economics
Takes a Structural Path

One discipline among the social sciences did not wait for the fifties before reacting to structuralism: economics. Of course, unlike the other social sciences, economics did not draw its model from linguistics. Economists were ahead of others in formalizing their research and were thus able to serve as examples for other disciplines in search of scientific rigor. Lévi-Strauss borrowed the idea of a model from economics in order to give priority to the scientific aspect of structural anthropology.

Economics, however, did not play the role of a pilot science during the period when structuralism was at its height even if it was at the time the most advanced discipline in terms of the mathematization required by most of the social sciences. Exchanges did exist and Lévi-Strauss's use of theoretical modeling was one such example, but economics nonetheless remained rather removed from the important debates being carried on in the sixties about the structuralist paradigm. This relative marginality resulted from the fact that the mirage of the period was the extension of the phonological model, but institutional divisions in the social sciences were such that economists found themselves housed with jurists and both were cut off from literature. "The rue Saint-Jacques really was a very deep river running between economists and literary types. By contrast, contacts with historians were already going on in the Sixth Section of the École Pratique des Hautes Études."[1] In 1958, Fernand Braudel proposed the creation of a university for the social sciences broadly conceived; his proposal was rejected, and the decision to separate letters and the social sciences more narrowly from the law school and the school of economics created a long-standing gulf. Economics could not be a hub discipline in the structural paradigm.

And yet, economic science produced highly axiomatic results even if it did not spend a long time pondering the epistemological conditions of the discipline's creation. Microeconomics in the fifties managed a rather complete axiomatization around the idea of a general equilibrium, which appeared to be a totally formalized structure. In economics, there was "a form of structuralism that met the logical conditions of scientificity, in terms of the criteria of the logical construction of propositions, and that led to results having universal value."[2] The very success of this axiomatization and its practical applications contributed to the lag time in problematizing the results of microeconomics, which, for the most part, remained removed from any critical reflection about its postulates.

The Marriage of State and Structure

Postwar changes in the relationship between the government and the market in France also pragmatically strengthened the idea of structure in economics. At a macroeconomic level, much thought was devoted to the range of possibilities for government intervention. "This was the golden age of Keynesianism."[3] But in the eyes of the Anglo-Saxon tradition, which is marginalist, and where state intervention must be limited to the periphery of a general equilibrium that is considered a given, the situation in France was unusual. After the Second World War, the government that had emerged from the National Council for the Resistance attacked macroeconomic models. Long-term plans, territorial redefinitions, and the nationalization of private enterprise would profoundly change the mechanisms of the French economy.

Economic structures themselves needed to be rethought in order to definitively change the overall flows of demand and, therefore, levels of activity. At that point, because the state was ostensibly directing national reconstruction and economic modernization, it took charge of the important structural transformations. These imperatives fueled activities that were propitious for regrouping and made possible the creation of "a veritable French school of economics."[4] This was one of those rare moments when energies came together, in an area that more generally favored fragmented research in a number of directions, in order to examine the unavoidable interconnections between the period's economic and social problems.

La Revue économique was one of the major hubs for this reorganization. Directed by François Perroux, Jean Weiller, Jean Lhomme, and the Marchal brothers, the editorial board also included Fernand Braudel, and thus symbolized the organic links of a dialogue begun between economists and historians of the *Annales*. The state created a series of new administrative structures following the war's end in order to effectuate the necessary structural reforms and enlighten public authorities about the short and middle term. The Institut National de la Statistique et des Études Économique (INSEE) was created in order to generate economic predictions, and then, in 1952, the Treasury created its own programs (Service des Études Économiques et Financières [SEEF]), which later became the Direction de la Prévision et du Plan, with its economic research centers, the CREDOC (Centre de Recherche en Documentation) and the CEPREMAP (Centre d'Études Prospectives d'Économie Mathématique Appliquées à la Planification). The government's use of economic expertise "took two directions: setting up a national accounting mechanism and creating macroeconomic planning models."[5]

The consequences of this organic alliance between the state and the theoreticians and practitioners of macroeconomics underscored the breach with the university of the humanities, and particularly with literature. Claude Gruson, Pierre Uri, Alfred Sauvy, and François Perroux created teams that included relatively few university representatives by contrast with the numbers of civil administrators and engineers coming from the Grandes Écoles. Prospective models of the national economy were developed, therefore, at the highest levels of administrative power in search of a certain harmony between the different sectors of the economy and the mechanisms of production.[6]

Valorizing the structuralist method was therefore quite effective among economists, but their outlook was generally foreign to the viewpoint of literary scholars, and the formalization of their research removed them further still. And yet, this situation did not prevent the creation of a number of bridges making dialogue possible between economists and the rest of the social sciences. François Perroux played a fundamental role in this.

Where the Paths Converged: François Perroux

As of 1955, François Perroux was a professor at the Collège de France. He had created the ISEA (Institut de Science Appliquée) in 1944 and his review, *Les Cahiers de l'ISEA*, was receptive to philosophical—and, more particularly, epistemological—debates and included articles by Claude Lévi-Strauss and Gilles Gaston-Granger. François Perroux's influence was twofold. He borrowed the notion of a generalized economy from Merleau-Ponty but contributed to its dissemination among economists. He also proposed a concept of structure to those liberals who deified a perfect market in which prices operated without restrictions. "The structure of an economic ensemble is defined by the network of links between simple and complex units and by the series of proportions between the flow and the stocks of elementary units and the objectively significant combinations of these units."[7]

Europeans massively used the structural paradigm in political economy around the 1930s, in reaction to the 1929 crash. But even before the idea of structure was generalized in political economy, Henri Bartoli astutely remarked that "structural sociology and structural economics were contemporary with the birth of sociology and political economy."[8] The idea of structure was born in the seventeenth century out of the correlation between the different economic givens seen as so many elements of an overall coherence guiding economic life.

Auguste Comte had already placed the physiocrats among the initiators of "social physics." And then Marx sought to distinguish the laws of capital by invoking such structural notions as modes of production, social classes, and the social relationships to production. He attempted to get beyond a simple description of observable facts in order to discern "the internal organization of the capitalist mode of production, in its ideal."[9] If Marx used the idea of structure to organize a purely conceptual theoretical model, he in no way forgot the other end of the chain; the model is linked to the economic reality of the stage of development of the productive forces in a given social system. The structure in question after 1945 in the French school of economics, on the contrary, relied more on empirical and observable facts than on theory, and more closely resembled the methodology of historians than that of anthropologists. This was altogether clear in the work of François Perroux, who defined structure by the proportions of flow and stocks of basic units, and that of René Clémens, who saw structure in the "proportions and value relations between costs, prices, revenues, and money in a given context."[10]

The German Ernst Wagemann had already used the notion of structure systematically in the thirties. Economists had adopted his definition, notably in France, beginning in 1936 with the structural reforms of the Popular Front. In France, structure was considered "the most permanent."[11] Structure is what resists rapid changes, what makes for an economic situation and inflects it without identifying with it. Structure is marked by the slowness of what are generally cyclical economic rhythms set into motion by deep mechanisms. François Perroux adopted this vision of structure as an invariant, or as a variant with relatively mild fluctuations, and saw structures as "ensembles of slowly moving quantities, sets of kinds of behavior or of relatively stable behaviors."[12] During a 1959 colloquium led by Roger Bastide,[13] André Marchal proposed his own more dynamic perspective in opposition to François Perroux's static notion of structure. Marchal's approach was based on relativizing those economic laws that are valid according to the type of structure or between two structural limits within an economic system in which a certain multidimensional combination evolves.[14]

André Marchal examined how the idea of structure had made its way back into contemporary economic thinking.[15] He saw in this a quest among economists to explain the big historical changes of twentieth-century capitalism: the transition from a competitive capitalism to a monopoly capitalism, the 1929 crash, and decolonization. The conjunction of all of these changes made it necessary to move beyond the models that eliminated all external elements.

Attempting an Economic Anthropology

André Nicolaï's work must be seen within this context of global confrontation. He defended his thesis in 1957, although his reflection on the notion of structure dated back to 1948, his last year in high school.[16] He had been very excited by the debate between Tarde and Durkheim and saw in their work a problem that would remain central to all of his later work: the polemic between the importance of behavior (Tarde) and that of structures (Durkheim). Nicolaï said to himself then that "both are partly right because society stubbornly remains composed of agents who, at the same time, seem to be acted upon by society."[17] In order to continue thinking, using this contradiction as a basis, he was led to a position that went beyond a strictly economic viewpoint; when he found *Tristes Tropiques* in 1955, he was delighted. Not only did he enroll in economics, but in political science as well, and at the Sorbonne he took philosophy, sociology, and psychology courses with Piaget, Lagache, Merleau-Ponty, and Gurvitch, and finally found himself at the heart of the structural confluence by the end of the fifties. He was a precocious structural economist, slightly atypical by virtue of his receptivity to all the social sciences and by his desire to establish a structural economic anthropology.

Econometrics

But there was an intermediary level between concrete reality and structure, which the economists more than others developed. This was the level of the model, a necessary mediation that produces the most developed formalization. It is here that economics, in the process of becoming econometrics, becomes a completely formalized language. "Constructing mathematical models became one of the most prestigious branches of economic science, to the immense benefit of the discipline and—why not admit it—to its great misfortune as well."[18]

The International Society for Econometrics dates from 1930, but it was only after 1945 that econometric models really developed. Certain historical events contributed to their development, and the models were perfected, for example, during the "great aerial bridge over West Berlin."[19] When Stalin blocked all but aerial access to and from Berlin in 1948, an econometric model had to be designed in order to organize a continual routing of airplanes to keep the population in West Berlin from starving. This kind of operational research significantly broadened the use of mathematics as applied statistics in economic models. Collecting statistical information became much more sophisticated and was important for the extended application of econometric models. Lévi-Strauss was fascinated by this operational efficiency and the capacity to take reality into account in a purely formal language. It was at the intermediary level of model making especially that economists in the fifties participated in the structuralist paradigm, more so than when they invoked a structure's reality, which is bascially nothing more than a way of accounting for the permanence of certain situations. Econometrics enables us to discern a certain number of aporias that become obstacles for the enterprise as it comes up against the limits of formalism in the social sciences: "Not only does mathematization push the intellectual undertaking to free itself of reality and to yield to a sort of deductive euphoria deeply contemptuous of patient, factual observation and any enthusiasm for analysis, but it also imposes some very severe syntactic limits."[20]

A number of economists hypostasized their tools when they adopted an econometric methodology, and some even went so far as to take these instruments for reality itself. Everything that could not be measured was meaningless. Historicity, which is part of the structural paradigm, was clearly eliminated since nothing can be foreseen in this scheme of things once the model perfectly reproduces itself, except variations in quantity. The same obstacle arises: how to construct an analytical apparatus of simple self-reproduction, a truly self-regulating machine that considers all human activity to be meaningless except for the initial structure, as well as any history of this action. Gilles Gaston-Granger very quickly recognized the danger of a formalism that creates such an illusion. It "comes from the fact that once the themes have been determined through axiomatic abstraction, we want to confer an ontological privilege over the operations, which, paradoxically, gave birth to them."[21]

Twenty-one

Get a Load of That Structure!

At the end of the fifties, before structuralism was being spoken of, the reference to structure was everywhere in the social sciences. At this point, certain representatives of convergent research interests chose to evaluate the situation and draw up a balance sheet on the use of the concept. The evaluation provided the occasion for the first important multidisciplinary meeting, which gives a good idea of how disciplinary boundaries were becoming increasingly porous—a situation that a good many researchers had already been using to their benefit. Because man was the common object of a whole series of disciplines, the conceptual approach that was taking shape, and that was overriding studies on intentionality or consciousness, suggested that it was possible to see a common approach take shape that would encompass all thinking in the social sciences. The air was redolent with the possible and proximate victory of the ambitious goal of paradigmatic unity.

Two important meetings took place in 1959. In January, Roger Bastide organized an important colloquium on the idea of structure.[1] Maurice de Gandillac, Lucien Goldmann, and Jean Piaget presided over a colloquium at Cerisy on the confrontation between genesis and structure.[2] The reference to structural binarism, which was already being invoked rather frequently, was becoming the necessary path for any researcher to take at sites of innovative research such as the Musée de l'Homme, the Sixth Section of the École Pratique des Hautes Études, and certain courses at the Collège de France. At that point, the search beyond sememes and mythemes for other *emes* was general.

The colloquium organized by Roger Bastide set the scene for a broad confrontation over the use of the concept of structure in diverse disciplines. Étienne Wolff argued that the notion corresponded to a biological given: "Living beings include a whole hierarchy of structures."[3] He defined several scales of biological structure, of the arrangement of cells in tissues, of tissues in organs, and that of the "ultra-structures" made visible by the electronic microscope. Although the level of observation could be defined, the passage from one structure to another remained mysterious and therefore a matter for theoretical speculation. Émile Benveniste gave a paper on linguistics, making clear that linguistics had played a fundamental role in diffusing the paradigm, which was no longer even that of structure in the eyes of this pioneer discipline: structure had become *structural*, and finally *structuralism*. Benveniste recalled the innovators: Saussure, Meillet, the Prague Circle, Jakobson, Karcevsky, and Trubetzkoy, who had already defined phonology in structural terms as early as 1933: "Contemporary phonology is characterized above all by its structuralism and its systematic universalism."[4]

Lévi-Strauss, for his part, considered that anthropology had brought about the decisive changes that made possible the discovery of the structural arrangements at the heart of the social order. He disputed George-Peter Murdock on these grounds, and rejected the possibility of simultaneously studying structure and process, holding that such an idea belonged, "at least in anthropology, to a naive philosophy."[5] Daniel Lagache recalled that structuralism took shape in psychology in reaction against atomism and around the psychology of forms, of Gestalt psychology. "It was in this context that structuralism became one of the dominant characteristics of contemporary psychology."[6]

Robert Pagès, for his part, recalled for the audience how the idea of structure in social psychology had been polysemic, and how frequently Jacob-Lévy Moreno had used it in sociometrics. Henri Lefebvre gave a paper on the use of structure in Marx in which he made it appear that Marx was the important forerunner of the current revolution, quoting the preface to his 1859 *Contribution to a Critique of Political Economy* (1859). Even Raymond Aron placed himself within this structural perspective by invoking his desire to see political science rise to a higher level of conceptual abstraction. He regretted that the structures in question were still too dependent on a concrete political reality and expressed the wish that "we might discover the basic functions of every political order at a later stage of abstraction."[7] Other participants demonstrated the fecundity of the structural approach in their particular discipline: Pierre Vilar in history, Lucien Goldmann in the history of ideas, François Perroux and André Marchal in economics.

The Consecration of Cerisy: Genetic Structuralism

The second confrontation took place in 1959 in Normandy, at the sixteenth-century château cum colloquium center known as Cerisy-la-Salle. The question this time was less one of determining which discipline had gone farthest in its use of the idea of structure than of comparing the ideas of structure and genesis. The colloquium organizers considered that their work lay in the wake of the structuralist break but they refused to see the social as static and sought instead to reconcile dynamic potentialities and permanent factors, in other words, to bring history together with structural coherence. They were the bearers of a genetic structuralism: "Genetic structuralism appeared for the first time as a fundamental philosophical idea along with Hegel and Marx."[8] Goldmann situated the second stage in the genesis of this new method in the development of phenomenology and especially of Gestalt psychology.

Somewhat earlier, Lucien Goldmann had applied genetic structuralism in his remarkable study on the links between Jansenism, Pascal's *Pensées*, and Racine's theater.[9] He situated the work of these two writers in relation to the far more vast significant structures of the different currents of Jansenism and the social antagonisms of the seventeenth century. Unlike Lévi-Strauss, however, Goldmann no longer saw the search for structures as incompatible with the search for genesis, and he thus opened up another direction for structuralism's development, one that was more receptive to history. Jean Piaget, another adherent of genetic structuralism and one of the colloquium organizers, criticized Gestalt for its immobility as much as for its Lamarckism, wherein structure was completely ignored. He argued for the inseparability of genesis and structure based on his work in child psychology: "There are no innate structures; every structure implies a construction."[10]

Maurice de Gandillac was the third of the colloquium organizers. He voiced some criticism of Jean-Pierre Vernant's paper on the Hesiodic myth of the races. Setting himself squarely in a genetic perspective, de Gandillac criticized Vernant for giving too much weight to the internal structure of Hesiod's myth to the detriment of history: "I wonder if we can go as far as you have in eliminating temporality from the interpretation of the myth of races."[11] Vernant, who also sought to reconcile history and structure, answered by arguing that Hesiod does indeed use temporality, but not our linear and irreversible temporality.

Structural Anthropology and Its Hegemonic Ambitions

Structure and genesis squared off at Cerisy. The colloquium had the merit of bringing to light very early on one of the major themes of the future debates concerning the relationship between history and the structural paradigm. The debate is fundamental and there are two sets of issues. The first was the much-disputed place of the discipline of history and the second the manner in which the West conceived its relationship to history. In this respect, structuralism posed a double challenge for historians.

When Lévi-Strauss reprinted a whole series of articles in *Structural Anthropology* in 1958, the collection was something of a manifesto. His opening article dated from 1949 and defined the ties between ethnology and history.[12] Lévi-Strauss's remarks were in the line of François Simiand's 1903 challenge to Durkheimian sociology; he observed that history had not renewed itself since, whereas sociology had metamorphosed itself, particularly through the prodigious progress that had been made in ethnological research.

The 1929 break with the *Annales* was forgotten in passing, doubtless for the sake of the polemic in order to better discredit a discipline that, in his eyes, was condemned to monographs and ideographs. Lévi-Strauss demonstrated that structural anthropology distinguished itself from evolutionism by breaking with the biological model and by hypothesizing a radical discontinuity between nature and culture. Not that he challenged the validity of history; in this respect, he disagreed with the functionalist school, and particularly with Malinowski, for having too easily sidestepped historical givens in favor of functions: "For to say that a society functions is a truism; but to say that everything in a society functions is an absurdity."[13] Faced with the excess of history in the diffusionist method and with the functionalists' negation of history, Lévi-Strauss proposed a third direction for structural anthropology.

He showed that ethnography and history are related by their object (alterity in time and space), by their goal (to go from the specific to the general), and with respect to their methodological demands (the critique of sources). They therefore resemble each other, but if they are to work in concert their distinctions would have to be made in the relationships between ethnology and history, two disciplines with distinct but complementary perspectives. "History organizes its data in relation to conscious expressions of social life, while anthropology proceeds by examining its unconscious foundations."[14] What made the unconscious accessible to ethnology, as we have seen, was the linguistic model, and especially phonology.

What also became clear through these distinctions was that only ethnology claimed a scientific, nomothetic project for itself, defined by the transition from the specific to the general, which alone allows the transition from the conscious to the unconscious. The ethnologist must therefore appropriate historical materials in the same way that he uses ethnographic inquiry, but he alone can claim to have access to "the complete range of unconscious possibilities. These are not unlimited."[15] The traditional opposition between history and ethnology, based on the distinction between the type of sources, between the study of societies without writing systems and those with a written culture, is of only secondary importance in Lévi-Strauss's view. Rather than the object of study, it was the orientation of the scientific project that was fundamental, and we can see how Lévi-Strauss's project challenged historians, especially since he considered the ethnologist to be no more than the first step toward a final synthesis that alone could forge a social or cultural anthropology that aims for a comprehensive understanding of man from the hominids to the present. *Structural Anthropology* coherently grouped together a number of articles dealing with anthropology's place in the social sciences, the relationship between language and kinship, artistic representations in Asia and America, magic and religion—in other words, a range of very diverse objects that seemed to ignite what Lévi-Strauss called a "Copernican revolution . . . which will consist of interpreting society as a whole in terms of a theory of communication."[16]

The structural version of anthroplogy proclaims its hegemonic intentions in the realm of knowledge about humankind, and Lévi-Strauss defines it broadly enough to describe all levels of social reality: "But as soon as the various aspects of social life—economic, linguistic, etc.—are expressed as relationships, anthropology will become a general theory of relationships."[17] This point of view lets anthropology receive its analytic models from mathematics, the formal language par excellence. By grouping complete series of variables as a group of permutations, the structuralist programs aspired to discover the very law of the group under study. In this analytic structure, the group's structure is understood through the procedure of repetition, based on the invariable whose function is to flush out the structure of the myth from its diverse enunciations. Here again, history and ethnology are opposed in their capacity for modelization. Structural ethnology can claim a mechanical modeling: "Anthropology uses a 'mechanical' time, reversible and noncumulative,"[18] whereas history must limit iself to a contingent, noniterable temporality that requires statistics. The time of history "is statistical."[19]

Those societies that Lévi-Strauss calls cold resemble mechanical machines that infinitely use the energy shaped at the outset—the clock, for example; hot societies resemble thermodynamic machines, such as the steam engine, which functions through temperature differentials. They produce more work, but consume more energy by progressively destroying it. This last society seeks ever wider and more numerous differentials in order to go forward and renew its sources. Temporal succession should influence the institutions in cold societies as little as possible. The most radical and destabilizing challenge Lévi-Strauss makes to historians is that structural anthropology leans on what is considered the most modern and the most efficient advances in the social sciences. Having resolutely situated anthropology on cultural grounds, Lévi-Strauss takes advantage, with respect to historians, of having a theoretical perspective that should one day make it possible to decode the inner structures of the brain. There is a kind of structuralist materialism in him, for, according to his analyses, structure is occasionally considered to be an analytic grid and, at other times it springs directly from concrete reality: "Claude Lévi-Strauss is a materialist. He constantly says as much."[20]

Structural anthropology can therefore flourish without boundaries, according to Lévi-Strauss; it makes it possible to move beyond the traditional culture/nature split. Similarly, structural anthropology can cast its net more widely to consider the whole of humankind. The structuralist manifesto of 1958 doubly challenged history and philosophy in this respect. Philosophy, which reflects in the first place on how the human mind functions, sees its object of inquiry co-opted by anthropology, which, in the name of an enterprise that has the advantage of scientificity, claims, at the end of its long road, to reach mental fortresses and their internal structures. The greatest advance made possible by Lévi-Strauss in the history of anthropology was "to work, in the first place, on relationships. This was structuralism's own contribution; it amply demonstrated the tremendous fecundity of this orientation. To work on relationships more than on objects made it possible to escape typology and typological classification, which had long been obstacles for anthropology."[21]

Ontologizing Structure

In 1959, Claude Roy considered Lévi-Strauss's quest to be a modern revival of "the old and untiring quest for the Grail of the Argonauts of the intellect, the alchemists of the mind: seeking the Grand Correspondence, the pursuit of the First Key."[22] Roy saw Lévi-Strauss as the great lama, the shaman of the twentieth century. There was a certain bitterness in this backward quest for the philosophers' stone; Lévi-Strauss had not forgotten the nightmare history had become, and in his disenchantment he sought to escape the present. Jean Duvignaud pictured Claude Lévi-Strauss as "the vicar of the tropics,"[23] who adopted in his own name the nostalgic dream of an original purity among the first men of the Savoyard vicar (Jean-Jacques Rousseau).

Lévi-Strauss answered Duvignaud's 1958 criticism of the structuralist method for which he proposed a pluralist approach to society, in a letter in which he defended, and even carried further, his point of view: "I don't know what human society is. I work on certain permanent and universal modes of human societies, and on certain levels of analysis that can be isolated."[24] Duvignaud raised a criticism dealing with the problem of the status of freedom and the place of collective dynamism in the anthropological project. In the same letter, Lévi-Strauss answered that "the question is not pertinent. The issue of freedom has no more meaning at the level of observation at which I place myself than it does for someone who studies man organically."[25]

For Lévi-Strauss, the issue was definitively removed from structural anthropology and he took the natural sciences as his epistemological model. Man, therefore, can only attest to his own impotence, his inanity before mechanisms that he will eventually render comprehensible but over which he has no control. Lévi-Strauss's position resembled the scientist illusion of the positivists, for whom theoretical physics embodied scientificity.

In a somewhat similar way, by taking phonology as its model, structural anthropology rejected any form of social substantialism and causality in favor of a notion of the arbitrary. It aimed more toward the meanders of neuronal complexity, which seem to hold an ontological key, the veritable structure of structures, the final underpinning of structurality.

Lévi-Strauss's Linguistic Underpinnings: A Strategic Choice

Georges Mounin used *Structural Anthropology* to define Lévi-Strauss's ties with linguistics during the period covered by the articles, which is to say between 1944 and 1956. He questioned the validity of the linguistic ideas used by Lévi-Strauss and, as a linguist, argued that in this volume Lévi-Strauss essentially borrowed the ideas of structure and opposition from phonology, whereas these "are not specifically linguistic."[26] Moreover, Lévi-Strauss rejected functionalism, and this prohibited him from linking these ideas to that of function, which is central in phonology. Identifying phonemes with signifying elements has no linguistic relevance: "The phoneme only helps to construct a morpheme's signifier; it is not part of the signified."[27] Even if Lévi-Strauss found many parallels between kinship structures and structures of language to the point of saying that "treating marriage regulations and kinship systems as a kind of language,"[28] he still remained reticent, as an anthropologist, about any reductionism in the service of linguistics. In 1945, he counseled against "hurrying to transpose the linguist's analytic methods,"[29] and refrained, in 1956, from wanting "to reduce society or culture to language."[30]

Georges Mounin presented Lévi-Strauss's relationship to linguistics as confused, clumsy, and full of regrets, albeit supremely clever, for Lévi-Strauss had no intention of becoming a linguist; he wanted to use the powerful thrust of linguistic rigor to propel the much broader project of structural anthropology. In this respect, Fernand Braudel understood much more clearly the intention, the stakes, and the risks of Lévi-Strauss's strategy. Braudel was a historian, and he was careful to preserve the historian's position at the forefront of the social sciences. At the same time, he was aware that this was a real challenge, and could threaten the position of the *Annales* school within the Sixth Section of the EPHE, over which he had presided since the death in 1956 of Lucien Febvre. He answered Lévi-Strauss in a manifesto-article that appeared at the end of 1958 in the *Annales*: "Économies, société, civilisations." In it, Braudel argued for the *longue durée* as the common language of the social sciences that the historian would federate.[31] This answer or riposte from the historians significantly turned historical discourse in the direction of a structuralization.

History Veers toward Structure

Before the structuralist challenge, historians had already shifted their centers of interest. When Marc Bloch and Lucien Febvre created the review *Annales d'histoire économique et sociale* in 1929, they were already adopting Durkheim's program, and the result was a change of direction toward a longer *durée*, toward examining phenomena and their underlying causes in depth, which had been too easily buried by the postivist school in favor of a short-winded history narrowly conceived as politico-military.

The fashion for structures emphasized this shift in the historical discourse away from the tendency to valorize change and toward an attention to immobile stretches of time. As early as his 1947 thesis, "The Mediterranean and the Mediterranean World at the Time of Philippe II,"[32] Fernand Braudel had altered the historian's vision by relegating the hero of the period, Philippe II, to a minor role and by focusing on immobile stretches, on the fixed points of the geo-historical framework of the Mediterranean world.

In the line of François Simiand, and therefore of the Durkheimian school, Ernest Labrousse's 1949 thesis, "The French Economic Crisis at the End of the Ancien Régime,"[33] written in the Division of Letters and Social Sciences, had similarly shifted the historian's vision; he had resituated the revolutionary crisis of 1789 within a triple temporality of seasonal variations embedded within cyclical oscillations that were, in their turn, integrated into movements of *longue durée*. Labrousse had thus made it possible to add a structural situationalism to François Simiand's use of economic circumstances: "The historian-economist was struck with the frequency of repetition."[34] Not that events were eliminated; but they underwent a procedure of elucidation as an end point that should be explained by statistical curves: "Our history is at once sociological and traditional."[35] And yet, Ernest Labrousse reigned over the Sorbonne during the fifties and directed much historical research oriented toward a social and economic history attentive to structural phenomena.

It was in this context, with elements drawn from both an economic situation and a structure set into a dialectic, that Pierre Vilar undertook his research on Catalonia. He had been an ENS student in 1925, had published his thesis in 1962,[36] and in a Labroussian perspective, he directed a seminar at the Sorbonne on the idea of structure: "The whole problem in history is to combine structure and circumstances. Therefore, I reflected a lot on structures. Claude Lévi-Strauss interested me when he showed that he was observing things that were structurally logical."[37] If the historian borrowed a logical and abstract dimension from anthropology, he nonetheless kept to a concrete and observable content, and within his field favored phenomena of crises like abcesses of fixation, or like so many poles around which structural givens crystallized, as if these poles dynamized them. The research was rigorous and relied heavily on strong statistical information and had a comprehensive ambition: its name was Ernest Labrousse in the fifties. "We were all anxious to ask him for thesis subjects—Maurice Agulhon, Alain Besançon, François Dreyfus, Pierre Deyon, Jean Jacquart, Annie Kriegel, Emmanuel Le Roy Ladurie, Claude Mesliand, Jacques Ozouf, André Tudesq . . . ," Michelle Perrot recounts.[38] For Perrot, Labrousse incarnated modernity, and she visited him in the spring of 1949 in order to propose a subject dealing with feminism—a subject that made her master smile. He suggested instead that she work on the workers' movement during the first half of the nineteenth century.

For Michelle Perrot, Ernest Labrousse incarnated a concern for rigor, a concern to reach beyond the altogether too familiar impressionism of the discipline of history: "Labrousse wanted to rediscover causality and laws; this was in keeping with both Marxists and positivists."[39] Given this outlook, Labroussian historians were very receptive to the structuralist phenomenon and to the anthropological challenge of the end of the fifties. They were on familiar ground when they read Lévi-Strauss, and in a similar quest for invariants, even if their object was different by nature: "There is a phrase in Claude Lévi-Strauss that I used in my thesis, 'Workers on Strike, France (1871–1890),' at the beginning of the section entitled 'Structures,' and that amounts to saying that when there are laws somewhere, they must be everywhere, a fundamental remark for the social sciences."[40]

Historical Anthropology: Jean-Pierre Vernant

The structuralist undertaking broadened after Jean-Pierre Vernant's lecture at Cerisy in 1959. Vernant had passed the *agrégation* in philosophy in 1937 and came, in fact, rather late to Greece, in 1948, but he did not leave his field of study to become a Hellenist. He had been a disciple of Louis Gernet and Ygnace Meyerson and recognized the triad of Émile Benveniste, Georges Dumézil, and Claude Lévi-Strauss as his other masters. His research was psychohistorical; he was interested by mental forms, which he called "the interior man," and investigated the nature of work, technical thought, the perception of the categories of time and space in the imagination, and the imagery of ancient and classical Greece. "Man is made of the symbolic. Social life only functions through symbolic systems, and in this respect I am profoundly structuralist."[41]

Following the publication of *Structural Anthropology*, Jean-Pierre Vernant therefore gave a paper at Cerisy on structure in the Hesiodic myth of the races, and his article was published shortly thereafter.[42] Vernant's article had an explicitly structural thrust, which was doubly enriched through discussions with Georges Dumézil about trifunctionality and by the revolution that Lévi-Strauss had realized in his study of Amerindian myths.

Vernant sought to apply his analytic grid to Greek myths and in so doing effected a major methodological shift that created possibilities for an entire productive school that took shape around him, establishing a historical anthropology of ancient Greece. In making the work he was analyzing comprehensible, he did not proceed like classical Hellenists, who sought to date the traditions they found in their work, but focused instead on explaining the fundamental articulations and the code underpinning the myth in question. The myth of the races opens Hesiod's *Works and Days*; it proposes a theogony that recounts how the archaic order of Greece can be explained by the successive battles between generations of divinities, until Zeus took command and established an immutable order. Hesiod's tale therefore appears chronological, following the succession of the races of gold, of silver, of bronze, of iron, and finally of heroes.

Jean-Pierre Vernant reduced and displaced the myth. In the first place, he held that the five ages correspond in fact to a functional tripartition "whose dominance over Indo-European religious thought has been demonstrated by Georges Dumézil."[43] Hesiod, therefore, framed his thinking in a tripartite structure when he reinterpreted the myth of the races. But, above all, Vernant took up binarism, Lévi-Strauss's oppositional framework, in order to show that time does not unfold chronologically in the Hesiodic vision of the races, but according to "a system of antinomies."[44] A binary structure opposing *diké* (justice) and *hubris* (exaggeration) is repeated during each age. Hesiod's tale, in this framework, has a didactic mission with respect to his brother, the cultivator Perses, to whom he speaks in order to preach the value of work as destiny and respect for *diké*—a lesson that applies to all social categories in Greek society.

Vernant's demonstration depended on reorganizing mythic material in order to bring out the major principles at work in Hesiod's mythic discourse: "The *diké/hubris* opposition is put to a melody, in music, through a Dumezilian functional tripartite organization."[45] For Jean-Pierre Vernant, Hesiod's founding myth was a plea for justice, made necessary because it took place during a period of transition during which the Greeks were in search of what is just and what is not just, and at a time when the old forms of *diké* no longer held.

Vernant did not propose a purely formalist or antichronological approach, therefore, because he referred the myth to a concrete geopolitical situation in which it is like "the presage of a universe in which the law of the polis, the political *nomos*, will be the fundamental element."[46] He therefore successfully combined an analysis of a mythic discourse with a sociohistorical context, giving it the value of a symptom, thereby reconciling history (genesis) and structure. Vernant later again emphasized the trifunctionality of the tale's internal structure, however, as a result of criticism he received:

> I would no longer say trifunctionality because if it functions for the first two ages (gold and silver), which do indeed represent sovereignty and the bronze race and the race of heroes and war, it is not the same for the iron race, which is more complex than the third function of production. This was the time of Hesiod and it was therefore not topical.[47]

Vernant was therefore obliged to reintroduce historicity into his analysis by considering the fifth age in the chronological succession of the four others. He admits to having gone too far in structuralizing the historical vision, but his rereading nonetheless made it possible to dialectize the *diké/hubris,* justice/exaggeration dichotomy, which is essential for analyzing categories of thought in ancient Greece.

Lévi-Strauss's Consecration

A chapter came to a close on January 5, 1960, on the occasion of Lévi-Strauss's inaugural lesson at the Collège de France: the heroic age of structuralism was over, while broad vistas of the paradigm's intellectual triumph stretched ahead. The entrance of the man who at the time embodied the rigor of structuralism's scientific program symbolized its success; this was official recognition of the rich effervescence that was under way, a decisive consecration at the dawn of the sixties.

This venerable institution was also undergoing a minor internal revolution by creating, for the first time, a chair for social anthropology. It is true that Marcel Mauss had taught at the Collège, but he taught anthropology from a chair in sociology.

In his inaugural lesson, Lévi-Strauss defined his project in line with Ferdinand de Saussure's discussion of semiology. This social anthropology took as its true object the very broad spectrum of the life of signs at the heart of society. He clearly expressed his debt to structural linguistics, mobilized as the hard scientific underpinning of his own anthropological project. He also expressed the global nature of his program by carefully avoiding becoming disconnected from the social realm and reality for the sake of the symbolic nature of his object: "Social anthropology . . . does not separate material culture from spiritual culture."[48] Moreover, he considered that the neuronal universe would offer the key to understanding the true sources of the symbolic universe: "The emergence of culture will remain a mystery so long as we are unable to understand, at the biological level, the brain's modifications of structure and function."[49]

Beyond this scientific thrust, Lévi-Strauss's lesson was also part of a particular moment in French historical conscience, or of "Western bad conscience. In a breathtaking way, Claude Lévi-Strauss orchestrated this grand theme of third-world sentimentalism and the structuralist sails were filled with third-world winds."[50] Pierre Nora's evaluation was confirmed at the end of Lévi-Strauss's inaugural lesson, for he declared in this rather confined enclave, where his words were like the odor of sulfur:

> You will allow me, therefore, dear colleagues, after having rendered homage to the masters of social anthropology at the beginning of my lesson, to reserve my final remarks for the savages whose obscure tenacity provides us with the means of assigning their real dimensions to human acts: men and women who, even as I speak, thousands of kilometers from here, in some savanna eroded by brush fires or in a rain-drenched forest, return to their camp to share a meager pitance, and together evoke their gods.[51]

Lévi-Strauss ended this very beautiful reminder of his field experience with the wish to remain within the Collège de France as both a student and a witness to these Indians of the tropics condemned to extinction by our civilization, the last of the Mohicans.

If the Collège de France represented the ultimate consecration for Lévi-Strauss, it was also a trompe l'oeil; the real research teams were at the university and the Collège alone did not resolve the problem of isolation or the possibility of creating a discipleship. This was not Lévi-Strauss's fate, however, for he immediately created a laboratory for social anthropology, which depended on the CNRS, the Collège de France, and the EPHE and which meant that he was immediately surrounded by researchers able to benefit from the prestige of the Collège. He was well aware that in order to realize such an ambitious project he needed solid institutional bases.

This was the context in which, in 1961, Lévi-Strauss created a new review, *L'Homme*, so that there would be a French counterpart to *Man* in England and the *American Anthropologist* in the United States. By his choice of codirectors for this professional anthropological publication, Lévi-Strauss clearly laid out his ambitions for a scientific structural anthropology, as well as his program. Two other professors from the Collège de France joined him on the editorial board: Émile Benveniste represented structural linguistics as the very model of scientificity on which Lévi-Strauss determinedly based his work, and Pierre Gourou, a tropical geographer, clearly represented the old vitality of the French school of geography in the Vidalian tradition. Lévi-Strauss made another attempt at the takeover the Durkheimians had tried at the beginning of the century of a school of geography long on the wane because it had joined forces with the *Annales* historians. Lévi-Strauss quickly enlarged his team, which he thought was a bit too much of a "Collège de France club," and asked André Leroi-Gourhan, Georges-Henri Rivière, and André-Georges Haudricourt to join. The absences were significant, for there were no historians, despite the fact that their work had drawn much closer to the anthropological program since the creation of the *Annales*. Lévi-Strauss's answer reflected the institutional stakes dividing the two disciplines: "In 1960, history and ethnology, which had come so much closer together, were, dare I say, rivals for the public's attention."[52]

The same year, Lévi-Strauss's interviews with Georges Charbonnier gave an idea of the ambitions of his program and of the metamorphosis that he hoped for in the social sciences in general, which should draw their inspiration from the natural sciences, going so far as to identify with them: "We might say that ethnology is a natural science or that it aspires to shape itself based on the example of the natural sciences."[53]

Crossing the Rubicon to join the natural sciences supposed a relationship with progress, history, and man that sought to reduce them in order to give precedence to a quasi-mechanical model; this in the framework of a cooling down of temporality and of a significance that escaped the individual and established itself on the basis of a logical time, without his knowledge. The structuralist challenge to the social sciences did not lack for grandeur. Throughout the fifties it had clearly demonstrated its fertility by embracing different figures of alterity. On the strength of its promises, this program was soon to flourish, during the sixties.

Part II

The Sixties:
1963–1966, La Belle Époque

Twenty-two

Contesting the Sorbonne: The Quarrel of the Ancients and the Moderns

On the threshold of the sixties, the aged and venerable Sorbonne continued to reign undisputed over the country of the mind. Indeed, it engaged only with great difficulty in any discussion of its orientation. The Sorbonne oversaw the heritage of a literary method whose concern for historical and philological exactitude had made it appear rigorous and modern in the nineteenth century. But university erudition, strengthened by an already ancient break, turned a deaf ear to the epistemological challenge that had begun to raise its voice in the fifties. Faced with triumphant positivism and the atomization of its method, the structuralist thrust took on the guise of veritable anti-mandarin trench warfare whose primary weapon was the construction of more modern and holistic scientific models.

This combat reached its climax in May 1968, when the old edifice collapsed. The weight of the Sorbonne had relegated those who contested it to a position of marginality, forcing them to seek out support and new disciplinary alliances, to define an ambitious program and the broadest possible readership/electorate in order to surround, deflect, and eject the mandarins in place. Institutionally, therefore, "structural linguistics embodied the contestation of modernity with respect to the dominant model."[1] For those invested with the role of preserving the dominant model, the role of reflection on language was entirely secondary, not to say elementary, insofar as it had been limited to language acquisition in the early classes of primary school.

Since linguistic mastery was considered complete, reaching the crowning study of literature was removed from studying its mechanisms. The study of literature, indeed, was limited to purely aesthetic considerations removed from linguistics, which could, however, be part of the program of studying foreign languages. Linguistics was simply a technical tool, dismissed with a certain condescension from the noble literary environment of creative genius. "In the traditional curriculum of literary studies, the study of language was dependent on and inferior to work on the literary text."[2]

André Martinet Returns

The only real, noteworthy exception in the aged institution was André Martinet's course in general linguistics. He had come back from the United States in 1955 and was internationally known. His notoriety, however, made little impression in the traditional humanities, where he was suspect and barely tolerated by those who initially confined him to a small enclave where, they believed, he would be forgotten. He was finally given a course to teach at the old Linguistics Institute, but in a small classroom that could hold only about thirty students. The room quickly overflowed with students and André Martinet immediately found himself directing about thirty theses of Africanists who were looking for a way to describe their languages. Since walls cannot be moved, university authorities had to find a bigger classroom for Martinet, who every year required more chairs for students who poured into his courses. In 1958, he was given Guizot lecture hall but it was only adequate for two years. In 1960, he held class in the Descartes lecture hall, which could hold up to four hundred students. "In 1967, the Descartes amphitheater was too small and they gave me Richelieu which, if you include the annexes, can hold up to six hundred people."[3] His trajectory within the Sorbonne clearly reflected the growing enchantment with linguistics in the sixties.

Richelieu consecrated Martinet. Despite his complaints about the inhuman amount of work, his course had become requisite for anyone wanting to become a modern semiologist, especially because, in addition to his universally recognized pedagogical talent, he was an exception in France. An entire student public could arm itself in his courses for the antimandarin criticism that was to grow throughout the sixties. "We were young, we were against those who were old, and it happened that the avant-garde movement of the time was structuralism so, let's become structuralists."[4] For the young generation, structuralism played a role of stripping things clean and became a provisional morality much in the manner of Descartes.

In a context of contestation against the powers that be, the attacks were once again directed against any form of vague psychologism among the specialists of traditional history, "the veritable pox of the French university and not only among literature people, but also among philosophers."[5]

A Lonely Innovator: Jean-Claude Chevalier

Jean-Claude Chevalier, a young teaching assistant in French grammar, defended his thesis, "The Idea of Complement among Grammarians," in 1968.[6] The preface carefully presented the term "epistemology" in quotes as if he were handling an explosive element in his milieu. He used the central idea of the period, rupture, and recalls the euphoria of contestation as something like a "hygienic pleasure."[7] But theoretically, he was looking for a conceptual break, a way of moving things forward in a new direction. This conception of a future rupture led to valorizing breaks in the past. Chevalier therefore saw a certain discontinuity in 1750 among grammarians, who until then had only used the term "origin," and henceforth would use the idea of complement. "Things shifted from a morphological system to a semantic system of syntax, implying a considerable change."[8]

Jean-Claude Chevalier did not, however, think of himself as an innovator at the time. He was just doing the work of an honest historical grammarian and he was quite unaware of the fact that Louis Althusser and Michel Foucault were engaged in similar work. Even at that point, however, Julia Kristeva remarked in *Critique* that Jean-Claude Chevalier's work was an essential element in shaping the rupture that was winning over all the avant-garde intellectuals.

Todorov Encounters the Void

With the exception of Martinet's enclave, which was limited to teaching how language functioned, nothing was going on at the Sorbonne in literature using the new methods of structural linguistics. When the young Bulgarian Tzvetan Todorov arrived in Paris in the spring of 1963, he was utterly discomfited by the resistance he encountered.

Todorov had come from the University of Sofia after finishing his university studies, and he was looking for an institutional setting in which to develop research on what he was already calling the theory of literature. For him this meant thinking about literature without drawing on external elements, be they sociological or psychological, but he might as well have been looking for a needle in a haystack. Bearing a letter of recommendation from the dean of letters in Sofia and confident of getting a positive response, he contacted the director of the Sorbonne to learn about the possibilities there. "He looked at me as if I came from another planet and explained to me, quite coldly, that there was no literary theory going on in his university, nor were there any plans for it in the future."[9] Rather confused, Todorov thought at the time that there had been some misunderstanding and he asked if there might be a program in stylistics, but the dean wanted him to specify in which language. This conversation between deaf men continued and Todorov began to feel increasingly uncomfortable because "I couldn't say to him, French stylistics, since I was stuttering in an entirely doubtful French. He would have told me to go and study French first."[10] Of course it was a question of general stylistics and the Sorbonne director reiterated that this field of study did not exist.

It was only thanks to completely fortuitous circumstances that Todorov finally managed to find a place in Paris, where what was to be called poetics constituted a field of study. Having established rather pleasant contact with the director of the Sorbonne library (thanks to her father, who was a librarian in Sofia), Todorov began to take heart by plunging into the holdings of the library. The librarian informed him that her nephew's work might help introduce him to the aleatory paths of Parisian modernity. So Todorov went to meet the nephew, François Jodelet, who was a teaching assistant in psychology at the Sorbonne. Jodelet took him to meet another assistant at the Sorbonne who was working in literature and whose name was Gérard Genette. "So I met Genette. He immediately understood what I was looking for and told me about someone who was working on this sort of thing: Roland Barthes. He told me that I had to take Barthes's seminar."[11]

Literary Dissatisfaction

If you studied English at the Sorbonne, you stood a chance of coming into contact with structuralism. Marina Yaguello came to the Institut d'Anglais in 1963 in this way, at the same time that Antoine Culioli, who had been an assistant in Nancy until then, was appointed. Culioli's work on Old English and on vowel variation made it possible not only to take a synchronic approach, but an approach that was also "completely structuralist insofar as when each vowel moves, the whole system moves with it."[12]

Linguistic training was not aimed at the majority of French literature students at the Sorbonne. Françoise Gadet was enrolled in literature but deeply dissatisfied by the teaching, and had gone to one of Antoine Culioli's classes to take notes for a friend who was absent. The course was a revelation for her. "I said to myself, there things are really rigorous and demanding."[13] Gadet therefore chose to do a linguistics certificate at the *Licence* level and found herself with Martinet. She switched from literature to structural linguistics because structuralism meant choosing rigor. "When you experienced the atmosphere in the Sorbonne in the sixties, you understood that there was nowhere else to go. When you understand just how much of a graveyard it was, you understand why structuralism was so appealing."[14]

Professors of literature at the time included, among others, Gérard Castex, Jacques Deloffre, Marie-Jeanne Durry who was a poet and Apollinaire specialist, and Charles Dédéyan, an Armenian prince who taught comparative literature. They were all conscientious professors but they emptied their lecture halls after a single class. "I saw it with my own eyes in Dédéyan's class. Fifty people had been at the first class and three were at the second," recalls Philippe Hamon who, like so many in his generation, chose linguistics in the mid-sixties. "It was the first time that a science called human could attain such a degree of rigor; the discourse was clear, it could be demonstrated, repeated, and reproduced."[15] Élisabeth Roudinesco began studying literature at the Sorbonne in 1964, and quickly felt the same dissatisfaction. She had to face the fact rather quickly that her interests were in no way sustained by the classes she took: "When you studied literature, the line of demarcation was: have you read the latest Barthes? There were two camps. Besides, what they taught us was idiotic."[16] In literature at the Sorbonne, therefore, there was a very marked split between two languages and two types of interest. The widening rift between the teachers and their students provoked a considerable degree of frustration but also created a buildup of tension that would later explode. Literature students were not alone in their frustration, however, for philosophy students were equally dissatisfied. As François Ewald described things, "The Sorbonne was a complete void,"[17] and he was dissatisfied with Raymond Aron's haughty, sardonic sideward glance at Jean-Paul Sartre's *Critique of Dialectical Reason.*

This feeling of cosmic void was so palpable that François Ewald and his friend François George conceived of a project—which never bore fruit—of starting a review along the lines of *Les Cahiers pour l'analyse,* and which would be entitled *Les Cahiers pour l'époché.* They wanted to express the feeling of the end of history, of a world on the wane, which completely corresponded to the new structuralist sensibility. Ewald had quickly encountered this sensibility through the people he knew at Ulm from *Les Cahiers pour l'analyse.* At the Sorbonne, he took a course with one of the members of that group, Jacques-Alain Miller, as well as Lacan's seminar. "This makes me a child of structuralism. I was raised on Bachelard, Canguilhem, and French epistemology."[18]

This deep sense of expectation was answered by the dynamism in the social sciences and their veritable explosion in the sixties. But should we see in the attraction of literature students, historians, and philosophers to structuralism an expression of the growing pains of sciences worried about institutionalization and seeking to drape themselves in greater rigor? "I would sooner speak about the senility of the social sciences because I don't see how they would be considered inaugural," answers Roger-Pol Droit, who saw in the structuralist ambition the high point of Durkheimianism in sociology and anthropology and would take a quarter century to discover an instrument of objectification, provided by the linguistics of the thirties. "It's more a question of a belated history in which the social sciences probably discovered something like the expression of their modernity."[19] Of course this desire for renovation can be considered in relation to an older Durkheimian exigency, but insofar as this tradition had only been half-successful, its program, renewed by linguistics, was the banner of modernization at a Sorbonne that remained largely indifferent to change.

The Foyers of Modernity

The sixties offered a particularly effervescent spectacle in the strategy of circumventing the principal academic institution. Innovation hailed from the periphery: it reached Paris via the provinces, or took root in marginal enclaves of the capital: "This university is incapable of doing anything new."[20] The philosopher Cournot had already observed during the Second Empire that the French university, vital until the Renaissance, almost provoked the reform that would culminate in the development of universities in northern Europe. But since then, whenever the habitus of *Homo academicus* needed a slight push, a new institution had to be created: the Collège de France, the ENS, the EPHE, and the CNRS. The events of the sixties therefore bore this legacy, which required a revolution to reform a system. Even at the very pinnacle of the paradigm, the celebratory concert of publishing houses, reviews, and the press should not make us forget that the traditional institution kept its grip on legitimacy. "Structuralism never reigned; it would be incorrect to say that it did, and especially in literature."[21]

Institutional frameworks did eventually provide the context for much research that was breaking with the past and making it possible for a great deal of work to be accomplished on many fronts with a common, new orientation. Textual structurality was shifting the search for textual genesis more and more radically, function was replacing the notion of oeuvre; literary analysis came to adopt the Russian formalists' notion of immanence. A common program allowed for very different kinds of research, which depended on the linguistic model to unseat the preeminent creative subject, considered fundamental until that point. The structural totality of the text was becoming most important, but a text whose internal rationality necessarily escaped authorial grasp because its enunciation escaped authorial knowledge. In the name of logic or aesthetics, criticism tended to become confused with an essentially descriptive thrust; different levels of resemblance or opposition were brought into relationship, or criticism was specifically linguistic. The decade that began in 1960 was therefore a particularly intense period for the linguistic model, which was principally structuralist, and its methodological effort.[22]

Strasbourg was one of the high spots of this structuralist renewal and Georges Straka, professor of philology, was its central figure. Straka was a friend of Greimas and he published semiotic articles in *Les Travaux de linguistique et littérature*,[23] a review created in 1963 with an initial print run of one thousand issues distributed by Klincksieck. He organized colloquiums, brought French and foreign linguists together at Strasbourg, and made their work known thanks to Klincksieck's support, as well as through the influence of the University of Strasbourg, which had already seen the great historiographical revolution of the *Annales* in 1929.

The university at Besançon was the other site of innovation and convergence, but its vitality was completely contingent; the youngest recruits were forced to take up their walking stick and begin their careers in excentric universities, and Besançon was a particularly distant and enclosed location. Young researchers such as Bernard Quémada, Georges Matoré, Henri Mitterand, and Louis Hay who were condemned to work together found themselves there. Interdisciplinarity was deliberate and bridges were built between professors in the departments of letters and sciences in order to apply laboratory methods to the social sciences. "An interdisciplinary dialogue went on everywhere, in the train, at restaurants. Henri Mitterand, who was always practical-minded, said that if *Les Cahiers du rapide 59* were ever published, they would be far superior to most of the institutionalized journals."[24] There was a real hunger for learning and for belonging to modernity at Besançon, something that characterizes a young and enthusiastic generation. "We were interested in all the new things that came our way."[25] The works of Barthes, Greimas, and Lévi-Strauss were all very enthusiastically received during this period of high intellectual tension. Alongside the Germanist Louis Hay, there was young Henri Mitterand, a grammarian and philologist who remembers the publication of Jean Dubois's thesis, "Political and Social Vocabulary in France between 1849 and 1872,"[26] as a fundamental event. Dubois incited an entire generation to look for parallels between discursive structures beyond the structures of class and vocabulary. The dynamism at Besançon made it possible to reach beyond the university enclave; before becoming a place to which everyone swarmed, Besançon was a place where a whole intellectual community, including Parisians and foreigners, could meet and thereby minimize the geographical distance between people like Jean-Claude Chevalier in Lille, Jean Dubois in Rouen and then Paris, and Greimas in Poitiers.

There were, of course, significant nuances in the work being undertaken. Barthes was the big reference point of the period, and he was more interested in how codes worked in a text than was Greimas, who wanted to find the system behind the text that commanded the working of the human mind. But, beyond these differences, there was "this setting into place of the critic as an explorer of immanence,"[27] a notion developed by Knud Togeby, a professor in Copenhagen who was a disciple of Louis Hjelmslev. Togeby had published *Immanent Structures of the French Language*[28] in 1965, and the term quickly became the rallying cry of an entire young generation of new critics.

Clearly, the east of France was in its heyday and the winds blew with some strength. As of 1960, Nancy also became a dynamic research center when Bernard Pottier created a Society for Automatic Translation, which attracted linguists and scientists to a colloquium on the topic as early as 1961. This branch of linguistic analysis would convert professional scientists to linguistics. In the early sixties, Maurice Gross, an engineer at the State Arms Laboratory who was assigned to the Center for Calculus, remarked: "I didn't have the vaguest idea about what a linguist was. I didn't even know that such a thing existed."[29] Automatic translation made it possible for Maurice Gross to become a linguist and to leave for Harvard in October 1961 where he met Noam Chomsky. The period was also propitious for research teams and for a certain reorganization of research that could only be carried on at the periphery of the great institutions but that compensated for the absence of modernization at the Sorbonne.

The French Communist Party still wielded some political influence at the beginning of the sixties, and many intellectuals were active in its ranks or were satisfied with their roles as fellow travelers. However, one important Communist linguist named Marcel Cohen was responsible for a Marxist research group that included a good number of the structural linguists. The group met regularly at the homes of its different members, including Jean Dubois, Antoine Culioli, Henri Mitterand, and André-Georges Haudricourt, among others. Quite quickly, however, political changes as much as Marcel Cohen's concept of linguistic work, which was considered too restrictive, created a diaspora among the old Marxist research group: "Cohen's idea of Marxism was sociological and Durkheimian. . . . Marcel Cohen always thought ill of the Americans."[30] According to André-Georges Haudricout, who recognized the importance of this group at the time, Cohen's sectarianism had a significant impact on the group's cohesion: "Poor Cohen was very totalitarian: for him, there was the party and the others."[31] The group turned its curiosity to the Russian formalists of the twenties and toward Soviet linguistics—Vinogradov—with the idea of constructing a sociology of language that would not encompass the structuralist ambitions. Whence its rather swift disappearance, despite its major role as a place for fruitful encounters.

Growing Effervescence

The excitement that was taking hold in a number of areas was a veritable explosion of curiosity, which could not express itself in the official Société de Linguistique de Paris (SLP). In 1960 the Société d'Études de la Langue Française (SELF) was created in Paris by three auditors of Robert-Léon Wagner's course: Jean-Claude Chevalier, Jean Dubois, and Henri Mitterand. Robert-Léon Wagner, a professor at Hautes Études, was decisive for diffusing structural linguistics in France. He was a medievalist who had been trained as a philologist and was the first to introduce Benveniste, Jakobson, and Hjelmslev in his seminars. "He played a seminal role."[32]

The SELF was born of necessity and in reaction to a sarcastic re-mark made by Michael Riffaterre, a professor at Columbia University who was quite disappointed by Jean-Claude Chevalier's personal li-brary. Chevalier decided therefore to have a small group of friends pool their discoveries. Every month it met to hear presentations by semanticians like Greimas, lexicologists like Guilbert or Dubois, syn-tacticians like Chevalier, or stylisticians like Meschonnic. Articles ap-peared shortly thereafter. This "public welfare committee among the lost"[33] would quickly grow. Its disappearance in 1968 was due not to failure but, on the contrary, because its catalytic role had succeeded, given the importance of the movement that was under way.

Other groups came together in the sixties, among them Enseigne-ment pour la Recherche en Anthropologie Sociale (EPRAS) at Hautes Études, where, in 1966, Greimas created a two- or three-year program of experimental teaching at the master's level with the help of Oswald Ducrot and Christian Metz, and the Association Internationale de Linguistique Appliquée (AILA), created in 1964, where seminar par-ticipants numbered as many as two hundred. "The seminar in Nancy in 1967 brought crowds of researchers. Practically the entire future team at Vincennes was there."[34]

The Sixth Section at the EPHE was another breeding ground for renewal, especially with Roland Barthes's seminar, which in 1964 addressed the question of cuisine. Barthes had been named *directeur d'études*[35] in 1962 for a research project titled "Sociology and Semiol-ogy of Signs and Symbols." Beyond the particularly active work in literature, Lévi-Strauss's work also spurred much new research.

Published in 1958, *Structural Anthropology* had a triple effect on the literary world in ferment:[36] the fecundity of the phonological model in one of the disciplines of the humanities, the anachronic reading of the Oedipus myth, and the myth's transformational formula. Two years later, Lévi-Strauss directly addressed a literary work with a polemical article titled "Vladimir Propp's *Morphology of the Folktale*," which had many repercussions.[37] And in 1962, his famous collaborative study with Roman Jakobson on Baudelaire's "Les Chats" was published, demonstrating that the sonnet is entirely determined by phonetic choices.[38] These incursions into literary territory revealed the ability of the method to contend with a vast area, in the name of a general semiology. These were so many confirmations of the scientificity and promises of their program for those working in literature and newly converted to linguistics.

In 1962, Jean Rousset's *Form and Signification*, subtitled *Essays in Literary Structures*,[39] also lent support to the immanence of literary analysis. In keeping with Paul Valéry's thinking and writing, which became the major literary reference for the new aesthetics, Rousset adopted the idea that form is rich in ideas. "It is the structure of the work that is inventive."[40] Rousset avoided any subjective judgment of a work in order to better concentrate on discerning its formal structures, borrowing not from linguistics but from the renewed literary criticism and reflection on rhetoric of Léo Spitzer and Gaëtan Picon; his work would be important in the program of literary structuralism. He took one of the important ideas of the literary structuralism of the sixties from Léo Spitzer's German stylistics, which was to consider an isolated work as a complete and self-sufficient organism whose inner coherence can be studied: "*Madame Bovary* is an independent organism, an absolute, a whole that can be understood and elucidated by itself."[41]

Jean Rousset broke with the kind of criticism that went beyond the work and dissolved the work in its context and genesis to the extent that everything except the work itself was present. This restoration of the literality of the work would be firmly invoked against the representatives of traditional literary history. The weapons of this new criticism were initially found in Jungian psychoanalysis, archetypes, and authorial imagination, taking inspiration largely from Gaston Bachelard's intuition, and later from Jean-Pierre Richard's thematic criticism and Georges Poulet's systematized reflection on temporality. Later, this new criticism looked to linguistics for the weapons that would enable it to adopt a rigorous scientific program.

Twenty-three

1964: The Semiological Adventure Makes a Breakthrough

The year 1964 marked the end of the Sorbonne's undivided reign. Peripheral and marginal activity won its first important victory thanks to the spectacular rise in the numbers of students enrolled in letters and the social sciences in the mid-sixties—an effect of the baby boom.

Nanterre was created in 1964, and this new campus gave a good number of the renovators the chance to hold a university job near Paris. Bernard Pottier and Jean Dubois, both linguists, made their way into the institutional ranks this way. This was the beginning of a shift that gained numbers and speed and drew peripheral institutes like the EPHE toward departments of letters. Whereas Strasbourg and Besançon had already clearly understood what was taking place, things in Paris took on an entirely different cast, of course. General linguistics was simultaneously starting to have an institutional existence independent of language departments and traditional philology, and consequently attracted a considerably broader audience than the narrow scope of specialists. Linguistics seemed at that point to be the common denominator for anyone involved with language.

Jean Dubois played a major role in this, particularly since he was an editor at Larousse, a tenured professor in a Parisian university, and a member of the selection board at the CNRS, a post that put him into frequent contact with Louis Guilbert, Robert-Léon Wagner, Algirdas Julien Greimas, Bernard Quémada, and so on. In addition, he directed research projects, selected members of Nanterre's linguistics department, and was on the tenure-granting board for a whole generation of French linguists. He was also a close friend of Roland Barthes, who had known his brother Claude Dubois when they were both at the sanatorium. Although their background and political leanings were not always consonant—Bernard Pottier was conservative and worked in Spanish while Dubois was a member of the French Communist Party and his field was French linguistics—the overriding feeling was one of belonging to a community of structural linguists. "One day, Pottier came to find us, saying, come help, Martinet is in trouble at the Sorbonne, and Dubois and I left to save him."[1]

Jean Dubois was responsible for a number of dynamic research groups, which counted among their members linguists like Claudine Normand, Jean-Baptiste Marcellesir, and Denise Maldidier; he was even able to attract specialists from other disciplines to linguistics. He recruited Joseph Sumpf, for example, as an assistant in the linguistics department at Nanterre in 1967 to do sociolinguistics. Sumpf had been working at the CNRS since 1963 in educational sociology, and at the Centre d'Études Sociologiques, where Liliane Isambert was his director. He was also in Pierre Naville's seminar, where the question of the necessity of formalization for reaching the notion of structure was being discussed. There were anthropologists as well in this same seminar, including Claude Meillassoux and Colette Piot. "Naville's ideas about formalization came from Saussure and Piaget, but I couldn't say that it was his major concern."[2]

Joseph Sumpf worked on the function of the philosophy class in the French school system. His research led him to create a corpus of interviews and papers from classes, and he went to see Jean Dubois with this material to work out a method of analysis. "Jean Dubois introduced me to linguistics and to Harris, and this was the basis on which he recruited me to Nanterre."[3] Structuralism thus became a particular approach to analyzing a mass of documents comprised of signs or traces; it offered a tool for discerning their internal coherence.

Lecturing before a group of Tunisians in 1965, Michel Foucault described this process as "deixology," the analysis of a document's internal constraints: "It is a question of finding what system determines the document as a document."[4] When considered an essential level of human practices, deixology established "the methodological importance, the epistemological importance, and the philosophical importance of structuralism."[5] One of the characteristics of the structuralist revolution was to redefine the traditional split between a literary work that has been critically classified and consecrated and the remains of the fact of writing. Rather than splitting these two aspects of writing, all writing traces were considered in a relationship that established the literary work as a complete document. Desacralized, it became nothing other than language, a simple writing effect upon which another act of writing is superposed. This discursive economy modified the contours of disciplinary boundaries, which are in fact effaced to bring a fundamentally linguistic analysis to the fore. Literary analysis became important in its synchrony, true to the Saussurean bases of linguistic analysis, but to the detriment of a temporal approach. No longer perceived as an expression of its time but as a fragment of space in the internal logic of its own mode of operation, the literary work was approached in terms of contiguous, syntagmatic, and paradigmatic relationships. External or contextual causes, indeed causality itself, fall to the wayside before questions of the simple communication of a range of different codes organized around a given number of poles.

Communications 4: A Semiological Manifesto

In 1964, an issue of *Communications* was published that presented the structural linguistic model in literature as the program of the future. Issue 4 of *Communications* was a veritable semiological manifesto. In it, Tzvetan Todorov wrote his first article in French: "La description de la signification en littérature." In it he defined a stratigraphy of analytic levels and differentiated between phonematic distribution, where content has no impact, and a grammatical level, which he defined as the form of the content whose substance is a matter of semantics and which plays a decisive role for meaning in literature. Todorov suggested taking a radically formalist approach, and although he acknowledged that literature bears traces of other signifying systems deriving from social or national life, "the study of these systems obviously remains outside literary analysis strictly speaking."[6]

In the same issue, Claude Brémond examined the possibilities and limits of formal analysis using Vladimir Propp's *Morphology of the Folktale*. He argued for an autonomous semiology to replace traditional content analysis. Propp had transcribed approximately a hundred Russian folktales according to a list of thirty-one functions that made it possible to give an exhaustive account of the actions in the entire corpus of folktales examined. Brémond argued for a method of formal analysis that would be a descriptive tool, in contrast to the concerns of traditional literary historians: "In their obsession with resolving questions of genetic ascendency, they forget that Darwin was only possible after Linné."[7]

Propp's method was particularly suggestive for Brémond, who was interested in understanding the conditions under which it becomes possible to make generalizations, or rules. However, Brémond adopted some of Lévi-Strauss's criticisms of 1962 and rejected Propp's teleological hypotheses, which certainly allowed him to create a more perfect model, but the cost was high since he could not include all of the material of folktales. Reducing themes to their invariant function necessarily limited his choices. Brémond preferred to differentiate the levels of analysis in order to adopt a methodical approach to narration: on the one hand, the classificatory work, that of the comparative study of different forms of narrativity, and, on the other hand, establishing a relationship not between forms but between "the narrative stratum of a message and the other strata of meaning."[8]

Roland Barthes's "Les éléments de sémiologie" came out in this same issue of *Communications*. This article translated a seminar he had given in the Sixth Section of the EPHE and was directed toward a wider audience of researchers. But it became a manifesto for the new science. The theoretical presentation was also a framework for Barthes's research since he was in the process of writing *The Fashion System*.[9] Barthes was enjoying a veritable "methodological euphoria"[10] at the time and even abandoned his own writing in order to undertake research with scientific aspirations. Caught between his writer's sensibilities and his aspirations as a semiologist, Barthes suppressed the writer in himself more strenuously than at any other time. "There are two phases in Roland Barthes. In the first, he believed in the necessity and possibility of establishing a science of man. In the same way that the natural sciences were forged in the nineteenth century, couldn't the twentieth century be the century of the sciences of man ?"[11]

In its article form, what later became *Elements of Semiology* gave a didactic presentation of Saussure's and Hjelmslev's teachings with an eye toward constructing this new semiological science. Barthes used Saussure's oppositions between language/speech, signifier/signified, and syntagm/system, and remained strictly orthodox in his structuralism in this regard. He described three distinct levels of structure (language in Saussure's sense), norm (language as material form), and use (language as a group of habits of a given society). It was thanks to Hjelmslev that the idea of language, based on this trilogy, could be radically formalized and replace Saussure's language/speech dichotomy with structure/use.

Of the linguistic revolution, Barthes retained the general concern for constructing a new science, and reversed Saussure's vision of semiology as the future of linguistics. He saw the semiological program as a subset of linguistics[12] and called for all the research being done across disciplines to clearly bear witness to the capacity of linguistics. Semiology, the science of the future, appeared as the science par excellence of society in that it signifies: "The sociological implications of the language/speech concept are clear."[13]

However, Barthes did not see the first positive signs of the creation of semiology in sociology. While other disciplines were giving clear signs of their interest, sociology remained recalcitrant toward the notion of immanence. Barthes saw these signs in the history practiced by the *Annales* under Fernand Braudel, who distinguished between event/structure; in the anthropology of Lévi-Strauss, who adopted the Saussurean postulate of the unconscious nature of language; in the psychoanalysis of Lacan, "for whom desire itself is articulated as a system of signification."[14] For Barthes, sociology defined itself as a socio-logic in which meaning is the product of the process that brings signifier together with signified whether it be in a Saussurean or a Hjelmslevian perspective.

Four disciplines played important roles in this semiology of the future: "Today, economy, linguistics, ethnology, and history form a quadrivium of pilot sciences."[15] Semiology was to delineate its own boundaries and limits and would be organized around the principle of pertinence, which meant the field of signification of the objects analyzed in themselves based on a situation of immanence. The corpus would have to be homogeneous, therefore, and would, by definition, reject all other systems, whether psychological, sociological, or whatever. This science would be ahistorical: "The corpus should eliminate diachronic elements as much as possible; it should coincide with a state of the system, a slice of history."[16] And the instrument used in this search for meaning was to be found primarily in connotative linguistics, which adopted the Hjelmslevian opposition between

Jean-Paul Sartre (photo Roger-Viollet, copyright Lipnitzki-Viollet)

Cerisy Colloquium, 1955: "What Is philosophy?" From left to right: Kostas Axelos, Martin Heidegger, Mrs. Heidegger (copyright Archives de Pontigny-Cerisy)

Cerisy Colloquium, 1956: "Theory of History." From left to right: Unknown, Raymond Aron, R. P. Danielou, Claude Lefort, Jean-Claude Michaud (copyright Archives de Pontigny-Cerisy)

Roman Jakobson (photo Éditions de Minuit)

Claude Lévi-Strauss, 1963 (photo Magnum, copyright Henri Cartier-Bresson)

Louis Hjelmslev (photo Éditions de Minuit)

Georges Gurvitch (photo Presses Universitaires de France)

André Martinet, 1957 (photo Presses Universitaires de France)

Jean Piaget (copyright press and information service of the University of Geneva)

Jean Duvignaud (copyright Universal Photo)   Algirdas Julien Greimas (photo Éditions du Seuil)

Paul Ricoeur, 1961 (copyright Universal Photo)

Michel Serres (photo Éditions de Minuit)   Pierre Bourdieu (photo Éditions de Minuit)

Louis Althusser (photo D.R.)

The office of *Tel Quel*. From left to right: Jean-Loup Dabadie, Jean-Edern Hallier, Jean-René Huguenin, Renaud Matignon, Jacques Coudol, Jean Thibaudeau, Philippe Sollers (photo Éditions du Seuil)

Jacques Lacan (photo Éditions du Seuil)

Edgar Morin (photo Éditions du Seuil)

Roland Barthes (photo Magnum, copyright
Henri Cartier-Bresson)

Michel Foucault, 1963 (photo Éditions Gallimard, copyright André Bonin)

Pierre Nora (photo Éditions Gallimard,
copyright Jacques Robert)

Georges Balandier (photo Presses Universitaires de France)

Georges Dumézil (photo Éditions Gallimard, copyright Jacques Sassier)

Cerisy Colloquium, 1964: "Man and the Devil." Maurice de Gandillac, Catherine Backès-
Clément (copyright Archives de Pontigny-Cerisy)

denotation/connotation, and which Barthes had already used in "Myth Today."

In order to better consolidate this ambitious project of constructing a semiological program, Barthes assembled the major part of the articles he had written as chronicler between 1953 and 1963 in *Critical Essays*. The collection can be read as a semiology in gestation, articulated by trial and error, a form of scientific bricolage that focused more intensely than ever before on the problem of the sign, influenced by Jakobson's binary thinking and Trubetzkoy's analyses in terms of differential positions. "Barthes's internal revolution became apparent at that point, between 1962 and 1963."[17]

Barthes Defines Structuralist Activity

Barthes defined his structuralism in this collection of articles as something that could not be limited to a school because this supposed a nonexistent community of research and solidarity among authors. How, then, could one define structuralism? "Structuralism is essentially an activity. . . . The goal of all structuralist activity . . . is to reconstitute an object in such a way as to reveal the rules by which the object functions. The structure is therefore, in fact, a simulacrum of the object."[18] There was thus a common goal of this activity, bringing together the diversity of disciplines engaged in the search for structural man, beyond the singularity of each researcher. Structural man was a producer of meaning, and the method used would essentially address the act of producing meaning more than the content of meaning. Structuralism was "an activity of imitation,"[19] a mimesis based on an analogy not of substance but of function. Barthes invoked a number of precursors, including Claude Lévi-Strauss, Nicolai Trubetzkoy, Georges Dumézil, Vladimir Propp, Gilles Gaston-Granger, Jean-Claude Gardin, and Jean-Pierre Richard. In addition, it was now possible to move beyond the distinction between artistic and literary work and scientific work. In this respect, Barthes placed this activity that uses linguistics to construct a science of structure on the same level as the one that created Butor's writing, Boulez's music, or Mondrian's painting; all belong to the same simulacrum of the object that semiology examines.

Barthes's approach was very Saussurean. Structuralism was not a simple reproduction of the world per se, but generated new categories that are irreducible to either reality or rationality. Structuralist activity referred to function, to an examination of the conditions of thought, of that which makes meaning possible, and not its specific content. And in its effort to uproot natural and immutable meaning from its ideological base, the structuralist program embodied a radical critique of the dominant ideology, which presented itself as something natural and immutable.

A semiologist was charged not with deciphering some underlying meaning already present in a work, but with accounting for the constraints imposed on its sense-making operations and the conditions of its validity. Deconstructing ideology and established meaning by attacking their monolithic status in order to pluralize them were so many forms of a radical historicism that is systematized in Michel Foucault's work, together with an ahistoricism characteristic of the synchronic position. Structuralism was much more than a school, in Barthes's view; it marked a true shift in the evolution of consciousness. "Structuralism can be historically defined as the passage from a symbolic consciousness to a paradigmatic consciousness,"[20] which becomes apparent in a comparative approach, not on the basis of meanings defined by their substance, but on the basis of their forms. For Barthes, phonology was the science par excellence of this paradigmatic consciousness, the model of models. "It is [phonology] that, throughout Claude Lévi-Strauss's work, defines the structuralist threshold."[21]

A Critical Vocation

This change in the sixties cannot be reduced simply to a shift among the disciplines in the social sciences; it was also the expression of a period during which the intellectual, that is to say, the writer, could no longer argue from a critical perspective or revolt in the same way as during the immediate postwar period. The issue was no longer to subvert the entire social order. Henceforth, revolt "is really the whole, the stuff of all our truths, I mean what we might call Western civilization."[22] Barthes's critique, like that of all the structuralists, worked on destabilizing dominant Western values, on making a radical critique of petit-bourgeois ideology, of opinion, and of the doxa. This paradigmatic consciousness or consciousness of paradox, which tried to shake the doxa, had to evaluate and dismantle from within logics and models, modes of being, and modes of appearance of ideological constructions. Its object was the superego of dominant rationality and its connotations, which required a thorough understanding of how language functions.

The angle of attack seemed more effective than simply rejecting past values in the name of avant-garde literary principles destined to be very quickly assimilated into the system in place: "Any avant-garde is quite easily and quite quickly co-opted. Particularly in literature."[23] The consumer society that spread during the fifties had such a capacity for rotating goods that it embraced cultural goods as well; never was the move from an avant-garde—that is to say a radical break—to a commercial object so swift. Assimilation provided the mechanism of self-regulation in this culture and "the windows at Hermès and the Galeries Lafayette are surreal."[24]

It became increasingly difficult, and virtually illusory, to escape the web of the technical society and the culture of mass consumption in order to express a cry, a revolt, or a refusal. Doubtless this was one of the reasons that semiology, as a discourse with scientific and critical aspirations, became something of a refuge, and which, for want of being a Rimbaud, a Bataille, or an Artaud, made it possible to dismantle the mechanism of domination from an irrecuperable position of extraterritoriality in the name of scientific positivity. Subverting language necessarily meant using language itself and constituted the first step in breaking down the barriers between literary genres: the novel, poetry, criticism. All these forms of expression are textual and therefore from the same analytic grid of paradigmatic consciousness: "I believe that now we are beginning a revolt that is more profound than prior revolts because, perhaps for the first time, this one affects the very instrument of revolt, which is language."[25] In this sense Barthes saw himself as participating in the writer's enterprise with other means. The obvious tension in him between the writer and the semiologist never completely killed his literary aspirations, even when he examined such diverse objects as cuisine or fashion and its language, the technical language of linguistics. In 1964, his program elicited ever-growing enthusiasm. Semiology appeared to be the modern means of literary creation in the second half of the twentieth century.

Twenty-four

The Golden Age of Formal Thinking

Closest to the hard sciences and to mathematical language, semiotic structuralism was the most formalized branch of structuralism. It was also the most ambitious. As Algirdas Julien Greimas, the program's first promoter, understood it, semiotic structuralism was not just a simple offshoot of linguistics, but sought to encompass all of the sciences of man. "From the beginning, I have always intended that semiotics go beyond linguistics, which is only one part of it."[1] Greimas remained faithful to Saussure's vision in this, believing that he could unify anthropology, semantics, psychoanalysis, and literary criticism under a single banner.

For those linguists who gave courses at the Institut Poincaré at the Faculté des Sciences de Paris, proximity to mathematicians and logicians was institutional. Antoine Culioli gave a seminar on formal linguistics beginning in 1963. Greimas taught there, as did Bernard Pottier, Jean Dubois, and Maurice Gross. Greimas's seminar focused on semantics, which until then had been considered to be extraneous to traditional linguistics.

> This was where, little by little Nicolas Ruwet, Oswald Ducrot, Marcel Cohen, and then Tzvetan Todorov came together. There was also an important person named Lucien Sebag, who died, unfortunately, during the summer when we had thought of giving a seminar together. We wanted to establish a link between anthropology, semantics, and psychoanalysis. Sebag committed suicide and I have never forgiven Lacan for that.[2]

Greimas's *Structural Semantics* came out in 1966, the year of all the structuralist hits. It grew out of the seminar that he had given at the Institut Poincaré from 1963 to 1964 and emphasized a general semiotics embracing all signifying systems. This finally resulted in a certain receptivity of linguistic research to quite different fields. The futile dialogue in which the two masters of French linguistics, Greimas and Martinet, were engaged quite clearly indicated their differences. "I get lost when I read Greimas. Semiology likewise goes in all directions at once."[3] Martinet wanted to limit himself to describing how language functions and he set clear boundaries on linguistic research. Greimas responded: "Martinet is a big peasant who knows his own field well. When someone wanted to study music or painting, I sent them to Martinet, who told them, 'Study phonetics and come back in a year.' A fairly unappetizing prospect!"[4]

The Roland Barthes of *Elements of Semiology* very clearly adopted Greimas's view of general semiotics, even if he was institutionally ahead of his Alexandrian master in the Sixth Section of the EPHE, to which he had Greimas elected in 1965, with Lévi-Strauss's help. Once Greimas became a *directeur d'études* and after *Sémantique structurale* came out, semiotics began to gain institutional support in France, thanks once again to Lévi-Strauss, whose work sketching out the structuralist program was more advanced and who was also already better ensconced, with contacts in high places.

In 1966, a research group took shape around Greimas as the semio-linguistic section of the Laboratory of Social Anthropology of the EPHE and Collège de France, which is to say, around Lévi-Strauss and his team of anthropologists. Oswald Ducrot, Gérard Genette, Tzvetan Todorov, Julia Kristeva, Christian Metz, Jean-Claude Coquet, Yves Gentilhomme were all involved.[5] In addition to research, there was some very high-powered semiotic teaching, based on general linguistics, mathematics, logic, grammar, and semantics.

Structural Semantics: Greimasism

Structural semantics "was always the poor cousin of linguistics,"[6] if we look at how many hurdles it had to overcome before its specific object and methods were established, and the fact that it only came on the scene at the end of the nineteenth century. To overcome these handicaps, Greimas anchored semantics on the most rock-solid formal grounds possible, which were those of logic and mathematics, "which linguistics cannot ignore."[7] He adopted the model of Saussure's most formalist heir, Hjelmslev; "Claude Lévi-Strauss said that before he began writing, he always read three pages of Marx's *Eighteenth Brumaire*. I used to read a few pages by Hjelmslev."[8]

Greimas adopted the mathematical notion of discontinuity, and contrasted two different analytic levels: the object of the study, language, and the linguistic instruments that constitute a metalinguistics. From a Hjelmslevian point of view, everything takes place in two metalanguages: the one descriptive, with meanings formulated in language, and the other methodical. This approach implied two new instruments or denominations with respect to Saussure's definitions. Greimas differentiated signifying *phemes* from the *semes* of the signified, considering them to belong to different levels. He also reexamined the signifier/signified unit split into two heterogeneous levels. "Once the communication has occurred, the junction between signified and signifier is destined to be dissolved if the analysis of one or the other levels of language is to proceed even a little bit."[9] The *seme* becomes the minimal distinctive unit making the construction of lexemes, paralexemes, syntagms, or other elements possible.

Another concept that Greimas borrowed from logic, isotopia, reveals how entire texts belong to homogeneous semantic levels that can be interpreted as structural realities that become visible in language. "These techniques are comparable, for the social sciences, to algebraic formulation in the natural sciences."[10] This model seemed to offer the possibility of allowing the social sciences to acquire the same degree of scientificity as the hard sciences. But this meant that structural semantics needed to dissociate itself from any humanist perspective and replace intuition with verification. A speaker's intentionality fell by the wayside, dissolved within a subjectless hierarchy of contextual interweavings.

The other implication of structural semantics, which had already been apparent in Saussure but which Greimas made quite clear, was its nonhistoricism. Structural semantics sought to extract an atemporal and organizational structural reality from the real, whatever the contextual framework or signified content might be: "We can reasonably suppose that the achronic organization of contents that we encounter in areas quite unrelated to each other should have a general scope. Because this model is uninterested in contents . . . we must consider it to be metalinguistic."[11] Greimas hoped to move beyond the contingency of the events in human history in order to write a structural history purged of all traces of empiricism. During the structuralist phase, his was the most scientistic semiotic project for it went furthest in its desire for scientificity made manifest by the onmipresent mathematical terminology—"procedural algorithm," "rules for establishing equivalences," "conversion rules"—and its function was to be a model of rigor.

We find this logical and scientific approach in Lévi-Strauss and in Lacan, whose two projects most closely approximated scientific structuralism. The recurrent structuralist notion of rupture lay at the heart of semiotics since it established the division between two structures belonging to two different realities, but "how can we go from an immanent theory of language to an immanent theory of meaning in general? How, in other words, can we infer the binarism of meaning from the binarism of signs?"[12]

Claude Brémond proposed an answer to these fundamental questions.[13] He differentiated between two stages of analysis in Greimas's reading of Propp: the first was inductive based on the model of *Morphology of the Folktale*: "Greimas considered the sequence of functions outlined by Propp in order to discern—and his idea has some merit—a better-structured system of basic oppositions."[14] Greimas contributed a certain number of useful tools, by distinguishing, for example, between the actors and actants among Propp's characters on the basis of their operational level. This let him build a mythical actantial model with six terms, which was more effective than Propp's seven characters.

But Greimas did not stop there. He quickly went on to a second stage of deductive abstraction where he argued for the a priori existence of a transcendent principle that would make it possible to go step by step from this principle to its concrete, textual manifestations. There were two basic ideas here: the semiotic square, which was Greimas's basic unit of meaning, and the idea of a semiotic generation of meaningful objects. Brémond saw the square as "completely sterile," more a "mystical idea than a transcendent principle,"[15] and nothing justified its extrapolation from Propp's model, which would be the model of models for any text in general, but especially for every possible written and unwritten text. "Ultimately, this simple postulate is like the head of a pin on which the diversity of the entire universe is made to rest."[16]

The semiotic square, a recasting of the Aristotelian square of opposites and oppositions, became an explanatory matrix for an indefinite number of narrative structures. "This is the most flagrant case of an irrefutable theory, as Popper explains it."[17] The semiotic square usually imposed an initial structure on a narrative, whether filmic or textual, letting it land on its feet since anything could be put in the four corners of the square without any verification whatsoever. "The use of the semiotic square has always shocked me a bit. I think it is justified at the end of an analysis, but surely not at the beginning."[18] With the semiotic square, the empirical world and the referent could be kept at bay so that the kernel of intelligibility, the principal and invisible key of all signified reality, could be discerned. Meaning was therefore directly derived from a structure that was immanent to it.

Paradoxically, the semiotic program that united Propp, Lévi-Strauss's analysis of myths, and Hjelmslev's *Prolegomenas*, and that presented itself as the most comprehensive semiotic program, disappointed its promises. Greimasism quickly seemed to become hermetically locked in an increasingly confidential abstraction. The orthodox believers rapidly dwindled in number as Greimas's theories mobilized the most sophisticated, meticulously logical strategy that produced very disappointing and often tautological conclusions. "I remember that, as part of the jury, I presented the summary of a very thick thesis by a very well known student of Greimas, on marriage. The conclusion was that marriage is a binary structure. This is true, in a certain way, but is this a conclusion that requires a thousand pages of analysis?"[19] If Greimasism did not have a particularly brilliant destiny, Greimas himself remained one of the major sources of hope for the structuralist enthusiasts of the sixties. For Jean-Claude Coquet, who had met Greimas at the University of Poitiers where they taught together during his last year there, "*Sémantique structurale* was an absolutely brilliant book, full of ideas, one of the major works of the period."[20]

When Greimas left Poitiers, he also left a student who was working on a *diplôme d'études supérieures* to Jean-Claude Coquet. François Rastier was very close to Greimas, who considered him to be his spiritual son. "Rastier informed me about structural semantics. That was how I came to know Greimas and I was fascinated by his intellectual dexterity and the force of his convictions."[21] The kind of linguistics most often practiced at the time eliminated the subject and history. Given this, Greimas seemed to be the most radical, and therefore the most scientific, and his success sidelined Émile Benveniste's approach to structural linguistics. Hjelmslev's model, which Greimas adopted, was in fact based on the production of a text baptized "normalized," or "objectivized." In order to arrive at this pure, scientific object, Greimas eliminated all dialogic signs or forms referring to a subject (first and second person pronouns, for example), which meant that he was left with third person canonical enunciations. And for the sake of a uniform present, he also normalized texts by eliminating all reference to time. The criterion for dissociating anteriority and posteriority became the vague reference to a distant past: "Whence Greimas's interest in folktales and mythic narratives, which were easier to work on."[22] But there was a steep price for the quadruple negation of the first person pronoun, of the subject, of intersubjective dialogue, and of the here and now with respect to space and time, and Greimas's theory rather quickly ran onto the shoals of an impoverished narrative reality, in favor of an ontologized structure.

Would semiotics be able to create such a unifying program for the social sciences? Its scientific imperialism was certain but its cohabitation with structural anthropology in a single institutional laboratory was short-lived.

Barthes the Semiotician

Greimas had a disciple between 1960 and 1964 who already enjoyed significant notoriety: Roland Barthes. This was the period when Barthes repressed his vocation as a writer and used Greimas's theory in order to better approximate a rigorous and scientific discourse. But Barthes was an essentially intuitive thinker, and he needed to rationalize his feelings; Greimas was the person who seemed to go farthest in this direction. "You can't understand anything about Barthes if you don't understand that even when his thinking appears most abstract, he is really just covering up his affective choices."[23] Saussure's binary model fit Barthes like a glove since he thought in dichotomies, and always set a valorized term against a devalorized term: the good and the bad; someone who is attractive and someone who is not; the *écrivain* and the *écrivant*; taste and distaste, and so on. But if Barthes would later give free rein to his feelings, they remained underground in the early sixties when he was articulating the principles of a semiological program that were consonant with Greimas's theses.

We can also understand Barthes's phase of theorizing and scientism in terms of a desire for university respectability. Even if he succeeded quite quickly and brilliantly, he never joined the ranks with the traditional diplomas. His quest for recognition generated a veritable work ethic in him, and behind the dilettante that the specialists saw was a deeply ascetic man devoted to work. "He was basically the opposite of a bohemian and led a typically petit-bourgeois life; he had an absolute need not to be upset by unexpected events."[24] At the beginning of the sixties, then, Barthes worked on the topic he would have wanted to have worked on as a *thèse d'État* had he continued his university work: fashion. He had tried to find a thesis director and, accompanied by Greimas, visited André Martinet: "I almost directed *The Fashion System* as a thesis. I gave him my O.K., all the while saying that this was not linguistics."[25] Given Martinet's relatively unenthusiastic response, Barthes went to see Lévi-Strauss to ask him to direct his thesis. Greimas again went with him, and waited like an anxious father in a nearby bistro to hear how things had gone. "Barthes came out after half an hour saying that Lévi-Strauss had refused."[26] Their disagreement had to do with the limited breadth of the project since, for Lévi-Strauss, Barthes's work only dealt with a written system of style and not with a general system. Barthes, on the other hand, believed that nothing significant existed beyond the realm of the written. Barthes's hopes of university recognition were dashed, but in 1967, Seuil published the book, the labor of six years from 1957 to 1963. Because it was like a thesis for him, even if it did not have that tag, this book was particularly meaningful for Barthes. His spiritual father confided that "we looked at his book together three times and reworked it each time."[27]

So this was both theoretically and affectively the expression of a significant period in his relationship with Greimas. *The Fashion System* bears the marks of this relationship and appeared from the outset as a methodical work set on examining spoken—rather than worn—clothes, which was the basis for the divergence with Lévi-Strauss. Barthes essentially worked on the style system as a metalanguage, in Hjelmslevian terms. The transition from real to written clothing, by way of the clothing-image, was made with the use of shifters, an idea Barthes took from Jakobson. Shifters "are used to transpose one structure into another, to go from one code to another code, if you will."[28] But Barthes used the idea in a very particular way since he was not referring to a specific message. He also designated three shifters for moving from one code to another: the principal shifter was the "sewing pattern," the second the "sewing program," and the third is the one that "makes it possible to go from the iconic structure to the spoken structure, from a representation of a piece of clothing to its description."[29]

Formalist assumptions of normalizing the functional uses of language led Barthes to give priority to the written piece of clothing because it was the only one that could give rise to an immanent study free of any practical function: "For these reasons, I have decided to examine the verbal structure here."[30] He defined his objects, consisting of newspapers from 1958 to 1959, and exhaustively sifted through *Elle* and *Le Jardin des modes*. A strictly orthodox Saussurean, Barthes reproduced the language/speech duo by opposing the clothing-image, located on the speech side and therefore inappropriate for scientific consideration, and the clothing-text, which is on the language side and therefore an object eligible for scientific inquiry.

Barthes anchored his analysis in the opposition developed by Hjelmslev: "The problem raised by the coincidence of two semantic systems in a single enunciation was dealt with primarily by Hjelmslev."[31] He adopted the separation between the expressive level (E) and the level of contents (C), brought together by the relation (R); this gives rise to a multilevel analysis of denotation and connotation, of the language-object and of the metalanguage. Fashion was thus caught up in a process of formalization and therefore of desubstantification, giving Barthes access to the essence of fashion, which appears as a system of signifiers, a classificatory activity cut off from the signified. "Fashion therefore immediately proceeds to a sort of sacralization of the sign: the signified is separated from its signifier."[32] Fashion functioned on the basis of a double postulate. Because it was, on the one hand, a naturalist system, it could be interpreted as a logical system. The popular press practiced a naturalized fashion with an infinite number of fragmented references to a dream world and its utilization, whereas a more "distinguished" press practiced fashion in a purer manner, freed from all ideological underpinnings. At the end of his long study, Barthes made it manifestly clear that the full signified represented the signifier of alienation, and he thereby drew sociological conclusions without falling prey to sociological reductionism. The fashion system translated a semiology characterized by its elaboration of a taxonomy. The novelty, however, was that this taxonomy was made in order to dissolve the subject in language.

Jean-François Revel took the work ironically, and used a syllogism to illustrate its thesis: a rat nibbles the cheese but the rat is a syllable and therefore the syllable nibbles the cheese. "A structuralist rat, nothing impossible about that, of course. But if the rat writes, can he still eat cheese? It is up to the sociologists to tell us."[33] However, the book was well received in general. Raymond Bellour interviewed Barthes in *Les Lettres françaises*,[34] and Julia Kristeva saw the book as a step toward demystifying the science of the sign: "Barthes's work subverts the main current of modern science: thinking the sign."[35]

Kristeva applauded Barthes for his radical interrogation of all metaphysics of depths, and for separating signifier and signified in favor of the relationship between signifiers, which was in fact part of Lacan's reading of Saussure when he invoked the signifying chain. Thanks to *The Fashion System*, an entire generation could imagine that it was possible to undertake similar investigations in other particularly vast fields. If Barthes was able to isolate the *vestemes* in written/described fashion, why not flush out the *gustemes* and other distinctive units at all levels of social practice?

In 1967, the response to Barthes's work was spectacular and a veritable collective fervor took hold of his semiological program. But Barthes soon distanced himself from his own pronouncements and ambitions and, leaving Greimas to occupy center semiotic stage, returned to his vocation as a writer, which for him was the goal of a structuralism that would have been meaningless had it not subverted scientific language from within. "Structuralism's logical continuation can only be to rejoin literature not as an object of analysis, but as an activity of writing. . . . It is therefore up to the structuralist to transform himself into a writer."[36] The need to write as the result of Barthes's methodological exigency in 1967 presupposed another renaissance, which came to be the very principle of his writing: the pleasure principle.

In an interview with Georges Charbonnier in 1967, Barthes answered a question about the book of the year. Would it be a mathematical work, given that the public relished formal thinking to the point that the social sciences would quickly consume themselves? "The final phase is that they question their own language and become, in their turn, writing."[37] Although Barthes did not renounce this liberating aspect of generalized formalization—the triumphant relegation of all referents to the dustbin of insignificance, the intersection of work and fate in a Mallarméan line between writing and formalization—he nonetheless admitted that "literary writing maintains a sort of referential illusion that makes it delicious."[38] By his taste for writing as a figure of the other's desire, an erotics of language based not on reality but on the illusion of the referent, we see that Barthes's writing in 1967 was already setting the stage for a radical change that would become apparent in the Barthes of post-May 1968.

An Ideology of Rigor

Hjelmslev inspired the semiotic program in France, but other influences were also at play during the golden age of formal thinking. There was, for example, a spectacularly successful mathematical epistemology in France, known for the mathematician Bourbaki. Bourbaki's mathematical structure, however, appeared as an antididactic form occulting the origin in the historical and empirical sense of mathematical knowledge. "The logic of its presentation and the context of the justification are far more important than the context in which the discovery was made or in which the investigation took place. The entire empirical and tentative aspect of mathematics is systematically eliminated in favor of a purely formalist presentation."[39] This new approach even gave rise to an important teaching reform at the beginning of the sixties, called new math; but it was a disaster and even its author repudiated it.

The Bourbaki ideology certainly contributed toward a structuralist mentality and activity, which Pierre Raymond called an ideology of rigor. Bourbakism made it clear that the splendors of the mathematical edifice were such that even those who might be able to appreciate them were held at arm's length: "Where the links, the concatenation, the imbedding of propositions are given as a sort of subjectless, objective necessity whose internal weaving is to be analyzed without understanding the properly historical process of mathematical discovery."[40] The French found this model particularly fascinating, showing how much Louis Hjelmslev, the major linguistic inspiration for the semiotic school in Paris, valorized mathematics as a science. Semiotics was therefore complicitous with Bourbakism in its search for the codes and messages exchanged around points of emission, and in its concern to constantly extend the formalization of communication phenomena.

The other model in this area from which structuralism drew its concepts and methods was cybernetics. Cybernetics became increasingly productive in the era of mass communication and cast an aura around the structuralist program. Cybernetics offered a potential bridge between math and the social sciences, and provided a framework for some especially wide-ranging investigations. It was a true interdisciplinary crossroad that addressed notions from algebra, logic, and information theory and game theory.

A certain osmosis existed, therefore, between a desire for formalization that found the very expression of a split from the referent in mathematical language, and formalist research in the visual arts, music, literature, and architecture, coming from the East. "It was a period when Lacan and Chomsky sold as well as the popular mystery stories written by San Antonio. I remember that I was living in Puteaux and I would go buy my books at the drugstore on the Neuilly bridge. That's where I bought Desanti's *Mathematical Idealities*[41] and Lacan's *Écrits.* "[42]

These formal models proposed that all boundaries between mathematical, logical formalization and the social sciences be effaced. Jean Piaget offered a particularly good example of a will to place psychology in a continuum using mathematics. With this end in mind, Piaget established a circular diagram of scientific knowledge that ended with a single and interdependent idea of the different sciences. Such a circle made it possible to link mathematics, physics, biology, and psychology.[43] The semioticians were utterly fascinated by logical formalization, which they adapted to language. The temptation to borrow in this way was strengthened because computer programs were addressing problems having to do with language, and logicians had the advantage of having come up with almost perfect formalizations in their thinking about linguistic operations. "The temptation was therefore quite strong to try to adapt these logical formalizations to language, but I think that it was a sort of capitulation."[44]

Although he never denied that formalization and model making were necessary, Oswald Ducrot held that a properly linguistic conceptualization should be the starting point, but that it should not, for example, be limited to differentiating true from false. If there is a tendency in language to construct true propositions and to link them through the reasoning process, other dimensions of language must also be taken into account and that logicians tend to ignore. "A remark that Antoine Culioli made about this had a big influence on me. One day, he said, 'truth—I don't know what that is.' "[45]

Lacan: A Bend in the Road toward Logic

In 1965, logic took up where the Saussurean linguistic model left off via another discipline, psychoanalysis. Jacques Lacan's text, "La science et la vérité" showed how much the École Normale Supérieure and Jacques-Alain Miller had determined the direction in which things would go. Beginning with Gottlob Frege, Miller wanted to uncover the concept of structural causality that Althusser emphasized in his reading of Marx, as a basis for applying Lacan's notion of suture. Frege, in his *Foundations of Arithmetic* (1884), had established modern symbolic logic by criticizing the empirical method. Symbolic language should be dissociated from all reference to any conscious subject. "Logic is that which is conceived or constructed outside any intuition; logic is that which is general to the point of belonging to every language such that no language could be conceived without it."[46] We can easily understand Lacan's interest in the work of a logician who excluded the psychological subject, even if Frege, who initiated a philosophy of language, was more appreciated by the Anglo-Saxons than by the French.

According to Élisabeth Roudinesco, when Jacques-Alain Miller articulated Frege's concept of the zero and that of its successors with Lacan's theory of the signifier, he recast Lacanian thinking. The consequences were political and theoretical: "Theoretically, Lacanian thinking becomes the model par excellence of the capacity of Freudian thinking to elude the ideals of psychology. Politically speaking, this recasting makes it possible to designate adversaries who are considered to be deviants with respect to a doctrine that represents scientific normalization in its all-powerful singularity."[47] After having used the rise of the social sciences to decenter the subject with Saussurean linguistics, Lacan radicalized his reading of Freud even further in order to avoid becoming the agent of constructing the social sciences, with the attendant risk of reestablishing a humanism of an unalienated subject.

In Kurt Gödel's logic, a theorem of incompleteness makes it possible to perceive the idea of truth as eluding complete formalization. "He infers that the experience of the Cartesian doubt marks the subject with a split between knowledge and truth."[48] This turning point heralded the transition from a me-theme to a matheme, and is at the origin of many topological manipulations. For some, this formalization had less to do with clinical psychoanalysis than with its transmission, and was more a didactic concern for rigor and method: "It is clear that Lacan does not use these objects as mathematical objects. They have a purely metaphorical status."[49] For others, the topological turning point was much more important because it made it possible for Lacan to better grasp the structure of the subject: "For him, the subject's structure is topological; he said so."[50]

This structure, which had for centuries been represented as complete by the figure of the sphere, in fact better approximates the aspherical and incompleteness. This view of the subject gave rise to the multiple topological manipulations designed to turn the sphere around in order to finally reach the subject's true structure as fundamentally split within the topology of knots.

Notwithstanding their differences, Claude Lévi-Strauss, Algirdas Julien Greimas, and Jacques Lacan were the most scientific of the structuralists in the mid-sixties, the most radically turned toward the search for a deep, occult structure, whether the metaphor be Lévi-Strauss's *enceintes mentales* as the structure of structures, Greimas's semiotic square, or the aspherical structure of Lacan's subject. These were the three crowning points of formal thinking, all part of the same adventure seeking to establish the social sciences on the same footing as the natural sciences within the city of science.

Twenty-five

Great Confrontations

Barthes/Picard

A Homeric combat that best reveals the issues of the period was waged between Roland Barthes and Raymond Picard. This was an important joust, with the new criticism contesting the old Sorbonne. The pivotal figure was that classic of classics, Racine, who had become an object of contention and scandal.

Would the venerable Sorbonne allow itself to be dispossessed of its patrimony in that realm of predilection known as tragedy by those very individuals who could not distinguish between journalistic scribbling and national literary treasures? Surely such provocation could not go ignored for *francité* was outraged. The confrontation occurred in the mid-sixties between two protagonists with different institutional ties and statures. Raymond Picard belonged to the venerable Sorbonne and Roland Barthes raised his voice from a modern but marginal institution. The stage was set and all the elements assembled for the duel, which was cast like some great Racinian tragedy of the twentieth century. The important combat deepened the differences between the two camps. Literary history was no longer the same after this, caught in the vise of two languages, each a stranger to the other.

The French Book Club published Roland Barthes's *Racinian Man* in 1960 and an article on Racine came out in the *Annales* that summer.[1] Three years later, Seuil published both pieces as *On Racine*, together with a third piece on the same topic, and it was only then that they received public acclaim. The Sorbonne could accept the fact that the new criticism addressed the new novel, but that it sought to appropriate the representative of classicism and of tradition in order to experiment with the incendiary effects of its analytic grid, its mixture of linguistic methods, psychoanalysis, and anthropology, bordered on scandal. "If you want to do literary history, you cannot touch the individual Racine."[2]

That Barthes published his article in the *Annales* already gave a clear idea of how he aligned himself in his approach to literary history, appealing to Lucien Febvre against the tenets of literary positivism. He adopted Febvre's combat against historicizing history, against the domination of events, in order to defend the necessary dissociation between the history of the literary function and the history of writers of literature. To do so, Barthes raised the same problems that Febvre had sketched out when he expressed the desire to study a writer's context, his ties with his public and, more generally, the elements of a collective *mentalité*, what Febvre called the mental equipment of a period. "In other words, literary history is only possible if it is sociological, and if it is interested in activities and institutions, and not in individuals."[3]

Barthes adopted the *Annales* idea about an active criticism that does more than assemble and collect documents and archives, asking questions and subjecting the material to new hypotheses. Just as history, for Febvre, was a history problem, Barthes held that a literary critic had to be paradoxical and raise contemporary questions when addressing any literary work, thereby participating in its undefined impact. Barthes read Racine analytically and structurally, therefore, and no longer saw the author as a cult figure, but rather as a field of investigation for validating new methods.

The structure of Racinian man was Barthes's object and it was revealed through Barthes's careful and attentive dialectic of space, and particularly through a logic of places. The interior spaces of the bedroom, that mythic retreat separated from the antechamber—the scenic site of communication—by a tragic object (the door), the object of transgression, were contrasted with the exterior spaces of death, flight, and events. "In short, in Racinian topography, everything converges on the tragic site, but everything gets mired in it."[4]

Based on this topo-logic, tragic unity took shape not so much in the individual singularity of Racine's characters as in the function defining the hero as enclosed. "He who cannot go out without dying:

his limits are his privilege, his captivity is his distinction."[5] This functional, binary opposition separating interior and exterior also made it possible to distinguish between Eros and the Eros event. Eros was a peaceful and sororal love rooted in childhood, whereas the Eros event was sudden, expressing itself violently and without warning, producing ravishing effects that provoke a tragic alienation, which, according to Barthes, was Racine's true subject. "Racinian disorder is essentially a sign, which is to say, a signal and a communication."[6]

A whole dialectic of the logic of places unfolded in this mythic combat of shadows and light in terms of contiguity and hierarchy. The Racinian hero was driven by the need to prove his ability to make a break; his heroism depended on his capacity to do so. His own infidelity created the hero who, like a creature of God, appeared locked in an inexpiable battle between the Father and his son. Barthes quite convincingly demonstrated that Racine substituted the word for praxis, for the offstage event; verbal communication became the source of disorganization, the very site on which the tragedy unfolded and consumed itself. "The fundamental reality of the tragedy is therefore this word-action. Its function is clear: to mediate the Power Relationship."[7]

Barthes used Jakobson's binarism as much as Freudian categories, together with a structural synchronic approach, and the Sorbonne's most erudite Racine scholar had a particularly violent reaction to all of this. Raymond Picard, author of *The Career of Jean Racine*, editor of the Pléiade's publication of the complete works of Racine, and great Racine specialist, published his answer in 1965 in the evocatively entitled work, *New Criticism or New Imposture?* Picard focused especially on Barthes's excessive use of psychoanalytic decoding for understanding Racine's theater and quickly lowered a chaste veil over the heroes whose secret and frustrated sexual passions had been revealed: "We must reread Racine in order to recall that his characters are, after all, quite different from those of D. H. Lawrence. . . . Barthes has decided to discover an unbridled sexuality."[8] Picard sliced through Barthes's systematization, denounced his avowed inability to speak the Truth about Racine, and therefore refused him the right to say anything whatsoever about an author about whom he had no expertise. For Picard, Barthes was "the instrument of a criticism that operates by instinct,"[9] that uses a pseudoscientific jargon to make inept and absurd assertions in the name of biological, psychoanalytic, and philosophical knowledge. Picard denounced the tendency toward generalization, toward taking a single, concrete example for a category of universals in a critical game that confuses everything. For Picard, the mixture of impressionism and dogmatism set to a modernist rhythm of indetermination "makes it possible to say absolutely any stupid thing."[10]

Picard was not personally attacked by Barthes's study, but he counterattacked nonetheless, as self-appointed spokesman for the Sorbonne. The institution was irritated by this structuralist agitation and wanted to see Barthes, who had become an idol, pilloried before being rejected. The violence of the polemic against him rather surprised Barthes: "I was not expecting such an attack from Picard. I never attacked university criticism, I simply set it apart, named it."[11] For Barthes, the assault was provoked by the issue of university exams in literature. New criticism was dangerous because it questioned the absolute, intangible nature of the criteria used to establish a comfortable canon of knowledge, which was so certain of its values and methods. He saw the attack against his book as a defense of verifiable knowledge measured in terms of eternal truths.

A whole generation of structuralists sided with Barthes, of course, and wholeheartedly embraced his cause against the aged Sorbonne.

> On the human level, we were always on Barthes's side. Today, I would not say that Picard was entirely wrong intellectually, but he was entirely wrong when it came to his aggressivity. Barthes and Greimas were not *agrégés* and they could not enter the university. Barthes's thesis had been refused. As for the linguists, they had no career options and many of them suffered because of that. They were the victims of a veritable interdiction. French scholars of the time were mostly conservative politically, and governed by university scruples.[12]

Picard's answer showed just how hermetic academic discourse was, and it once again demonstrated its stubborn hermeticism in the face of new issues and questions.

Aesthetics professor Olivier Revault d'Allonnes kept score, and in the spirit of reconciliation, told himself that all the polemicists were right. He did not want to choose between Lucien Goldmann's sociological perspective, Charles Mauron's psychoanalytic viewpoint, Raymond Picard's biographical approach, and Roland Barthes's structuralist outlook. "They are all right. All of that exists in *Phèdre* and perhaps that is what makes it a great work. To recall Adorno's metaphor, great work can tolerate layering."[13] At the time, as Louis-Jean Calvet pointed out, Picard was well received by the media. Jacqueline Piatier wholeheartedly supported him in *Le Monde* and referred to "Roland Barthes's surprising interpretations of Racine's tragedies."[14] *Le Journal de Genève* relished Picard's counterattack: "Roland Barthes KO'd in one hundred and fifty pages."[15] Barthes suffered from these attacks at the time because he could not bear the polemic. He confided to his friend Philippe Rebeyrol: "You know, what I write is playful, and if I am attacked, there's nothing at all left."[16] But the polemical debate, which Picard turned into a public event, boomeranged against the old Sorbonne.

Soon, an enthusiastic generation of students would have the opportunity to contest academic wisdom. Barthes answered Picard in his *Criticism and Truth*, published in 1966, at the height of the structuralist paradigm. The book was clamorously heralded by the press, and bore the question "Should Barthes Be Burned?" on the promotional band encircling the cover. The drama was therefore carried to an extreme, and Barthes once again played the role of the virtuous innocent risking being burned at the stake. It was an opportunity to fire up an entire intellectual community around the ambitious program proposed in *The Elements of Semiology*, which thus reached a vast public. This time, Barthes answered without sparing the polemical tone.

He denounced the fact that within "the literary state, criticism needs to be as restrained as the police."[17] Barthes saw Picard's criticism as an expression of the most traditional literary history, clinging to a vague notion of "verisimilar criticism," which stands on its own, and thus has no need to be supported by evidence. This notion included references to a critic's objectivity, to his taste, and to the clarity of his argument. Barthes characterized this type of literary history as the old criticism: "These rules are not of our time: the last two come from the classical age, the first from the era of positivism."[18] He also attacked the postulate according to which the literary critic should limit himself to the literary level. Here, Barthes forayed beyond immanentist proclamations in order to defend content and the external elements that shed some light on the general economy of the literary text and required some knowledge of history, psychoanalysis, and anthropology. Unlike the positivist method, Barthes defined the critical act as an act of writing in the full sense of the work, a work on language. And in so doing, by bringing the writer and critic together, he weakened the boundaries, limits, and prohibitions that differentiated writing genres.

Barthes took a double line of defense against Picard. He invoked the rights of the critic as writer and bearer of meaning, a veritable creator by virtue of his own active reading; this critic/writer represented a more scientific discourse that no longer considered writing as decorum, but as a source of truth. The structuralist current supported his argument, with references to Lacan, Jakobson, and Lévi-Strauss. Influenced by the work of deconstruction in the social sciences, he proposed and made himself the spokesman for a "science of literature," as opposed to a traditional literary history.[19] A science of the conditions of the content rather than of the content itself, which is to say, of its forms. Not surprisingly, Barthes took linguistics as the model for his science: "Its model, obviously, will be linguistics."[20] The author is displaced by the language, which has become the true subject, making the search for a hidden sense and ultimate meaning vain because it assumes an idea of the subject that is, in fact, an absence. "Literature never bespeaks anything other than the subject's absence."[21]

In proclaiming the birth of a new historical era based on the unity and truth of writing, Barthes spoke for the ambitions of an entire generation that saw in the explosion of the critical discourse of the social sciences a mode of writing that, properly speaking, rejoined literary creation. He shook up a university discourse that preferred to turn a deaf ear to an increasingly insistent voice. Even after 1966, the distant echoes of these battles and gambols reverberated, and René Pommier's violent remarks clearly revealed the breach that Barthes had successfully made into academic knowledge—a true robin announcing the spring of 1968.[22]

Lévi-Strauss/Gurvitch

The other notable confrontation of the sixties pitted Lévi-Strauss against a whole area of sociology that was reluctant to be cast in the structural mold, even if it was familiar with the notion of structure. This sociology was greatly influenced by the highly colorful personality of Georges Gurvitch. It was another front in the battles of the moment and was essential for Lévi-Strauss, who absolutely needed to persuade sociologists to join him if he hoped to bring all the sciences of man together around an anthropology that had become structural. The polemic between Gurvitch and Lévi-Strauss was, therefore, quite lively because the theoretical and institutional stakes were important; not surprisingly, it crystallized around the notion of structure.

Gurvitch had laid out his idea of social structure in 1955, and defined it much as Murdock had done, as a phenomenon designating the idea of coherence among social institutions.[23] As a phenomenon, the idea of structure can be compared with or contrasted to other terms. For Gurvitch, social classes had to be distinguished in their structure as well as in their organization, and these social structures became the objects of an ongoing process of destructuring and restructuring. When they are involved in a process, they are also part of a dialectic. For Gurvitch, the social encompassed and extended beyond structure, and was irreducible to it: "It is incomparably richer than [its structure], and its fullness implies the unexpected even more."[24] Gurvitch criticized structuralism at once for its reductionism and impoverishment of reality and as something static that crushed society's immanent movement beneath its weight.

Lévi-Strauss's retort was particularly stinging. "By what authority does M. Gurvitch appoint himself as our mentor? And what, in fact, does he know about concrete societies? As a pure theoretician, Gurvitch is interested only in the theoretical aspect of our work."[25] Which should take precedence, the singularity of an event or the permanence of structure? This debate had recurred in sociology ever since Durkheim and Tarde, and was once again evoked at the heart of the confrontation between Lévi-Strauss and Gurvitch. An article by Gilles Gaston-Granger that was widely cited in the sixties paid considerable attention to it.[26]

Gilles Gaston-Granger, an epistemologist, defined the alternative apparently opposing a perceptual comprehension of the world and an intellectual conception of the scientific approach, and in this regard he contrasted Gurvitch with Lévi-Strauss. "For Gurvitch, a structure is, in a certain way, a being, where for Lévi-Strauss, it is only a model."[27] Gurvitch refused both mathematical tools and formalization and considered structure to be a phenomenon, whereas for Lévi-Strauss it was a question of a learning tool. Gaston-Granger considered Gurvitch to be an Aristotelian, whereas Lévi-Strauss represented "the party of a mathematics of man."[28] Gaston-Granger did, of course, point out the danger of reifying a learning tool and transforming it into the object of knowledge in the social sciences, but the risk was to be taken despite the potential danger: "The risk must be run."[29] Gaston-Granger finally opted for structuralism even if he maintained a critical distance and criticized Lévi-Strauss for having gone from analytical models to universalizing diagrams, and running the risk of reintroducing a certain ontologization into the instruments of conceptualization.

Thirty years have passed since he published his article and Gaston-Granger is freer now than he was at the time because he did not want to ruffle Gurvitch's sensibilities. Today, he considers that Gurvitch was "infinitely small next to Lévi-Strauss, and the bearer of a scholastic void."[30] As for Lévi-Strauss, Gaston-Granger had only warned him against the danger of considering structures to be more real than reality, much like Plato; he nonetheless hoped that a great sociology or structural anthropology would be created and discover the key to a scientific understanding of social man. Today, Gaston-Granger is less optimistic about the results of Lévi-Strauss's program: "I think that Lévi-Strauss's work did not yield what I had hoped it would."[31]

Gaston-Granger is severe and he does not fully admit how important Gurvitch was for a whole generation of sociologists and anthropologists. Of course, Gurvitch was something of a megalomaniac, whose rather natural vanity made him consider only his own work as worth taking seriously. Roger Establet, who became his assistant, was in fact supposed to have worked on that project: "I was supposed to give courses on his work."[32] His dogmatism was well known. "When he said that there were fourteen levels of structural depth, he did not mean thirteen or fifteen and he recalled with no little irony a Durkheim who had only found three."[33] But the hidden side of these dogmatic assertions reveals a touching individual, bludgeoned by history and driven by a consuming passion. Gurvitch lived on the rue Vaneau in the apartment where Marx had lived when he was in France; he was an exile in Paris and bought nothing except books, hoping one day to return to the Soviet Union. The conditions he stipulated for his return in his ongoing negotiations with Soviet authorities made him particularly sympathetic. He wanted to be able to speak in Russian to workers as they left the factories, and to be able to work in Russian archives in order to write a history of the Russian Revolution in the place where he had been a commissar of the people. He was, therefore, a sociologist forever cut off from the field in which he would have liked to work. Finally granted permission in 1964 (he had given up on the idea of addressing workers in Russian, on the advice of his wife), Gurvitch died before being able to realize his dream.

During this entire period, Gurvitch was the rather charismatic leader of a network that was more or less reticent about the structuralist vogue. The coterie included sociologists like Jean Duvignaud and Pierre Ansart, philosophers like Lucien Goldmann and Henri Lefebvre, and anthropologists like Georges Balandier. Most did not want to confront Lévi-Strauss head-on. The choice was rather between two emblematic figures of sociology: Raymond Aron and Georges Gurvitch. And yet, even in Gurvitch's group, the influence of structuralism spurred research and determined some methodological choices.

Lucien Goldmann, of course, was receptive to a structuralism that he qualified as genetic and receptive to history. But structuralism's influence was also palpable among sociologists such as Pierre Ansart even if Gurvitch was directing his thesis. "I have a very clear memory of the first day I heard structuralism discussed. It was a course that Georges Davy had given after having been at Lévi-Strauss's thesis defense. He gave an absolutely fascinating discussion on *The Elementary Structures of Kinship*, which he presented as a unique intellectual possibility."[34] And yet, Pierre Ansart, who had to do a complementary thesis on the birth of anarchism—which, moreover, he defended in 1969, after Gurvitch's death—freely elected a structuralist problematic. Influenced by Lucien Goldmann, he tried to construct a presentation of the structuration of a thought process about anarchism in its relationships with economic structures, practices, and contemporary worldviews. "For those of us seeking our way, structuralism seemed to offer something extraordinarily productive for our work."[35]

Structuralism did have a real influence on this group of left-wing sociologists, but it was the object of heated debate because of its demonstration of the dehumanizing process of our technical civilization. During a colloquium at Royaumont in 1960, the debate was quite lively; a consensus on criticism led by Gurvitch against structuralism brought together in a united front Jeannine Verdès-Leroux, Sonya Dayan, Pividal, Tristani, and Claude Lefort. Jean Duvignaud, who was close to Gurvitch, examined the correlation between structuralism and the place from which it emanated: "Many people were dragged into this conflict because there was something more than what met the eye. The question was whether or not a society could transform itself from within."[36] For Duvignaud, the famous epistemological break, which legitimated ideological structuralism so that it could either become official university doctrine or that of the intelligentsia,

reproduced the hiatus between the dominant laws of the technostructure and those of an eventual global change. "I will therefore say that
Lévi-Strauss's thinking has become true, even obvious, since, after having taken a detour via the natives, it once again found the very structures of the second industrial age."[37] Jean Duvignaud suggested the
idea that Lévi-Strauss ignored history less because he observed the
prevalence of relationships of reproduction, of a cooling of temporality among tropical cultures he called cold, than because of an intuition
about the changes under way in the postindustrial civilization at a time
when communication was carrying the day over change.

A Book Event: *The Savage Mind*

Another great intellectual duel pitted two sacred monsters of the
French intelligentsia against one another: Jean-Paul Sartre and Claude
Lévi-Strauss. Lévi-Strauss had been attentive when Sartre's *Critique
of Dialectical Reason* was published but had not objected at the time
to Sartrean philosophy, not because he had abandoned philosophy,
despite his remarks to the contrary, but because he was preparing a
severe and highly polemical response on his own anthropological turf.
Lévi-Strauss's answer was the final chapter of *The Savage Mind*, entitled "History and Dialectic," which became the masterwork in the
history of anthropology. *The Savage Mind* came out in 1962, as did
Totemism Today. Lévi-Strauss not only reacted to Sartre's theses, but
he continued to explain how the savage mind operated. He added
grist to the demonstration begun in "Race and History," by concen-
trating this time on a demonstration of the universality of mental
mechanisms beyond differences of content. In this respect, there was
an important shift from Lucien Lévy-Bruhl's theses contrasting the
prelogical mentality of primitive societies, characterized by the principle of participation, with the logical mentality of civilizations, governed by a principle of contradiction.

Contrary to anthropological tradition, Lévi-Strauss asserted: "The
savage mind is logical, in the same sense and the same fashion as
ours."[38] Long presented as the primitive expression of emotions, the
savage mind, here, was perceived in terms of the dimensions of the synthetic and analytic goals it assigns itself. The savage mind proceeds just
like the Western mind through the paths of understanding, and uses a
complete system of extremely varied distinctions and oppositions.

There are, however, two distinct but unhierarchized kinds of minds, distinguishable by two strategic levels. The savage mind, based on a perceptual logic and expressing itself in signs rather than in concepts, is a closed and finite system, governed by a given number of laws. Lévi-Strauss, to be sure, opposed this closed and circular system to open scientific thinking with its different relationship to nature. The savage mind belongs to a kind of thinking that binds words and things together in a relationship of redundancy. It understands the concrete world and is neither spontaneous nor confused, as was long believed. Its terrain of predilection comprised the daily activities in primitive societies, including hunting, gathering, fishing, and so on. "The richness of abstract words is not a monopoly of civilized languages."[39] Lévi-Strauss described the confusion of ethnographers when faced with the wealth of knowledge of Indian tribes and their capacity to distinguish, identify, and represent the animal and vegetable worlds in which they lived. The Hopi Indians had distinguished three hundred and fifty kinds of plants and the Navajo Indians more than five hundred. This kind of concrete mind made its classifications in a meticulously careful way so that this knowledge, organized in a complete system of prescriptions and prohibitions, could be useful for everyday life.

In *Totemism Today*, published the same year, Lévi-Strauss illustrated the central thesis of *The Savage Mind*. He showed that until then anthropologists had encountered an apparent aporia because they limited their observations about totemism to similarities between the animal or vegetable world and the human world, whereas the value of totemic classification lay in the structural homology it established between a natural and a social series. "The totemic illusion begins, first of all, by distorting the semantic field governing the same type of phenomena."[40] Totemism integrates binary oppositions and its function is to transform whatever might appear to create an obstacle to integration into something positive. Natural species are not selected because they are good to eat but because they are good to think about.[41] An osmosis exists between method and reality, a homology between human thinking and its object. Ethnographic research therefore becomes logical construction and can reach the level of anthropology—in other words, the search for the fundamental laws of the human mind.

Lévi-Strauss diverged here from Malinowski's functionalist interpretation, which only examined the naturalist, utilitarian, and affective dimensions when explaining that the deep interest that primitive societies showed for the animal and vegetable worlds comes from their primary preoccupation with food. Lévi-Strauss argued that the explanation lay at a deeper level than a simple identity mechanism, namely, the intersection of nature and culture: "Totemism postulates a logical equivalence between a society of natural species and a world of social groups."[42] Structuralism always flourishes, therefore, at the crossroads of nature and culture, upon which its project is built.

The Savage Mind was an immediate and spectacular success and helped to make the structuralist program better known beyond anthropological circles. It was so successful, in fact, that a journalist from France-Soir warned those of her readers who might be tempted to buy the book not to be misled by the reproduction on the cover of the Viola tricolor, called "wild pansy" (pensée sauvage). The lovely bouquet of flowers adorning bookstore windows might make potential readers think that the book was about botany, whereas, the journalist warned, this was really a very difficult essay. More seriously, Claude Roy considered Lévi-Strauss's book to be as important as Freud's Psychopathology of Everyday Life: "Freud brilliantly demonstrated that our madness obeys a logic that escapes the conscious mind. Claude Lévi-Strauss proposes a profound and new demonstration that shows that the apparent chaos of primitive myths and rituals in fact obeys an order and principles that until now have remained invisible."[43]

In a long article in Critique, Edmond Ortigues began by drawing an analogy between the methods of Paul Valéry and Lévi-Strauss. Both the poet and the ethnologist shared the same formal concern: "A like-minded family of minds: the same reticence with respect to history, both equally insistent about defending the sensitivity of the intellect against the intelligence of the emotions."[44] In his column in Le Monde, Jean Lacroix hailed this strictly scientific work but was somewhat skeptical of what he called "the most rigorously atheist philosophy of our time."[45] For him, this philosophy occasionally resembled a vulgar materialism that sees a reflection of the mind's liberty even in mathematical expression, that is, cellular activity in the cerebral cortex, which obeys its own laws. Le Monde gave the event considerable coverage; in addition to Jean Lacroix's article in November 1962, there was Yves Florenne's article of May 1962 and an interview with Lévi-Strauss on July 14 of the same year. Claude Mauriac reviewed the book in *Le Figaro*, and Robert Kanters enthusiastically reviewed it in *Le Figaro littéraire*, commenting judiciously that "the sciences of man today are the sources of the art of tomorrow."[46]

The structuralist community voiced its approval through Barthes's very favorable review of Lévi-Strauss's two 1962 works. Barthes applauded the substitution of a sociology of signs for a sociology of symbols, as well as the introduction of a socio-logic that was in keeping with the comprehensive semiological enterprise. Lévi-Strauss's merit was to have extended the field of human freedom to a realm that had escaped it thus far: "Claude Lévi-Strauss invites us to consider a sociology of that which is specifically human. It acknowledges that humans have the unlimited power to make things signify."[47]

Lévi-Strauss/Sartre

The Savage Mind was one of those rare moments when a book seemed to be a real irreversible event thanks to its capacity to transform our vision of the world and of others. Lévi-Strauss decided to publish his deferred attack on Sartre in this centerpiece of the structuralist program, a veritable riposte to *Critique of Dialectical Reason* that was particularly polemical. Sartre's charisma was targeted, along with the status of philosophy as the crown discipline, as well as the privileged position of the philosophy of history, and of historicism, eliminated from the structural perspective. History is nothing more than a narrative, condemned to ideography. Lévi-Strauss attacked Sartre's elevation of it as unifying and totalizing: "In Sartre's system, history plays exactly the part of a myth."[48] Experience, events, historical material all belong to myth and Lévi-Strauss could not understand why philosophers, and Sartre first among them, insisted on granting history so much importance. He viewed their fascination as something resembling the effort to restore a collective temporal continuity, in contrast to the ethnologist's method, which unfolds in spatial discontinuity.

For Lévi-Strauss, historical content was wholly illusive and mythical; since a historian chooses a given region or epoch, he can only construct local histories, without ever managing to achieve any sort of meaningful comprehensive history: "A truly total history would cancel itself out—its product would be naught."[49] Thus, no historical totality existed, but only a multiplicity of histories untied to a central subject, to man. History can only be partial or incomplete, and therefore remain partial, in the sense of being "biased."[50] This was a formal diatribe against the philosophy of history: its "alleged historical continuity is secured only by dint of fraudulent outlines."[51] History would only be the last refuge of a transcendental humanism and Lévi-Strauss invited historians to rid themselves of their vision of man as central, and even to give up history. "As we say of certain careers, history may lead to anything, provided you get out of it."[52]

Instead of history identified with humanity, Lévi-Strauss proposed the timelessness of the savage mind, which grasps the world in a renewed synchronic totality. Sartre did not directly respond to this attack, but Pierre Verstraeten analyzed Lévi-Strauss's work in *Les Temps modernes* in an article entitled "Claude Lévi-Strauss or the temptation of nothingness." Verstraeten argued that "Lévi-Strauss willingly mixes up the realms of semiology and semantics (or linguistics) by systematically applying the principles of semantics to all of semiology."[53] Lévi-Strauss proved the power of the dialectic negatively, by discerning how inane historical temporality was for him. Verstraeten therefore criticized Lévi-Strauss by taking his own idea of the imagination just as Lévi-Strauss had dubbed Sartrean philosophy as mythic. In 1962, this underlying battle between the two giants of the period led to Lévi-Strauss's triumph: the structural program took precedence over Sartre as the incarnation of historicism.

Ricoeur/Lévi-Strauss

The Savage Mind also stirred another important debate during the same period in the review *Esprit*. The editorial board immediately felt concerned and challenged by Lévi-Strauss's work and as representatives of a philosophy of the subject. *Esprit*'s director, Jean-Marie Domenach had created a philosophical group to study Lévi-Strauss's work over a period of months, in order to publish a special issue on him. There were articles by Jean Cuisenier, Nicolas Ruwet, and others, that put *The Savage Mind* into perspective, and the issue ended with a debate between Lévi-Strauss and the team that had worked on his work. Certain of Lévi-Strauss's remarks were edited out of the transcribed debate, such as this one: "My own formula is that of Royer-Collard: the brain secretes thought the way the liver secretes bile."[54] And Lévi-Strauss refused a second round of interviews or debate, which many foreign reviews repeatedly requested. Nonetheless, Jean-Marie Domenach was particularly grateful to Lévi-Strauss for having participated in this contradictory confrontation: "I appreciate his participation in this debate because I greatly admire his intellectual ability."[55]

Paul Ricoeur's article "Hermeneutics and Structuralism" clearly sketched out the two divergent positions. Ricoeur did not reject the scientificity of structuralism's work on the codes operating in languages and myths, but he did contest what he saw as a transgression of limits in the unjustified shift to generalization and systematization. For Ricoeur, the two levels needed to be clearly differentiated. The first was based on linguistic laws and formed an unconscious, nonreflective stratum, a categorical imperative that did not necessarily require reference to a conscious subject. Binary oppositions in phonology illustrated this level, as did elementary kinship structures—about which, moreover, Ricoeur acknowledged the validity of Lévi-Strauss's analyses: "The structuralist enterprise seems perfectly legitimate to me and removed from any criticism so long as it remains conscious of the conditions of its validity and therefore of its limits."[56]

With *The Savage Mind*, Lévi-Strauss generalized his enterprise, which worked as well in the tropics as it did in more temperate climes and resembled logical thinking. Yet Ricoeur contrasted totemic thinking to biblical thinking, which reversed the relationship between diachrony and synchrony. He did not suggest that subjective meaning should replace the objectivity of formalized meaning, but rather something he called the object of the hermeneutic: "Which is to say the dimensions of meaning that are opened by each of these successive returns; the question that is raised becomes the following: do all of these cultures equally offer as much to reconsider, repeat, and rethink?"[57] Ricoeur characterized the transition from structural science to structuralist philosophy as "Kantianism without a transcendental subject, indeed, an absolute formalism."[58] His hermeneutic took this stage of formal deciphering into account at the same time as it set a goal of making understanding the other coincide with self-understanding through the mediation of the interpretation of meaning, by a mind that ceaselessly thinks and rethinks itself.

Lévi-Strauss repeated and accepted the "Kantianism without a transcendental subject" in his reply to Ricoeur, but although he accepted the terms, he rejected the question of the meaning of meaning: "We cannot at the same time try to understand things from without and from within."[59] For Lévi-Strauss, the scientific phase of his work was the requisite taxonomy of societies, which meant that he could only go forward in those areas that had been sufficiently prepared.

The era of great debates had begun, and with it the question of disciplinary boundaries was raised. Caught up in the game of disciplinary confrontations, many would go from one to another and accumulate analytical tools and areas of competence; interdisciplinarity was on its way to becoming the new religion. In order to be a good structuralist, one had to be a linguist, an anthropologist, and have a bit of psychoanalysis and Marxism. The period was rich and intense; men and concepts became mobile, irrespective of boundaries and indifferent to customs agents. These were the forerunners of a structuralism that was more ideological than scientific; this malleability made it possible to acquire powerful positions and shake up the old Sorbonne. Indeed, Michel Foucault's election in November 1969 to the Collège de France, and Paul Ricoeur's defeat, can be seen as part of structuralism's propulsive force.

As the numbers of encounters and debates increased, different disciplines were forced to redefine their positions. André Green did just that for psychoanalysis when he called its practices into question on the basis of the then current opposition between history and structure.[60] Back to back, he dismissed Sartre, who denied a theoretical basis to psychoanalysis, and Lévi-Strauss, whose panlogical position led him to limit his considerations about man to his physical-chemical structure. A defender of the work of Freud, André Green demonstrated that history and structure could not be dissociated in psychoanalytic practice: "History is inconceivable outside of repetition, which itself refers to structure; structure, insofar as man is concerned, is not conceivable outside of man's relationship with his genitors, who constitute the symbolic and introduce a temporal-atemporal relationship that implies the historical dimension."[61] In this symphony of discord and friction, which produced anathemas and exclusive models, André Green's position of a well-tempered structuralism seemed like that of the sage who settles matters at a time of extreme positions when it was a question of pushing things to an extreme.

Twenty-six

Signifying Chains

The Schism

Between the schism in 1953 and his excommunication in 1963, Jacques Lacan consolidated his positions by anchoring them firmly in the flourishing structuralist paradigm. Indeed, this grounding became necessary while negotiations to affiliate the Société Française de Psychanalyse (SFP), which was finally created in 1953, with the International Psychoanalytic Association (IPA) foundered. It quickly became clear that the sine qua non of this affiliation would be the abandonment of Lacanian practice, and the pure and simple exclusion of Lacan himself, who had become the main obstacle to a general reconciliation.

Banished, Lacan gathered the faithful around and created the École Française de Psychanalyse in 1964, while another part of the SFP, led by Jean Laplanche, affiliated itself with the IPA in 1963 and became the Association Psychanalytique de France. What was true for Trotskyists was also true for psychoanalysts: the schisms and dissolutions became the yeast for the Lacanian movement. The secession of those who had been members of the SFP for ten years, in addition to being the result of the sought-after benediction of the IPA, followed a certain number of disagreements.

On the one hand, the practice of short sessions created great concern for the numbers of patients filling the waiting rooms. On the other hand, mixing individual or so-called didactic analyses with teaching also raised a certain worry about the risks of mixing the genres. "But above all, Lacan's unwillingness to give up anything having to do with his practices suddenly revealed their importance. . . . So, what in our (or my) naive eyes had appeared to be secondary was in fact the main issue."[1] A good many of Lacan's disciples would therefore go their way within other organizations.

Risk of isolation and marginalization became Lacan's major concern. Anyone who was not with him was considered to be necessarily against him. But Lacan needed to rise above things in order to give his charisma free rein. Exiled and banned, definitively excluded from his temple, Lecan identified himself quite simply with Spinoza, who had fallen victim to the same excommunication, in two stages: the *Kherem* of July 27, 1656, was the principal excommunication, followed by the *Chammata*, which forever excluded him from the Jewish community of Amsterdam.[2] In order to hone the image of the martyr, Lacan left his teaching position at Sainte-Anne Hospital.

Lacan was alone at that point, without his refuge of Colombey-les-Deux-Églises, but the author of the Rome Report returned as a hero and announced a new undertaking: on June 21, 1964, he established the École Française de Psychanalyse: "I establish, as alone as I have always been in my relationship to the psychoanalytic cause, the École Française de Psychanalyse." He obtained the protection of Fernand Braudel and Louis Althusser and created an outpost at the Sixth Section of the EPHE at the ENS. This institutional link allowed him to broaden his public considerably and, thanks to the philosophers, he found himself in an important strategic position on the intellectual playing field. Eminently aware of the absolute necessity of developing his public, he bowed to François Wahl's insistent request to publish the bulk of his writings, something he had always refused to do. Seuil began publishing in 1966.

Given Lacan's theoretical politics, he needed to find some support. Having failed with Paul Ricoeur,[3] he invited Lévi-Strauss to the opening lecture of his seminar in Dussane Hall at the ENS. Lévi-Strauss agreed to come despite very serious reservations about Lacan's style. Lacan therefore managed to transform his failure with regard to the IPA and the weakening of his movement in the wake of the split into a moment of glory symbolized by his teaching at the ENS. For five years, anyone who was anyone among with-it Parisian intellectuals rushed to see and hear the man who became the shaman of modern times. "Rejected by the international psychoanalytic movement,

Lacan's work came to have a central place in the French adventure of structuralism."4

The Signifier

The trace of structuralism in Lacan's theory of the unconscious is particularly noticeable in the role of the signifier. We have already seen that he adopted Saussure's notion of the sign in the fifties and modified the respective places of the signified and the signifier in order to valorize the latter. In his seminar on Psychoses (1955–56), Lacan made it clear that the signified was not free from the signifier but slid beneath it until it reached a point at which the patient's meaning became more clear, which he called a *point de capiton*; this is "what makes the signifier stop the otherwise indefinite slippage of signification."5 There is therefore no similarity between Saussure's and Lacan's signifier, even if the Saussurean signifier "is not only the homonym but also the eponym of the Lacanian signifier."6 Once it had become independent from the idea of the signified, the notion of the signifier took on even greater importance for Lacan at the beginning of the sixties, when the signified represented the subject for another signifier. "It was on December 6, 1961, exactly, during the seminar on Identification, that Lacan defined the signifier for the first time, by distinguishing it then and from then on quite clearly from the sign."7 It was not until 1964 and *The Four Fundamental Concepts of Psychoanalysis* that the signifier really came to occupy the place of the subject for another signifier that it kept from then on.

The signifier, then, occupied the place and site of the subject, whose existence is given as the absent cause for its effects, that is, the signifying chain by which it makes itself intelligible. The subject is not reduced to nothing, but rather to the status of nonbeing; it is the non-signifying foundation of the significance of signifiers, in other words their very condition of existence. It is the analyst's job to restore the internal logic of this signifying chain, for no one of the discrete elements can in and of itself represent meaning. A subject for another signifier, the signifier only fulfills its function by constantly being effaced in order to let another signifier take its place. Lacan represented this chain by making S become S2, which represents the signifying chain, and S1 the additional signifer that pushes it forward. The subject, however, is nowhere, or in the place of the signifier that it supplants, given that that place is to be nowhere. Transcribed as a slashed $, out of step with itself, the subject is forever split; it occupies the fourth term of the signifier's structure and is just as eccentric with respect to what is said. This object is represented as the *objet petit a* [object little o] (for other).[8]

Lacan's profound interest in the signifier is thus key and took off in the sixties as a fundamental stake in the structuralist vogue. The context revealed what Jean-David Nasio called the "umbilical" meaning of an idea, or the conditions under which an idea is born and evolves.[9] An entire dialectic developed on the basis of this signifying structure, according to a double logic of places and forces, and established the primacy of the signifier over the signified. The world became little more than a fantasy in which things are subordinate to words. Even if Lacan's definition of the signifying chain freely interpreted Saussure's ideas, it was nonetheless part of a more general structuralist conception that atomized the realms of discourse and instituted the order of things on the basis of the order of words. Only the signifier of lack holds the world together, the Thing that Lacan took from Heidegger in order to designate the quadripartite earth, sky, humans, and gods. "Thinging is the nearing of the world,"[10] but just as it did in Heidegger, the Thing "bears this fourfoldnesss because it is essentially constituted by a void."[11] The thread of the world was thus based on a central lack, which was the condition of its unity.

Objet petit a

One of the principal terms of Lacan's signifying structure is the *objet petit a*. Serge Leclaire considered this to be a major scientific discovery: "An invention worthy of the Nobel Prize, a veritable invention."[12] The innovation came in two steps. Lacan first referred to the "little other" as a mediating element between the barred subject and the Other, situated in an imaginary function. In the second stage, the little other became the *objet petit a*, as an object of lack, a metonymic object of desire, a simple signifier of desire cut off from its reference to a desiring subject and from any symbolic reference to an unconscious signifer. Lacan no longer attached the *objet petit a* to the imaginary, but to the Real as he understood the term, which does not mean reality but that which resists signification. "The Real is what is impossible."

For Lacan, this partial *objet petit a* was extremely important. He placed it at the level of the function of refuse and gave new meaning to the initial separation of the fetus, forever separated from the placenta, which is tossed into the trash bin. The libido is thus designated as a multiple chain of desires, trying in vain to substitute themselves for the initial separation. The *objet petit a* is put "in the place of the refuse of the signifying operation."[13] It has a relationship with all parts of the body that can be linked to the function of refuse, transition, or separation. *Objet petit a* as an object of desire ever reborn and always lacking became increasingly central to Lacan's thinking and came to incarnate the very object of psychoanalysis: "The object of psychoanalysis . . . is nothing other than what I have already set forth in the function that the *objet petit a* plays in it."[14] It is the object of the drive that makes the law of desire, as well as the phantasmatic object, function. "The *objet petit a* is the negative of the body."[15] Whatever its place in Lacan's framework, the *objet petit a* cannot be addressed as an isolated object, for it only exists through its articulation with the symbolic and the imaginary by way of the Real. Castration, however, determined the mode of this articulation and made it possible for desire to become manifest: "Castration is the law that organizes human desire like a partial truth,"[16] making it possible to enter into the order of the Law, linked to the Name of the Father, in other words to a figure that can be dissociated between that of the real father and the symbolic father.

In this respect, Lacan reversed Freud's vision of the Law as a prohibition: the Law was positive, the law of desire. In the early sixties, when he taught principally through lectures, Lacan favored writing, as did Jacques Derrida later, and identified the signifier with the letter (*The Purloined Letter*), completely in tune with Saussure. "The Thing becomes word, says Lacan, in the sense of motus: it is both speech and silence, which takes your breath away and overwhelms speech."[17] In analytic practice, the *objet petit a* has become a fundamental tool for certain analysts. "The *objet petit a* is useful. Analysts even say that, depending on the object, this or that drive can be deduced. It makes it possible to get desire going once again and to avoid despair."[18]

Lacan said of this *objet petit a* that it had to become the cornerstone of psychoanalysis rather the cornerstone of rejection. Even if he established the rules of a science while remaining fundamentally pessimistic about it, the object on which his science was based was synonymous with an unrecoverable loss; the *objet petit a* set the signifying chain going. So Lacan laid out the rules for investigating the signifying chain but held out no illusions about the analyst's ability to find what had been forever lost. An analysis is not just a positivist effort of memory; in place of the lost object there is an entire "construction made of signifiers, but what organizes them? The object as if it were lost."[19] For Serge Leclaire, the partial object is the necessary counterweight, by virtue of what it evokes as impermanent in order to escape the pure Signifier, to a Symbolic purged of its Imaginary dimension. This was one of Lacan's fundamental lessons and had the virtue of preventing any dogmatic closed-mindedness. "All the analysts who have really contributed something interesting have spoken about objects. Whether it be Freud, of course, or Melanie Klein, Winnicott, or Lacan."[20]

Lacan broached the question of meaning through the idea of signifying sequences. Interpretation always comes after the fact and is deferred with respect to what has been said. This temporal difference makes recourse to the *objet petit a* necessary as a substitute for detaching meaning in the relationship between the signifier and signified. We might even wonder if Derrida did not simply borrow this *objet petit a* for his notion of différance, so central to his work on deconstruction. For Lacan, the *objet petit a* became something like the means of recuperating the eliminated of the signified in the signifying chain. "It is the loss of this *objet petit a* as an object that provokes desire and as an object of desire per se that both makes the subject speak and is that about which he will speak, while always eluding him."[21] The analyst is therefore glad to be able to keep his patient's attention riveted to these *objets petit a*.

Yet even those analysts who were quite deeply affected by Lacan's teaching do not attribute the same importance to this *objet petit a*. "I don't do anything at all with the *objet petit a*."[22] André Green is clearly the most critical on this essential issue. In 1966, he published an article in *Les Cahiers pour l'analyse* on the *objet petit a* in which he clarified Lacan's perspective on it as well as that of Jacques-Alain Miller on the relationship between (*a*) and the suture, based on Frege. This was the period when Green, while still a member of the Société Psychanalytique de Paris (SPP) and of the IPA, was fascinated by Lacan's work: "The love I felt for Lacan lasted seven years."[23] André Green is the current director of the SPP and has therefore had an entirely fascinating and receptive career, given how deeply he was affected by Lacan's teaching, even though he maintained his theoretical and institutional distance. His position changed and he became increasingly critical of Lacanian positions for theoretical reasons. "As time went on, I was less and less in agreement with him, but he affected me quite profoundly."[24]

Green began going to Lacan's seminar in 1961 and was at the same time interested in Winnicott, whom he had discovered at the Edinburgh conference in July of that year. Although he was conceptually interested in the *objet petit a* at the time, today he is quite critical about this aspect of Lacan's thinking: "I don't think that psychoanalytic theory can be satisfied with a theory about partial objects. By eliminating the so-called total object, the Other capital O is once again necessary and this Other is nothing other than God."[25] Green was interested in Lacan's Augustinian sources and particularly in Saint Augustine as read by Pascal in his *Writings on Grace*, doubly infused with religion and mathematical formalism.[26] He also saw this double polarization in Lacan, who gave his spiritual forebears, and not the church, which he criticized, a chance to renew themselves. "The structural approach (the question of the *Filioque*) should come first and it alone makes it possible to have an exact idea of the function of images. Here *De Trinitate* is just like a theoretical work which we can take as a model."[27] Lacan's rereading of Freud referred to a pure Signifier that can be read through the lens of religion. In the place of Freud's castration anxiety, Lacan gave castration an ontological status derived from the Name of the Father, together with the trinitary order of the Subject—Real/Symbolic/Imaginary—giving a Christian cast to his reading. Indeed, Lacan was quite familiar with the Bible and, insofar as the Great Other is concerned, its position with respect to the drive chain remains undetermined, a pure extraterritorial Signifier, the veritable equivalent of the soul: "Lacan reverses Freud's appreciation of Goethe in *Totem and Taboo*: 'In the beginning was the action.' He admitted that he preferred a formula taken from Saint John: 'In the beginning was the language.'"[28]

Other readings are possible. Alain Juranville, for example, also recognized the figure of God in the pure Signifier, not a religious God but the God of absolute reason. However, the Thing's location outside the world as an incarnated Signifer refers back to fullness as God's *jouissance*, beyond the world's closure in Saint Augustine. Lacan's position of radical if dialectical idealism was confirmed when he posited the world as fantasy or when he referred to its unity as an initial lack or to a causal chasm. The Signifier-master was everywhere and no-where; it escaped the worldly world and at the same time could be located within it. Like God, it was only a Name, albeit an essential Name because it was the condition of being in this world insofar as castration, as a symbolic operation, must be endured. All of Lacan's efforts to decontextualize and to eliminate the organic dimension of Freudian theory and to take refuge in linguistics, and then in topology, as so many intellectual and formalizable means of approaching the question, can therefore be seen as so many secular efforts to achieve a rule, a Law made by a regular member of the clergy who had attained salvation after having blocked all the other roads that did not lead to the Big Other.

Reading Lacan this way could explain why so many Jesuits, and not the least among them Michel de Certeau or François Roustang, as well as Catholics like Françoise Dolto, joined in the Lacanian adventure. "I see in Lacan a new encounter with that whole Catholic, post-Tridentine, theological intelligence, in the sense of an awakening regarding the question of the Trinity,"[29] remarked Jean-Marie Benoist, a philosopher who shared this feeling with Philippe Sollers. Both considered that Lacan had made a post-Tridentine opening possible, that of baroque thinking. Many Christians thus followed Lacan, "believing that they were working for God, until the moment they realized that Lacan was only working for himself."[30]

This religious dimension was carefully occulted during the structuralist period when the issues were science, theory, and formalization. And yet, specialists of the history of religion attended the seminars. Bernard Sichère, for example, did not believe that Lacan was trying to give a Catholic reading of Freud, but that he was, in fact, the only one to believe that, at the risk of going mad or suffering the return of the repressed in its most fanatical and frightening forms, the religious question was unavoidable. And this at a time when the major concern was to wring the neck of Western metaphysics. "This is not to say that psychoanalysis should be religious. But to ask why one of the last important works of Freud was, precisely, *Moses and Monotheism*."[31] On this point, both Freud and Lacan attributed to religion a centuries-old function of effectively mediating between forbidden sexual reality, and they wondered whether this discourse had the same place in contemporary society. Yet, Lacan confronted a total symbolic where nothing had replaced the mediating role of religion. Neither a political discourse nor a scientific discourse can replace the dominant fictions that organize social life, and Lacan therefore assigned this role to psychoanalysis, this lucid placeholder, "ideally, because psychoanalysis cannot be a religion."[32]

Affect

The signifying chain effectively eliminated the insignificant dimension of affect. This was another of the points on which André Green criticized Lacan. In 1960, at Bonneval, he heard Jean Laplanche and Serge Leclaire on the unconscious and he shared Laplanche's reservations about the linguistic conception of the unconscious. At the same time, and with respect to affect, Lacan announced at Royaumont that "in the Freudian field, in spite of the words themselves, consciousness is a feature as inadequate to ground the unconscious in its negation (that unconscious dates from Saint Thomas) as the affect is unsuited to play the role of the protopathic subject, since it is a service that has no holder."[33] So Jean-Bernard Pontalis asked André Green to write on affect for *Les Temps modernes*; his article was published in 1961. Green took up the question more broadly in a work published in 1970:[34] "For me, Lacan gives an anti-Freudian version of the unconscious."[35]

For André Green, the richness of Freudian theory was based on the heterogeneity of the signifier. Freud did not consider the signifier to be an array of internally homogeneous, interchangeable terms such as one finds in language, but a series of levels of different materials. Green insisted on distinguishing, as Freud did, between the material of the psychic representations of drives (endosomatic stimulation) and the preconscious (the representation of things with the representation of words that corresponds to them). The clearly distinct levels may not always translate from one to the other. "The proof is that there are psychosomatic problems that do not have representations."[36] And yet, according to Green, with Lacan we return to a Platonic conception linking things to a linguistic essence. Where Freud saw heterogeneity, Lacan saw homogeneity and went so far as to introduce intellectuals to a clean unconscious. However, according to Green, the analyst's work is to account for complexity. Eliminating affect in favor of a purified Signifier explains why Saussure was considered to be the dawn of modern consciousness on this point. In order to establish the scientificity of linguistics, Saussure was also obliged to eliminate the referent, speech, the individual, and the diachrony. There was a price to be paid for the birth of modern linguistics; making the meaning of language less vital was the parallel to be drawn with Lacanian psychoanalysis. Lacan used the Saussurean rift to negate affect and to leave on the sidelines other possible linguistic sources that took affect more into account: Saussure's disciple Charles Bally, for example.[37]

In structural linguistics as in Lacanian psychoanalysis, affect was forced to the sidelines by an ever-increasing formalism. A sense of mastery could be maintained as long as the field was limited and homogeneous. And yet, "affect is something over which we really have no control; it is evanescent, diffuse, slippery, full of disorder and noise. That is why it seems fundamental to me."[38] In his *Studies on Hysteria*, Freud emphasized the need to get to the affective origin of traumatic memories. Serge Viderman used the metaphor of the crystal ball so dear to the structuralists and considered psychoanalysis to be closer to the smoke than to the crystal ball. Negating affect, the barred *objet petit a* could simply be the result of an essential aspect of analysis that Lacan needed to use but that he also wanted to guard against, even going so far as to repress it: transference.

Lacan was so concerned with formalizing and purifying the analytic situation that he reduced transference as much as he could, for it created the most aberrant sentiments, and difficult to rationalize. He banished the term "countertransference" by placing it in the category of the analyst's desire. "He refused to let us talk about or use the term."[39] Freud's relative laconism on the subject became a pretext that made it easier for Lacan to purge the term. Was it also in order to guard against his personal tendencies toward an overflowing affectivity, working out his theoretical justification after the fact in order to contain his own affective drives? But although transference was to be contained in an analysis, Lacan recommended it in the teaching of psychoanalysis. The first yearbook of the École Freudienne made it quite clear that teaching psychoanalysis succeeded only when transference operated. But it changed at this point to become a vector of knowledge free of all sentiments, referring back to "the subject who is supposed to know." The Lacanian subject was disincarnated, and the familiar structuralist theme of the negated individual once again made its presence felt. "The Lacanian operation is double, which is to say perfectly contradictory. On the one hand, it has to maintain subjectivity, . . . and on the other, to empty this subjectivity of all incarnation, humanization, affectivity, and so on, in order to turn it into a mathematical object."[40]

Jean Clavreul believed André Green's criticism of affect to be unfounded. Of course, Lacan always refused to take any pleasure in the delights of intersubjectivity where one hates or loves oneself, but this did not mean that he was indifferent to affect, since he never stopped speaking about love, hate, and love-hate, and he even devoted an entire seminar to anxiety. "But what Lacan showed us was this kind of dependency of affect with respect to the game of signifiers."[41]

Serge Leclaire also remained unconvinced by André Green's critique of Lacan for eliminating affect, which he found too imprecise and to which he preferred the idea of economy or of drive-inspired movement: "I remember a debate with Green in which I had proposed some other formulations, saying that one is affected to a job or receives ones affectation, but to make it a cornerstone, no."[42]

And yet, Lacan used affect in the transference that he promoted among his disciples. He did not hesitate to mix genres in this context, for whatever he learned through a personal analysis was immediately reinjected into the organizational circuit of power and knowledge in the name of the imperative of didactic transmission. Reacting against this tendency, "the French Psychoanalytic Association is the only association in the world in which there are no didacts, in which analysis is considered a personal issue."[43]

The key institutions Lacan created were interesting for the way they lent dynamism to analytic know-how, rather than letting it sluggishly coagulate into a dogma. Analytic work became a source of renewal and debate. The conventions of transmission, supervision, and multiplication of cartels were so many tools and points of observation. "I have said of la passe [transmission] that it was a site for observing the transferential situation."[44] There were two types of cartels: work groups with at least three and no more than five people, with either an additional person (the "extra one") or the "plus one," so that each of the individuals in turn became the "plus one" onto which the transference was made without the presence of any additional person. Above all, this made it possible to pursue unfinished analytic work and to sweep away illusions, but the unconscious returned in another swing of the pendulum. For Claude Dumézil, Lacan pointed out a difficult path, the only possible one, which required that the toys used along the way be destroyed; but this was the only way to keep the possibilities of analytic research open.

Twenty-seven

Mythology's Earth Is Round

Lacan placed the signifying chain at the level of the unconscious; Lévi-Strauss situated it in the constant reutilization of myths. This recycling made it possible to understand the meaning of mythology through the matrix whose transformations resemble the unconscious operations of condensation and displacement. Lévi-Strauss saw mythic structure as the product of a veritable syntax of transformations. In the tetralogy he devoted to myths, *Mythologiques*, he pursued his argument, which diverges from the dominant symbolist theory of the early twentieth century, symbolist theory, which viewed the mythic story as an object cut off from its environment and which tried to root out the occult meaning of each term of the mythic tale. Lévi-Strauss also tried to get beyond functionalism, and particularly Malinowski, who tried to take account of the social function of myths in their specific context. Instead, he integrated the study of myths into a symbolic system, but emphasized the idea of system, structure, and construction by cutting the myth into minimal units, which he called *mythemes*, and which he arranged into paradigms. He essentially attempted to decode mythic discourse internally and, unlike the functionalists, he studied each myth independently of the conditions of its communication and function. By studying the full range of myths, he hoped to find their common structure.

Myths must be understood by juxtaposing their differences and variations, an approach that would be consonant with Vladimir

Propp's 1928 suggestions. Comparing mythic analysis to Penelope's labors, Lévi-Strauss intimated that the work of decoding was infinite, whereas the conclusions to be drawn were relative: "As happens in the case of the optical microscope which cannot reveal the ultimate structure of matter to the observer, we can only choose between various degrees of enlargement."[1]

The Myth as a Mode of Derealization

Lévi-Strauss did not believe that myths were the best material for working out a comparison between infrastructure and the unconscious psyche, but that they could provide a key to the constants of the human mind since they, more than any other object, escaped external determinism and social constraints. Seen this way, myths, even more than kinship structures, provided a propitious terrain for study and were a better means of reaching the structures of the human mind: "They make it possible to discover certain operational modes of the human mind which have remained so constant over the centuries and are so widespread over immense geographical distances, that we can assume them to be fundamental."[2] Their meaning would be the product of a signifying chain, and, in the manner of Lacan's concept of the unconscious, the signified, while not excluded, slips beneath this chain. The environment was not really negated in this signifying system, but could play a local role in the communication of the mythological message, and which operated internally in its resistance to reality: "The syntax of mythology is absolutely free within the confines of its own rules. It is inevitably affected by the geographical and technological substructure."[3] Beyond the diversity of the societies that spawned them, myths could be taken as a group, a mode of derealization, an uninterrupted flow of representations to be examined in their internal variations, "in the author's fascination with myths which, in the last resort, all say the same thing."[4] They referred to a double unity: unity of the system in which they were integrated and unity of the message to which they referred, expressed by the relationship of the message to itself and to another message, thereby doubling the emphasis.

Myth's Signifying Chain

Lévi-Strauss started working on Amerindian mythologies relatively early on. In 1951, he began teaching in the Fifth Section, where the theme was religious sciences, at the École Pratique des Hautes Études

(EPHE) and his first seminar was entitled the Visit of Souls. "My ideas on mythology took shape at the École [Pratique] des Hautes Études."[5] In his 1955 article "The structural study of myths,"[6] he laid out the methodological principles according to which the constituent units of myth are not isolated relations but bundles of relations whose combination produces meaning: "We have reorganized our myth according to a time referent of a new nature . . . a two-dimensional time referent which is simultaneously diachronic and synchronic."[7]

Anthropology was no longer to seek an ultimate meaning or the essence of myth in an invariant, but should define each myth by the accumulation of its versions as constituent parts of the signifying chain that alone is capable of substituting a beginning of interpretative order to initial chaos. Repetition revealed the myth's structure and was a function of one or many codes disclosing the mythic substance of the message.

The Savage Mind, published in 1962, was a prelude or general introduction to the later tetralogy. In this early work, Lévi-Strauss presented the mythic mind as being as structured as the scientific mind and every bit as able to think in terms of analogies and generalizations. He attacked Jung's theory of archetypes and the notion of the collective unconscious, and laid out his own ambition of sketching the construction of a "theory of superstructures,"[8] based on juxtaposing many explanatory systems and on reintroducing the individual myth, as a single element in a process of general transformation, into the signifying chain of other myths. One element was therefore substituted for another in the signifying mythological chain and internal shifts within the mythic system became necessary. In this way, he adopted the binary oppositions between marked or unmarked terms, a notion borrowed from phonology, and above all the notion that meaning results from position, so many analytic tools borrowed from linguistics and applied to myth. More than ever, linguistics became the heuristic model.

The anthropologist's work, therefore, must consist in "organizing all the known variants of a myth into a set."[9] Repetition acquired a special status since it was essential for revealing the very structure of the myth in its synchronic and diachronic dimension. "Mythical thought is therefore a kind of intellectual *bricolage*,"[10] continually recuperating the debris of events. Lévi-Strauss attacked the quest for ultimate origins because he considered the object of the analysis to be to define each individual myth by the ensemble of its versions. He therefore opened up a limitless and indefinite quest for the primitive mind, whose lively imagination organized material in new ways, inverting or substituting ideas integrated into increasingly complex combinations.

Social reality, however, dropped out of the anthropologist's purview in this game of slipping beneath the signifying chain in which distinctive oppositions take their place within the structure and establish the structurality of the signifying chain. References to the ecosystem or to social organization only made sense once they were integrated into the signifying chain, which, by definition, was constructed at a remove from referential reality, which is always held at some distance.

Saussure had excluded the subject, similarly eliminated from this scientific perspective. "The subject is an epistemological obstacle"[11] for Lévi-Strauss. There was no place for a "cogito"—"Myths are anonymous"[12]—and Lévi-Strauss pursued his enterprise of decentering a subject dominated by the mythological universe that speaks in him but unbeknownst to him. Man is only a pertinent level of analysis insofar as he reveals the organic constraints inherent in his mode of thought: "The problem therefore is to define and categorize these *enceintes mentales*."[13] Although he addressed other objects of study, Lévi-Strauss had in fact pursued the same goals since his work on kinship. His oeuvre was coherent, straddling the borderline between nature and culture and bent on establishing the natural bases of culture (and making it possible to transform anthropology into a science of nature freed from the reins of a philosophy that, at each step along the way, was being repudiated and treated as an object of derision and of repeated polemics).

The Myth of Reference

Having established the bases of his method, Lévi-Strauss really began his study of the vast field of Amerindian myths in 1964, with *The Raw and the Cooked*. He opened with the Bird-nester's aria, a myth of the Bororo of central Brazil, which became his myth of reference and the basis for the study of 187 myths belonging to about twenty tribes, which together constituted a series that answered the question of the origin of cooked food, of cuisine.

A son, guilty of incest with his mother, is sent by his father to confront the souls of the dead. The son accomplishes his task with the help of a good grandmother and various animals. Furious that his plans had been foiled, the father invites his son to come with him to capture the macaws that nest on the face of a cliff. The two men arrive at the foot of the rock; the father erects a long pole and orders his son to climb it. When the son had barely reached the place where the nests were perched, the father knocked the pole down, leaving his son to the vultures. The birds devour the son's buttocks, after which they save him. Once back in the village, the son takes revenge by transforming himself into a stag and rushing at the father so furiously that he impales him on his antlers. He then gallops toward a lake and drops his victim into it; all that remains of the gruesome feast are the bare bones at the bottom of the lake and the lungs, which float to the surface in the form of aquatic plants. The son also takes revenge on his father's wives, including his own mother.

Decoding: Culinary Mediation

Lévi-Strauss's method resembled Freud's interpretation of dreams, isolating each sequence of the myth and comparing it to other sequences in other myths. And yet, an anthropologist's questions differ fundamentally from those of an analyst: the interpretation focused less on the son's incest than on the oppositions between sensorial qualities, based on their binary organization. The Bororo were apparently not interested in guilty incest in this myth or in the veritable guilty party or the perpetrator of the incest, who appears as the hero of the myth; they were interested in the father who wanted to take revenge on his son and who was mortally punished. The object of the myth, according to Lévi-Strauss, lay not in what it recounted explicitly but in the explanation of the origin of cooked food—even though this theme was apparently missing—because cooking is the mediating operation par excellence between heaven and earth and between nature and culture. Myths about the origins of fire bespeak a double binary opposition between the raw and the cooked and between the pristine and the corrupted. The link between raw and cooked has to do with culture, whereas the link between the raw and the rotten has to do with nature. Fire is an essential mediator for the beginning of cooking and works in two ways. It unites sun and earth and saves man from what is rotten, but it also eliminates the risks of a situation that would lead to a burned world. The basic rule of Lévi-Straussian interpretation was to focus on the myth's internal organization and to arrive at paradigmatic sets based on different mythemes. In order to reveal the meaning of this myth of reference, a deeper rationality had to be brought to bear, drawn from the search for permuting sets, articulations of sign systems manifested in a long mythic series; whence the long comparative quest to establish a meaningful series.

Taking as starting points observable, empirical categories such as the cooked, the raw, the humid, the rotten, and the burned, Lévi-Strauss restored conceptual tools and abstract ideas, behind his ethnographic observations, which elucidated the way primitive societies think. Although he took ethnographic observation quite seriously, Lévi-Strauss nonetheless considered theory to be most important. Discernible qualities of mythic discourse have a logical existence that reiterates the five senses in five fundamental codes. The mythic mind was structured like a language in a way that recalled Lacan's definition of the unconscious: "By taking its raw material from nature, mythic thought proceeds in the same way as language which chooses phonemes from among the natural sounds."[14]

The Infra- and the Supraculinary

In *From Honey to Ashes*, the second volume of his *Mythologiques*, Lévi-Strauss moved from the oppositions between material qualities to oppositions between full and empty, container and contained, internal and external. The analysis became more complex as the less obvious myths were discussed, for while they said the same thing, they meandered and took more detours on their way to saying it. These myths reflected a new dimension of a culture's transition to society: from the paleolithic economy to a neolithic economy, from the hunter-gatherer society to an agrarian society. Lévi-Strauss explored the same realm of cooking with honey and tobacco, but in a roundabout way, for they appear, "each in their different ways, culinary paradoxes."[15] The Indians considered honey to be a ready-made food, a given of nature, making it a natural infraculinary object. The symbol of a descent toward nature, honey could be good but it could also be poisonous. Ambiguous, therefore, it engendered risks illustrated by the "girl who was crazy about honey" myth with its reference to the seduction of the natural order over human culture and the danger of its dissolution in the natural order. Unlike honey, tobacco is a supraculinary product, whose function is to restore the relationship between the natural and cultural orders that honey can undo. As the smoke rises sinuously, tobacco restores what honey undid by rising toward culture. Lévi-

Strauss made a second shift in his distinction between a symbolic level of immediately obvious images and a new category of the imagination that came into play and required an image that symbolism did not offer: "We see all the important mythic scenes backwards, a little as if we had to decipher the subject of a tapestry from the interwoven threads which we see on the back."[16]

Human life had to find its precarious balance somewhere between the two perils of a natureless culture and a cultureless nature, each of which posed the threat of famine. Setting the nature/culture relationship, initially considered as a fact and then as the order of things in *The Elementary Structures of Kinship*, into a dialectical relationship was here perceived as a myth culture needed in order to create itself with and against nature. "I have changed rather a lot since then through the influence of the progress made in animal psychology and the tendency to make ideas of a cultural nature intervene in the sciences of nature."[17] The nature/culture opposition shifted; from an immanent property of reality, it became an antinomy belonging to the human mind. "Opposition is not objective; it is men who need to formulate it."[18] The ethnographic context was no more than a frame, the beginning of a reflection that had to free itself from the popular customs, beliefs, and rituals whence myth arises, in order to reach a higher level of abstraction so that "the context of each myth consists more and more of other myths."[19] Honey and tobacco, unlike the static ideas of the raw and the cooked, represent dynamic imbalances: they are temporal rather than spatial oppositions.

The Culinary Moral

With his third volume, *The Origin of Table Manners*, Lévi-Strauss cast his net more widely than the geographical zone that until then had been limited to South America; he now included North American Indians in an even more complex comparative study of myths that studied the opposition between the different ways according to which the terms were used, whether together or separately. Culinary mediation continued to be the general focus, but in this volume morality made its appearance as a new and central object. After the material and formal levels, this was the third level involved in describing what was now a logic of propositions.

The ordered world is also a threatened world; it suffices to displace the boundaries or transgress the safe distances. Every infraction can create disturbances in any universe, be it natural or cultural; appropriate customs therefore play a regulatory role. Lévi-Strauss contrasted the ethics of the West, where individuals respect hygiene in order to protect themselves, and the ethic of societies called primitive, where hygiene is respected so that others are not victims of one's own impurity. The "savage," unlike the "civilized man," shows a greater humility toward the order of the world. After the origins of cooking and its derivations, therefore, Lévi-Strauss addressed the different ways of preparing and eating dishes. Each stage along the way illustrates the fact that "culture is not defined as a realm but as an operation, one that makes of Nature a veritable universe. . . . This operation is a mediation that is both separated and united."[20] Nature was therefore constantly acculturated and culture, conversely, naturalized; mythic thinking operated in both directions in this instance.

The Tetralogy

The Naked Man came out in 1971, the fourth and last volume of the remarkable tetralogy and the end of a seven-year-long effort. The press applauded the event. *Le Monde* published a complete dossier including an interview with Lévi-Strauss by Raymond Bellour, articles by Hélène Cixous ("Le regard d'un écrivain"), by historians Marcel Détienne and Jean-Pierre Vernant ("Eurydice, la femme-abeille"), and by the linguist-musicologist Nicolas Ruwet ("Qui a hérité?"), as well as an article by Catherine Backès-Clément.

Even television viewers could watch what *Le Figaro* called a "serious Sunday": Lévi-Strauss was the guest speaker. He decided to show off the Laboratory of Social Anthropology he had created, showing viewers bits of the fieldwork of François Zonabend, Pierre Clastres, Maurice Godelier, and Françoise Izard. *The Naked Man* as well as the entire *Mythologiques* were unanimously hailed, and Lévi-Strauss thus joined Wagner in the register of the social sciences.

The fourth volume at first seemed out of joint with the first three, for it was no longer a question of cooking or of culinary metaphors. But in fact the four volumes were linked by a profound unity, and it was clear for Lévi-Strauss from the outset that if the first term of the *Mythologiques* was *raw*, the last would be *nude*, for at the end of this mythological journey, he found the equivalent of the Bororo myth of reference. Moreover, "if the transition from nature to culture, for the Indians of tropical America, is symbolized by the transition from the raw to the cooked, for the Indians of North America, this transition is symbolized by the invention of clothing, ornaments, costumes, and, beyond all this, by the invention of commercial exchanges."[21] The South American hero reduced to the state of nature—or to the state of rawness—had his parallel in the North American hero reduced to the state of nudity.

The Naked Man revisited the determinisms of the economic infrastructure and the tetralogy reached its apex: "This rounds off my analyses of a vast system, the invariant elements of which can consistently be represented in the form of a conflict between the earth and the sky for the possession of fire."[22] The decisive and founding element was therefore a mortal hero's capture of fire from the heavens, willingly or not. The earth oven appears as effectuating the double conquest of fire and of earth by the culinary art of cooking. A veritable pivot of these mythic tales, the earth oven plays the role of a formal pattern. "Consequently, at this stage, the image of the earth oven as a supreme manifestation of culinary art . . . marks the transition from the state of nature to the constitution of society."[23]

In the finale of The Naked Man, which was like a contrapuntal response to the overture of the first volume, Lévi-Strauss reminded the reader of the methodological necessity of effacing the subject in order to reach mythic structure. And, by attacking the subject, he once again took up the polemic he had never really ceased waging against the pretensions of philosophic discourse. Lévi-Strauss answered those critics who accused him of dessicating and impoverishing the human universe with his formal reductions of messages shaped by the societies he studied:

> However, for too long now philosophy has succeeded in locking the social sciences inside a closed circle by not allowing them to envisage any other object of study for the consciousness than consciousness itself. . . . what structuralism tries to accomplish in the wake of Rousseau, Marx, Durkheim, Saussure and Freud, is to reveal to consciousness an object other than itself; and therefore, to put it in the same position with regard to human phenomena as that of the natural and physical sciences, and which, as they have demonstrated, alone allows knowledge to develop.[24]

This criticism also sought to achieve the status of a natural science able to discern the conditions governing the operations of the human mind through anthropology, among other things. The internal tension between nature and culture was reiterated in Lévi-Strauss's own discourse, between his own ambition to read the intangible laws of the neuronal nature of the human brain and his undying desire to be a creator who had chosen the social sciences as a realm of study in which to create something artistic.

This tension is palpable in the very composition of *Mythologiques*, conceived on the basis of Wagner's tetralogy.[25] *The Raw and the Cooked* dealt with the origins of cooking and once again repeated the theme of the genesis of the world, of the Law, and of *Das Rheingold*. *The Origin of Table Manners* corresponded to *Die Walküre* in its treatment of kinship and of incest and how to avoid it. *From Honey to Ashes* corresponded to *Siegfried* as an acculturation of savagery. *The Naked Man*, of course, corresponded to *Die Götterdämmerung*, a return to origins after the disappearance of the system constructed to reach the finale. The musical analogy is present from the definition of the project to study myths in "La structure des mythes," where Lévi-Strauss compared the mythological object to a musical score that should be read vertically and horizontally. *The Raw and the Cooked* was dedicated to music and took the figure of a fugue. The musical reference was even more explicit in *The Naked Man*: "I have tried to construct with meanings a composition comparable to those that music creates with sounds."[26]

Music and mythology in Lévi-Strauss mirrored one other, from the invention of the fugue whose composition was reflected in the myth. "With the death of myth, music becomes mythical in the same way as works of art."[27] And yet, the scientific if not scientistic perspective of the program of structural anthropology was constantly repeated with greater optimism about its powers of analysis: "structuralism offers the social sciences an epistemological model incomparably more powerful than those they previously had at their disposal."[28] Philosophy was the obvious target for it had always given priority to the subject, "that unbearably spoilt child who has occupied the philosophical scene for too long now."[29]

Naturalist Structuralism

If Lévi-Strauss rediscovered man, it was as human nature. In *The Naked Man*, he used his research on vision and on the cerebral cortex, which demonstrated that the data of perception are repeated as binary oppositions. Binarism, therefore, became not simply an external logi-

cal apparatus slapped on reality, but a reproduction of corporal operations, "and if it constitutes an immediate property of our nervous
and cerebral organization, we should not be surprised that it also supplies the best common denominator for making human experiences
coincide that might seem superficially to be utterly different."[30]

Lévi-Strauss hoped to awaken on Judgment Day to find himself
among the natural sciences. But the price for such an accession would
be the elimination of all narrative content from the signifying chain of
myths and, like phonemes, the reduction of mythemes to oppositional
values. Scientific conquest would then be based on compatability or
incompatability but it led Lévi-Strauss to a "logical formalism"[31] that
contributed to setting mythemes into relationship with each other
within a myth. Formalism established the syntagmatic link and the su-
perposition of mythemes taken from different myths, which constitute
paradigmatic groups. The mind reiterated nature because it was nature; their complete isomorphism blurred the traditional lines of demarcation between these two orders of reality. In this respect, we can
talk about Lévi-Strauss's radical materialism. Indeed, he remarked
that if he were asked about the signifier to which the signifying chains
ultimately lead, "the only reply to emerge from this study is that
myths signify the mind that evolves them by making use of the world
of which it is itself a part."[32]

Causality was clearly at work in these mythological links, but it
was neuronal and implied, by definition, that the semantic content of
mythological propositions be kept at a complete distance from their
social referent. Not that this referent was absent from *Mythologiques*,
of course, because these volumes include all the available ethnographic information that Lévi-Strauss had, but it was only as pertinent as a simple decor, the basic material that was used without
determining the mode of thinking. Because the logical constraints
governing mythic utterance could only be seized at the grammatical
level, this was the only pertinent level for mythic necessity, and the
only possible means of reaching the *enceintes mentales*. Through the
symptom that it represented, grammar revealed that which it avoided
saying. A myth's truth consists "in logical relations which are devoid
of content or, more precisely, whose invariant properties exhaust
their operative value."[33] Lévi-Strauss could thus avoid the specular
relationship between social reality and myths. He escaped—and he
was right to do so—the mechanisms of reflective thought; but he re-

placed them with an internal mythological logic obeying only neuronal constraints.

The necessary autonomy of culture from society was pushed to
the limits of its logic, until it became entirely independent. The phonological model became the theoretical basis for extracting social content, for favoring the code over the message. "The proposition according to which the elements that form the myth lack independent
meaning follows from the application of phonological methods to
myths. In fact, the absence of meaning is a characteristic of phonemes."[34] His analogy between mythology and music lent support to
Lévi-Strauss's ambition to have a theory that is constructed, detached
from an object. The result was a fascinating monument—Lévi-
Strauss's work itself—but its cost was the loss or abandonment of the
principles of any hermeneutic perspective. Logical reductionism required eliminating affect from the signifying chain, just as it had for
Lacan. Thus, the sexuality of Amerindian societies was put to everything except sensual ends. It answered a "dialectic of opening and
shutting,"[35] and therefore opened onto a desexualized world where
sexuality was everywhere. The parallels between Lévi-Strauss's and
Lacan's structural procedures were once again clear, and made patent
by Lacan's similar affirmation that "sexual relationships do not
exist." The subject was negated, an insubstantial site, delivered up to
the anonymous thinking unfolding within it. This mind could be better understood so long as the subject "dissolve, like a spider, in the
threads of its structural web."[36]

A Machine That Abolishes Time

History is the other important omission in the *Mythologiques*. Lévi-
Strauss saw a particular relationship between myths and temporality.
Mythology and music, "indeed, are instruments for the obliteration of
time."[37] The object Lévi-Strauss chose to use in his polemical demonstration with philosophers was designed to unseat the priority, which
he considered exorbitant, that they gave to historicity. And yet history
was not absent much and we have already seen that Lévi-Strauss criticized functionalism for ignoring it, but it belonged to the realm of
contingency.

History's place was "the place that rightfully belongs to that irreducible contingency. . . . To be valid, any investigation which is entirely aimed at elucidating structures must begin by submitting to the

powerful inanity of events."[38] *Clio* was repressed, the first step in a scientific procedure; the dichotomies Lévi-Strauss established between necessity and contingency, nature and culture, form and content, all align structure and science, the event and contingency. Relegating historicity in this way did not belong to cold societies alone: Lévi-Strauss saw the "Greek miracle" (the transition from mythic to philosophical thinking) as a simple historical occurrence that meant nothing more than that it happened there and could just as well have taken place elsewhere since no necessity made it inevitable. At the end of his mythological adventure, Lévi-Strauss radicalized his position. The temporal order that myths reveal was not only time rediscovered, like some Proustian experience, it was "abolished."[39] "If taken to its logical conclusion, the analysis of myths reaches a point where history cancels itself out."[40]

We once again find that importance ascribed to presence that so characterized the structural paradigm, but this is a present that stretches out and dissolving past and future in a temporality nailed to the ground, static, a mind that refutes historical teleology as much as the idea of fleeing time in a reconciled present. Lévi-Strauss borrowed this idea of "man liberated from the temporal order" from Marcel Proust.[41] Both this liberation and refutation of history led him to the point of "reinstalling a philosophy of presence."[42] This presence was nothing other than the presence of nature that had forced out history, presence of the mind and of the universal genotypes that functioned like a binary machine; all of this a reinstatement in the living and present material of the human mind.

The Dusk of Men

The end of history sounds a crepuscular note in the finale of *The Naked Man.* At the culmination of this great work elucidating the mythological universe, the reader perceives the historical pessimism that, from the beginning of the undertaking, has inhabited Lévi-Strauss. Everything that had been so intelligently studied becomes nothing more than the ephemeral flowering of a world fated to meet its end, its ineluctable death. *Mythologiques* ends with the dusk of men, and echoes Wagner. These myths let the complex edifice appear as it "slowly expands to its full extent, then crumbles and fades away in the distance, as if it had never existed."[43]

Time unfolds in the very logic of its disappearance, inscribing its own abolition in a dusky setting. Lévi-Strauss realizes his initial conception of an anthropology as entropy: "The lyrism of death is the most beautiful, but also the most fearsome."[44] Having been revealed to itself at the price of a very complex conceptual unfolding, structure has no message to communicate to us other than that we must die: "This gigantic effort has therefore met its vain limits: it opens on NOTHING, which is the last word, and not accidentally so, of this sumptuous 'finale.'"[45] The polemic with philosophers, and with Sartre in particular, and the teasing and distant tone Lévi-Strauss sounded with respect to philosophy in general, should not, however, lead us to imagine that philosophy was absent in him.

Lévi-Strauss never stopped thinking of structuralism not only as a scientific method or a new sensibility that occasionally finds echoes in literary, pictorial, and musical creation, but also as a philosophy of the end of history, henceforth foreclosed. According to Jean-Marie Domenach, Lévi-Strauss "contributes to the destruction by killing, with his knowledge, this cultural vivacity, life, and vigor. The murderous side of this philosophy is atrocious. . . . Rather than finishing with hope or a renaissance, he ends by what I had called a requiem or a *de profundis*. The only thing that remains is to let writing sink into entropy."[46]

A sign of the degradation of the ideologies that inspired it, structuralism was the outline of a totalizing ideology in the making, an expression of synthetic thinking as well as its destruction in a vertiginous and deathly spiral.

Twenty-eight

Africa: The Continental Divide
of Structuralism

Lévi-Strauss, and numerous anthropologists after him, traveled all over the American continent using the structural grid in order to better grasp the unconscious dimension of the social practices of native populations. Those who turned their sights toward Africa held the structural paradigm at a greater distance because it did not adequately describe societies that had been colonized. Not only did researchers need to work on populations larger than those small Indian communities that had escaped genocide, but the interweaving of beliefs and local customs together with colonial institutions also led to phenomena of acculturation that made it rather difficult to reduce African social organization to binary oppositions; geographically, the area to which the structural paradigm could be applied was therefore rather limited. But there were structuralist Africanist anthropologists, and at the risk of being quite reductive, we might imagine a binary opposition between Lévi-Straussian Americanists and Africanist disciples of Georges Balandier.

Georges Balandier: Africanism

Georges Balandier trained a whole generation of ethnologists as Africanists. He had been trained in ethnology by Michel Leiris, who became his model, and belonged to the small circle of sociologists including Jean Duvignaud and Roger Bastide who met on the rue Vaneau at Georges Gurvitch's place. Balandier's conception of doing sociology in black Africa was informed by his militant anticolonialism and his work quite naturally addressed the political dimension of life. A victim of structuralism, Balandier paid quite dearly for his criticism of the dominant paradigm of the sixties. "I paid for it at the Collège de France. Claude Lévi-Strauss did all he could to find candidates who were the equivalent of what I could propose."[1]

And yet, Balandier and Lévi-Strauss had been close friends for six or seven years, until Lévi-Strauss was elected to the Collège de France. Despite their different methodologies and fields, they had had common activities. Both were involved, for example, in the International Council for Social Sciences, affiliated with UNESCO after 1954, and of which Lévi-Strauss was secretary-general and Georges Balandier the head of a research office. Their falling out was apparently due to a bad pun that reached Lévi-Strauss and for which he was unforgiving. "Everything degenerated because of a trivial incident, a sort of gossipy story."[2] What should not have been an definitive rupture took on the tone of a polemic as early as 1962 with a vigorous critique of Georges Balandier's inconsistency in the organization of his propositions.[3] The rift was never repaired; beyond the peripeteias and the ruffling of sensibilities, it symbolized two divergent points of view.

Georges Balandier was, in fact, deeply marked by postwar existentialism. A member of the Resistance during the Second World War, he had been associated with Michel Leiris and the Musée de l'Homme, and Leiris had introduced him to Sartre's entourage at *Les Temps modernes*. Balandier was not involved, however, in the great postwar debates because he left to do anthropology in black Africa in 1946. In Dakar, he became the editor in chief of *Présence africaine* and actively participated in decolonialization in Africa, during which he became "an active agent close to certain African leaders."[4]

What struck Balandier first when he went to Africa was poverty. He quickly looked to politics as a means of emancipation and came to believe that politics took precedence; he diverged from the structuralists. Balandier participated in history in the making and saw Léopold Sédar Senghor, Sékou Touré, Houphouët-Boigny, and Nkrumah practically on a daily basis. He discovered the figure of the other, of alterity, and of negritude as a culture that was different and was to be recognized as such, but at the same time, he immediately felt that he was participating in a moment in history that was coming to a boil not only because of growing hostility to the colonial framework and the desire for political emancipation, but also because of the historical demand of these peoples aspiring to reestablish links with their own precolonial history.

Africa was changing profoundly. Since the Bandung Conference on Asian and African nonalliance, the continent was rising up and the confrontations were increasing even as populations were growing poorer and shantytowns were spreading. Parties and unions were emerging in a world that until then had been organized by clans. The society Georges Balandier was discovering was therefore the very opposite of a society frozen in time: "I can in no way accept the idea that in these societies myth shapes everything and history is absent, in the name of a notion in which everything is a system of relations and codes, with a logic of possible permutations that enables the society to maintain an equilibrium."[5] To the contrary, Balandier discovered the movement and productivity of chaos, the indissociability of synchrony and diachrony. "I am learning that societies are not produced, they produce themselves; none escapes history even if history is made differently and even if there are multiple histories."[6]

Once he was back in France, Balandier joined the Sixth Section of the EPHE, where, in 1954, he set up a program on sociological studies in black Africa. He also became a member of the cabinet of the secretary of state, Henri Longchambon, in Mendès-France's government, where he was responsible for the social sciences. In 1961, Jean Hyppolite asked him to teach a seminar at the École Normale Supérieure at the rue d'Ulm, which he did until 1966. "Everything was bathing in structuralism, which had borne many things along with it in its course."[7] It was in this sanctuary of triumphant structuralism during the sixties that Balandier successfully attracted some geographers, historians, philosophers, and students of literature to anthropology, among them Jean-Noël Jeanneney, Régis Debray, Emmanuel Terray, and Marc Augé.

A whole generation that had protested against the Algerian war was drawn to Georges Balandier, whose charisma was linked to his ability to fit his theoretical practice and the disturbances of history and to avoid the ivory tower isolation of a scientific laboratory. He gave his first class at the Sorbonne in the fall of 1962. "The Africanism about which I lectured didn't concede anything to the structuralist mode."[8] In 1967, he published *Political Anthropology*[9] and his analysis looked beyond the classical vision of power as the simple management of repressive forces to include the imaginary and the symbolic. In this respect, his work in Africa was consonant with Marc Bloch's *The Thaumaturge Kings*, where the analysis focused on the transformed body of the king incarnating political power. Balandier emphasized politics and history, which structuralism had largely ignored. Indeed, having taken shape at a remove from things political, French structural anthropology had a particular blind spot for politics. Balandier therefore read the work of Anglo-Saxon Africanists starting in 1945: Meyer Fortes, John Middleton, Siegfried-Frederick Nadel, Michael-Garfield Smith, David Apter, J. Beattie.

He adopted Edmund Leach's criticisms of applying the structuralist approach to the study of political systems. In his work on the political organization of the Kachin, Edmund Leach had noticed an oscillation between the aristocratic and democratic poles that required constant variation and fine-tuning of the sociopolitical structure. "The rigorousness of many structuralist analyses is superficial and deceptive,"[10] because they are based on unreal situations of equilibrium. Although Balandier's thinking diverged from Lévi-Strauss's, he nonetheless agreed with Lévi-Strauss's criticism of Western ethnocentrism and its tendency to define politics in such a limited way that it was reduced to little more than an apparatus of the state. As early as 1940, Meyer Fortes and Edward Evans-Pritchard had established a dichotomy between stateless segmentary systems and state systems, the former among the Nuer of the Sudan, and the latter among the Tallensi of Ghana.[11]

But Balandier went even further in attacking a typology based solely on the principle of coercion. Instead, he proposed a synthetic approach to politics that included social stratification and kinship laws. He rejected the structuralist postulate of isolating variables in order to study their inner logic, preferring a total approach mixing the real, the imaginary, and the symbolic in a dynamic equilibrium that was, by definition, unstable. This perspective accorded a place and an importance to such notions as open strategies, thereby giving its authors some latitude in their choices; it could include the relationship between kinship and power through the interplay of marriage alliances conceived of as so many pieces of the political network.

Balandier took issue with anthropology's assertion that politics began where kinship ended. Such an approach let historical problematizing into the picture: "Anthropology, political sociology, and history have been led to coalesce their efforts."[12] It became possible to dialogue with historians. This dialogue occurred in 1968, when a television show called the *Lundis de l'histoire* presented Balandier's work and Balandier, along with Jacques Le Goff and Pierre Vidal-Naquet. Balandier's synthetic and diachronic approach in fact resembled the work of both of these medievalists, in which certain sources, like the epics, describe wars among pretenders to the crown as so many political issues. Balandier's definition of politics was therefore quite broad. "Politics as a means of ensuring the government of men must be distinguished from politics as a strategic means that men use. We too often tend to mix up these two levels."[13]

The Heirs of Balandier and Lévi-Strauss

It would be pointless to try to compare the respective impact and influence of Lévi-Strauss and Balandier. Clearly, the structuralist vogue carried Lévi-Strauss to his glory and left Balandier in the shadows, relatively speaking. And yet, historical injustice has to be rectified, for Balandier's influence was as important as it was on occasion misunderstood. Balandier launched quite a number of studies and careers and if Lévi-Strauss had his progeny, many of Balandier's, and particularly the Africanists among them, consider themselves to have a double paternity.

Marc Augé, the current president of the EHESS, was one such example. In 1960, while preparing his *agrégation* in literature at the École Normale Supérieure and unsure about the direction to take since he was attracted equally to philosophy and literature, he was going to both Lévi-Strauss's and Balandier's classes. He thought that ethnology might offer a middle road that could reconcile his taste for writing and his desire for a more speculative form of thinking. The opportunity presented itself, thanks to Balandier, to enter the ORSTOM, and in 1965 Augé left for the Ivory Coast. "It was my friend Pierre Bonnafé who suggested that I go and see Balandier, who was very attentive, and seductive because of his unusual background."[14] Augé received his training as an Africanist in Balandier's seminar but he did not sense a significant opposition between Balandier's perspective and Lévi-Straussian structuralism. "It's true that in those years, a critique of Lévi-Strauss was taking shape in Balandier's seminars, but I was too much of a novice to attach any fundamental importance to it."[15]

In the Ivory Coast, Marc Augé's sensibilities to colonialism and neocolonialism, which had profoundly affected the lagoon populations of the Alladian, were sharpened. In this respect, he was closer to Balandier in considering that history had a certain place in the equation, but his first object of study placed him more in Lévi-Strauss's camp since he was working on a monograph trying to recover the logic of kinship ties among the Alladian. His first concern, upon arriving in Africa, was to look for kinship rules. This

> would have reminded even the most myopic that transformation systems do indeed exist. . . . There are many variants, but they are all based on the common models of reference for occupying space, in the modes of residing in that space, and in the way power is transmitted. The West has the most purely lineal societies without any central authority, and, at the other end of the spectrum, a sovereign ruled at the head of an autonomous political power; all the intermediary systems can be found between the two.[16]

But his thinking quickly evolved and he worked increasingly on power and on the ties between politics and religion, themes that were closer to Balandier's work, although he never questioned the contribution of structuralism.

Dan Sperber, similarly, was trained by both Balandier and Lévi-Strauss and went from Balandier to Lévi-Strauss. A third-world militant who translated one of the earliest of Nelson Mandela's texts in 1963, Sperber turned to anthropology as a complementary science that would help him better understand the cultural dimension of political problems in the third world. "I was therefore first at Balandier's seminars at a time when the structuralists, or Lévi-Strauss, were no longer part of my thinking."[17] He finished his *Licence* in 1962, and then signed up with Balandier to do his *troisième cycle*.[18]

Dan Sperber left for England in 1963 to work with Rodney Needham, who initiated him, in fact, to structuralism. "Needham, on the one hand, and the empirical atmosphere in England, on the other, generated a very lively interest in structuralism."[19] Dan Sperber gave many presentations in Britain in which he defended and explained structuralism.

> I remember a talk I gave in a college at Oxford in which I defended the structuralism of the moment when General de Gaulle had refused to let the English into the Common Market. One of the professors said then, "Sperber does intellectually what de Gaulle did to us politically." At the time, I seemed to be defending something rather exotic and not altogether trustworthy.[20]

It was only upon his return to France in 1965 that Dan Sperber, who had joined the CNRS, started going to Lévi-Strauss's seminars on a regular basis. Today, he says that anthropology interested him at the time because of Lévi-Strauss, "not in the sense of simply being in agreement with him or sharing his convictions, but because thanks to him it was possible to raise general questions in a scientific way."[21]

Africanism Resists Structuralism

But many Africanists remained skeptical about structuralism. Claude Meillassoux, for example, had a very particular background that suggested once again how much the choice to be a professional anthropologist resulted from chance and opportunity more than any clear-cut university trajectory. Meillassoux was an untraditional Africanist whose training and activities were quite eccentric with respect to the profession of ethnology. After studying law and political science, he left for the University of Michigan's School of Business in 1948. Upon his return, he ran his family's textile business in Roubaix, in the north of France, but he found administration unsatisfying and left again for the United States, recruited by the *commissariat à la productivité*. Back in France once again, he became the intermediary between American experts and French businesses. In the early fifties, Meillassoux became a militant in the new, independent left and joined the CAGI (Centre d'Action de la Gauche Indépendante [Center for action by the independent left]), along with Claude Bourdet, Pierre Naville, and Daniel Guérin. He was looking for a job and Balandier needed someone to inventory the works by British functionalists on black Africa. "That was how I did my ethnology classes. I had an office on the Avenue Iéna. I wrote my index cards and had endless discussions with Georges Balandier."[22] Having been trained, after having taken Balandier's courses, Meillassoux joined a research project in the Ivory Coast in 1956 where he was to be responsible for the economic aspect of things.

In the sixties, after a seminar on trade and markets in West Africa organized by the Institutional African Institute (IAI), Meillassoux organized an international colloquium to which he invited, among others, Emmanuel Terray, Michel Izard, and Marc Piot. The colloquium was supposed to take place in the Ivory Coast but Terray was persona non grata there and Meillassoux, who did not want to give in to the government's orders, held it in Sierra Leone. After this, Michel

Izard suggested that Meillassoux give an unofficial seminar on Africa that would be called the Meillassoux seminar. By its very existence, it demonstrated that even theoretical splits could take second stage to more empirical considerations about ethnographic material collected through fieldwork. However, in keeping with Balandier's perspective, Meillassoux always remained very critical of structuralism as it triumphed in anthropology: "Primitive societies were used for all purposes and structuralism used them as material to push its ideas on the way the mind structures the rest, whereas this is, in a word, the way computers think. Binary thinking is bureaucratic thinking."[23]

In Meillassoux's view, Lévi-Straussian structuralism worked by analogy. For want of being able to construct its own problematic, Lévi-Strauss used different sciences, one after the other, to support his theses, and his disciples were always tripping over these trying to keep up with their master's frenetic movement, which was always one step ahead of them. "I went to Lévi-Strauss's courses at the Collège de France. He was a king who opened a door; the moment it seemed that the philosophers' stone had been found, he shut the door again and took up another subject in the next seminar. Still, it was fascinating because he came up with intellectually stimulating comparisons and combinations."[24]

Jean Duvignaud was also disappointed by the structuralist model in North Africa because it did not account for the complexity and changes in the kinship systems there: "My work in Chebika, in Tunisia, led me to take my distance from structuralism."[25] His work of four years was published in 1968.[26] Bertucelli used it as the basis for a very beautiful film called *Ramparts of Clay*.[27] Lévi-Strauss's review *L'Homme* criticized Duvignaud for having abandoned kinship structures, but it was not for not having tried to apply the analytic categories that Lévi-Strauss had developed. Duvignaud had not been able to apply them successfully. Close to the group of Gurvitchian sociologists and to Balandier, he was also very critical of the ambitions of the structuralist paradigm, which he considered to be a renewal of the Comtian positivist legacy, which culminated "in a sort of ontology of the visible."[28] The structuralist a priori met functionalism in its presupposition of a positivity of social coherence and through its holistic view of the social realm: "It is not at all clear that contestations, deviations, forms of subversion, revolt, eccentricities, atypicality, and figures of anomie can be integrated into the whole and are in the service of the whole."[29]

In the center of Chebika, Jean Duvignaud discovered a place that corresponded to no logic or rule, an empty zone where people wandered and waited; it challenged all reductionism and stymied the self-enclosed structural grid. The phenomenological perspective remained valid, according to Duvignaud, in its desire to define consciousness as the consciousness of something, recalling the hidden dimension of life behind formal logic. Without refuting the validity of some points of the structuralist method, Duvignaud suggested that this epistemology should include that part of collective experience that resists any particular determinism.

Structuralism Regains Africa

There was, therefore, an implicit spatial division of labor. When Michel Izard joined the CNRS and the Laboratoire d'Anthropologie Sociale[30] in 1963, he was more of an exception as an Africanist. Africanism was represented by Balandier on the one hand, and on the other by the sector of studies of systems of thought in black Africa established in the wake of Marcel Griaule by Germaine Dieterlin and taken up again by Michel Cartry. But structuralism's success was such that in 1968 the situation changed and Africanism managed to penetrate Lévi-Strauss's Laboratoire d'Anthropologie Sociale, "which must be tied to the entrance of Tarditz, who was probably the first Africanist close to Lévi-Strauss."[31] Including Africanists in the laboratory meant that Africa and structuralism were not incompatible, as a certain geopolitics of research might have suggested. The fact that today an Africanist, Françoise Héritier-Augé, heads the laboratory is quite significant in this respect. There are many homes in the African house, and for Jean Pouillon, who was also an Africanist in the lineage of Lévi-Strauss, "Balandier's Africa is not at all the one I know."[32] Moreover, the fact that many Marxist Africanist anthropologists, among them Emmanuel Terray and Maurice Godelier, were interested in structuralism would increase this current's influence throughout the sixties.

It is not at all clear that Africa defined the limits of structuralism, but it certainly suggested an analysis that was more attuned to political phenomena and to acknowledging social dynamics and history, perspectives that remained marginal if not repressed, in the structuralist current.

Twenty-nine

Reviews

One measure of the exceptional intellectual activity of the period was the vitality, number, and influence of the new reviews, which provided both a place for a special sociability and the perfect framework for valorizing the strength of the structuralist paradigm. These interdisciplinary reviews could circumvent traditional institutions, and provide a forum for exchange from which concentric circles of influence spread outward.

A review's inherent structural flexibility, its capacity to respond quickly to the most recent theoretical debates and battles, as well as to reflect the conceptual progress in thinking about these problems, enabled the various reviews to augment the structuralist successes well before these made the daily or weekly press. Those that were to transform readers in the social sciences into crowds of enthusiastic structuralists addressed a public of disciplinary specialists, or touted themselves as the embodiment of interdisciplinarity, or finally, were linked with a particular political ideology, which felt troubled by the structuralist phenomenon and invited a debate with its representatives. We have already mentioned the first issue of Lacan's review, *La Psychanalyse*, which came out in 1956 and carried the famous Rome Report, a text by Heidegger, and an important article by Émile Benveniste on the function of language in Freud's understanding of the unconscious.

The publication of philosophical and linguistic theses in a psychoanalytic review clearly indicated the intentions of the Société Française de Psychanalyse: "If psychoanalysis dwells in language, it must be receptive to dialogue. . . . Psychoanalytic receptivity to the human sciences is a gesture that puts an end to psychoanalysis's long-held position of extraterritoriality."[1] *La Psychanalyse* therefore had no intention of strictly limiting itself either to a well-established Freudianism or to the internal debates of the analytic corporation, but rather planned to present itself as an organ of structural modernity able to renovate Freudian thinking based on a dialogue with the other social sciences. We have also mentioned Lévi-Strauss's creation of *L'Homme* in 1961. Although *L'Homme* presented itself as a French anthropology journal, it sought a broader public than that of the professional milieu; its editorial board included Pierre Gourou, a geographer, and Émile Benveniste, the most popular and respected linguist of the period.

Langages

Linguistics was the pilot science for the structuralist renewal of the sixties. Although only one review—*Le Français moderne*—was founded between 1928 and 1958, during the decade from 1959 to 1969, no fewer than seven new linguistics reviews were created. They represented the culmination of the energetic work and thinking in linguistics going on in a number of areas in the discipline.

In 1966, the year of the structuralist consecration, André Martinet created *La Linguistique*[2] and Larousse began its own linguistics review, *Langages*.[3] The editorial board of *Langages* included some of the most illustrious names in modern linguistics and the team that worked on the review was drawn primarily from the meetings, seminars, and colloquiums in Besançon. Algirdas Julien Greimas, a veritable flag-bearer of structural thinking, conceived the project and proposed a thematic formula for the review whereby one or two specialists in the area being addressed would guest-edit each issue. Work sessions took place at his home and the project bore fruit thanks to Jean Dubois at Larousse.

Martinet's review was aimed at professional linguists, but *Langages* had other ambitions. From the outset, the structuralist method was supposed to reach the vast field of the social sciences, bring into contact, contrast, and unify the networks of research in the various disciplines. The first issue announced the very principles of linguistics as a pilot science. "The study of language is fundamental for the humanities, for philosophers, psychoanalysts, and people in literature, and this exigency calls for broad scientific information—this study encompasses all signifying systems."⁴ This very broad notion of an encompassing semiological project including linguistics as a subcontinent corresponded exactly to the program defined by Roland Barthes in 1964. Barthes was, in fact, the anonymous author of this opening of the first issue of the review. "It was really a very new type of 'linguistic' review. . . . It set linguistics in the broad cultural arena, an idea that had taken hold of Paris in 1966."⁵ The project was ambitious and sound, it relied on groups that had been working for a number of years in this direction, and it was receptive to different areas of thinking in their relationship with language—Nicolas Ruwet was working on music and language, Oswald Ducrot on logic, Henry Hécaen on medicine, Roland Barthes on literature, and Maurice Gross on artificial intelligence.

The mood was euphoric during the planning stages but the first issue led to a serious conflict because several schools were already disputing the paternity of modern thinking about language. Todorov was in charge of this inaugural issue bearing on "research in semantics," which gave considerable importance to Chomsky's theses. Greimas was so angered ("He [Todorov] produced an American issue")⁶ that he resigned from the editorial board. The rupture would not be overcome. Jean Dubois and Nicolas Ruwet would adopt increasingly Chomskyan positions; with Greimas gone, Barthes wanted to avoid getting involved in the dispute and, "as a result, sought one thing and one thing only, to escape."⁷ In the grips of a veritable implosion, the editorial board of *Langages* stopped meeting and it fell to Jean Dubois, who had some editorial power at Larousse, to continue. This episode notwithstanding, Dubois was able to begin a collection called "*Langages* at Larousse." At the high point of the structuralist vogue, it sold as many as five thousand copies, a sign of success that was all the more remarkable given the technical nature of linguistic discourse.

Communications

Communications was a major instrument for disseminating structuralist ideas. Born in 1961 at the Centre d'Études et de Communication de Masse (CECMAS) in the Sixth Section of the EPHE, which had been created in January 1960 at Georges Friedmann's initiative, *Communications* was a veritable symbiosis between sociology and semiology. The title expressed the major concern of the moment: deciphering the meaning of messages transmitted by the technology of information dissemination: press, radio, television, advertising, all the media, whose importance was growing considerably at the time. It was thus a matter of investigating modernity in which "technical civilization and mass culture are organically linked. . . . The contents, the substance pass, but the form, the being, and consequently, the meaning of the thing remains."[8]

Georges Friedmann edited the review and the members of his editorial board had diverse relationships with structuralism.[9] *Communications* published two programmatic issues—number 4 in 1964 and number 8 in 1966—prepared by a group around Roland Barthes. These were real syntheses of structuralist ambitions: number 4 included Barthes's "Les éléments de sémiologie," and number 8, in particular, was devoted to the structural analysis of a *récit* that came to be seen as a manifesto of the French structuralist school.[10]

Tel Quel

Tel Quel was founded in 1960, at Seuil, and quickly became the expression of structuralism's syncretic ambition.[11] It did not emanate from any particular discipline among the humanities and as such reflected the profound concern for synthesis during this period. Launched by writers and targeting an avant-garde intellectual audience, *Tel Quel* had been in the offing since 1958. "François Wahl had said that it would be the Parnassus of Napoléon III, this new Napoléon III embodied by General de Gaulle in 1958."[12]

On the cover of the first issue, *Tel Quel* took up a phrase by Nietzsche: "I want the world and I want it *as it is* [*tel quel*], and I still want it and want it forever."[13] This liminary declaration denoted an essentially literary intention, placing poetry "at the mind's acme."[14] The whole group had an essentially literary goal, but the word "science" set off the quote on the cover because the project sought to appropriate all avant-garde and modernist forms in the social sciences in order to advance a new kind of writing. During the sixties, structuralism embodied scientific modernity, whence a very encompassing subtitle: "Literature/Philosophy/Science/Politics." But the goal remained literary: "This periodic and contemporary political activity was always carried out in the name of literary creation, by writers."[15] The objective, therefore, was to influence literary creation and change the mode of writing by using the contributions of structuralism to support the new stylistics. *Tel Quel* was interdisciplinary from the start, therefore, a place where discussion and exchange were given priority, where the only principle was to reflect the avant-garde. The cornerstone of the project was rhetoric, a particular realm of knowledge made popular by structuralism.

Tel Quel took as its adversary classical literary history of the nineteenth and twentieth centuries: "To set ourselves apart from the reigning idea of literature in France in the postwar period, which was a literature of psychological restoration."[16] In this sense, the intellectual communion was unambiguous between the structuralist paradigm, which attacked the notions of the conscious mind, the subject, a mastery of history, and *Tel Quel*, which had recourse to the social sciences in order to destroy the idea of a harmonious and positivist literary history. The review was a crossroads and at the same time a surprising and curious mix of Lacan-Althusser-Barthesianism, so much so that it was often considered to be the organ of an imaginary structuralist international; in the sixties, Marcelin Pleynet, as the review's director, was invited to write an article on structuralism by a medical journal. The privileged position enjoyed by the unconscious and by formal structures was a time bomb that would eventually explode psychologism: "The best way to say that psychologism in literature was finished was to be interested in psychoanalysis."[17]

The strength of *Tel Quel* was to remain independent of all parties and institutions and to be without any particular disciplinary loyalty. The logic of the editorial board was to stay in the avant-garde, but insofar as the avant-garde always runs the risk of being recuperated, ingested, and digested by the system—"Run, comrade, the old world is behind you"—what resulted was a conception that was most often terrorist and that amounted to flattening the adversary (in general, the one that was closest at hand), and imagining that there was always a conspiracy brewing. *Tel Quel* gave free rein to a veritable terrorized terrorism, which Marcelin Pleynet summed up by saying, "It was always a matter of avoiding being surrounded."[18] And, curiously enough, even though it was born in 1960, *Tel Quel* had nothing to say about Algeria until it became the hard core of one of the most pro-Chinese positions in France.

The review's history is punctuated by extremely brutal ruptures, each of which resulted in the expulsion of valuable members of the editorial board. "In truth, the history of *Tel Quel* is not a history of exclusions but of the exclusion of individuals, which made it possible to include much broader fields of investigation."[19] Sollers was responsible for the first overtures, thanks to his position in support of the New Novel, which led to Thibaudeau and Ricardou joining the board. The second overture was to include poetics, with the introduction of Denis Roche and Marcelin Pleynet, who became secretary in 1962, replacing Jean-Edern Hallier, whose break would come in 1971, at a time when Maoism was triumphant, as "the failure of an attempt from the right to take over the review."[20]

During the period from 1962 to 1967, baptized a posteriori as the review's "formalist era," *Tel Quel* was strongly influenced by the rising wave of structuralism.[21] Barthes, who had formed a strong friendship with Philippe Sollers and Julia Kristeva, became closer to the editorial board and to the review, "which provoked a break between people like Genette, Todorov, and me, on the one hand, and *Tel Quel*, on the other."[22] For Barthes, the *Tel Quel* group was seductive; it incarnated modernity, and his friendship with Sollers and Kristeva was reinforced by their common publisher, Seuil, which published both Barthes and the review. It was under the "Tel Quel" imprint that Barthes's *Critique et vérité* came out in 1966, and at that point, Barthes remarked that "the review *Tel Quel* is a critical enterprise for me."[23] Jacques Derrida was also close to the review, which he supported and which published his texts. Lacanian discourse was very much in evidence in articles by Sollers and Kristeva, who were faithful auditors of Lacan's seminars.

Althusser's influence was palpable in *Tel Quel*'s rereading of Marx, particularly in the dialogue it undertook with the French Communist Party as of 1967, with *La Nouvelle Critique*. So were the pro-Chinese, pro-Cultural Revolution positions the review took, which hailed from an orthodox Althusserian perspective. Jean-Pierre Faye, who had joined the editorial board in 1963, left when its members became Maoists, and his departure was a crisis punctuated with insults. If the important breaks in the history of *Tel Quel* took place because of arguments about particular political positions, these remained secondary to a fundamentally literary goal.

The Communist Thaw

For the French Communist Party press, on the other hand, literature came after the application of the official party line. Not that this precluded the occasional article by someone from the outside in order to broaden the party's audience by attracting an intellectual readership. During these years of peaceful coexistence and of the beginning of de-Stalinization, *Les Lettres françaises*, the PCF literary weekly run by Louis Aragon and Pierre Daix, began to print articles of the avant-garde and of formalist thinking in order to break out of the socialist realist mold. "*Les Lettres françaises* and a certain avant-garde of the PCF were the first to make it possible for the literary avant-garde, the university, and structuralism to meet prior to 1968."[24]

Jean-Pierre Faye, for example, was a member of the *Tel Quel* group who regularly contributed to *Les Lettres françaises*, and he so successfully convinced the journal's board to take an interest in formalism that he was asked to publish an interview with Roman Jakobson. "I became quite close friends with Jakobson. As soon as he came to Paris, he got in touch with me."[25]

La Nouvelle Critique was the second PCF review that was open to debate. Created in December 1948 as an organ for theoretical struggle to be waged after the creation of the Cominform, this weekly publication for PCF intellectuals was the tool for a veritable normalization in the hands of its editorial director, Jean Kanapa. This was the Stalinist period, the period of the two sciences (bourgeois and proletarian), of Zhdanovism and of Lysenkoism. This kind of review would have ignored the structuralist challenge had it not been for the meeting in March 1966 of the central committee of Argenteuil, and then of the Eighteenth Congress of Levallois in January 1967. The result was a new position with respect to intellectuals. A "logic of receptivity replaced a politics of the besieged fortress."[26] Thanks to the new formula of 1967, *La Nouvelle Critique* therefore enjoyed relative autonomy with respect to the PCF leadership, and it acted as a headhunter in the social sciences. This quest for new alliances especially led the PCF intellectuals to valorize a history informed by the social sciences, and, as a result, Antoine Casanova organized a collective discussion in the review. He published a number of articles on this theme that were reprinted in a 1974 anthology entitled *Aujourd'hui l'histoire*. Here, alongside articles by Communist historians, were others by André Leroi-Gourhan, Jacques Le Goff, Jacques Bergue, Georges Duby, and Pierre Francastel.

As of 1967, *La Nouvelle Critique* thus became a place of debate, receptivity to modernity, and therefore to an encounter with structuralism. Of course, this PCF review never adopted structuralist theses, but it did discuss and comment on them. Even before the 1967 turning point, *La Nouvelle Critique* had opened its pages to certain positions and fundamental debates. It was there that Althusser published his famous 1964 article "Freud et Lacan," in which he had opened Marxist thinking to psychoanalysis and to Lacanian thinking.[27] These pages had also held debates on the relationship between humanism and Marxism in 1965–66. After Maspero's publication of Althusser's new reading of Marx, the debates in *La Nouvelle Critique* corresponded to the need to "decide, first of all, on whether to assimilate Marxism to a philosophical humanism, as Garaudy and Schaff asserted, or to assert its antihumanist and theoretical aspect, as Althusser maintained."[28]

In 1967, the new *La Nouvelle Critique* was invited by *Tel Quel* to join an enterprise of intellectual modernization. The PCF review enthusiastically accepted the offer, considering that its work was "of a high literary and scientific level," so much so that the Communists claimed that they were ready to learn from the *Tel Quel* writers, whose "work greatly merits our sympathy and can teach us quite a bit."[29]

This was a time of dialogue, but the PCF did not adopt all of the structuralist theses. In 1967, *La Nouvelle Critique* published four articles attacking structuralism, without directly attacking Althusser, who was a member of the party.[30] Pierre Vilar and Jeannette Colombel criticized Michel Foucault's *The Order of Things* for ignoring history; Georges Mounin criticized the broad and flabby dissemination of the linguistic model, and Lucien Sève argued for a scientific humanism against the Althusserian theoretical antihumanism.[31] *La Nouvelle Critique* did not adopt the paradigm, but it it did help to disseminate and discuss it, and this strategy attracted a certain number of intellectuals such as Catherine Backès-Clément, Christine Buci-Glucksmann, and Élisabeth Roudinesco to the PCF, which they perceived as a place where debate was possible. This turn in the relationship between the PCF and intellectuals was the result of a certain international thaw, but, as the party leadership saw it, it was also necessary because of the competition from the political and cultural activity of students, who would later reject it and establish their own theoretical development.

The Maoist Pole

The École Normale Supérieure on the rue d'Ulm in Paris was a sanctuary of protest, and Louis Althusser was its figurehead. Some disciples of the *caïman* of the philosophy *agrégation* began the *Cahiers marxistes-léninistes* in late 1965. Distributed by the Union of Communist Students, the *CML* bore this remark by Lenin in an epigraph: "Marx's theory is all-powerful because it is true." They were successful: the first printing of a thousand copies immediately sold out. However issue 8 created a serious crisis. Robert Linhart, a hard-line Maoist, an Althusserian, and a philosopher who specialized in economy, blocked it because he no longer recognized the review's mission of placing political struggle at the forefront when the issue was completely devoted to the power of literature and included articles by Aragon, Jorge Luis Borges, and Witold Gombrowicz. Linhart accused Jacques-Alain Miller of "only looking for an academic career, a bourgeois position of authority."[32] The year 1966 at Ulm saw a double break: Jacques-Alain Miller and his group established an epistemological circle that would publish *Les Cahiers pour l'analyse*, and a second break would affect the Union of Communist Students in November 1966, when its "pro-Chinese" wing was dissolved and had to form its own organization, the Union of Young Marxist-Leninist Communists (UJCML). With issue 9–10 of the *Cahiers marxistes-léninistes*, Dominique Lecourt became editor in chief, and references to Althusser became increasingly obvious. Issue 11 was entirely devoted to his work with, in particular, the publication of excerpts from *Matérialisme historique et matérialisme dialectique*.

As of issue 14, which was devoted to the Chinese Great Proletarian Cultural Revolution, the *Cahiers marxistes-léninistes* became the theoretical and political organ of the Young Communists Marxist-Leninist. The break with the PCF was consummated; the party was considered revisionist, according to the Chinese line. And yet Althusser, who remained a member of the PCF, nonetheless gave his blessing to his students by publishing an article in this issue on the Cultural Revolution, but without signing his name. Paradoxical as it might appear, given the distance between the respective positions of the exaltation of Maoist China on the one hand, and structuralism on the other, an entire generation of students was politically and theoretically fascinated by this symbiosis.

The editor in chief of the *Cahiers marxistes-léninistes*, Dominique Lecourt, embodied this double commitment. He had been accepted at the ENS in 1965 as a Hellenist but had converted to philosophy. A militant against the war in Algeria at the beginning of the sixties, within the UNEF (National Union of French Students) Lecourt was seduced by Althusser's positions. In 1966, along with four others, he founded the UJCML. "There was something in the themes of the Cultural Revolution that echoed a certain number of Althusser's positions."[33] Theoretical concerns were an essential vector of Dominique Lecourt's political combat; as early as 1967, he regularly went to Georges Canguilhem's seminar. Canguilhem "played an absolutely decisive role in my thinking."[34] Lacan was at Ulm, and Lecourt did not miss the show even if the Maoist militants were "rather overwhelmed by the relatively irreconcilable atmosphere of our proletarian ideals."[35]

These young ENS students wanted to find the same scientific rigor in their interpretation of Marx as Lévi-Strauss had found in the savage mind. But theoretical combat, like political combat, had to be ongoing, and this was what a certain number of Althusserians, including Dominique Lecourt and Robert Linhart, found unacceptable in issue 8 of the *Cahiers marxistes-léninistes*. Jacques-Alain Miller, François Régnault, and Jean-Claude Milner, who were in charge of the issue,

> appeared to be totally esoteric, and there was a split after awful sessions that probably lasted until three in the morning. We talked about the epistemological split and the Signifier. I remember especially one big meeting where Robert Linhart was talking with Jean-Claude Milner about the Signifier and unsignified of the Signifier for hours in order to know how it was materialistic. These discussions had a certain appeal.[36]

Out of this break finally came the review by the young generation of Althusserians, *Les Cahiers pour l'analyse*, which we might consider to be an Althussero-Lacanian review. It took a position of a combative structuralism as a totalizing philosophy, and its sources included Althusser, Lacan, Foucault, and Lévi-Strauss. The offspring of Althusser and Lacan were here. The editorial board included Alain Grosrichard, Jacques-Alain Miller, Jean-Claude Milner, and François Régnault, all of whom were members of Lacan's psychoanalytic association, the École Freudienne de Paris.

From 1966 to 1969, *Les Cahiers pour l'analyse* was engaged in an epistemological investigation into the scientificity of psychoanalysis, linguistics, and logic in order to construct *the* science, conceived as a theory of discourse or philosophy of the concept. Georges Canguilhem's remark opened the collective reflection on one of the issues:

To work on a concept is to vary the ways in which it can be extended, to understand and generalize it by incorporating certain exceptional traits, to export it beyond its original context, to take it as a model or, conversely, to seek a model for it—in short, to progressively confer transformations upon it that are regulated by the function of a form.[37]

Les Cahiers pour l'analyse in the sacred ENS on the rue d'Ulm was the most symptomatic emanation of the structuralist fervor of the sixties, in its unbounded, ambitions in its most radical scientistic experiments, in its most elitist appearance as an avant-garde/popular dialectic that claimed to speak in the name of the world proletariat, and which it used to legitimate the most terrorist and terrifying of theoretical practices.

Was it a caricature, a Ubuesque parody, or was this a serious enterprise that took the baton from the first structuralist period? Doubtless both, and it was this unharmonious mixture that inspired an entire generation of philosophers.

Thirty

Ulm or Saint-Cloud:
Althusser or Touki?

In the sixties, the challenge of the social sciences was taken up by philosophers, who would reappropriate the structuralist program and thereby maintain their domination of the intellectual field, avoiding the marginalization experienced by the classical humanities. The École Normale Supérieure was a sanctuary of intellectual legitimacy and an essential institution, for through it and its goal of transmission, structuralism could circumvent and disdain the traditional universities (even if the ENS was in the process of losing its unique stature as the institution responsible for shaping future leaders of the nation to the École Nationale d'Administration [ENA]).

ENS students were part of a double structure, depending on whether they were at the rue d'Ulm or at the school in the suburb of Saint-Cloud. At Saint-Cloud they could take courses with Jean-Toussaint Desanti, who encouraged his students to convert to the new disciplines, counseling them to be trained in one of the social sciences even if it might mean eventually giving up philosophy. Conversely, Louis Althusser constructed a theory in which philosophy played a central role, and he incited his students to test the validity of the different social sciences on the basis of a philosophy of the concept. Althusser, like Desanti, included the structuralist paradigm in his strategy, but this meant speaking in the name of philosophy, whereas for Desanti it meant more of a reconversion.

Saint-Cloud

Jean-Toussaint Desanti has a place in the phenomenological line. An heir to Merleau-Ponty, who had him read Husserl as early as 1938, Desanti joined the PCF after the war. "It was the experience of political struggle that led me toward Marx and his successors."[1] He had entered the ENS on the rue d'Ulm in 1935, where he met Jean Cavaillès, an important meeting for Desanti, who elected mathematics as a privileged philosophical object, and engaged essentially in work on epistemology. He concluded that philosophy was not an autonomous and founding discourse, but a second discourse. "In order to do philosophy seriously, we have to get to the heart of positivities—these are Desanti's words."[2]

The conflict in the sixties between these two philosophers was latent. Althusser was increasingly committed to Marxism-Leninism, while Desanti was disengaging himself, having broken with the PCF in 1958. Nonetheless, Desanti had helped the *agrégation* students at Ulm, including Althusser, to take the examination, and had even had Althusser get his PCF card after he had passed it: "I was the one who had him join the Party . . . alas!"[3] Desanti regretted having led Althusser into what he considered, as early as the end of the fifties, to be a dead end. He considered Althusser's work to be a true philosophical undertaking of complexifying Marxism, but that only had the effect of "slowing things down because this very elaborate enterprise of maintaining Marxism-Leninism is not at all adapted to the problems of our period. Who, aside from the Albanians, is a Leninist today?"[4]

Desanti combined structuralism and phenomenology in his search for mathematical idealities. He was not, however, trying to escape either the world or experience: "They are the form of an exigency that makes it possible for us to understand the productivity of this sort of object, ideal objects."[5] They are rooted in an area that is symbolizable from the outset and belong neither to the intelligible nor to the material world, but lie somewhere between the two. In his research on mathematical objects, Desanti used the contribution made, since the mid-nineteenth century, by the baring of structures and, since the beginning of the twentieth century, the contributions of the Bourbaki group, which had made it possible to construct symbolically defined problematic objects. "It is a poor structure from which extremely powerful theorems can be obtained that enables us to master chains of properties among fields of objects that are differentiated from the outset."[6]

In this respect, Desanti was driven by a desire to lay bare the structure, form, and unity. His theoretical project of establishing significant connections using the principles of closure and the rules of transition is related to the structuralist project. However, he did not give up on meaning-giving acts or on his eidetic quest for an area where meaning is preconstituted and therefore to be reactivated. He basically remained a phenomenologist.

> The necessity of having to link conducts to the determination of a underlying structure once again poses the question of the subject. The subject is not abolished because if it signifies nothing, there is no structure. Where experience is missing, there is no structure. Structure is that which shapes itself, is made and one wants to make, and this relationship must be understood. That is the problem we are facing today.[7]

Sylvain Auroux, an epistemologist in linguistics and a disciple of Desanti, chose a path reflecting the relationship of his teacher's work to philosophy and science. In 1967, he was accepted into *khâgne*, and took courses with Desanti, who initiated him into structuralism. "Structuralism was the anticulture and we bathed in it."[8] He entered the ENS in Saint-Cloud, passed the *agrégation*, did his doctorate in philosophy, taught high school for a while, and then entered the CNRS in the sciences of language. In so doing, he fulfilled the advice that Desanti had given him to get involved in a specific discipline, linguistics, and to become a research director at the CNRS and work with other linguists. "People like me always saw Althusser as an ideology maker. . . . He had managed this feat of giving a Platonic version of Marxism."[9]

Rather than constructing an epistemology outside of and critical of science, Desanti therefore encouraged epistemological work on sciences from within, which is what Sylvain Auroux later accomplished. "As Desanti said at the time, to be a philosopher of mathematics is to place oneself within mathematics."[10] Sylvain Auroux's conversion to linguistics did not indicate, however, that students at Saint-Cloud should abandon philosophy, particularly since Martial Guéroult was giving a very strict history of philosophical texts there at the same time.

Ulm

At Ulm, Louis Althusser was the tutelary figure for the new generation. He became an *agrégé* in philosophy in 1948, was the philosophy *caïman* responsible for preparing ENS students specifically for the *agrégation* examinations. Althusser, more than Desanti, considered that philosophy had a role to play vis-à-vis the modern social sciences, as a theory of theoretical practices able to evaluate the scientific validity of different disciplines in order to test the truth. Philosophy, for Althusser, should maintain its traditional role as the queen of disciplines, even if its discourse should change and address new problems. During the sixties, Althusser and his disciples played a central role in disseminating structuralism because they could meet the challenge of the social sciences, which prided themselves on their rigor and as the bearers of a certain modernity, by shepherding them into the traditional mold of a totalizing philosophical discourse as the bearer of truth.

Ulm therefore became the epicenter of a structuralist ideology, a very French symptom of the importance of the humanities in the university program. From this point of view, it was the ideal place for launching a counteroffensive against the aged Sorbonne. The very expression of excellence, the ENS incarnated the double advantage of traditional scholarly legitimacy and the most advanced modernism. "I remember quite clearly that university philosophy inspired tremendous weariness; it was a mixture of humanism and spiritualism," recalls Jacques Bouveresse, who had been a student at Ulm.[11] The appearance of what was called, at the time, the "good" social sciences came as a breath of fresh air, a real intellectual liberation. The remedy was not, however, to appropriate all the social sciences: there were the good ones (psychoanalysis, anthropology, and linguistics, the trio comprising the structuralist paradigm) and the bad ones (the traditional social sciences of psychology and sociology, the empirical sciences of basic classification), which were looked down upon with the greatest disdain.

The philosophers tried a takeover in these three innovative sciences. "The scientists who were involved accepted this, as is often the case, because philosophy, even if it is disdained, has the advantage of being able to conquer a broader public than the one scientists can ever hope to reach."[12] By renewing its problematic, philosophy could thus socialize the social sciences, which had the advantage of using a readable, rigorous, and formalizable discourse. The operation was so successful that philosophers refrained from carrying it out in the name of philosophy, which many at the time considered dead; instead, they substituted the word theory, as, for example, in the imprint by that name inaugurated at Maspero, and whose director was none other than Louis Althusser.

It was not a matter of becoming an anthropologist, a linguist, or a psychoanalyst, however, but of using the rigor of these disciplines to demonstrate their scientism in the name of a theory that was superior to these specific theoretical practices. This was an effort at internal subversion as much as of appropriation undertaken in favor of philosophers. Such an operation required a certain stealth, and that, according to Jacques Bouveresse, imposed a heavy price: "It was a time when one had the impression that a game was being played without any rules. You could say anything, without any rule for argumentation once a certain number of dogmatic presuppositions were accepted."[13]

Marx at Ulm

The first innovation made by the *caïman* at Ulm was to enshrine Marx among the holy of holies by including his works in the ENS, the institutional bastion for training the nation's prestigious elite. In 1960, Althusser published *Feuerbach's Philosophical Manifestos*,[14] and in 1961 he began giving his seminar on the "young Marx," in response to student demand. "The book on Montesquieu came out in 1959, and his first texts on overdetermination and on the young Marx came out in 1960. We asked him to give a seminar on the young Marx at the ENS."[15]

Students at Althusser's seminar included Pierre Macherey, Roger Establet, Michel Pêcheux, François Régnault, Étienne Balibar, Christian Baudelot, Régis Debray, Yves Duroux, and Jacques Rancière. For them, reading Marx like Aristotle or Plato was completely surprising at the time, even if the literal method of textual explanation continued to use well-known canons. If Althusser's disciplines expressed their enthusiasm about this "overwhelming originality,"[16] they also had political reasons to fight Garaudy since they had broken with the PCF leadership. This political dimension was fundamental for a generation that protested against the war in Algeria, and their feeling of communion was cemented by the intense sociability that prevailed among the boarders at the ENS. "It was a militant community. When Althusser published his first articles on the young Marx, we said to ourselves, "Here is a rigorous Marxist we can respect."[17] Again emphasizing the intensity of the social life within the school, a common theoretical undertaking began to take shape while preparing the *agrégation* examination. This was how "we decided that we would help one another for the *agrégation*."[18]

Althusser spent 1962–63 lecturing on the origins of structuralist thinking: Lévi-Strauss, Montesquieu, and Foucault. Jacques-Alain Miller talked about the archaeology of knowledge in Descartes; Pierre Macherey addressed the origins of language. Jacques Rancière, Étienne Balibar, Jean-Claude Milner, and Michel Tort also participated in this seminar.[19]

In 1964, Althusser changed his orientation and the seminar undertook a collective reading of *Capital*. "All that happened without ever giving a thought to the possibility of a publication. It was a free and disinterested activity."[20] And yet, this work, which was supposed to have been limited to a strictly confidential circle, was published by Maspero as *Reading Capital* and had remarkable repercussions. In 1965,

> we were in an unbelievable situation; we had become famous overnight without having tried. . . . It was a time when the exam readers for the *agrégation* found our names quoted in the students' exam papers as if we were important contemporary philosophers. We were immediately famous, and remained so through 1968, and I can assure you that we paid for it dearly.[21]

This work and its publication quite obviously had major political implications beyond the university, particularly in the confrontations occurring inside the PCF where, since 1963, Althusserian positions had come under sharp criticism from Garaudy. Ulm thus became a double instrument contesting the traditional university structure and the PCF leadership. Just as the linguists who were confronted with classical literary history had used structuralism, so here too it was used to protest the leading authorities, whose imprecision was denounced in the name of scientific rigor. A symbiosis took hold of the different disciplines at Ulm, the temple of structuralist ideas. Michel Pêcheux had acquired a solid linguistic background and many took Georges Canguilhem's courses and were therefore involved with epistemology. Everyone was familiar with Lévi-Strauss's work. "I had been interested in Lévi-Strauss somewhat in reaction to the norm imposed by the Certificat de morale et sociologie. There was a counter-culture side to it."[22] Althusser added a revisited Marx to this structuralist paradigm, and a return to Marx joined the ranks of the "returns to" Saussure and Freud. He had the excited feeling of finally being able to achieve a philosophical synthesis that could account for the different forms of contemporary rationality, beyond the social sciences.

In a confused way, Althusser was adopting the structuralist orientation while maintaining a critical distance in the name of Marxism. An internal tension existed from the outset in the concepts that were advanced, making it possible to understand why Althusser later spoke about a "flirtation" with structuralism that had gone too far. At the time, it was a question of using the momentum, the propulsion, the scientistic side of a rather optimistic linguistic positivism that thought it could interpret all reaches of knowledge with a total semiology, starting from a simple phonological model. But Althusser and the Althusserians, in line with Nietzsche via Canguilhem, were at the same time critical of those who believed themselves able to create such a metalanguage. This ambivalent captation made it possible to coast along on the crest of a structuralist wave, using those themes that brought disciplines and viewpoints together, while at the same time deconstructing them from within. "The somewhat enormous oppositions like subject/structure or the notion of a subjectless trial took on such importance because they served to mask the conceptual ambiguity within which we were operating."[23]

During these first years of working out their theory, the Althusserians leaned, however, toward scientism. The changes in political orientation that they hoped to see on the part of the PCF leadership were to be guided by science: "Science had to be placed in the driver's seat, as was said at the time."[24] The ambient climate of scientism emphasized further the enthusiasm of a whole generation that believed it was possible to synthesize modern rationality and philosophical problematization, and that lived it as an emancipation. Jacques Rancière was a student at the ENS in 1960, and he was immediately seduced by "the intellectual dynamism that was generated around Althusser,"[25] whereas until then, philosophy had been limited to Husserl and Heidegger. When he got to the ENS, "the generation that was taking the *agrégation* were all old-guard Heideggerians."[26] This was the last year during which Jean Beaufret, a disciple of Heidegger, was giving his course. The Althusserian new guard was receptive to new fields of knowledge, to broadening philosophical culture so that it took new objects into consideration, and to bringing about a radical break with everything that was based in any way on classical psychology. "For my generation, this corresponded to a kind of liberation from university culture."[27]

If structural linguists attacked literary history limited to the author and the work, and anthropologists and psychoanalysts circumvented models of consciousness, Althusserian philosophers also sought to joyfully bury humanism like the pitiful remnants of a bygone era of triumphant bourgeois thinking. Man was the object of a dismissal; he should surrender his arms and soul and submit to the various logics that condition him and of which he is only a miserable speck. By virtue of its challenge of the validity and the very existence of the subject, the Althusserian enterprise was utterly harmonious with the entire structuralist movement.

Lacan Shores Up the Breach

A powerful ally in this effort against humanism and psychologism penetrated the sanctuary on the rue d'Ulm in 1963, at the invitation of Althusser: Jacques Lacan. Lacan too was at war, but his war was being waged within a different institution—psychoanalysis. Banned from the institution, he was also excluded from the psychoanalytic apparatus (the International Psychoanalytic Association). Lacan and Althusser were to become a team that was as curious as it was fascinating for a generation that would become, in part, Althussero-Lacanian. Jacques-Alain Miller, the former director of the École de la Cause Freudienne, claims to have read Lacan at Althusser's urging,[28] when he was giving his seminar on the foundations of psychoanalysis in 1963–64, but which was essentially focused on Lacan. As we have seen, many Althusserians were to go from Marx to Freud and from Althusser to Lacan; *Les Cahiers pour l'analyse* was essentially the expression of this Ulmian Lacanianism, which evolved from Althusserianism. The Althusserians were split among themselves; there were those who remained strictly loyal to their master and who would remain in philosophy, such as Étienne Balibar, Pierre Macherey, and Jacques Rancière, and there were those who converted to psychoanalysis, choosing to exercise a particular discipline in a practical way.

Philosophy had once again lost a good part of its forces to a new, conquering social science. A whole Althussero-Lacanian current identified with a position known as antirevisionist: at one and the same time opposed to the Soviet and PCF revision of Marx and to the revision of Freud by the official heirs of the IPA. The symbiosis between these two currents was at once theoretical and strategic and led to a reliance on solid dogma and sacred texts. In the mid-sixties, the crowds of Chinese waving the little red book on Tiananmen Square would represent for them the hope for an end to the old world. Their leader Mao Tse-tung quickly became the harbinger of a new China, saluting the birth of a new world.

Mao Tse-tung thought, Lacan thought, Althusser thought—all united against ego thought. But by the end of the sixties, the Molotov cocktail was poised to welcome the radicalization of young French students.

Thirty-one

The Althusserian Explosion

Neither God, nor Caesar, nor the tribune—yet Louis Althusser seemed to many to be the supreme savior of Marxism. His was a difficult undertaking, a veritable wager that amounted to setting Marxism at the center of contemporary rationality but disengaging it from praxis and from the Hegelian dialectic so as to get beyond the current Stalinist vulgate based on mechanistic economism. To carry out this shift, Althusser used structuralism; he presented Marxism as the only form of thinking that could manage a global synthesis of knowledge and set itself at the center of the structural paradigm. The price therefore implied getting on the structuralist bandwagon by setting aside experience, its psychological dimension, models of consciousness, and the dialectic of alienation. Setting the referent on the sidelines took the form of an "epistemological break," resembling Bachelard's models of rupture. It differentiated the ideological on the one hand, from a science incarnated by historical materialism on the other. All the sciences were thus to be questioned on the basis of the foundations of scientific rationality and the philosophy of dialectical materialism in order to free them from their ideological setting. Based on the model of the arbitrariness of the sign with respect to the referent, science was to "satisfy purely internal exigencies,"[1] and the criterion of truth was therefore not to depend on a possible falsifiability of propositions.

Untethering Marxism from its own historical destiny in the early sixties provided a means of saving it from rapid decomposition by placing it at the center of science. It was one response to the need to abandon an official, dogma-bound, post-Stalinist Marxism with an onerous past. Althusser made it possible to complexify Marxism, to cross its adventure with that of social sciences that were in full swing, and to up the ante by presenting the theory of theoretical practices as the discourse of discourses. Louis Althusser offered the exciting challenge to a militant generation that had cut its teeth in anticolonial combats of resuscitating a scientific Marxism freed of the scoria of the regimes that had ruled in the name of Marxism.

From Jesus to Marx

Louis Althusser was born on October 16, 1918, in Birmandreis, Algeria. In 1939 he entered the ENS, and from 1940 to 1945 he was a prisoner of war in Stalag XA in Schleswig-Holstein, where he corresponded with René Michaud, who initiated him into Marxism. He continued his preparation for the *agrégation* after the Liberation; he was twenty-seven. *Agrégé* in 1948, he joined the French Communist Party at the same time, and decided to stay at the ENS on the rue d'Ulm, where he became the *caïman*, the person responsible for helping to prepare students for the *agrégation*. At the same time, he began working on a *thèse d'État* with Jean Hippolyte and Vladimir Jankélévitch, "The Politics and Philosophy of Eighteenth-Century France."

And yet, at the beginning, Althusser was a practicing Catholic, a member of Action Catholique, and confirmed in his religious convictions by his *khâgne* teacher in Lyons from 1937 to 1939, Jean Guitton. According to Guitton, although Althusser had returned from the war transformed, he nonetheless remained fundamentally true to his desire for a religious absolute, which he in fact displaced onto Marxism. The friendship between the two never waned, despite the distance between their respective positions and Jean Guitton's experiences of contestation at the Sorbonne, where he held a chair in the history of philosophy: "You taught me to enter a relationship with an idea, with two, to combine them, oppose them, unite them, dissociate them, to flip them like flapjacks, and to serve them up in an edible dish."[2] From 1945 to 1948, Althusser had been attracted both to the PCF and to a small group of Catholics from Lyons founded by Maurice Montuclard and headquartered in Paris.

Althusser's fascination with religion and mystical purity lasted until the drama of 1980 when he asked his friend John Guitton to intervene in his favor to meet Jean-Paul II. Althusser was granted a meeting with Cardinal Garrone, and Guitton, who had met the Holy Father, was given to understand that his request was granted. However, Althusser murdered his wife Hélène shortly thereafter and the project was aborted. A great reader of Pascal, Althusser was filled with the disquiet of a tragic mysticism and the unsolvable character of contradiction. Having abandoned Christianity, however, he displaced his quest for an absolute onto a purified Marxism, a crystalline philosophy that could counterbalance religious faith and get beyond metaphysics by substituting a total, exclusive, and rigorous science for it. "In his bedroom, I saw the works of Lenin next to those of Teresa of Avila. Regarding Althusser, I wondered about a problem that had always haunted me—the problem of change. Had Althusser changed in the secret and profound recesses of his being?"[3]

It was fashionable to ontologize structure during the sixties, and it enabled Althusser to shift the system of causality in use in the Marxist vulgate. Until then, explanations had been limited to a simple monocausal notion of reflection. Everything had to derive from economics, and superstructures were therefore considered to be simple translations of the infrastructure. Breaking with this purely mechanical view offered the double advantage of complexifying the system by substituting a structural causality for a simple relationship of cause and effect in which the structure determines what dominates. However, as Vincent Descombes explains, Althusser's analytic model also made it possible to save the Soviet economic model, still considered consonant with the socialist model and dissociated from any objectionable and autonomous political and ideological reality. Althusser could therefore make an even further-reaching critique of Stalinism than that of the official critique of the personality cult, but at a lesser cost because it saved the socialist base of the system in the name of the relative autonomy of the forces of production. Althusser quickly grasped the utility of structuralism for a Marxism in need of renewal and continued to regard the Soviet Union as a socialist country. "The structuralist doctrine was almost worked out at the ENS under Althusser,"[4] and it was represented by his disciples in *Les Cahiers pour l'analyse*.

Until then, structuralism had advanced within specific disciplines: anthropology for Lévi-Strauss, psychoanalysis for Lacan, linguistics for Greimas. With Althusser, it became possible to broaden horizons to include a structuralist philosophy that presented itself as such, and as the expression of the end of philosophy, the possibility of reaching beyond philosophy in the name of theory. Moreover, Althusser's conception of a separation between science and ideology coincided with and quickened the rapidly generalizing division between the techno-structure and the workers. The Althusserians "gave significant comfort to the split between the learned elite and the ordinary mortals, which, they implemented in their reviews and in their Maoist movement, which were hierarchized into groups with their relays and their grassroots committees: an organization that reflected that of French administration."[5] The project therefore took its place as part of the project of unifying the thinking that was going on about the social sciences, under the vigilant supervision of the philosophers. "There really was an attempt to construct a single problematic of the social sciences."[6]

Strategic Planning

There was also another—political—logic guiding Althusser's intervention in challenging the validity of the official PCF positions. As we have seen, between March 1965 and February 1966, *La Nouvelle Critique* became the locus of an important debate between Communist intellectuals about the relationship between Marxism and humanism. An important confrontation took place between Roger Garaudy, a partisan of a Marxist humanism, and Althusser, who argued for a theoretical antihumanism. "This controversy . . . appeared to us very concretely to raise the essential question of the theoretical status of historical materialism."[7] Jorge Semprun opened the argument against the Althusserian position by separating Marxist thinking, which is dialectical, from Althusserian thinking, which operates in terms of breaks. Using Marx's 1843 *Critique of Hegel's Philosophy of Law*, he showed that even the young Marx had never had an abstract notion of man, and that on the contrary, even as early as 1843, he defined man as an entirely social being. Michel Simon insisted on the dissociability of Marxism and humanism, even if he agreed with the Althusserian criticism of the use of the notion of alienation outside of the vague realm of ideology. He was careful to distinguish clearly between the abstract and universalizing humanism of the rising bourgeoisie and Marxist positions, but "humanism designates something that, in its deepest recesses, is essential for Marxism."[8] Pierre Macherey defended the hard line of Althusser's positions and proposed a clear position of rupture in place of the discourse of synthesis that was being outlined by certain party ideologues: "There is a break between the approaches of Semprun and Althusser."[9] He rejected any possible dialogue between two discourses that did not grant equal importance to the concepts being used. Using the same terminology was misleading because it addressed opposing ideas. The same was true for the term "praxis," which for Semprun referred to a real object, whereas for Althusser it referred to a theoretical object. Michel Verret also enthusiastically embraced Althusser's position: "Althusser emphasizes in a remarkable way that this humanism can only follow the theoretical destiny of alienation."[10]

Roger Garaudy had been warning against Althusser's sabotage of the young Marx since 1963, but his arguments were strongly contested by many party intellectuals. But the philosophers' meeting that took place in January 1966 at Choisy, without Althusser, made it possible to consolidate the team of ideologues who were part of the leadership around Garaudy: Lucien Sève, Guy Besse, Gilbert Mury, Pierre Boccara, Jean Texier. Each, at different levels, expressed disagreement with Althusser's positions. On this occasion, Garaudy strenuously attacked Althusser's notion of science, which he characterized as "outdated," "naive, scholastic, and mystical," as well as his "bloodless doctrinariness."[11]

A Marxist heretic in the eyes of the Communist Party apparatus, Althusser was isolated, and his isolation makes it easier to understand his strategic interest in suturing his positions to those of the structuralist wave, which had the enthusiastic support of intellectuals during the mid-sixties. Althusser offered the advantage of defending a "Cartesian Marxism made up of clear and distinct ideas,"[12] which made intellectuals proud to be Communists. A return to Marx and to his fundamental texts made possible by a purely theoretical and exegetical approach helped to attenuate the guilt feelings of being a Communist after the incontrovertible evidence of Stalin's crimes. "Althusser's work really represented a breath of fresh air."[13] The context was favorable for Althusser's theses because the PCF had been trying to establish a new relationship with intellectuals since the end of the fifties in order to abandon Stalinism bit by bit. Receptive to new forms of artistic expression and to the different avant-gardes, the party was breaking with socialist realism; in its openness to new theoretical exigencies, it was casting off the Lysenkoist delirium of the past. As early as 1959, Maurice Thorez announced the creation of a Center for Marxist Research and Study (CERM), which Roger Garaudy was to head up. The PCF was looking for a way to compensate for the losses it suffered from the trauma of 1956, by resuming the interrupted dialogue with intellectuals. Althusser arrived at a propitious moment, the culmination of a process that had begun with the decade and that gave intellectuals a special place in defining the new post-Stalinist line. But his theses went unadopted by the PCF central committee that met in March 1966 and that concluded, in fact, that "Marxism is the humanism of our time."[14]

Once the Garaudy line had triumphed, Althusser's work was carefully filtered by the party leadership and his texts disappeared from the shelves of the École Centrale des Cadres. This defeat was largely offset, however, by the tremendous dissemination of his work from the very place where Althusser would once again resume his theoretical efforts: the ENS on the rue d'Ulm. From Ulm, he could oppose the party leadership with a Marxist discourse fertilized by structuralism and worthy of the ranks of modern rationality.

Michel Pêcheux had been a disciple of Althusser in 1965–66, and the philosophy professor of Roger-Pol Droit, who, along with Guy Lardreau, Christian Jambet, and many others, was stimulated by Althussero-Lacanism, which seemed to incarnate the philosophy of the concept. Today, Roger-Pol Droit looks back on his training and his early philosophical years as

> a period defined by grids: grids in the sense of a conceptual framework of elucidation. We had the feeling that if we could just find the right overlay we would see what was invisible without the grid. The structure depended on this: it belonged to what was apparent in what we did not see, in the rainbow diversity of reality. And at the same time, theses are grids in the cellular sense of the word.[15]

The Althusserians had succeeded in making epistemology fashionable. It was a time when the epistemology of everything was being undertaken, such that one could say that it was no longer philosophy that was being done, but science. The situation was all the more paradoxical in that epistemology, by its hermetic discourse and the degree of expertise required in different fields, was generally limited to small circles: "I even saw Derrida once answer a question put to him about whether what he was doing was science say no, it was not, but that it could become that."[16] This was the scientistic context of Althusser's project, which also responded to the desires of a new generation that did not want to bear the burden of Stalinist crimes and hungered for an absolute. All of this made possible a paradoxical bringing together of an often mad political voluntarism—a desperate activism—and the notion of a subjectless process that resembled a mystical commitment:

> Just as for all religious persons, the subject tears itself from itself in order to become the agent of a process. I was raised by the Jesuits. It was clear that we were ripping ourselves from ourselves, and were no longer subjects before the great Subject that was the Process; this is how we saved our souls. It was completely feasible to reconcile these things.[17]

Althusser became a rallying point for an entire generation. For those who wanted to leave academicisms behind, he was a standard-bearer, an anchor: "I was a student from 1955 to 1960 and Althusser brought us a kind of illumination. It was extraordinarily stimulating."[18]

The Return to Marx

Maspero published two books in 1965 that were immediately and spectacularly successful and became the major references of the period: *For Marx*, a collection of articles by Althusser published in the "Théorie" collection, which sold thirty-two thousand copies; and *Reading Capital*, a collective work including, in addition to Althusser's pieces, contributions by Jacques Rancière, Pierre Macherey, Étienne Balibar, and Roger Establet. Maspero had been created in 1959, and we might wonder if Louis Althusser deliberately chose this house or if he came to it after having been rejected by the Éditions Sociales. According to Guy Besse, on the one hand, Althusser did not want to commit the whole of the party to his positions, which would have been the case had his book come out at the Éditions Sociales, and, on the other hand, his concern for efficiency would have led him to choose Maspero because its distribution network enabled him to reach a much broader public than simply that of the PCF. But it would seem that behind Althusser's attitude, which was at once daring and fearful, lay the party leadership's major roadblocks. "In 1979, Althusser told me that he had only published at Maspero after having been turned down elsewhere."[19]

So the Althusserians had achieved a "return to" Marx himself, a

Marx extracted from the commentaries and from the exegeses that had been made of his work up to then and that had blocked any direct knowledge of his positions. The act of reading Marx was the first of the shifts the Althusserians accomplished, and in so doing they fully participated in the structural paradigm by favoring the discursive realm and the internal logic of a self-enclosed system. Of course, Althusser's perspective was not linguistic, but he was part of this autonomization of the discursive sphere that must be approached on the basis of a new theory of Reading, inaugurated by Marx himself, ignored by the vulgate, and reactivated by Althusser.

This new practice of reading was baptized "symptomatic reading," using an adjective directly borrowed from psychoanalysis and from Lacan in particular, and which bespoke the more essential character of that which is invisible and refers to a lack or an absence. Althusser distinguished between two different modes in Marx's reading of classical political economists. First, he read the discourses of Ricardo, Smith, and so on, within his own categories of thinking in order to understand their lacunae and to establish their differences, thereby demonstrating what his predecessors had missed. This first reading allowed for "an inventory of possible agreements and differences."[20] But behind this was a more essential reading, beyond the observed inadequacies, lacunae, and silences. This second reading let Marx see where classical political economy had been blind even with its eyes open. He made patently clear those assertions his predecessors had left unproblematized and unquestioned. Marx thus made answers appear where questions had not even been asked, in a purely intratextual play. "The not-seeing is then included within the seeing; it is a form of seeing, therefore, in a necessary relationship with seeing."[21] Just as an individual neurosis can be expressed by a certain number of symptoms without any obvious or direct correspondence to their cause, so too political economy could see or take into consideration what it does.

There were two advantages to this kind of reading. On the one hand, it demonstrated a certain sensitivity to the need for linguistic rigor by seeking the key to the problem within the text itself, by problematizing the text and its internal logic; and, on the other hand, it offered a method that, similar to Freudian analysis, considered that the most essential reality is the least obvious. Althusser's reading was situated neither in the absence of the discourse nor in what it makes explicit but somewhere in that gray area between the latent and manifest discourses, which only a particular kind of listening or reading can bring to light. If the error concerns seeing, sight depends on structural conditions, the conditions of discourse, the range of possibilities of what is said and what is unsaid. This shift borrowed as much from Michel Foucault as from Lacan: "Althusser did nothing more than reemphasize the ideas of Foucault and Lacan again."[22] The model of making a dialectic of visible and invisible space came from Foucault's *Madness and Civilization*, which Althusser invoked at the beginning of *Reading Capital*, not only with regard to the relationship of the interiority of shadows, darkness, and light, but also with respect to the attention paid to those apparently heterogeneous conditions that organize branches of knowledge into disciplinary units: "Terms that recall some very remarkable passages of Michel Foucault's preface to his *Madness and Civilization*."[23]

The Epistemological Break

Althusser also borrowed Bachelard's idea of an epistemological rupture, but he made it more radical by adopting the term "break" in order to emphasize its trenchant quality. He took his analytical model for reading Marx from scientific epistemology. Bachelard applied this notion notably to physics, and more precisely to quantum mechanics, to express the distance separating scientific knowledge and perceptual understanding.

Althusser extended the idea, broadening it into a general concept that applied to the history of any of the sciences, making it clear that the discontinuities on which any particular scientific edifice was built needed to be discerned. In his concern to present Marx as the bearer of a new science, Althusser saw a radical split between a young Marx still mired in Hegelian idealism, and a mature, scientific Marx. Yet, "Bachelard never would have spoken about a split between a science and a prior philosophical construction."[24] According to Althusser, Marx reached a scientific level at the point when he managed to rid himself of the ideological and philosophical legacy with which he was imbued. Althusser even laid out the phases of the process and very precisely designated 1845 as the moment of the caesura that permitted Marx to become scientific. Everything before 1845 is the work of the young Marx, a Marx before he was Marx.

The young Marx is therefore marked by the Feuerbachian theses of alienation, of generic man. This was the period of a rationalist, liberal, humanist Marx closer to Kant and to Fichte than to Hegel. "The first works suppose a Kantian-Fichtean kind of problematic,"[25] centered around the figure of a man destined to his freedom and who must restore his lost essence in the thread of a history that alienates him. He must resolve the contradiction of his alienated rationality, incarnated by a state that remains deaf to the demands of freedom. Despite himself, this man realizes his essence through the alienated products of his labor and he must complete this realization by once again taking possession of this alienated essence in order to become transparent to himself, a total man finally realized at the end of History. This reversal came directly out of Feuerbach: "The fundamentals of the philosophical problematic are Feuerbachian."[26]

According to Althusser, Marx rejected the notion of founding history and politics on an essence of man in 1845, when he adopted a scientific theory of history based on entirely new explanatory concepts such as social formation, the forces of production, relationships of production, and so on. At that point, he eliminated the philosophical categories of the subject, essence, and alienation and made a radical critique of humanism, which was considered to be part of the mystifying ideology of the ruling class. This was the mature Marx of the period between 1845 and 1857, and his evolution made the great scientific work of his mature years possible, for *Capital* is a veritable science of the modes of production, and therefore of human history.

This fundamental break in Marx's work was perceptible thanks to the shift from praxis to epistemology. Thanks to *Capital*, Marx broke definitively with ideology and his work thus came to make a scientific contribution the equal of Newton's *Principia*. "We know that a pure science exists only if it is ceaselessly refined. . . . This purification and this liberation are acquired only at the cost of a constant struggle against ideology itself."[27] Whereas until then Marx's work had been considered to be a return to the Hegelian dialectic from a materialist perspective, Althusser made a term-by-term comparison of Hegel's and Marx's dialectics; Marx did not simply stand Hegelian idealism back on its feet, he constructed a theory whose structure was in all ways different, even if the terminology of the negation and the identity of opposites, and of getting beyond contradiction, suggested certain similarities in procedure. "It is absolutely impossible to maintain the fiction of the reversal, even in its apparent rigor. Because, in truth, even as Marx reversed them, he did not maintain the terms of the Hegelian model of society."[28]

This discontinuity between Hegel and Marx let Althusser break with the Stalinist economist vulgate, which was satisfied with substituting the economic sphere as an essence for Hegel's political-ideological essence. But this criticism of the mechanisms of Marxist thought was made in the name of the construction of a pure and decontextualized theory, which, as such, made it possible to achieve the status of a science. Dialectical materialism, for Althusser, was the theory that established the scientificity of historical materialism, and it had to be preserved from the ideological contamination that constantly threatened it. "We see that it can no longer finally be a matter of reversal. Because we do not get a science when we overthrow an ideology."[29]

Historical materialism was therefore the science of the scientificity of sciences. And a historian can only find perplexing this obvious scientism that runs through Althusser, even when he is, like Pierre Vilar, deeply committed to the construction of a Marxist history. "There is a progression in Marx's thinking that absolutely does not occur around a break. I completely disagree with such an idea, which in fact belongs to Foucault's work."[30]

Althusser certainly wanted to escape the Stalinist vulgate, which had a tendency to see everything as a reflection of economic relationships, by making a purified scientific field autonomous. In this regard, he produced a veritable renewal of Marxist thought. But by offering a system that was closed in on itself, Althusser precipitated the crisis.

> This sounded the death knell for a certain Marxism because, after coming full circle, things went around in circles. If Marxism is alive, it is not because it is satisfied with exhuming scientific concepts. This dimension contributed to a certain decline of Marxism, which, paradoxically, it had wanted to save. How can you construct a Marxism that is fundamentally a reflection on history with a profoundly ahistorical method.[31]

If Althusser finally sawed off the branch he was sitting on, he did nonetheless inspire a momentary second wind in Marxist thinking and comforted a whole current of modernist intellectuals in search of a radical break that was as much theoretical and institutional as it was political.

A Structured Totality

Rather than the mechanistic vulgate of the theory of reflection, Althusser proposed a structured totality in which meaning was a function of the position of each of the elements of the mode of production. He could therefore acknowledge the specific efficacy of the superstructure, which was dominant in certain cases, and in all cases in a relationship of relative autonomy with respect to the infrastructure. By unhooking the superstructure from the ideological-political sphere, Althusser could save the socialist base of the Soviet Union because its relative autonomy "could explain quite simply, in theory, that the socialist infrastructure could, for the most part, evolve without being harmed during this period of errors affecting the superstructure."[32] As they said at the time, you don't throw out the baby with the bathwater, and although one could legitimately speak about Stalinist crimes and of a savage repression against the masses by those in power, it was not yet possible to talk about exploitation and the failure of a system that remained fundamentally and miraculously preserved at the level of its infrastructure, safe in the face of a bureaucratic degeneration affecting only the highest reaches of Soviet society. To Hegel's ideological-political totality, Althusser opposed the complex, structured totality of Marxism, which, depending on the historical moment, was hierarchized differently in terms of the respective places of ideology and politics, for example, in the mode of production, even if economics was always determinant in the final analysis.

With Althusser, structure became plural, transforming a single temporality into multiple temporalities. "There is no general history, but only specific structures of historicity."[33] Thus there were only differential temporalities, with each one autonomous in its relationship to the whole: "The specificity of each of these times and of each of these histories—in other words, their relative autonomy and independence—is based on a certain type of articulation within the whole."[34]

Althusser participated in the deconstruction of history, and in so doing he was part of the structural paradigm, not by denying historicity but by breaking it into heterogeneous units. To his way of thinking, the structured whole was dehistoricized and decontextualized in the same way that, in order to achieve the status of a science, that which is ideological had to be detached. Knowledge (Generality III) is only possible through the mediation of a body of concepts (Generalities II) that work on an empirical prime matter (Generality I). Such an approach assimilated the object of analysis of Marxism to the objects of the physical and chemical sciences and implied a total decentering of the subject. "This meant mixing up experimental sciences with what are called the social sciences."[35]

Structural Causality

In general, structuralism tried to avoid simple causal systems, and in this respect Althusser's work was consonant with structuralism. Leaving the theory of reflection behind, he proposed to combine what was internal to the structure of the mode of production. And yet he did not abandon the search for a causal system, which was indispensable for establishing the scientific character of his theory, but defined a new determination, which he called structural causality or metonymic causality: "I believe that when it is understood as the concept of the efficacy of an absent cause, this concept is admirably well suited for designating the absence as structure in the effects under consideration."[36]

This concept of the efficacy of an absence, a structure defined as the absent cause of its effects, reaching beyond each of its elements in the same way that the signifier goes beyond the signified, belonged to the aspherical structure that defined the Subject for Lacan, constructed on the basis of a lack, of the loss of the first Signifier. This dialectic around a void is found in Lacan and in Althusser, and the principle of explanation, which is of course unfalsifiable, can accommodate any kind of situation like an open sesame. Here, the purification of Marxism reached the highest degree of a metaphysics that "also makes sacrifices to a hidden God in the name of the struggle against theology."[37] This structuralist philosophy, which endows itself with all the appeal of scientificity in order to renew Marxism or Freudian thinking, also ontologized structure with idea of structural causality. It becomes a fact that "structures are deep causes and the observable phenomena of simple surface effects; . . . these structures therefore have an ambiguous status."[38] They are, in fact, occult entities insufficiently substantial to act since, as structures, they are only pure relations; but, moreover, they are too solid to be structures in Lévi-Strauss's sense of the term, and thus make it possible to account for observable phenomena in terms of causalities.

Lacan is everywhere in Althusser's work and the strong current of Althussero-Lacanianism at the rue d'Ulm was based on a theoretical matrix that made a symbiosis of the two possible: from the symptomatic reading via the structural causality, which is absent from its effects, to overdetermination, another fundamental conceptual tool that Althusser imported from psychoanalysis. "I did not forge this concept. As I have indicated, I borrowed it from two existing disciplines: linguistics and psychoanalysis."[39]

This notion was central, providing the Marxist contradiction with its specificity and making it possible to account for the structural totality, the transition from one structure to another in a concrete social formation. Along with overdetermination, Althusser borrowed other Freudian concepts as well, such as condensation and transference, which make their way into Marxism. This intrusion let Althusser multiply the contradiction, if not to dissolve it. It "corroded . . . the comfortable arrangements of the logos of contradiction."[40]

Theoretical Antihumanism and Antihistoricism

The appetite for Althusser's theses also corresponded to a moment in which the conception of the Subject was taking off from the theoretical horizon. The structuralist program had already managed to reduce, dethrone, and split the Subject, and generally make it insignificant; with Althusser, Marx took his place alongside those who, on the basis of the social sciences, were carrying out and developing this decentering of man in every way. "In a strict relationship to theory, we can and should speak openly of Marx's theoretical antihumanism."[41] The notion of man loses all meaning as it is reduced to little more than a philosophical myth, a contemporary ideological category of the rise of the bourgeoisie. Reading *Capital* in a theoretical antihumanist perspective would set in place essentially structural categories; these were Lacanian in Althusser and Lévi-Straussian for Étienne Balibar. "In *Reading Capital*, I had somewhat imitated a certain number of models for constructing concepts that, although they were not taken from Lévi-Strauss, made it possible to discover, surprisingly, a comparative method in Marx's texts. There are aspects of Marx that are structuralist before structuralism."[42]

Balibar in fact made an essential contribution in the collective anthology *Reading Capital*, in which he studied the fundamental concepts of historical materialism. He elucidated Marx's theses on the basis of a theoretical apparatus in which the methodological presuppositions of Lévi-Straussian structuralism became readily apparent.

Marxist notions were reconstructed from purely formal determinations, as they are in the phonological model, and evolved according to a system of purely spatial pertinent differences that excluded material nature, the concrete substance of the objects in question. Just as for kinship structures, empirical descriptions of observable reality counted less than defining the mode of production as "the differential determination of forms, and defining a 'mode' as a system of forms that represents a state of variation."[43] Setting the referent aside therefore lent an essentially formal aspect to the approach, making it possible to claim a greater latitude for applying it to all possible cases. "This combination—practically mathematical— . . . will incite us to speak about a perfectly unexpected structuralism here."[44] In a pure interplay combining forms and pertinent differences, Étienne Balibar did, nevertheless, agree that economics played the fundamental role, that of determining the relationship of relationships, that of the structural causality.

This theoretical elaboration made a science of the modes of production possible because it could achieve a high degree of abstraction and generalization and at the same time make use of a system of pertinent causality. In such a science, the Subject shone by its impertinence; indeed, it is simply impossible to find, an exquisite corpse cast out with the ideological bathwater: "Men only appear in the theory as supports for the relationships implied in the structure, and the forms of their individuality only appear as the determined effects of the structure."[45] The structural paradigm lends some support to this decentering, which also claims a philosophical heritage in Spinoza and his definition of attributes, which function like pertinent characteristics within the mode of production in Marx. A subjectless process, therefore, according to the Althusserians, shapes the course of history.

Not only the Subject, but all historicist notions of history went unrecognized for their potential perversion of the sought-after theoretical scientificity: "The fall of science in history here is only the indication of a theoretical fall."[46] Althusserian antihistoricism evolved over a number of stages, including the decomposition of temporalities and the construction of a totality articulated around pertinent relationships within a general theory. But this totality in fact became immobilized without recognizing structure in the same way that Lévi-Strauss's cold societies were immobilized, without recognizing what was going on in their internal contradictions or in the potential for getting beyond them. By metonymy, the state of structure was substituted for the cadaver of the subject, which had disappeared along with its historicity. Since this atrophied and frozen structure had to be attached to something, Althusser anchored it with the status he gave the notion of ideology, which served as a pivot much as the symbolic did for Lacan or Lévi-Strauss. Althusser used it as an invariant, atemporal category, like the Freudian unconscious, and therefore had free rein to complexify the kind of purely instrumental relationship used in the Marxist vulgate's view of the dominant ideology as a simple instrument of the ruling class.

A Subject of Substitution: Ideology

Althusser elevated ideology to the level of a relatively autonomous veritable function making it mechanically irreducible to what underlay it. But setting ideology at a distance also meant its hypertrophy as a transhistoric structure invoked in order to construct theory. By induction, then, the efficacy of the ideological led to the creation of subjects absolutely subjected to the place to which they were assigned, like so many mystified objects of occult forces represented by a new subject of history: ideology.

This was the period when everything was ideology: feelings, behavior . . . Nothing escaped the critique of ideology, which became a totalizing category within which an impotent individual operated. The only escape from what could have been a vicious circle in a closed system, the only way of getting out of this labyrinth, was, for Althusser, through the epistemological break, the sole thread that made the advent of science possible.

Marxism, as a theory of theoretical practices and as the ideological detergent in the name of science, allowed for an entire generation to reconcile its political commitment with a truly scientific exigency that, in its purity, resembled a metaphysical desire for an absolute. We can readily understand how such a thinking machine could attract those avidly in search of critical arms.

Thirty-two

Marxism's Second Wind

This new Althusserian reading represented a youthful cure for Marxism and rid it of its tragic cast. Everyone used the mature Marx to turn him into the harbinger of the scientificity of his discipline, as the remarkable sales of the very theoretical *For Marx* attested. Moreover, the totalizing conception of Althusserian thought gave each discipline the feeling that it was an active participant in a common adventure. Marx became the intersection of all research, a veritable common denominator in the social sciences.

In philosophy, Althusser received the exemplary and completely unexpected support of Alain Badiou, a brilliant philosopher who was close to Sartre, who thus once more lost one of his disciples, carried away by the structural wave. Badiou published an enthusiastic article on the (new) beginning of dialectical materialism in *Critique*.[1] "This article was very favorable and everyone was quite surprised by such a reversal."[2] Alain Badiou was pleased with the harmony generated by the new Althusserian theses and by the political context. He discerned three types of Marxism: a fundamental Marxism based exclusively on the young Marx of the *Manuscripts of 1844*, a totalitarian Marxism based on dialectical laws, and, taking Althusserian thinking as its realization, an analogical Marxism for which *Capital* is a privileged object and that "uses Marxist ideas in such a way as to undo their organization. He in fact considered the relationship between the base and the superstructure . . . as pure isomorphs."[3] After the publication of

his article, Badiou was invited by Althusser's work group to participate in a philosophy course for scientists that was to be held at the
ENS during the academic year 1967–68. Lecturing to an enormous
crowd, Badiou presented his ideas of the model.

This symbiotic synergy between political commitment, epistemological reflection, and a new approach to Marxism carried beyond the
Latin Quarter to most French university campuses. In Aix-en-Provence,
Joëlle Proust, who was about twenty at the time and working in epistemology with Gilles Gaston-Granger, discovered *For Marx* with a
passion and discussed its new theses in her work group. "We were
completely convinced. We felt that we were discovering the theoretical
possibilities linked to political positions and inseparable from structuralism that seemed to offer the key for interpreting a range of different fields. What was fascinating was that it worked in linguistics, so
we all did some linguistics."[4]

Such a return to Marx's work and to the internal construction of
his texts cannot but recall the principles of Martial Guéroult's method.
For a whole generation of philosophers, this kind of reading meant
the possibility of breaking with a form of teaching that tended to water
down the specificity of philosophical problematization itself and to
analyse purely doxographic influences. Althusserian structural Marxism laid the foundations for a new era in philosophy, but all the fields
of knowledge experienced a serious jolt in 1965. Althusser's model,
which made use of the structuralist vogue, became in its turn, the
launching pad for other efforts to transform the human sciences.

Althusserism in Linguistics

Michel Pêcheux, a friend and disciple of Althusser, thought that the
best way to do philosophy in the sixties was to do it in the social sciences. In this regard, he was somewhat of an exception among the
ENS disciplines. Appointed to a CNRS social psychology laboratory
at the Sorbonne, under Pagès, he belonged to a discipline that, at
the time, had the reputation of being the worst of horrors in the eyes
of Althusserians. As a student of Althusser and Canguilhem, he was
something like the Trojan horse of psychologism. In 1966, Pêcheux
met Michel Simon and Paul Henry, two researchers from another
social science laboratory in the Sixth Section of the EPHE, under the
direction of Serge Moscovici. The three of them together worked on a
critique from within of the classical forms of the social sciences. "We

had become sort of an informal team and we worked together practically all week long."[5]

Michel Simon had been a technician in the laboratory and later became a researcher, while Paul Henry, who had been trained as a mathematician, was interested in ethnology. He had gone to see Lévi-Strauss in 1962, just after having finished his *Licence* in mathematics, to discuss his interest in taking up ethnology. Henry had found Lévi-Strauss appealing because of his use of mathematical models and his will to construct an encompassing communication theory. Lévi-Strauss advised Henry to do linguistics and to get a certificate in ethnology. When Henry entered the social psychology laboratory, he, like Pêcheux, had a critical perspective. He was surprised by the use of mathematics and the proliferation of equations without any conceptual constructions, and his research projects were increasingly oriented toward linguistics, toward the structures of language and the notions of what is implicit or presupposed. These placed him at the heart of the structuralist problem. "We were interested in structuralism because it was a way of critiquing social psychology, and particularly by the notion of the subject."[6]

Led by Pêcheux, this little work group tried to apply Althusser's theses to linguistics. Many others worked on this as well, particularly at Nanterre: Régine Robin, Denise Maldidier, Françoise Gadet, Claudine Normand. Michel Pêcheux initially published two articles in *Les Cahiers pour l'analyse* under the pseudonym of Thomas Herbert, first in 1966 and again in 1968.[7] This theoretical work was part of the double return to Marx that Althusser had undertaken and the return to Freud carried out by Lacan, and was to be used as a framework for the publication of a book that became a methodological manifesto. Pêcheux's *Automatic Discourse Analysis*, published in 1969,[8] served as a bridge to Althusser's thinking, making it accessible to linguists. Pêcheux also argued for the notion of a break in the process of establishing a science, and he took the example of technical practices that only later became scientific practices, such as stills or scales. Scales were long used for commercial transactions before Galileo used them as an object for the theory of physics. "This process is exactly what Pêcheux called the 'methodical reproduction' of the object of a science."[9]

For Pêcheux, this second stage was the true realization of science; he was convinced that the human sciences were merely ideologies and that philosophically based criticisms of them were useless. He hoped to transform them from within by providing truly scientific instruments adapted to their specific field. However, the proximity between this ideology belonging to the social sciences and political practice in its ability to reproduce social relationships made it necessary to give priority to discourse, the specific instrument of political power. This hidden tie between political practice and the social sciences needed to be examined. "Pêcheux totally rejected any idea of a language reduced to an instrument for communicating meanings that exist or could be defined independently of it."[10] The orientation that Pêcheux gave discourse analysis took its place within the Althusserian notion of ideology, transformed into a veritable subject of discourse, a universal element of historical existence. His goal was to make the link between language and ideology explicit. He "placed himself between what we might call the subject of language and the subject of ideology,"[11] at the core of the problem of a structuralized Marxism.

Althusserian Thinking in Anthropology

Alain Badiou's conversion to Althusserianism brought with it another. The anthropologist Emmanuel Terray had also been rather a Sartrean early on and a great admirer of *Critique of Dialectic Reason*. Later, Terray would transform anthropology from a Marxist-structuralist perspective. He had taken courses with Althusser at the ENS but had left Ulm in 1961, just before Althusser began teaching Marx. When Althusser's theses were published, Terray was in the Ivory Coast doing fieldwork, and it was his friend, Alain Badiou, who kept him current. "I read *For Marx* and *Reading Capital* then with great interest and excitement."[12] Althusser's article "Contradiction and Overdetermination" in *For Marx* seemed the most fundamental to him because it made it possible to tear Marxism away from questions of origins and metaphysics in order to make it an instrument of scientific analysis. But what would influence Terray's anthropological perspective more than anything was Étienne Balibar's article "The Fundamental Concepts of Historical Materialism," in *Reading Capital*.

Terray later tested the validity of the concepts of mode of production, relation of production, forces of production, and their articulations while doing his fieldwork. "Reading this text, I wrote the second part of my book, *Marxism and Primitive Societies*.[13] This was a rereading of Claude Meillassoux's work using the conceptual grid that Étienne Balibar had proposed."[14] Before publishing his book, Terray sent the manuscript to Althusser, who not only considered it to be pertinent but immediately understood how much it would affect the work being done in anthropology. From then on, Terray was included in the circle of Althusserians.

An ethnologist and friend of Terray, Marc Augé, was also working in the Ivory Coast at the time, and he also joined the Althusserian vogue. "Althusser was enormously influential because he appeared to be a liberator, a model of nuance with respect to the Marxist vulgate."[15] In his monograph on the Alladians, Augé had also tested the pertinence of the Althusserian model, but only in notes,[16] although today he recognizes his discomfort in this exercise of making a theoretical projection of a reality ill adapted to his reading grid at the time: "It did not correspond to what I was looking at empirically, which is to say, people who wondered about death, illness, and the beyond."[17] This manner of questioning was therefore quite eccentric with regard to the instruments being used in Althusser's form of structural Marxism, even if there was a real change in anthropological receptivity to an entirely new manner of thinking about social and economic fields.

Althusserianism in Economics

Althusserian thinking also made inroads in economics. Under Althusser's direct influence, Suzanne de Brunoff published *Money in Marx*,[18] a book that was contemporaneous with *Reading Capital*. But it was especially Charles Bettelheim's work that was spectacularly influential at the time. Bettelheim took Althusserian categories of contradiction between the relations and forces of production in order to demonstrate—and in this he distinguished his work from that of Althusser—the reestablishment of the capitalist mode of production in the Soviet Union. Using the invariant of the separation between producers and owners of the means of production—the basis of business organization in the Soviet economy—he deduced the domination of capitalism in social organization. Taking a structural Marxist perspective, meaning became positional, defined by the polarity between the proletarian and the bureaucrat, who, like the capitalist, finds himself on the other side of the structure. Bettelheim's work was also interesting because it reduced the dominance the Marxist vulgate attributed to the forces of production and underscored, to the contrary, the principal role played by social relationships in the very organization of production.[19] Bettelheim and Balibar agreed on this point to consider the level of the productive forces also as a relation of production. Bettelheim questioned the neutrality of the productive forces, a thesis that Robert Linhart later took up in his study on the inherent contractions in the development of Soviet socialism in *Lenin, Peasants, and Taylor*.[20]

Linhart demonstrated the opposition between the construction of a socialist reality and the application that Lenin, as early as 1918, wanted to make of Taylor's model, which involved a clear division between a technocratic leadership and the workers. This application of Taylorism overwhelmed the technical division of work at the same time as it tore the workers' own knowledge out of their hands in order to transfer it to a bureaucratized management.

And yet, because the Althusserian theses were so intensely theoretical, it was impossible for them to make a decisive and immediate incursion into economic territory, although economists would be deeply jolted by Althusser's ideas after the shock wave of the May 1968 movement.

Althusser Introduces Lacan

It is also to Althusser's credit that psychoanalysis came to the fore of French intellectual life, thanks to his 1964 article "Freud and Lacan," which came out at the same time that Lacan relocated his seminar to the ENS on the rue d'Ulm.[21] Althusser's position made it possible to open Marxism up to Freudian thinking and to put an end to the separation imposed by the Stalinist rejection of psychoanalysis. With Althusser, the return to Freud took the form of a recourse to Lacan, for both were engaged in a similar enterprise of epistemological elucidation and ideological critique and both were waging a war against humanism and psychologism in the name of science. This similarity was also apparent in their renewal of a particular kind of reading of the basic works of Marx and Freud.

"The return to Freud was not a return to the birth of Freud but to the mature Freud."[22] What Althusser appreciated in the Lacanian approach was that Lacan saw a break in Freud's work that resembled the one he perceived in Marx's work: "Lacan's first words are to say that by virtue of his principles, Freud founded a science."[23] But a science needs it own object; it cannot be constructed as a simple art of accommodating leftovers. After Freud's discovery of this specific object, the unconscious, Lacan, according to Althusser, took a step forward in constituting psychoanalysis as a science by considering that the transition from a biological to a social existence was to be inscribed in the register of the Law of Order, which is to say, language. According to Althusser, Lacan's contribution lay in the priority he accorded the symbolic over the imaginary: "Lacan made clear this crucial point: these two moments are governed, dominated, and marked by a single Law, that of the symbolic."[24]

Shifting the ego out of the center and subordinating it to an order eluding consciousness recalls Althusser's reading of Marx wherein history is a subjectless process. In this way, an Althussero-Lacanism could explode and make Marx and Freud the great thinking machine of the sixties. A renewed Marxism received its second wind, fanned even further by the aftermath of May 1968.

Thirty-three

1966
Annum mirabile (I): A Watershed Year for Structuralism

> Everything started falling apart as of 1966. A friend had talked to
> me about *The Order of Things* and I made the mistake of opening
> it. . . . I dropped Stendhal, Mandelstam, and Rimbaud, the way one
> fine day you stop smoking Gitanes, in order to read the authors that
> Foucault was discussing—Freud, Saussure, and Ricardo. I was in-
> fected. The fever did not stop and I loved this infection. I did not
> want to get better. I was proud of my knowledge, like a louse on the
> pope's head. I was talking about philosophy. I called myself a struc-
> turalist, but I was not going around shouting my head off since I was
> still uncertain; the slightest jolt would have shaken me. I spent my
> nights teaching myself the principles of linguistics and I was quite
> happy. . . . I was gorging myself on syntagms and morphemes. . . . If
> I happened to have any discussions with a humanist, I wiped him out
> with an epistemic blow. . . . I spoke the names Derrida or Propp in
> an emotional and almost trembling voice, preferably during autumn
> evenings, like an old soldier caressing the flags he has wrested from
> his enemy. . . . Jakobson was my tropics and my equator, Émile Ben-
> veniste my Guadeloupe, and the proairetic code my Club Med. I
> thought of Hjelmslev like a steppe. . . . It seems to me that I was not
> the only one to have gotten lost in these detours.[1]

Twenty years later, Gilles Lapouge describes the real Saturday
night fever of the sixties for a structuralism that had reached its
zenith. All the energy of the social sciences converged at that point to
irradiate the perspective of research and publication around the structuralist paradigm. The year 1966 was the "central reference point. . . .
At least in Paris, we could say it was that year when lots of things got

mixed together, and it was probably a decisive year for the most specialized research areas."[2] The year 1966 can be consecrated as the structuralist year; if we can talk about the descendants of 1848 or of 1968, we have to include those descendants of 1966, who were just as turbulent. "I am a child of 1966."[3]

Publishing in the Kingdom of Structure

The activity in publishing houses in 1966 gave a clear idea of the veritable structuralist explosion going on everywhere that year and it appeared to be a real seismic jolt. The number of major works was impressive: Roland Barthes published *Critique et vérité* at Seuil, his famous reaction to Picard's attack, and about which Renaud Matignon wrote in *L'Express*: "This is the Dreyfus Affair of the world of letters. It too had a Picard, whose name was even written the same way, and his 'J'accuse' has just been published."[4] For Matignon, Barthes's work holds a place in the history of critical thought equal to the one accorded the Declaration of the Rights of Man in social history. There was no real French civil war to decide whether Barthes or Picard was right, but the intellectual world found itself very much divided that year along those lines.

Greimas published his *Structural Semantics* at Larousse that year. "Thanks to Dubois, my semantics has become structural in big red letters. He told me, 'You will sell a thousand more copies if you add the word structural.'"[5] Adding the adjective "structuralist" was a good sales pitch in the mid-sixties. Everyone was affected, including the "trainer of the French soccer team, who declared that he was going to reorganize the team according to structuralist principles."[6]

François Wahl, Roland Barthes's close friend and editor at Seuil, managed to persuade Lacan to publish his writings in an anthology: "The *Écrits* were published because of me, to tell you the truth. I found myself de facto in a central role, speaking purely in a topographical sense."[7] This enormous nine hundred-page volume, written in a baroque and hermetic style, consecrated Lacan as the "French Freud" in 1966. When the reviews starting coming out, 5,000 copies had already been sold and Seuil quickly had to reprint the *Écrits*. They continue to sell well: 36,000 volumes had been sold by 1984. In 1970 the two-volume paperback was published and it broke all records for this kind of book, selling 94,000 copies of the first volume and 65,000 copies of the second volume.

Still at Seuil, in the *Tel Quel* collection, Tzvetan Todorov made the work of the Russian formalists known to a French public with his *Theory of Literature*, with a preface by Roman Jakobson. Gérard Genette published *Figures* in the same collection.

The real event of the year, however, was Michel Foucault's *The Order of Things*. Its success was unprecedented: the book was out of print within days. "Foucault is selling like hotcakes: 800 copies of *The Order of Things* in five days, during the last week of July (9,000 copies in all)."[8] Published in April of 1966, *The Order of Things* sold 20,000 copies during that year alone; in 1987, it sold 103,000 copies.[9] Given the difficulty of the work, this was entirely exceptional.

Thanks to Foucault's work, Pierre Nora, who had just joined Gallimard, began the Library of the Human Sciences collection in 1965:

> I was profoundly convinced that there was a movement taking place in what we called the sciences of man. Different disciplines were beginning to converge around a common set of problems based on the fact that when men speak they say things they are not necessarily responsible for, and end up doing things they did not necessarily want to do, that forces they are not conscious of course through them and dominate them. . . . Moreover, a second movement was going through the research being done: this was a sociopolitical content, which gave this knowledge a potentially subversive value.[10]

At the same time and in the same collection, along with Michel Foucault Pierre Nora brought out Élias Canetti's *Mass and Power*,[11] and Geneviève Calame-Griaule's *Ethnology and Language*.[12] Émile Benveniste's *General Linguistics* also became the great reference work of the moment and brought its author out of his isolation at the Collège de France.

Pierre Nora did not, however, want to limit himself to being a simple spokesman for structuralism. He was taking Raymond Aron's seminar at the time and asked Aron to prepare a book that would come out in 1967, *The Stages of Sociological Thinking*.[13] And yet, the fact that he was director of Gallimard's social sciences publications in 1966 made him, despite himself, structuralism's standard-bearer. He tried, unsuccessfully, to draw Lévi-Strauss into his circle: "When I got to Gallimard, I went to see him to try and bring him along. For reasons that are not important here, he did not want to come to Gallimard."[14] In 1966, Payot decided to publish Georges Dumézil's *Ancient Roman Religion*,[15] which was originally to have come out at a

German publishing house. Pierre Nora immediately understood how important it was to publish a work by Dumézil in the structuralist fever of the time and went to see him. "Pierre Nora intervened. He made me. I am a creation of Gallimard."[16]

Even if certain houses, such as Seuil or Gallimard, appeared to be the spearheads of the structuralist publishing enterprise, others also participated in the explosion of 1966. Éditions de Minuit published Pierre Bourdieu and Alain Darbel's *Love of Art*.[17] Éditions François Maspero, which had stunned everyone in 1965 with *Reading Capital* and *For Marx*, published *For a Theory of Literary Production*[18] by Pierre Machery, an Althusserian. Presses Universitaires de France reprinted Georges Canguilhem's thesis, *Normal and Pathological*,[19] which had initially come out in 1943. Nor were historians silent in this rising tide of structure. The *Annales* school also published a certain number of major works during this same year of 1996, including Emmanuel Le Roy Ladurie's *The Peasants of Languedoc*,[20] published at the École Pratique des Hautes Études (SEVPEN), and Pierre Goubert's *Louis XIV and Twenty Million Frenchmen*,[21] published by Fayard. The master of the *Annales* school, Fernand Braudel, took advantage of this infatuation with the long haul and structures to have Armand Colin republish his *The Mediterranean and the Mediterranean World at the Time of Philip II*.[22]

The year 1966 was one during which the apprentice structuralist reader had to read constantly. Every day brought another work to the harvest; a number of reprints came out that were also considered absolutely indispensable reading for a good structuralist. Gilles Gaston-Granger's *Formal Thinking and the Human Sciences*[23] (Aubier, 1960) was an example. "When I got to the Sorbonne in 1965–66, I asked people two or three years older what I should read. Everyone told me that I had to read that book, which was being quoted everywhere."[24] The same was true for Jean Rousset's *Form and Meaning*[25] (Corti, 1962), which was essential for an entire generation, and in which the author proposed to analyze the production of meaning within texts based on their internal formal structure.

Reviews in the Kingdom of Structure

The year 1966 was also one of intense structuralist activity in reviews. Hundreds were created. The first issue of *Langages* came out in March 1966 and presented the scientific study of language as an essential dimension of culture. This project focused on the interfacing of various disciplines interested in problems of language. Similarly, *Les Cahiers pour l'analyse* was published by the Cercle d'Épistemologie de l'École Normale Supérieure in early 1966, and the Note to the Reader, signed by Jacques-Alain Miller for the editorial board, clearly expressed its ambition to construct a theory of discourse for all the sciences of analysis: logic, linguistics, and psychoanalysis. The first issue focused on truth and included Lacan's famous text "La science et la vérité," which was reprinted in the *Écrits* published by Seuil. Issue 3 of *Les Cahiers pour l'analyse* came out in 1966, and in it Lacan clearly placed himself within the structuralist movement, in an answer he gave to philosophy students: "Psychoanalysis as a science will be structuralist to the point of acknowledging a rejection of the subject in science."[26] Analytic discourse should therefore be used to construct a theory of science.

Communications 8: An Ambitious Program

But the major review-event was issue 8 of *Communications*, devoted to the structural analysis of the *récit*, which included articles by the semiology luminaries of the day: Roland Barthes, Algirdas Julien Greimas, Claude Brémond, Umberto Eco, Jules Gritti, Violette Morin, Christian Metz, Tzvetan Todorov, and Gérard Genette. *Communications* 8 was not just a simple issue, it was a program. Barthes wrote an introduction to the structural analysis of the *récit* and designated linguistics as the founding model for "dechronologizing" and "relogifying" narrative within a structural logic. Greimas located the structuralist enterprise at the intersection between semantics and a Lévi-Straussian analysis of myth. His contribution, written as an homage to Lévi-Strauss, was supposed to complement to the anthropologists work in its constitution of elements for a theory of interpretation for mythic narrative: "The recent progress in mythological research, thanks especially to the work of Claude Lévi-Strauss, includes a considerable number of materials and elements of reflection that belong to semantic theory."[27] Greimas put himself on Lévi-Strauss's turf and addressed the Bororo myth of reference, which had been the basis for the first volume of *Mythologiques, The Raw and the Cooked*. But he shifted the perspective, and, rather than arguing that narrative was the unity of the mythological universe, he considered that universe from

the angle of narrative unity in order to explain the descriptive processes at work in it.

This Hjelmslevian approach to the material that Lévi-Strauss had
studied in order to understand immanent structures did not sit particularly well with Lévi-Strauss, who did not feel he needed a lesson in
rigor, even when it was given by a semantician like Greimas. Shortly
thereafter, Lévi-Strauss dismissed the team of semioticians headed by
Greimas, which he was housing in his social anthropology laboratory
at the Collège de France. He could not continue to keep a team under
his roof that thought it did things better than he did by creating a synthesis between his own paradigmatic approach and Propp's syntagmatic analysis. "Greimas did not understand that the two things were
completely different."[28] He paid a heavy price for his lack of understanding. Lévi-Strauss's structures were not, in fact, narrative structures. He did not study the linear, syntagmatic links of a myth whose
constitutive elements of a paradigmatic structure were picked here
and there: "Mythic structure is something completely external to narrative form and is altogether of capital importance."[29]

Vladimir Propp's work on folktales provided the other important
model of narrative analysis. *Morphology of the Folktale* appeared in
Russian in 1928 and became the great inspiration for the structuralist
method, especially after it came out in France in 1965 at Seuil. It was
translated into English in 1958 and had attracted Lévi-Strauss's attention as early as 1960.[30] Lévi-Strauss explained Propp's method in his
article and was enthusiastic about what he called its prophetic quality,
but critical of the distinction Propp drew between folktales and myth.
For Lévi-Strauss, the folktale was the degraded, weakened version of
the first myth, and the fact that it lent itself to the most diverse permutations made it less appropriate than the myth for structuralist analysis. But Lévi-Strauss especially criticized Propp's formalist vigor, and
contrasted it with the structuralist method: "Formalism destroys the
object. Propp ends up discovering that there is, in fact, only one folktale."[31] Lévi-Strauss took issue with formalism because it ignored the
complementarity between signifier and signified that Saussure had
pointed out, and he essentially criticized Propp for his method, although he did acknowledge and emphasize the importance of Propp's
work, which became one of the matrices of thinking in the context of
literary semiology.

Propp responded in the Preface to the Italian edition of his book, which came out in 1966. "*Morphology of the Folktale* and *Theory and History of Folklore* were two parts or two terms of an important work."[32] In fact, Lévi-Strauss did not consider that the morphology of the folktale was presented as the prelude to a historical study that is its inevitable complement. This second work, published in the Soviet Union in 1946, was carefully ignored in France.[33] Gallimard published it only in 1983, a clear sign of how, in the sixties, a historical approach was carefully overlooked.

Claude Brémond had already based his study on the narrative message using Propp's method in issue 4 of *Communications* in 1964, and in 1966 he again used Propp's work to define the logic of possible narratives.

> I first had Madame Jakobson's translation of Vladimir Propp and indeed found that it was very interesting insofar as it implied a shift in the mechanics of narrative and of characters toward functions. So I began to think about this approach without ever considering that what I was doing fit into the structuralist project. There are narrative structures, of course, but they do not represent more than simple logical constraints or ways of creating the drama of the story. For me, you do not need to look for anything more.[34]

In his 1966 text, Claude Brémond sketched out a typology of elementary narrative forms that corresponded to universal categories of human behavior, and from this he constructed a possible classification of narrative types around a basic referential structure that then undergoes a process whereby it is made more complicated or adapted to this or that spatial or temporal situation.

Umberto Eco's piece clearly revealed one of the ambitions of structuralism to decipher everything rather than limiting the corpus of the great literary works to the usual canons. Eco chose Ian Fleming's popular 007 James Bond series. *Casino Royale*, the first volume in the series, which came out in 1953, served as the unvarying matrix for all the later books. Eco was interested in James Bond's sustained popularity, and instead of giving the general analysis and valorizing its ideological aspects, he demonstrated that the series was, above all, rhetorical. Fleming's world is Manichaean because of its convenience in the art of persuading the reader. "Fleming is not reactionary because he uses a Russian or a Jew as a bad guy; he is reactionary because he uses formulas."[35] Eco shifted the reactionary label generally attached to

Fleming in order to describe the fable, a genre in which inherent dogmatism leads to inevitably reactionary forms of formulaic thinking.

For his part, Todorov used the work of the Russian formalists to create categories of literary narration within the framework of something that was no longer a literary study, but a study of literariness, not a direct reading of works but of the possibilities of the literary discourse that made the works possible. "This is how literary studies can become a science of literature."[36]

Gérard Genette investigated the boundaries of narrative using Aristotelian and Platonic definitions of how these boundaries operate in the work of such contemporary writers as Philippe Sollers or Jean Thibaudeau who experimented with and proclaimed the end of representation, and announced perhaps the definitive end of the age of representation. Taken together, these contributions provided an immense scaffolding for literary research, which would be used to contextualize the dominant discourse of classical literary history with a vengeance, fueled by the apparent collectivity of the project and its promise of constructing a truly new science.

Les Temps modernes

When Sartre's *Les Temps modernes* devoted a special issue to structuralism, its sweeping success was consolidated.[37] Jean Pouillon wrote the Introduction, beginning with the incontrovertible fact that structuralism was in vogue: "Fashion is exasperating in that by criticizing one is also yielding to it."[38] For Pouillon, the phenomenon expressed two important ideas: totality and interdependence, or the search for relations between different terms, not in spite of, but in light of, their differences. Structuralism was therefore a matter of "looking for the relations that give a positional value to the terms that they bring together in an organized set."[39] Marc Barbut wrote about the meaning of the term "structure" in mathematics, and recalled Lévi-Strauss's use of the analogy of a system of four classes in his analysis of the Kariera kinship system.

Greimas contributed an analysis of the relationship between "structure and history" in order to emphasize that the Saussurean dichotomy between diachrony and synchrony lacked pertinence, and he contrasted Hjelmslev's notion of structure as an achronic mechanism. He also responded to the criticism of structuralism's ahistoricism and recalled Fernand Braudel's three temporalities of structure, moment, and event to salute—without in any way agreeing with the use to which it was put—the beginning of a reflection on the problem as well as historians' effort to integrate structure. "Such a view, unfortunately, does not stand up to close examination. . . . First of all, we do not see how to sustain the argument according to which that which lasts longer is more essential than that which does not last long."[40] According to Greimas, everything, for a structuralist, is located at the level of a metalinguistic model, and in this context, the historical dimension is relegated to the role of "background."[41]

Maurice Godelier reiterated the pertinence of the link between Marx and structuralism. Marx "presages the modern structuralist current,"[42] and he is therefore understood, thanks to Lévi-Strauss's work, as the true precursor of the structuralist paradigm because he made it possible to dissociate visible social relationships from their underlying logic. Not only did he prefer structural analysis to historicism, but he finally furthered the contradiction by locating it in "two structures that were irreducible to one another: the forces of production and relation of production."[43] Pierre Bourdieu laid out the bases of a sociology of intellectual thought and of artistic creation that, he argued, should encompass more than the traditional opposition between internal and external aesthetics by using a rigorous structural method: "The intellectual realm enjoys a relative autonomy, which justifies the methodological independence of the structural method when it considers this realm to be a system ordered by its own laws."[44]

Alétheia

Alétheia published its special issue on structuralism in February 1966. It included an article by Maurice Godelier on contradiction, and an article by Lévi-Strauss on scientific criteria in the social sciences and the humanities. Kostas Axelos contributed an article on Lucien Sebag's attempt to reconcile Marxism and structuralism, and Georges Lapssade wrote a piece on Hegel. Roland Barthes presented structuralism as the possibility of "defetishizing the old—or concurrent—knowledge."[45]

Esprit

Esprit had devoted an issue in 1963 to Lévi-Strauss's thesis and in December 1966, the review organized a conference whose proceedings were published in May 1967 in a special issue on structuralism.[46] *Esprit* invited its readers to ponder this rather complete panorama. Jean-Marie Domenach viewed the structuralist phenomenon as an enterprise that destabilized the terms by which philosophy had operated until then, particularly in its view of consciousness. He raised the question of how the challenge of those on the left to the foundations of the established system can be reconciled with their political stuggle, for if men are moved by a system that constrains them and cannot assure some autonomous consciousness, in the name of what can they continue to protest? The complexities and contradictions of the structuralist phenomenon explained its attraction. "Structuralism has two faces: one expresses the epistemological sufficiency of our period and the other expresses the anxiety of an absence, the tides of darkness."[47]

But *Esprit* remained reticent and critical of the notion of the death of man and his dissolution in the structures surrounding him. On the one hand, Mikel Dufrenne placed the neopositivism in vogue in a France that was belatedly discovering Anglo-Saxon logical positivism, and interpreting it in its own way, on the same plane as antihumanism. "Contemporary philosophy cries: hands off of man!"[48] On the other hand, Paul Ricoeur recognized that the structural triumph was costly; scientificity was accompanied by two major exclusions: the act of speaking—Saussure's elimination of speech in his study of language—and history. And without repeating the wanderings of either mentalism or psychologism, he suggested moving beyond this amputation; thus, "reflecting on language would mean considering the unity of that which Saussure untethered, the unity of language and of speech."[49]

Sartre Breaks His Silence

Jean-Paul Sartre was mute in the face of this unbridled passion for structuralism, alone in his silence as each successful publication weakened the bases of his existentialist philosophy a bit more. In 1966, Foucault, at the height of his glory, shelved Sartre along with nineteenth-century philosophers. This was too much for Sartre, who decided to break his silence and wage war, on the occasion of a special issue of *L'Arc* that was devoted to him.[50] Bernard Pingaud wrote the Introduction, in which he reviewed the radical changes that had taken place over the previous fifteen years, during which time philosophy had been supplanted by the social sciences: "We no longer speak about consciousness or the subject, but rather about rules, codes, and systems. We no longer say that man makes sense, but that meaning comes to man. We are no longer existentialists, but structuralists."[51] Sartre responded to Pingaud's questions, and the polemical tone of his remarks reflected his anger as well as the difficulty of his position. On the great success of Michel Foucault's *The Order of Things*, Sartre remarked that "the success of his book proves that people were expecting it. However, truly original thinking is never expected. Foucault brought what people needed: an eclectic synthesis in which Robbe-Grillet, structuralism, linguistics, Lacan, and *Tel Quel* are each used in turn to demonstrate the impossibility of historical thinking. But what was being targeted behind the attack on history, of course, was Marxism. The issue was the creation of a new ideology, the last barrier that the bourgeoisie can still erect against Marx."[52]

Following this somewhat reductionist assault, Sartre pondered his remarks, and clarified: he did not totally reject the structuralist method, so long as it remained mindful of its limits. If, for Sartre, the mind could not be reduced to language, it remained a fundamental part of his philosophy and corresponded to a constitutive part of the practico-inert. Even if Lévi-Strauss's work found grace in Sartre's eyes, he still answered the polemic against him that Lévi-Strauss opened in *The Savage Mind*, by considering that "structuralism as Lévi-Strauss conceives and practices it has significantly contributed to history's current fall from grace."[53] For Sartre, Lacan fully belongs to structuralism insofar as his decentering of the subject is linked to the same discrediting of history: "If there is no longer any praxis, there cannot be any subject. What do Lacan and the psychoanalysts who come after him tell us? That man does not think, he is thought, just as for certain linguists he is spoken."[54] He nonetheless recognized Lacan's debt to Freud, for the status accorded the subject in Freud was already ambiguous, and the psychoanalytic cure in principle presupposed that patients let themselves be acted upon by abandoning themselves to free association. Althusser also came under attack for his ahistoricism because he privileged the concept of atemporality at the cost of historicity, without fully understanding "the permanent contradiction between the structure of the practico-inert and man, who turns out to be conditioned by it."[55]

Finally, Sartre attributed this tremendous development and energy of the social sciences around the structuralist paradigm to an American import, an ideological adaptation of a technocratic civilization in which philosophy has no place: "You see what is happening in the United States: philosophy has been replaced by the social sciences."[56] During the same year that President Johnson sent B-52s to bomb North Vietnam on a daily basis, we can appreciate the extent to which Sartre's evaluation could be insulting to the structuralist musketeers.

In fact, this affair created a scandal because Sartre's viewpoint on the successive attacks on his philosophy since the early sixties was ardently solicited. *Le Figaro littéraire* dramatized the gravity of the situation, brandishing on its cover: "Lacan Judges Sartre." Lacan answered ironically in an interview, and relativized Sartre's position: "I don't consider myself at all with respect to him."[57] Lacan simply refused to credit any notion of a homogeneous structuralist group: "Who is going to believe that we are working together?"[58] It was not an issue of plotting, of course, but of an intellectual debate, and Jean-François Revel, who had virulently criticized structuralist theses in his articles in *L'Express*, titled his report on the dossier on Sartre in *L'Arc*: "Sartre on the Ballot." He recalled "King Lear, repudiated and despoiled by his daughters,"[59] and to the Sartrean analogy of the correspondence between the rise of a technostructure and the success of an antihistorical and negative doctrine of the subject, he added the political parallel between a Gaullism in which the French citizen is spoken when his role is limited to listening to General de Gaulle incarnate the voice of France during his famous press conferences.

Structuralism Crosses the Atlantic

The year 1966 also saw a number of important colloquiums and symposia. The château at Cerisy remained a sanctuary for intellectual activity; in 1966 it was the site of a colloquium on the topic "Current Paths of Criticism." Plon published the proceedings two years later.[60]

In September 1966, on the shores of Lake Leman in Geneva, a francophone philosophy congress was organized on language, and the discussions focused on presentations by Émile Benveniste and Mircéa Eliade. Others, beyond the confines of Europe, were also beginning to be touched by the fever of French structuralism. In October 1966, under the auspices of the Humanities Center at Johns Hopkins University, an important structuralist ceremony unfolded. This was the first structuralist crossing of the Atlantic to reach the New World.

Americans, having quite correctly perceived the multidisciplinarity of the phenomenon of critical thinking in France, invited the representatives of the different sciences of man:[61] Lucien Goldmann and Georges Poulet in sociological literary criticism, Roland Barthes, Tzvetan Todorov, and Nicolas Ruwet in literary semiology, Jacques Derrida in philosophy for his work on Saussure and Lévi-Strauss, published in *Critique* at the end of 1965,[62] Jean-Pierre Vernant for his historical anthropology of ancient Greece, and Jacques Lacan for his structuralist rereading of Freud. The symposium was published several years later in the United States.[63]

Roland Barthes was quite clearly singled out as one of the stars of the effervescence in French intellectual life. He spoke about the repression of rhetoric in the nineteenth century and how its replacement by positivism had long separated the paths of literary theory and the theory of language. Within this framework, he outlined the historical roots of the rise of interest in a reflection upon language and the new interfacing between literature and linguistics, which he called semiocritical, based on writing as a system of signs in a relationship of objectivation. He recalled the new frontiers to be conquered in the exploration of language using the modern symbiosis that structuralism had achieved between linguistics, psychoanalysis, and literature.

Jean-Pierre Vernant addressed Greek tragedy by demonstrating that tragedy cannot be interpreted unless its context is understood, but not in the classical sense of the term: "What I call context is not something that is outside the text, but that underlies the text. As we read and decipher the text itself, we realize that its semantic fields force us to consider elements that are outside the tragedy and that give meaning to it."[64] Vernant insisted on the necessity of starting with the internal, hermetic structure of the text, but also on the need to bring to light all the verbal, semantic, and ideological play that makes the specific effects of tragic discourse possible.

Vernant met Lacan for the first time in Baltimore. It was a meeting that was not to be repeated, even if shortly thereafter, while Vernant was vacationing on Belle-Ile, he was surprised to see three Lacanian messengers arrive and explain that he absolutely had to attend the master's seminar. "They were explaining to me that I was doing the same thing as Lacan was doing without knowing it—which proved that I needed a good psychoanalysis. I told them that it was a little late, but they insisted that Lacan was very interested in my work and that he read it quite attentively."[65] Lacan, whose discourse was already difficult to understand in his native tongue, insisted on speaking English in Baltimore, despite the fact he did not speak it fluently, making his talk even more hermetic. Still, he appeared as the great guru of structuralism.

Thirty-four

1966
Annum mirabile (II): Foucault
Sells like Hotcakes

The publishing event of the year and the summer blockbuster was, without any doubt, Michel Foucault's *The Order of Things*. Sartre had said that the book was predictable, but neither Foucault nor Pierre Nora, his editor, had foreseen anything like what happened. The first printing of 3,500 copies, which had come out in April, quickly sold out, and 5,000 copies were reprinted in June, 3,000 in July, and 3,500 in September. Michel Foucault was borne along by the structuralist tide and his work came to embody the philosophical synthesis of the new thinking that had been developing for fifteen years. If the author later put some distance between himself and the structuralist tag, which he considered insulting, in 1966 he considered himself to be at the heart of the phenomenon: "Structuralism is not a new method; it is the awakened and troubled consciousness of modern thought."[1]

Pierre Dumayet invited Foucault to appear on an important television literary show of the period, *Books for Everyone*, where he spoke in the name of the founders of a collective rupture in which he, together with Lévi-Strauss and Dumézil, considered that Sartre "still belonged to the nineteenth century because his entire enterprise tries to make man adequate to his own meaning."[2] Foucault's remarks emphasized his consonance with the new ambitions of structuralism. He claimed that philosophy had been dissipated in other activities of the mind: "We are coming to an age that is perhaps one of pure thinking, of thinking in deed, and disciplines as abstract and general as linguistics or as fundamental as logic, or even more, literature since Joyce, are activities of the mind. They do not replace philosophy, but are the very unfolding of what philosophy was in the past."3

Foucault defined his archaeology of the social sciences (the book was originally to be subtitled *An Archaeology of Structuralism*) as the expression of the will to make our culture appear in a position of strangeness similar to the way we perceive the Nambikwara described by Lévi-Strauss. It was not at all a question of tracing the continuous and logical lines along which thinking had unfolded, but rather of discerning the discontinuities that made our own cultural past appear as fundamentally other and foreign to us, thanks to this restored perspective. "This is the ethnological situation that I wanted to reconstitute."4 Moreover, Foucault attacked any effort to identify with the purely ephemeral figure of man, a figure at once recent and destined to quickly disappear. God was dead, and man was destined to follow him, nudged along by the very sciences whose legitimacy is based on his existence: "Paradoxically, the development of the social sciences invites us to witness the disappearance of man rather than his apotheosis."5

The epoch was clearly fascinated by the death of man, and many were ready to join the funeral procession. The successive negations of the subject in Saussurean linguistics in structural anthropology and Lacanian psychoanalysis found in Foucault someone who could reinstall the figure at the very core of Western cultural history, but as an absence, a lack around which the epistemes unfold.

The Foucault Effect

Foucault's reception was a flamboyant event. Jean Lacroix saluted his work as "one of the most important of our time,"6 and Robert Kanters dubbed it "an impressive work" in *Le Figaro*.7 François Chatelet, in *La Quinzaine littéraire*, considered the book to be a philosophical event that revolutionized thinking. Reading Foucault's work would lead to the birth of "a radically new perception of the past of Western culture and a more lucid notion of the confusion of its present."8 In *L'Express*, Madeleine Chapsal evocatively entitled her three-page article "The Greatest Revolution since Existentialism,"9 and Gilles Deleuze wrote a three-page review in *Le Nouvel Observateur*: "Foucault's idea: the sciences of man were not created when man

took himself as an object of representation, nor even when he discovered his own history—to the contrary, they were created when he dehistoricized himself."[10]

Foucault was of course very much in demand to explain this
death of man that the press quite generously attributed to him alone.
In answer to a question about when he stopped believing in meaning,
asked during an interview given by *La Quinzaine littéraire*, Foucault
answered: "The breaking point came on the day when Lévi-Strauss
for societies and Lacan for the unconscious showed us that meaning
was probably only one sort of surface effect, a shimmering, a froth,
and that what profoundly coursed through us, what existed before us,
what maintained us in time and space, was the system."[11] Raymond
Bellour strongly supported Foucault's theses, whereas his party, the
PCF, was clearly less enthusiastic. But Bellour enjoyed a certain autonomy in *Les Lettres françaises*, where he interviewed Foucault. Bellour
considered Foucault to be the initiator of a true revolution in the history of ideas when he restored the logical totality of the ideas of a period and when he relegated to the dustbin of history what had been
considered until then to be the bible in this field, the famous "Hazard"
and his *Crisis of European Consciousness*.[12] Bellour quite lucidly discerned the writer beneath the philosopher, and appreciated the dazzling style: "This era will have seen the birth of a new kind of writer,
under the guise of the decipherers of meaning."[13]

In all of his numerous interviews and lectures during 1966, Foucault continued to shelve Sartre alongside nineteenth-century philosophers and to firmly place himself alongside Lévi-Strauss, Dumézil,
Lacan, and Althusser—the writers and researchers who embodied the
modernity of the twentieth century. Which fully justified Didier Éribon's remark: "It seems clear that Foucault considers himself to be a
full member of the structuralist galaxy,"[14] even if it was a very special
structuralism based not on the existence of structures, but a "structuralism without structures,"[15] leading François Ewald to say that
Foucault was never a structuralist and that his project was to combat
the idea of structure and therefore of structuralism. For Ewald, Foucault's whole enterprise was to make politics possible, whence his hostility to the very idea of structure: "Structure is one of the forms of the
important historical subject, of the grand identity running through
history, whereas Foucault quite clearly explained that that is what he
wanted to destroy."[16] This internal tension, as yet unfelt by Foucault

in 1966, arose from his ambiguous position as a philosopher who placed himself at the center of the social sciences in order to subvert them from within. But, far from challenging the structuralist phenomenon, his position was reinforced by structuralism, even if Foucault disagreed with the scientism that the others in the movement sought to legitimate their discipline.

Transitory and Ephemeral Man

Above all, *The Order of Things* was an heir to Georges Canguilhem's work. Foucault also argued that scientific history should be based on discontinuities and on the Nietzschean deconstruction of established disciplines. His radical rejection of humanism bespoke the Nietzschean base. Man, as an active, conscious subject of his history, disappeared. His recent return and discovery presaged his proximate end. His centrality in Western thinking was merely an illusion, dissipated by studying the many different kinds of conditioning that he underwent through history. Decentered, man becomes relegated to the periphery of things, under the influence of many forces, such that he disappears in the froth of time: "Man is probably no more than a kind of rift in the order of things. . . . It is comforting, however, and a source of profound relief, to think that man is only a recent invention, a figure not yet two centuries old, a new wrinkle in our knowledge."[17] Foucault undertook to historicize the manner in which the illusion known as man took shape, born only in the nineteenth century. For the Greeks, what existed were the gods, nature, and the cosmos; there was no room for a conception of a responsible subject. For Plato, the fault could be attributable to an error in judgment or to ignorance rather than to individual responsibility.

Similarly, there was no room for man in the classical episteme. Neither Renaissance humanism nor the rationalism of the classics could conceive of him—there had to be a rift in the configuration of knowledge for man to come to have a central place there. Western culture conferred a central role on man, who appears as the king of creation, the absolute referent of all things. This fetishization is particularly clear in philosophy, where the Cartesian ego introduced the subject as substance, the container of truths, reversing the ancient and medieval scholastic problematic of error and guilt. "Subordination is reversed, and it is error that becomes relative to fault: to make an error . . . is to openly assert, by means of the free and infinite will, the meaningful contents of understanding that remain confused."[18] And yet, as Foucault, following Freud, commented, this man has experienced many serious narcissistic wounds in the history of Western thought. Copernicus, discovering that the earth was not at the center of the universe, revolutionized thinking and set back the primitive sovereignty of man. Later, Darwin, discovering the proximity between man and simian, reduced man to the phase of an episode in a biological time that he does not comprehend and that leaves him behind. Finally, Freud discovered that man cannot know himself alone, that he is not fully conscious, and that his behavior is determined by an unconscious to which he has no access, yet which makes his words and actions comprehensible.

Man therefore found himself progressively dispossessed of his attributes, but he reappropriated these breaks in the realm of knowledge in order to forge so many instruments with which to reassert his domination. In the nineteenth century, he appeared as a starkly palpable, perceptible object, at the confluence of three forms of knowledge: Propp's philological apparatus, Smith and Ricardo's political economy, and Lamarck and Cuvier's biology. The singular figure of a living, speaking, and laboring subject appeared at that point, the product of this triple knowledge and the holder of a central place among these new sciences, their necessary figure and common signifier. He could then be restored to his sovereignty over nature. Astronomy made physics possible, biology made medicine possible, the unconscious made psychoanalysis possible. But, for Foucault, this recent sovereignty was necessarily illusory and short-lived. On the heels of Freud, who had discovered the unconscious dimension of individual behavior, and of Lévi-Strauss, who sought to explore the unconscious of collective social practices, Foucault set off in search of the unconscious of the sciences where we believe our conscious minds dwell.

Such was the Copernican revolution he wanted to realize in order to demystify humanism, which for him was the important perversion of contemporary times: "Humanism is the Middle Ages of the modern era."[19] Foucault saw the philosopher's main role as removing the epistemological obstacle of the privilege granted to the cogito, or to the subject as consciousness and substance. He fully theorized the constitution of a true philosophical base bringing together the different semiotics oriented around the text and subjecting man to a network dissolving him despite himself: "Let us be done with this old philosopheme of human nature, with this abstract man."[20] This was Foucault's perspective, and it corresponded with Lévi-Strauss's evocation of the fleeting figure of man: "The world began without man and it will end without him."[21] Moreover, Foucault paid homage to Lévi-Strauss when, through ethnology, he made it possible to dilute man by successively undoing all his efforts at positivity. Ethnology and psychoanalysis hold privileged positions in our modern knowledge, Foucault remarked. "One may say of both of them what Lévi-Strauss said about ethnology: that they dissolve man."[22]

This obituary might appear paradoxical at a time when the social sciences were exploding, but Foucault conceived psychoanalysis and ethnology to be "countersciences,"[23] and their valorization was consistent with the structuralist paradigm, which portrayed them as the main keys to modern understanding. In this respect, the structural revolution was "the guardian of man's absence."[24]

Multiple and Discontinuous Temporalities
Decentering or dissolving man created another temporal and historical relationship in which time became plural and immobile. External conditions that determine human practices were also observed differently.

> Will the history of man ever be more than a sort of modulation common to changes in the conditions of life (climate, soil fertility, methods of agriculture, exploitation of wealth), to transformations in the economy (and, consequently, of society and institutions) and to the succession of forms and usages of language? But in that case, man is not himself historical: since time comes to him from somewhere other than himself.[25]

Man thus endures multiple temporalities that escape him, and in which he can be no more than a mere object of these pure external events. Consciousness became the dead horizon of the mind. The unthought was not to be sought in the depths of the human mind; it was the Other for man, within him and outside of him, next to him, irreducible to him, fleeing "in an unavoidable duality."[26] Man was articulated on the already-begun of life, of work, and of language, and thus he found to be closed the paths leading to what would be his origins and his beginning.

Modernity, for Foucault, lay in this recognition of the impotent and inherently illusory theology of the man of the Cartesian cogito. Having removed the hero and cultural fetish from the pedestal upon which our culture had placed him, Foucault took on historicism. Foucauldian history is no longer a description of evolution, a notion borrowed from biology, nor a tracing of progress, a moral-ethical notion, but rather an analysis of the many transformations at work, a tracing of discontinuities, like so many instant snapshots. This deconstruction resembled a Cubist enterprise, exploding history into a dehumanized constellation. Temporal unity became little more than a fiction obeying no necessity. Indeed, reversing historical continuity was the necessary corollary to the decentered subject. "The human being no longer has any history: or rather, since he speaks, works, and lives, he finds himself interwoven in his own being with histories that are neither subordinate to him nor homogeneous with him. . . . the man who appears at the beginning of the nineteenth century is 'dehistoricized.'"[27] Self-consciousness dissolved in the discourse-object and in the multiplicity of different histories.

Foucault proceeded to deconstruct history in the manner of Cubism, breaking it up into a dehumanized constellation. Temporal unity was now nothing more than a fiction; it obeyed no necessity. History belonged to the sole register of the aleatory, to contingency, as it did for Lévi-Strauss, both unavoidable and meaningless. And yet, unlike Lévi-Straussian structuralism, Foucault did not elude historicity. He even considered it to be a privileged zone for analysis, the perfect site for his archaeological investigation, but in order to point out the discontinuities vexing it, beginning with the important fractures juxtaposing coherent synchronic slices.

Epistemes

Foucault located two important discontinuities in the episteme of Western culture: that of the classical period in the mid-seventeenth century, and that of the nineteenth century, which inaugurated the modern era. Areas as diverse as language, political economy, and biology gave indices that, if correctly read, revealed these alterations in the order of knowledge. At every stage, Foucault separated what belonged to the realm of the conceivable from what did not. "The history of knowledge can be written only on the basis of what was contemporaneous with it."[28] The discontinuities that Foucault indicated, insofar as any form of evolutionism was eliminated, became so many enigmatic figures. These were true rents in the fabric, and it was enough to localize them and discern their modalities without asking how they emerged. Indeed, how events came to occur remained fundamentally enigmatic in Foucault's work. "Such a task implies the calling into question of everything that pertains to time, everything that has formed within it, everything that resides within its mobile element, in such a way as to make visible that rent, devoid of chronology and history, from which time issued."[29] Discontinuity appeared in its specificity, irreducible to a system of causality because it was cut off from its roots, an ethereal figure that emerged from the morning fog of the creation of the world.

Foucault's approach radically broke with any search for origins or for any system of causality. He substituted a polymorphism that made it impossible to restore a historical dialectic. *The Order of Things*, his archaeology of the social sciences, sought to explain how this new configuration of knowledge emerged, based on a method that was the most structuralist form that Foucault's thinking took and that led from one episteme to another, from one discursive tissue to another in an unfolding in which words led to other words. The synchronic dimension of this eminently structuralist approach of valorizing the autonomous discursive realm over the referent made it possible to locate the significant coherence between discourses that do not immediately appear to share anything except simultaneity. "He showed me the audacity of the intellectual comparison between biology, astronomy, and physics. . . . Contemporary sociology today does not have this expansive power."[30]

Foucault's episteme, however, raised the most questions. Not only the unresolved question of understanding how to proceed from one episteme to another, but also the question put to Foucault himself: on the basis of which episteme does he speak? This idea, omnipresent in 1966 in *The Order of Things*, was so contested that it disappeared from Foucault's later work. His archaeology sought the fault lines, the significant ruptures in the continental plates of knowledge: "What I am attempting to bring to light is the epistemological field, the *episteme* in which knowledge, envisaged apart from all criteria having reference to its rational value or to its objective forms, grounds its positivity and therefore manifests a history."[31]

The Representation of the Represented

The first configuration of knowledge that Foucault addressed was the episteme of the Renaissance until the sixteenth century. Knowledge at the time was based on the same, on repetition, on the representation of what is represented. The basis of knowledge in Western culture was similitude. The relationship of the idea to its object was doubled: "The universe was folded in on itself."[32] Many procedures of similitude existed in this episteme: the proximity of site, simple reflection, analogy, and the interplay of sympathies—all could assimilate very diverse things to a fundamental identity. The sixteenth century superimposed semiology and hermeneutics in a form of knowledge that was complete, with unlimited similitude or reference to resemblance, but at the same time reduced because it was constructed as a simple addition: "Sixteenth-century knowledge condemned itself to never knowing anything but the same thing."[33] Nature was merely a figure reflecting the cosmos; erudition and divination belonged to the same hermeneutic.

This episteme would shift in the sixteenth century because of a rent affecting the old kinship between words and things, the site from which man could be born to himself and become a particular object of knowledge. The change was figured by Don Quixote's quest, his attempt to read the world in order to demonstrate the truth of books. He pitted himself against the nonconcordance between signs and reality, against the perfect discord that brought his utopia up short. Nonetheless, this tilter against windmills stubbornly persisted in his desire to decode the world through its dated grid, and his adventure became doubly significant as it unveiled the birth of a new configuration of knowledge and the historicity of language. Don Quixote's experience of words and things and the inadequacy of his form of knowledge could lead to madness in its indifference to differences: "Words wander off on their own, without content, without resemblance to fill their emptiness; they are no longer the marks of things."[34]

With the new episteme of the classical seventeenth century and Cartesian rationalism, the analogical hierarchy gave way to critical analysis. Resemblances became comparative. "Western reason is entering the age of judgement."[35] A general science, a theory of signs, became possible in the classical episteme by using a mathesis for simple structures for which algebra was the universal method, and a system of classification for complex natures. A general grammar was born with this critical order: "The basic task of classical discourse is to give names to things, and with this name, to name their being."[36] A science of language arose out of this new distance between words and things. Similarly, natural history, inseparable from language, was born. Divided into three classes—mineral, vegetable, and animal—natural history did not yet cleave the living from the nonliving. The classical episteme was also characterized by the birth of the analysis of wealth, which resembled the analysis of natural history and general grammar. Whereas economic conceptions of the Renaissance made monetary signs correspond in quantity and weight of the metal elected as the standard of exchange, things changed during the seventeenth century. Exchange became the basis for the birth of mercantilism. Gold became precious because it was a form of money, and not the reverse, as had been believed in the sixteenth century. Money took its value from its pure sign function.

The Episteme of Modernity

At the end of the eighteenth century and at the beginning of the nineteenth, this episteme was once again shattered. Our modern episteme was born of the same disjunction that forced all of Western thinking to shift. The new sciences that appeared in the nineteenth century constructed their objects in a realm removed from observation. Life, work, and language became so many "transcendents." The analysis of wealth was supplanted by political economy. Adam Smith embodied the first important shift: what circulates as things could be referred to work. "From Smith onward, the time of economics is no longer to be cyclical time of alternating impoverishment and wealth . . . but the time of capital and production."[37] Ricardo completed this advent of political economy by ensuring that, at the heart of economic thinking, work determined value, not as a sign but as a product.

A similar revolution took place in natural history and made the birth of biology possible. Jussieu and Lamarck no longer defined characteristics on the basis of the observable but on an internal principle of organization that determines function; this implied a transversal cut within the organism to see the vital organs below the superficial organs. Biology became possible, and Cuvier used the discovery to assert the primacy of function over organ.

In the realm of language, an epistemological revolution took place with the appearance of philology. No longer limited to its representational function, the word now belonged to a decisive grammatical whole. "The language is then defined by the number of its units and by all the possible combinations that can be established between them in discourse; so that it is a question of an agglomeration of atoms."[38]

The Era of Relativism

The succession of epistemes up to our own era, this historicization of knowledge and of man—a figure that only became possible in the last epistemological configuration—led to a historical relativism for Foucault, similar to that of Lévi-Strauss. Just as there is no inferiority or anteriority between primitive and modern societies, there is no truth to be sought in the different stages that constitute knowlege. There are only historically distinguishable discourses: "Since the human being has become historical through and through, none of the contents analyzed by the human sciences can remain stable in itself or escape the movement of History."[39] The foundations of contemporary knowledge, represented by disciplines that are themselves structures used in verifiable scientific practices, are only temporary, transitory configurations. Paradoxically, this absolute relativism that completely historicizes knowledge is turned against the historical approach in favor of a fundamentally spatial conception, a purely synchronic epistemological space that must separate inside from out, but that turns its back on duration, and therefore on history.

Foucault invited us to turn an eye on temporality that was as cold as the one the ethnologist turns on primitive societies. The misunderstanding with historians arose from the fact that Foucault took no reality or historical referent into consideration, but only considered the internal modulations of the discursive realm. The level of discourse was the only one he saw in this nominalist approach, which considered the word to be something practically physical, like a thing, and replaced the thing. Discourse and documents were no longer to be considered documents, but monuments: "The text is a historical object like the trunk of a tree."[40] His approach led him to valorize the internal coherence of successive epistemes and to ignore the processes of transformation and mediation. Diachrony and discontinuities remained, therefore, fundamentally enigmatic.

The Order of Things was written during Foucault's most structuralist phase. This was the period when the sciences of sign systems flourished and during which, behind the description of the succession of different epistemes since the classical period, he discerned the repressed of each of these stages of Western culture, their modes or order, their historical a prioris and hierarchies. Just as Lévi-Strauss perceived the unconscious of social practices in primitive societies, Foucault deciphered the unconscious foundations constituting Western knowledge, thereby prolonging the Kantian effort to "shake us out of our anthropological slumber."[41]

In order to escape from this anthropological space and from finite analysis at the empirical transcendental level, Foucault conferred a special status on three different disciplines at the end of his book. Psychoanalysis reconsidered and corrected by Lacan, ethnology, revised by Lévi-Strauss, and history, reconsidered and deconstructed by Nietzsche. *The Order of Things* closed, therefore, on the episteme of structuralism, which offered itself as the realization of modern consciousness.

One noteworthy absence in this program was entirely consonant with the structuralist moment: Marx was relegated to the episteme of the nineteenth century.

> At the deepest level of Western knowledge, Marxism introduced no real discontinuity; it found its place without difficulty, as a full, quite comfortable and, goodness knows, satisfying form for a time (its own), within an epistemological arrangement that welcomed it gladly (since it was this arrangement that was in fact making room for it). . . . Marxism exists in nineteenth-century thought like a fish in water: that is, it is unable to breathe anywhere else.[42]

There was an important break between the position of Foucault, who tried to diverge from the Marxist model as much as from the phenomenological model, and that of the Althusserians, who were trying to give Marx a second wind. They were clearly divided and their divergence was such that they provoked a major rupture in the history of science. Foucault had to justify his position because the Althusserian group of the ENS epistemological circle considered it a provocation. Later, he rectified things with *The Archaeology of Knowledge*. "When he wrote *The Order of Things*, he was unaware of Althusser's reading of Marx, whereas in *The Archaeology of Knowledge* he speaks of a Marx revisited by Althusser."[43] Foucault's position in 1966 was wholly in line with the ambient structuralist theorizing. By speaking of the primacy of pure reason and of the representation of the structures of experience articulated on the constitution of epistemological objects, he gave it a philosophical answer.

Thanks to this, Foucault appeared as the potential spearhead of all the structuralists united in their battle against the philosophy of meaning, against humanism and phenomenology, by raising again the question of the relevance of philosophy, as Kant had done, and considering it in its critical and demystifying capacity.

Thirty-five

1966
Annum mirabile (III): Julia Comes to Paris

When the twenty-four-year-old Julia Kristeva arrived in Paris in a snowstorm just before Christmas 1965 with only five dollars in her pocket, this young Bulgarian woman never imagined that she would become the Egeria of structuralism. Indeed, the structuralist period was, along with everything else, an encounter between a daring cultural adventure and a talented woman. It was a propitious moment. Kristeva's arrival in France near the beginning of 1966 plunged her into a veritable cultural whirlpool that would rivet her with the passion of a foreigner cut off from her native Bulgaria. Circumstances would lead her into the eye of the cyclone. The French were interested in and responsive to the Russian formalist texts that Todorov was publishing, and in the political and literary events unfolding in Eastern Europe at a time when East-West relations were thawing. This was the context in which Kristeva was awarded a French government scholarship by General de Gaulle and began to work on what seemed to be the very expression of modernity in France at the time: the New Novel. She began writing her thesis with Lucien Goldmann, but very quickly direct contact with semiological thinking, then in full flower, led her to deconstruct her subject of study in order to work on narrative and on the constitution of the novel as a genre. From that point on, she was a full-fledged participant in the intellectual fervor of the day.

A Taste for Formalism

Kristeva attended Barthes's seminar at the Hautes Études and also went to Lévi-Strauss's Laboratory for Social Anthropology, which housed a section on semio-linguistics. She met Philippe Sollers there. "I will always see her as she appeared to me then, very charming. There was something quite striking about her, her grace, her sensuality, this union between grace and physical beauty and her capacity for reflection. From this point of view, she is unique in history."[1]

Their union sealed Kristeva's intellectual place within *Tel Quel*, the most active and provocative group in 1966, which placed her at the center of the who's who of Parisian intellectuals. She met her compatriot Todorov, became friends with Benveniste, discovered Lacan, thanks to Sollers, and went to his seminar. Sympathetic to the PCF or at least to its intellectual fringe (*La Nouvelle Critique, Les Lettres françaises*), she argued for Marxist positions and, after some months, became the spokesperson for structuralism's pretentions to generalization, a surprising mixture of semio-Marxo-Freudian thinking that embodied the intellectual avant-garde's desire to revolutionize the world . . . through writing. It was a foreigner who was to best express this ambition, the most Parisian foreigner in the capital. Philippe Sollers, whom Kristeva would marry in 1967, was interested in literary semiology at the time. In 1966 he wrote up a presentation that he had given on Mallarmé on November 25, 1965, in Barthes's seminar in which he proclaimed Mallarmé to be the great initiator of the current rapprochement between literature and literary theory: "For Mallarmé, literature and science are henceforth in close communication."[2]

Tel Quel's entire project was part of the Mallarméan legacy: an experimentation with literature beyond genres and limits, literature as the expression of self-consciousness in death, a veritable suicide after which language claims its rights and reaches beyond the limits of the subjectivity of the author's consciousness. Mallarmé was attuned to rhetoric and to philosophy, and invited semiological reflection all the more so since *Le Livre à écrire* sets the impossible as its horizon. Only scintillating fragments remain, glittering in a foreclosed future that, according to Mallarmé, "is never more than the flash of that which should have happened before or near the beginning."[3] Mallarmé opened a vast program of formal thinking, that of a literal revolution, of a return to rhetoric, of a return of the East, of the "return to," and of the arrival from the East of a certain Julia Kristeva. According to Jean Dubois, "this taste for formalism is the expression of a profound tendency that predates even structuralism. As a young *agrégé*, I was interested in formal structures, and if I was a good Greek and Latin grammarian, it was because these are formal structures."[4]

A Toast to Literature

The excitement of 1966 quickly affected Julia Kristeva, but her status of foreigner gave her a certain lucidity that enabled her rather quickly to point out the two important aporias of the structuralist paradigm: history and the subject. Mikhail Bakhtin's work was particularly useful for her in this. The year 1966 was indeed a special one for literary thinking. Althusserian thinking had even appropriated literature, which Pierre Macherey considered as an object of production in *For a Theory of Literary Production*.[5] Macherey examined the new figure of the literary critic, who, during the structuralist era, had stopped being a second skin and had become practically a writer: "The critic is an analyst."[6] The critic's task comprises the deciphering and reconstruction of meaning; it is no longer restricted to the role of simply restoring the meaning that had been deposited in a literary work. Although Macherey did not adhere to the principles of the general formalism of the period, and even saw "a Platonic reminiscence"[7] in them that led to derealizing things, he was in favor of reading literature as Althusser and his group read Marx. It was not a matter of looking for the philosophers' stone hidden behind the text, but of saying what the text says without saying it: "A true analysis . . . should encounter something that is never said, an initial unsaid."[8]

Literature, decidedly, was in its heyday, the center of a major theoretical wager during the year of Barthes's response to Picard in *Critique et vérité*. Gérard Genette, however, argued for a more subtle position, apparently preferring a peaceful coexistence based on a complementary division of labor between hermeneutics on the one hand, and structuralism on the other. There would thus be a division of the literary field between a literature capable of being experienced by the critical consciousness of hermeneutics, and another distant and rather indecipherable literature that became the privileged object of structural analysis: "The relationship that brought together structuralism and hermeneutics could be one of complementarity rather than a mechanical separation or exclusion."[9] Genette clearly defined the reversal taking place at the time by identifying the shift from a temporal to a spatial determinism. The new structural sensibility was essentially characterized by its rejection of historicity and its withdrawal into a slack present whose shape needed only to be outlined: "Each unit is defined in terms of relationship and no longer in terms of filiation."[10] Like Pierre Macherey, Gérard Genette was particularly critical of the way the psychologism that held sway in classical literary history took an individualist approach, paying exclusive attention to works and authors at the expense of the networks of literary production and those of reading. "The conditions of its communication are produced at the same time as the book . . . ; what makes the book also makes its readers."[11]

When *Écrits* came out that year, it provoked many conversions to a Lacanized Freudian thinking. Gennie Lemoine, one of the members of the *Esprit* team who had been with the review since 1946, left it to join Lacan's school in 1966. Antoinette Fouques was writing her thesis with Barthes on the avant-garde at the time and she converted to psychoanalysis as soon as she read the *Écrits*. "I could almost say that I knew Lacan before Freud."[12] At the end of the *Écrits*, Lacan republished an essential article that had already come out in January 1966 in the first issue of *Les Cahiers pour l'analyse*, "Science Truth." In it he rejected the fashionable notion of "human sciences" because it recalled for him the state of servitude that Georges Canguilhem had already pointed out with respect to psychology.

But the repugnance with which the "human sciences" inspired Lacan evaporated once they became invested and metamorphosed by structuralism to imply a new notion of the subject. "The subject is, shall we say, internally excluded from its object."[13] During this structural year, and despite a move toward logic that had begun in 1964, Lacan still leaned heavily on Lévi-Strauss: "The loyalty that Claude Lévi-Strauss's work displays with regard to this structuralism will only be considered in our thesis to limit us for the moment to its periphery."[14] Shortly after, Lacan evoked the "Lévi-Straussian graph" to explode the subject. Descartes's famous *ego* would have had no other existence than one of denotation. According to Élisabeth Roudinesco, in 1966 Lacan was still suffering from insufficient recognition, which would explain his search for support, whether from Lévi-Strauss or from Foucault, whose *Birth of the Clinic* he mentioned in the *Écrits*,[15] without falling into what he would later qualify as the "structuralist banquet."

Julia Kristeva therefore traversed a Paris jolted by structuralism, the sanctuary of exchanges among those who enthusiastically shared the impression of belonging to a new world of the concept, beyond the notion of substance and disciplinary deep-rootedness, in the sole abyssal vertigo of the infinite game of relationships and their combinations, shaking boundaries and settling in as close as possible to the limits, on the threshold of the ever-receding and ever-inaccessible realm of the possible.

The Solitary Path of Maurice Godelier

Freud and Marx were the two important tutelary figures in question. Lacan's reading and his return to Freud became absolutely fundamental for the indispensable renovation of Freud's work, in the same way that Althusser's reading of Marx was a return and a revision of the master. But there were also some hybrid cases, and Maurice Godelier was one of these. Godelier sought a way to reconcile two approaches that might seem antagonistic at the outset, for he tried to create a synthesis between Lévi-Strauss and Marx in order to return to Marx. And his effort was every bit as much a renewal and just as structural as the efforts of Lacan and Althusser.

In 1966, Maspero published Godelier's *Rationality and Irrationality in Economy*,[16] but the second part of his work was a group of articles that had appeared between 1960 and 1965 in *La Pensée* and *Économie et politique*, which is to say prior to Althusser's rereading of Marx. Godelier distinguished between Marx's hypothetic-deductive and dialectical methods. He had not awaited Althusser's return to Marx; his solitary undertaking was part of an oeuvre that displays a certain solidarity with Lévi-Strauss's structural anthropology. "I reread *Capital* alone at a time when no one was interested in rereading it."[17] Having come from an *agrégation* in philosophy, Godelier had studied economics for three years and tried to create an economic anthropology that would make it possible to undertake a comparative theoretical study of different economic systems over time and in space, based on a widely accepted definition of political economy that would include all dimensions of social life. "There is no economic rationality in itself nor any definitive form or model of economic rationality."[18]

Of course, in the context of the sixties, it was surprising that no common activities were ever undertaken by Althusserians and Godelier, given the great proximity in their points of view. Godelier, however, did go to the rue d'Ulm one Sunday morning to the initial meeting of an important collective research program led by Althusser. "A monstrous operation unfolded there before our very eyes. There was Althusser, the sacred interpreter of the sacred work, assigning tasks to everyone. Badiou was supposed to take care of the Marxist theory of mathematics, Macherey was to take care of the Marxist theory of literature . . ."[19] According to Emmanuel Terray, Godelier had an unfavorable reaction to the group because he was suspected of seeking an impossible compromise between Marx and Lévi-Strauss.

If ideas circulated quickly in 1966, and if all roads led to structuralism, it was not easy to discern who held center stage, a potentially hegemonic position in this cultural cauldron. The positions were dear and the risk of falling into the pot relatively high. The game had to be subtle. No, clearly, a structuralist Paris was an impossible wager.

Part III

A Hexagonal Fever

Thirty-six

The Postmodern Hour Sounds

Imperceptibly, over the course of the twentieth century in the West, a new relationship with temporality was taking hold. At the same time, European domination and its role as a model for the rest of humanity were on the wane. At the beginning of the century in Vienna, at the heart of the old, decadent Hapsburg empire, a new ahistorical culture was bursting forth.[1]

The First World War had decisively redrawn the old economic maps in favor of the non-European powers. Europe underwent a crisis of consciousness as it realized that the uninterrupted linear evolutionism of its own historicity had been broken when it had been obliged to pass the baton of modernity to the young American power. In 1920, Spengler's *Decline of the West* relegated Europe to its proper provincial place, a Europe that was beginning to experience the unstable foundations of nineteenth-century evolutionism.

Heirs to the Lumières and the Aufklärung, the social sciences were enjoying their belle epoque, progressing toward the age of perfection and of reason triumphant. The tenants of immobilism or of change had all concurred on a general shape of the future of progress, whether Saint-Simon, Spencer, Comte, or Marx. August Comte saw outlined against the horizon of humanity a theological state, succeeded by a metaphysical state, and finally a positive state. For Karl Marx, the transition from slavery to serfdom to capitalism culminated with socialism. These certainties about constructing the future in a progressive perspective would founder in the face of the tragic reality of a twentieth century that, in 1920, had not yet run out of surprises for Eurocentrism.

The Second World War and the Holocaust further traumatized a West that had scarcely dressed its wounds when it saw its leading position in the world challenged by whole continents shaking off the colonial yoke. A denuded Europe problematized its dramatic past against a background of increasingly radical pessimism. And at each new jolt, Europe mourned the very idea of a future of rupture.

A Futureless Present

A dilated present made the past present. A new kind of relationship to historicity developed; the present was no longer the anticipation of the future but the arena for a possible recycling of the past. "When the difference of the future is no longer to be sought in the present, we suddenly discover it coming from behind, backwards."[2] Only when the question was no longer the search for something in the past that made another construction of the future possible could the relationship between past and present be relaxed, when the future was screwed shut, weighed down in a present equilibrium condemned to infinitely repeat itself. The taste for novelty, the publicity picture of our daily life, made it possible to further dilute every possible future alterity.[3] Having rejected all historical teleology and all meaning given to the history of humanity, the distant enticements of the "world that we have lost," of the Middle Ages magnified as the site of alterity linked to the search for the roots of identity, could be rediscovered.

A new, ethnological consciousness was needed to replace historical consciousness as this decentering of European culture and metaphysical deconstruction unfolded. The West was beginning to examine its nether side, the ways in which the unconscious made itself palpably present by its very absence. Freud had discovered the laws of the unconscious underlying our society and Durkheim had deciphered the unconscious of our collective practices. Postmodernity therefore was built around this quest for underlying mechanisms and targeted the deconstruction of the humanism that Michel Foucault had characterized as medieval, using this triumphant epistemological revolution of the sixties in order to glorify it: "Structuralism is not a new method, it is the awakened and troubled consciousness of modern thought."[4]

Reason Loses Its Charm

A fundamental pessimism, a sort of negative theology, was nourished by the provincialization of Western reason and realization of the irreducible logic of resistance of other logics, and of cultural plurality. "Those who were disappointed by Western reason"[5] countered the optimistic belief in rationality by falling into a sort of nihilism or reflection on limits made at the intersection between sense and nonsense. It was a complex situation confusing personal idiosyncrasies born of disillusionment and rejection but still bearing the marks of its contestatory beginnings. Theorizing man's incapacity to master his collective or personal history, underscoring his incompleteness, the defunct pavane of Western reason also heralded a more rigorous effort whose lucidity was greater than that of Western reason itself. This is what was clearly at work in Lévi-Strauss's exhuming of primitive societies, what gave Lacan a capacity to care for his patients, what allowed Foucault to work on prisoners, the forgotten, and the repressed. The ruse of reason worked at its own decentering.

The relationships between the structuralist paradigm and the disillusionment of the period are therefore complicated, not a mirror reflection of each other, but rather the scientific mind developed autonomously with regard to the context. To argue for their equality would be "like saying that Einstein's relativity is a disillusionment based on the idea that everything is relative."[6] And yet another piece must be added to this context of ambient disenchantment preceding the explosion of structuralism, which is the exhaustion of the evolutionist, phenomenological, functionalist paradigms and the search for an epistemological renewal. The law of evolution itself was seen to be comprised of successive ruptures and models and programs surpassed, conveying a veritable history of theoretical failures. In the same way that the West was discovering a nonlinear history, the social sciences were no longer thinking of themselves as successive accumulations of layers of sedimentation.

The Ideology of Suspicion

The twentieth century is the century of ruptures, breaks, and radical shifts. It has led to a fundamental pessimism with respect to history and to the onset of the postmodern era. We would agree with Jean-François Lyotard, who dates the rupture of Western evolutionism in

1943,[7] the year of the final solution, a radical plunge into horror. No one could henceforth ignore Dachau and Auschwitz, said Adorno. Technological modernity became a steamroller, a planetary death machine enmeshed in an ideology of suspicion. In addition to which, the reality of the totalitarian system behind the Iron Curtain was laid bare as the underside of the ostensible model. Beyond reason, implacable ruses muzzled the hopes of creating a better world and this observation of a necessary discontinuity: "We must start from the beginning."[8] It was no longer possible to naively exalt the continuous progress of freedom and human lucidity, nor to sustain the humanist vision according to which man is the perfectible master of his destiny, marching directly toward perfection. In place of that rosy future stood the approach of partial changes whose limits and possibilities needed definition.

From Budapest to Alexandria by way of Algiers, 1956 witnessed a procession of disillusionments. In France, songs of Liberation were silenced and a certain collective hope dimmed. Only the voice of the master who ended all hope sounded and resounded as he awaited the moment in 1958 when he could call for a new national leader, this general who presented himself as the incarnation of the "incarnation." The fifties were to deal a new hand to French intellectuals. "After 1956 . . . we were no longer obliged to hope for anything."[9]

Not that the decade was more propitious for bringing forth positive changes. If, during the space of a springtime in 1968, the international movement had infected French society, the year ended with the Soviet boot crushing another spring, the Prague Spring. A new wave of intellectuals was to fully feel the brunt of this new jolt. "I was in New Guinea in 1968, and I cried when I heard that the Russians had invaded Czechoslovakia. . . . We saw how legitimacy was established with tanks rather than with democracy; it was all over."[10] Revolutionary hopes, exposed to the forces of oppression, took on a mythological cast for an entire generation, reduced to a fantasy and repressed like a nineteenth-century myth. These important experiences of limits invoked by the intellectuals were irreversibly eroded in Western society, which no longer thought of itself as belonging to what Lévi-Strauss called a warm history, but rather seemed to borrow from primitive societies, in order to favor a cold relationship to an impaled and immobile temporality.

The Death of Evolutionism

Revolutionary eschatology dissolved with the resistances, blockages, and inertia of our society. In the same way that political will and commitment were discredited, a similar theoretical discredit tainted all things historical. The structuralist paradigm would be constructed and flourish from this negation of historicity and quest for origins, from the genesis of the reflection on temporal rhythms. It would freeze movement, cool off history, and anthropologize it when "the natives become the indigents."[11]

Western fascination with the unchanging lifestyle of the Nambikwara that Lévi-Strauss had resurrected in a certain way, a West breaking with its historicity, revealed the beginning of the postmodern period. The very idea of progress as a unifying phenomenon underwent a form of disinfection. Pluralized, progress was no longer perceived as the driving force of social evolution. And without refuting certain advances, these were no longer part of a total problematization of society. This deconstruction lay behind a true intellectual revolution inaugurated by structuralism, particularly through anthropology and the idea of the equivalence of the human species. This was a fundamental shift from Lévy-Bruhl to Lévi-Strauss. It demonstrated that, beyond the tropics with their plurality of lifestyles and thinking, all human societies were the complete and hierarchy-free expression of humanity. This aspect of the structuralist revolution remains, and it gave a new perception of the world in which all forms of social organization were considered equal, abolishing distinctions between inferior and superior or befores and afters. Thanks to structuralism, the idea of progress lost significant luster. "In order for there to be a notion of progress, there had to be primates at the beginning. . . . This was acquired thanks to structuralism, something we no longer realize because we do not see the transition clearly. It is a given; it has become something obvious."[12] Granted, it was easy to go from relativity to relativism, but whatever the position, perceiving the Other as a partial manifestation of the human Universal meant abandoning the historical vision of nineteenth-century evolutionism. The human sciences replaced the consciousness of a model Europe poised at the vanguard of human progress with a critical consciousness that dethroned the Subject and History, and that turned consciousness upon itself, or rather, upon its nether side, its repressed. This egalitarian notion burst forth during the postwar period, and with decolonization it was here to stay. It was a completely new idea that redefined the geopolitical points of the globe. The perception of humanity became eccentric as a result for the Western intellectual; no longer read from within, identity was projected into an external space. This inflection of perspective required a dialectical relationship between spaces, and that the anthropologist's glasses be trained on the universe of the Other.

Temporality Slides into Spatiality

There had clearly been a radical break with the Enlightenment and the belief in continuous progress as Condorcet had imagined it.[13] Western man had been at the center of the conception of knowledge and judgment before his anthropocentric viewpoint was decentered. The seeds of this revolution had been planted at the end of the nineteenth century by new structures of scientific thought, pictorial perspective, and writing, all of which favored discontinuity and deconstruction. From the arbitrariness of the Saussurean sign to the new mathematical and physical models to quantum theory to the Impressionists' dislocation of classical perspective, followed by that of the Cubists, a new vision of the world imposed discontinuity: the referent was held at bay.

Western reason was being gnawed at from within and tending toward plurality as of the late nineteenth century, no longer conceived of as a reflection, but rather as a discontinuous succession of different structures. Psychoanalysis emphasized this phenomenon by demonstrating the discontinuity between the unconscious and the conscious requiring the presence of a third element in the analytic context. An infinite unfolding of epistemes replaced the unitary view of evolutionism.

The shifting ideas between the nineteenth and twentieth centuries further accentuated these changes. Nineteenth-century European historicism had seen human history as a liberation from the laws of nature, whereas the twentieth century once again took its distance from history in order to retether itself to nature, perceived as "a regulatory ideal in the paradise to be rediscovered."[14] The battles waged by man in the name of the noble values of freedom and equality were thus considered doubtful, incomplete, and most often destined to failure.

Historical consciousness was repressed by a planetary, topographical consciousness. Temporality shifted into spatiality. Being removed from the natural order gave way to a search for unvarying logics born of the nature/culture joining. The prospect of a foreclosed future generated a quest for an immutable human nature with evident constants—Lévi-Strauss's *enceintes mentales*, ecosystems, the *longue durée*, structures, the extension of the notion of geographicity—and the natural paradigm took its revenge. "Today we see how the de-sacralization of history leads to a resacralization of nature by communicating vases."[15]

The ruptures were tragic and provoked a need for and a return to cultural, ethnic, and natural constants for protection. This approach sought even more to protect against history, to be free by clinging to an identity that anchors rather than constructs history from a signifying diachronic logic. Those uncertain moments of history, the cult of the past, the restorations occulting superficial ruptures transformed man as the subject of his history into an object of history that he could not understand. The relationship between men, as a result, is "subjected to a zoological status."[16]

Western society underwent a number of changes during the interwar years that further upset the relationship between past, present, and future. The future was reduced by computerized programming to little more than a projected reproduction of the present, but it was impossible to think a different future. The end of territories and the beginning of a society beyond national soil contributed to the state of temporal weightiness, a cooled relationship to temporality. "What we called the acceleration of history fifty years ago . . . has become the crushing of history."[17] Similarly, this atemporal relationship became fragmented into myriad uncorrelated objects, a segmentation of partial and disarticulated knowledge, a disaggregation of the general field of understanding, and the gutting of any real contents. This socio-economic mulch would particularly nurture a structural logic, symptomatic reading, logicism or formalism that would find its coherence elsewhere than in the world of flat realia.

Some, like Henri Lefebvre, saw a direct link between structuralism's success and the implantation of a technocratic society. In his view, structuralism played the role of an ideology legitimating a social caste, the technostructure of the new industrial state, the justification of its location at the highest levels of authority, and the theorization of the elimination of history. Structuralism would thus be the harbinger of the end of history for a middle class that had managed to reach a position of domination. An ideology of constraint and of the weight of the structural on human liberty reduced to common property, it reflected the consumerism in which the citizen would cede his or her place to the consumer. The social universe and the representation of the world that it engendered were thus magnificently connected with the mortification of the European left, which, in the sixties, averted its gaze from history and from notions of progress. Structuralism therefore answered a social need; it crystallized a particular historical situation in which shifting attention toward the figure of the "savage" no longer responded to a need for exoticism but to the desperate search for the truth of humanity in a universe where the future seemed to be foreclosed.

As early as 1967, François Furet had seen that the intellectual milieu of the Marxist left was the most receptive to the structuralist vogue.[18] According to Furet, this milieu had an inverted relationship whereby it could express nostalgia for a Marxism that was being abandoned little by little to the rhythm of revelations about the gulag, and, thanks to structuralism, find some compensation for the same determinist ambition to universalize and totalize, but without the burden of history. According to this hypothesis, structuralism would express a very specific historical moment, an intersection characterized by political immobility and the consolidation of systems.

The death knell had sounded for progress; the structuralist fervor led to a calling into question of dialectical thought. Philosophers contributed new readings that were to cast doubts on the Hegelian foundations of their analyses. In their place, a symptomatic reading made it possible to perceive an epistemological break between the "young Marx," who is still Hegelian, and the "mature Marx," scientifically mature, a structuralist before his time. "A nondialectical culture is in the process of taking shape."[19] At the same time, François Châtelet was reducing the dialectic to rhetoric and Gilles Deleuze was announcing "an ebb of dialectical thinking in favor of structuralism."[20] Today we customarily say that the ebb of ideologies has made it possible for a hundred structuralist flowers to bloom. In the same way that the limits of praxis resulted in man's decentering, an immantentist reading of the social sciences saw the sources of scientific rigor in the decentering of human practices.

Repetition Compulsion

Posthistory brought a new relationship with a dilated present that appears as ahistorical, an eternal recycling of different configurations of the past. This present offered a hermetic horizon, for it could only re-produce itself in the dominant presentism. The fashion for commemo-ration clearly illustrated this new relationship with historicity. Mem-ory repressed history, which was no longer the search for origins in order to generate future possibilities, but the simple reminder of the universe of signs of the past living in an immutable present. Signs that referred to each other and whose only referents were those sites of memory, so many traces left in the space of a past, perceived some-where over the horizon of an impassable split. We experience "the end of what we were as an affirmation: the adequation of history and memory."[21] These sites of memory kept their symbolic value and in-vited an archivistic relationship to the past. They were not revisited so as to be reconstructed, but were simply considered as the remains of a repressed past that had disappeared.

A radical discontinuity separated the memory of an ever-indefinable past, invisible as reality except for its multiple material signs, from a slack present that recycles, commemorates, and remembers. The rela-tionship to temporality was thus split and memory became memories, fractured for want of a breakwater constituting a full, collective mem-ory. History flowed back into the moment, thanks to the unification of lifestyles and *mentalités* when there were no longer any true events, but only a profusion of "news." The present plunged its roots into the past through a purely museographical relationship, without concern-ing itself with the outlines of a definition of the future. It thus destabi-lized the very function of historical discourse as the connection be-tween past and present.

Postmodernism established a relationship to history resembling that of a senile individual who can do little more than collect souve-nirs, remaining forever cut off from all possibility of a future project. Structuralism's success therefore corresponded to a general phenome-non of civilization and should be ascribed as much to the establishment of a technocratic society and to the birth of Herbert Marcuse's one-dimensional man as to the reification of man reduced to his con-sumerism. In this respect, and without being reducible to that, humanity was the ideology of nonideologies, the end of revolutionary ideologies, of colonial ideologies, and of Christian ideologies. But in the sixties this aspect was the unsaid, the unconscious of profound changes that only become evident in the eighties. This process of pacification, this end of meaningful breaks, closed the present in on itself; what came to dominate was the feeling of satisfaction, of marking time, of a society where "the new is greeted like the old, where innovation has become banal."[22]

Discourses of Legitimation in Crisis

Both a fundamental pessimism critical of the illusions of reason and a desire to deconstruct everything that presented itself as total coherence, categorical imperative, and natural order subjected to the decompostion of a radical critique, spurred the retreat of history and the crisis of discourses of legitimation that characterize postmodernity. The very notion of reality was called into question. Since everything that touched these categories elicited only disillusionment, reality was repressed into meaninglessness. Structuralism was, in this respect, one stage in the process of deconstruction, by its faculty of derealization. Public space was imperceptibly transformed into a space of advertisement in the era of the simulacrum, at the same time as all the poles of reference were vanishing, so many spatiotemporal frameworks for the values we had believed to be eternal and universal.

Paul Virilio saw in philosophy's search for the hidden face an echo of an aesthetic of disappearance in which the reality effect supplants reality. Every metanarrative is in crisis in the postindustrial or postmodern society because of a generalized skepticism. According to Jean-François Lyotard, this transition to a new economy of discourse occurred at the end of the fifties in Europe when "reconstruction" was coming to an end.[23]

With modern technologies of communication and the informatization of society, knowledge shifted and became the inseparable face of the power of the deciders, the programmers, who little by little relegated the old traditional political class to a lesser role. In this context, the question of legitimation deviated and provoked a crisis of the major narratives. "The 'crisis' of scientific knowledge . . . represents, rather, an internal erosion of the legitimacy principle of knowledge."[24] Deconstructing the One, the metadiscourses, yielded to a proliferation of multiple discourses unassigned to any single subject, simple language games, a seamless fabric. The humanist perspective dissolved and was replaced by a performative stake, a "legitimation by the fact."[25]

A Crepuscular Vision

Structuralism responded to this crisis of legitimation discourses by reducing human ambitions to something of only provincial proportions, simple participants without any particular privileges, living beings on the planet, subjected to a history that no longer belongs to them, at the geological level. Lévi-Strauss was the most eminent representative of this fundamental pessimism, of this retreat of man. One of the most critical observers of the evolution of Western modernity, he contrasted it with a profound skepticism and pessimism that placed him in the long line of conservative thinkers stretching from Edmund Burke to Philippe Ariès. "I would gladly accept the reproach of pessimism, on the condition that the adjective 'serene' is added."[26]

This jaded view was further underscored by Lévi-Strauss's own position as an anthropologist who watched his field disappear beneath his very feet with the staggering blows of an often forced acculturation. At the beginning of the nineteenth century there were two hundred and fifty thousand natives in Australia, but in the mid-twentieth century there were only forty thousand survivors of hunger and illness. Between 1900 and 1950, ninety tribes disappeared in Brazil. These disappearances from the specific ethnological field forced the ethnologist to consider his own society, to which he could certainly apply his methods of analysis, but based on the uniformity of modernity that imposed its laws. Lévi-Strauss therefore observed an atmosphere of something that was ebbing. After the dusk of the gods, it was the turn for humans: "The day is coming when the last of the cultures we call primitive will have disappeared from the face of the earth."[27] At the end of his four volumes on myths, a disabused Lévi-Strauss concluded with an involution of the resources of the universe/nature/home combination, which ended "before collapsing in upon themselves and vanishing, through the self-evidence of their own decay."[28]

As early as 1955, Lévi-Strauss had warned the West of the disasters, of the underside of its euphoria in the thirty glorious years. With *Tristes Tropiques*, he was offering to make primitive societies live again, to remove them from the mire beneath "our garbage" flung in the face of humanity, the concrete that takes root everywhere like dandelions, the pauperization of the slums, deforestation. This is a sad score card of a conquering, lesson-giving civilization, a civilization of death behind the hypocrite face of adventure and of encounter with the Other. Lévi-Strauss's structural anthropology attacked the Lumières and their pretension to a universal message.

In a similar fashion, and on a speculative rather than an ethnographic level, Foucault expressed this same desire to shake up universalism. "I dream of the intellectual who destroys facts and universals."[29]

The Richness of a Closure

Whether defined by Lévi-Strauss or by Foucault or by all of new structuralist thinking, and despite its tremendous diversity, this new problematization took root in this retreat of history characteristic of postmodernity, in this pessimism that was not only serene but productive. For want of a historical perspective, once having destabilized the status of man and taken its distance from the reality of the real, structuralism preferred closed systems in which methods with a scientific vocation sought refuge, an inaccessible place, repressed and removed from consciousness. An increasingly complex social reality and an inability to identify any unifying logic favored this withdrawal into the search for a unity in the hidden face of reality. Revealed meaning fell into insignificance. It was no longer part of the closed field of this universe of signs that, removed from the referent, referred back and forth among themselves in the absence of any material causality. The truth of the closed system could no longer be sought by some hermeneutic whose starting point was revealed meaning, but it was to be understood in the relationships and interrelationships between signs within their specific and limited structure, and the interplay that it defined between the signs.

This web of relationships excluded historical contingency just as it excluded the free play of initiative. If structural linguistics provided the preferred model of approach, there was nonetheless some resemblance between the cybernetic approach, which decenters the finalist and anthropocentric perspective in order to give precedence to the processes of self-regulation, a combination of a physics of relationships, the games and replays of the same and the other, decentered humanity that only held an illusory place. "We must break this network of appearances that we call man with all our might."[30] At the moment when the social sciences seemed fascinated by the cybernetic model, the human variable in its psychological and historical components lacked consistency and was replaced by a rigorous method that sought to reach a level of efficacy equal to that being practiced in the hard sciences. The closed system that became necessary would pay a heavy price for setting the real world at a distance. And yet, it would be remarkably effective in the receptivity it would inaugurate in the field of knowledge.

In its quest for the unconscious dimension of social practices, structuralism would open the universe of signs of the symbolic, of collective representations, and of customs and rituals in their internal logic, and from the nonexplicit strata find the traces of human activity. Acceding to these new objects and pluralizing them would help shatter systems of causality: "The structural method has made it possible to triumph over causalisms or simplistic determinisms."[31] The unifying coherence of social history faded as well, sinking into the quicksands of the unifying and plural structural combinatory, a dialectical game of the same and of the other inaugurating the new era of a posthistory.

Thirty-seven

Nietzschean-Heideggerian Roots

One philosopher was intensely aware of the impasses of history at the heart of a nineteenth century in which Western history reigned triumphant, and that was Nietzsche. He clearly understood that the thinking of the moment was preparing the advent of the despotic state. German unity was realized, but at the price of a militarized and aggressive Prussia. Nietzsche's *Untimely Meditations* (1873–74) addressed the dangers of history, by which he meant two different definitions of the term: historicity (*Geschichte*), and the understanding of historical change. Nietzsche theorized the suicide of Western history and the death of *Homo historicus*. Instead of the theodicy leading to the creation of the coldest "of cold monsters," the state, he put forth an argument in favor of multiple, local, and present values, a return to sources in a Europe bastardized by successive racial mixtures and whose universalizing message had been deformed by the radical exit from historicity. During the same period, Darwin was demonstrating the simian origins of the human species. Anthropocentric perspective and metaphysical thinking were thus both being put to the test by scientific discoveries.

Nietzsche's nihilistic discourse could flower and challenge the outlook of the triumphant Lumières like a narcissistic wound following on the heels of the Copernican-Galilean revelation that the earth was not at the center of the universe, and rock Western metaphysics. The evolution of reason would thus lead to its other side, to a realization of the non-sense, the relativity, and even the relativization of the figure of man. Nietzsche dispatched history as well as the dialectic of reason.

Later, Heidegger renewed the Nietzschean legacy in his radical critique of modernity. His thinking was rooted in Oswald Spengler's *Decline of the West*, a depiction that Heidegger, affected by the trauma of the First World War and the ensuing debacle in the Weimar Republic of the twenties, pushed to its paroxysm. He plotted the trajectory of the Forgetting of Being, of a constant repression underlying the prevalence of being. Man no longer had access to the revelation of truth insofar as each manifestation of truth "is at the same time in itself a dissimulation."[1] In this view of things, history was nothing more than the sad unfolding of reason, mystified since the original crack. The theme of the eternal return found its echo in the Heideggerian notion of *a perennis* philosophy, a veritable remake of the same based on the question of why there is Being rather than nothing. The answer was that there was no answer. As a philosophy of impotence, this philosophy signaled our incapacity to answer without reappropriating the "Scriptures and the Holy Roman and Apostolic Church, which does not, however, mean that Heidegger was a believer."[2]

Both of these philosophies, moved by a profound pessimism, sought to establish the end of philosophy. "It looks as though everything is becoming chaotic, the old becoming lost to us, the new proving useless and growing ever feebler."[3] For Nietzsche, the faculty of reason that made it possible to decenter man still nourished his illusion of omnipotence, salving the wounds it inflicted each time a bit more. Similarly, the Forgetting of Being was further accentuated by the development of modernity and the generalization of technicity.

The Anti-Lumières

These two thinkers presented themselves as anti-Lumières. Nietzsche denounced the brutal violence of the Lumières philosophy that culminated in the French Revolution. In his eyes, any brutal change or revolutionary break could only elicit a vision of barbarism: "It is not Voltaire's moderate nature . . . but Rousseau's passionate follies and half-lies that called for the optimistic spirit of the Revolution against which I cry: 'Écrasez l'infâme.'"[4] Here Nietzsche defended the moderate and progressive philosophers against those radical philosophers who worked toward the fulfillment of the Revolution. But Nietzsche's work, like that of Heidegger, was essentially a radical critique of the

Lumières. Both attacked a certain notion of historicity as a bearer of progress, for if history has any meaning at all, it is that we are inexorably moving toward a decline. The conscious mind is encumbered by history and must free itself in order to judge the present. "He sends the dialectic of reason packing."[5] Underlying the Lumières' claims of universality, Nietzsche saw the immanent and hidden roots of the will to power. Becoming was meaningless, or rather an apprenticeship in the tragedy of the world, which is its very essence. "History resides in us like camouflaged theology."[6] Meaninglessness clearly led man to impotence, to a nihilism assumed by an aristocratic and powerful elite making any illusion of human action moot. The human spirit of rationalization was perceived as continuous with religious spirit; substituting reason for God would have been equally illusory. The effort at human mastery was therefore absurd.

For Nietzsche, humanity began its decline with the beginning of Greek thought, and Socrates, who appeared in *Ecce Homo*, was the very symptom of decadence. Instincts and Dionysian hubris are contrasted to Socrates' ethic, which would later be embodied by religious morality in order to repress and suffocate vital drives. The entire history of civilization therefore unfolds according to an internal logic of castrating reason and a mystifying morality. Philosophy must discover the creative drive shrouded beneath the mask of civilization. Nietzsche favored forgetting in order to be rid of the illusory and mystification: "Thus it is possible to live almost without memory, and to live happily moreover, as the animal demonstrates, but it is altogether impossible to *live* at all without forgetting."[7] Filled with a fundamental pessimism and hostility to historicity, Nietzsche also nourished a visceral hatred of the masses and of revolution.

Nietzsche described his thoughts in his correspondence with a German officer during the 1870 siege of Paris. He considered war to be a useful test of virility, but the awful spectacle of the Paris Commune, the "slaves'" revolt, and their breaking of rules frightened him. General insurrections lead straight to "barbarism" he wrote in 1871–73 in his preparatory notes for an essay on the future of teaching establishments. Those dispensers of earthly happiness, the socialists of the late nineteenth century, could only perfect the metaphysical cast of mind at work in all of Western history and therefore make it veer toward decadence and catastrophe. But laying bare the illusions of the metaphysical era also revealed an unprepared and weak individual in the grips of the ephemeral, a striking contrast to the false happiness of the metaphysical ages. Whence the temptation to be borne toward the construction of a better future, a future that is always part of a comforting illusion: "That better future which one wishes for mankind must necessarily be in some respects a worse future for it is folly to believe that a new higher stage of mankind will write in itself all the excellences of earlier stages."[8]

Socialism was Nietzsche's true enemy: "Socialism is the fanciful younger brother of the almost expired despotism whose heir it wants to be."[9] "The poison of this disease which is presently contaminating the masses with increasing speed as a socialist scabies of the heart."[10] Since history at the close of the nineteenth century seemed to guarantee the irresistible success of the socialist movement, history needed to be eliminated in order to better destroy the dangers threatening the West and was thus assimilated at once to a mystification, to decadence, to a smell of rot, and to a paralyzing straitjacket. In the middle of a historicist century, Nietzsche was a radical partisan of the dissolution of the category of the new, the thinker of the end of history.

Nietzsche was therefore a precursor of the triumphant postmodernity of the mid-twentieth century. He was already sketching out the deconstruction of the unified, total framework of historical movement, which yielded to the immobility of a slack present in which histories undergo a process of atomization and multiplication when they are only constructed on an individual basis: "Nietzsche and Heidegger . . . laid the necessary foundations for constructing an image of existence in response to the new conditions of nonhistoricity or, better yet, of posthistoricity."[11]

The Forgetting of Being

In the 1930s, Heidegger took up Nietzsche's critique of modernity in his lectures. Heidegger, like Nietzsche, saw history as little more than the unfolding of a slow decline whose roots harken back to the Greeks in the constant Forgetting of Being. In his 1957 *The Principle of Reason*, Heidegger critiqued two forms of historical thinking. He qualified the first as the metaphysics of history, which imagines that freedom operates in historical evolution, metaphysical insofar as it presupposes man at the center of the historical process—a belief that Heidegger clearly considered to be an illusion, a metaphysics of subjectivity. In the second place, he attacked Hegelianism as a teleology in which reason slowly revealed itself to itself through history, as simply another form of metaphysics that subjects history to the principle of reason, a variation that also reintroduced the Subject into a central position—not because this subject mastered a process that more often than not victimized him by its ruses, but because he could come to understand its significance. However, man modeled meaning on the structure of his own human reason rather than that of Being, which remained confined within Forgetting.

In place of these approaches, which Heidegger characterized as metaphysical, he proposed the history of Being, a history without a history, the simple unfolding of that which is presented through its successive images, meaningless, without either filiation or periodization. To conceive of history, he used the metaphor of a trunkless, rootless rosebush flowering in the springtime. A profusion of buds described shattered history, with neither a subject to infuse the historical unfolding with meaning nor an underlying, occult subject whose traces would have to be sought.

In *Being and Time* (1927), the temporality of Being was placed alongside that of a progressive decline leading to an apocalpyse, in which, as we know, Heidegger participated. Degradation is structural in human history: "Belonging to the very being of *Dasein*, degradation is an existential."[12] From his rectorate speech to his interview in *Der Speigel*, Heidegger never stopped reiterating his Cassandra-like warning against the decline (*Verfall*) in which the West was inexorably becoming mired: "The spiritual force of the West eludes us and its edifice trembles, the dead appearance of culture crumbles."[13] To this involution, Heidegger contrasted the strength of rootedness, tradition, and country; they must be so many breakwaters of resistance against the technicity of the modern world that carries away the totality of being with which the being-there of Being is dissolved. If the history of Western civilization is the history of a progressive forgetting of Being, the twentieth century is the culmination of this amnesia.

For Jürgen Habermas, Heidegger's critique of modernity, technicity, and mass civilization was unoriginal because it simply appropriated the repertory of received ideas of the generation's conservative mandarins. Habermas situated the drift leading Heideggerian theory to embrace National Socialism in what was, in 1933, a new investment in the categories of fundamental ontology. Until that point, *Dasein* had designated the being toward death in its singularity, whereas after 1933 it took on a collective sense of the reunited population. Heidegger also diverged from the path of triumphant reason and chose the sinuous path of an obscure world that "will lead nowhere." A conception of wandering to come nearer the paths leading to the realm of origins and of logos. This theme of wandering found no earthly culmination; these pilgrimages of the human "shepherd of Being" could only evoke a complete theological variation. "This explained how theologians were the first to adopt *Being and Time*."[14] Heidegger radically detached Being from empirical reality in the same way that he realized the end of history.

Antihumanism

If structuralism was fortified by this antihistoricism, Nietzsche and Heidegger radically critiqued humanism, in which the figure of man disappeared like so many grains of sand beneath the waves. At the beginning, there was the fracture Nietzsche created with the death of God, which destabilized the notion of an identifiable, definable human mastery and subject of history. He denounced the deification of man that replaced religion at the time of the Lumières and that continued throughout the nineteenth century.

If God was dead, no immutable human nature could exist as an *aeterna veritas* or measure of all things, and this relativism led Nietzsche to a radical nihilism. Moral judgment became impossible; on what basis could a norm be constructed? "When virtue has slept, she will get up more refreshed."[15] Ethical judgment supposed a freedom of action and a level of responsibility that man does not possess. Under such circumstances, individual judgment in any given situation became the sole criterion for action, the rest little more than the basis for subjugating the subject. "The complete unaccountability of man for his actions and his nature is the bitterest draught the man of knowledge has to swallow if he has been accustomed to seeing in acceptability and duty the patent of his humanity."[16] Nietzsche attacked humanism as a doctrine that assigned man the central role of subject as a full being, as the seat of the proof of self-consciousness. Here, Nietzsche translated the impossibility of relying on any transcendental foundation whatsoever, given the death of God.

Heidegger took Nietzsche's critique of humanism further. Man was fundamentally dispossessed of any mastery since his reality could only forever appear to him as something veiled. "The question: who is man? can only be raised in the questioning of Being."[17] This questioning led to indetermination and inaccessibility, except that here, man is the trace, the communion, the witness. The effectiveness of Heidegger's critique lay in emphasizing the fact that man's definition in no way gave him the capacity to free himself from the codes enclosing him in contingent definitions and in particular determinations. Ek-sistence preceded being and determined man's initial nothingness, and his vocation of universality.

Heidegger represented a major break from the vision of man as master and owner of nature. Later, Sartre would say, "If man, such as existentialism conceives him, is undefinable, it is because he is, first, nothing."[18] From this point on, the problem was posed and would give rise to two different interpretations of whether existentialism could be a humanism, as Sartre claimed, or if, as Heidegger believed, it leads to an antihumanism.

In 1946, Heidegger sent his *Letter on Humanism* to Jean Beaufret in which he clarified his thesis by cleaving the humanist interpretation of his thinking. Ek-sistence was not given to man like the Cartesian cogito, which is only a rationalist hyperbole to be reversed by the formula "I am, therefore I think." Man was in an inextricable alienation: "Man, exiled from the truth of Being, goes in circles around himself like a *rational animal*."[19]

Rather than assuming its position as the shepherd of Being, being in the world has been lost in being. In the twentieth century, this is translated by a universal technologization and generalization of modernity, the *Ge-Stell*, the setting into place of technology. As Heidegger saw it, man's fate was independent of himself; he was not autonomous in his subjective faculties and could only be attentive to the voice of Being. In this regard, the philosopher and the poet were presented as those who succeeded in being most proximate to this being-there of Being, most often presented as an abyss.

Being points to the human condition as being-toward-death, the first root from which the world of the mind arose. It thus displaced the point of view of the Cartesian cogito or of psychologism. No longer there where consciousness masters itself, Being was to be found in the cogito's conditions of existence. Whence Heidegger's criticism of Sartre's effort to determine the conditions of the cogito. This archaeology revealed man to be inexorably decentered and subjected to a history of which he is no longer the subject, but rather its object or its toy.

The Primacy of Language

In this quest for the beginnings of the thinkable, Nietzsche and Heidegger both thought that language and its laws played a particularly important role. Language had lost its original purity because it had been diverted by the functionality of being. The philosophical or poetic quest sought to complement this lack in order to rediscover the meaning of the lost logos. Because being masked the conditions of its reality, Heidegger favored using linguistic interpretation as the privileged medium of the history of Being. "Heidegger gives the phenomenological method the sense of an ontological hermeneutic."[20]

Language thus became the important object of study in a Heideggerian perspective. This clearly showed the fundamental roots of structuralism's generalization of the linguistic model to the entire range of the social sciences. Heidegger's influence was fruitful, but it was constructed at a distance from anything having to do with being. Moreover, his influence went unfelt for Charles Sanders Peirce's pragmatics as well as for the linguistic philosophy of Ludwig Wittgenstein or of John L. Austin.

For Heidegger, who was unfamiliar with the work being done in pragmatics, man did not speak, language spoke, while man was spoken. Consequently, his approach was nominalist and fetishized the discursive since language differentiated humans from the vegetable and animal realms, a distinction and a burden. Similarly, Nietzsche's critique of metaphysics also decentered the cogito from language presented in its "natural" rhetoric. Metaphoric and metonymic processes found a critique of unattainable truth, in place of which they offered the infinite interpretative labyrinth whose only value lay in the relativity of their site of enunciation. "Rather has the world become 'infinite' for us all over again, inasmuch as we cannot reject the possibility that it may include infinite interpretations."[21] This new area of interpretation had to avoid metaphysics, which was little more than an exaggerated quest for a genesis and origins in order to establish a continuity and causality around the unity of the subject. Nietzsche favored a deconstructive genealogy of the subject so as to decipher the conditions of belief systems based on what they occult or repress. This deconstruction aimed at unearthing the originary inscription of a primitive truth, which preceded its formulation; it sought every absolute that was supposed to bear the human being.

The Genealogical Program

Nietzsche, like Heidegger, privileged language as disenfranchised from all subjection to the imperative of truth. "With his aphorisms, Nietzsche establishes the return in force of censored and repressed elements, and puts them in perspective."[22] This Nietzschean genealogy had to take another approach to temporality and to the relationship to truth. Presented as the point-by-point antithesis of the Platonic approach, Nietzsche argued for the destructive use of reality rather than reminiscence/recognition, for the derealizing and dissociative use of identities against tradition, and for the destruction of truth in place of history-knowledge. "Genealogy is history as a concerted carnival."[23] Access to truths thus became doubly inaccessible. On the one hand, truths were no more than clouds of metaphors, metonymies, and anthropomorphisms that we believe to be stable, simple exchange values whose use value has been forgotten. On the other hand, the fiction of the cogito became the targeted site of the illusion: "There is no one who is innocent enough to still raise the question of the subject 'I' as Descartes did, as the condition of 'think.'"[24] For Nietzsche, the cogito was the model of metaphysical pronouncements and the hypostasis of the fictive subject whose polysemism he analyzed.

The genealogy valorized the territory of the sign, which was to be retraced as an unveiling of a unitary, metaphysical discourse. The meaning was unsheathed behind the ever-denied textual opacity. Having deconstructed the carnival masks, it was necessary to reconstruct the unbroken signifying chains of successive interpretations; these chains are no longer proposed as continuous, but on the contrary perceived as discontinuity, as symptoms, or as lacks. The genealogical approach favored the underbelly of what is spoken, the hidden face of the signifieds. It defined a game of displacement in order to disinvest and de-implicate the metaphysical content of the stratified layers of the signs. The genealogy sought to restore the conditions of discourse more than its contents. Both Nietzsche and Heidegger made this shift toward the discursive.

The Nietzsche-Heidegger Program Once Again

Heidegger's quest for logos and Nietzsche's genealogy converge here, and both nourished structuralist thinking. The critique of ethnocentrism and of Eurocentrism intensified during the fifties and sixties with the structuralist vogue, which adopted the Nietzschean-Heideggerian critical paradigm on its own; but behind the continual unfolding of triumphant reason lurked the image of the madman, of the savage, and of the child as so many repressed figures allowing reason to reign. Lévi-Strauss rehabilitated the savage mind; Jean Piaget looked at childhood no longer as the negative of adulthood, but understood as a specific age; Foucault rediscovered the long drift of madness before its internment; as for Lacan, he truly pulverized the Subject, demonstrating, contrary to the Cartesian cogito, that "I think there where I am not, therefore I am there where I do not think."

In *Thinking 68*, Luc Ferry and Alain Renaut systematized the intellectual structure of the sixties, even if they were mistaken in correlating May 1968 and this intellectual cast of mind.[25] The major thrusts of Nietzschean-Heideggerian thinking are here: the theme of the end of philosophy, which Derrida developed in order to free thinking from its captivity. He favored the writing of a pure trace, a mind "that does not mean anything," pure meaning freed from the signified. Also present are the paradigm of the genealogy, or the problematization, of the external conditions of production of discourse, rather than the examination of their contents. And there is the idea of truth as the sole means of verifying the adequation between a discourse and its content, an idea that, along with the referent, which is radically cast to the sidelines, loses any foundation. Finally, we witness the historicization of categories and the end of any reference to a universal. To this systematization, elucidated by Luc Ferry and Alain Renaut, must be added the disappearance of the name of the author and the meaning of his existence. The author is erased behind the laws of language, of which he is nothing more than one pole performing a composition that does not belong to him. We once again find an attack on the subject and on the enunciation of discourse, and it led to a new definition of the literary text and of the work of the critic, who must shift his gaze from the author to the text as a closed system.

Certainly, these shifts are at work between Nietzschean-Heideggerian thinking and structuralism. Thus, Heidegger's antihumanism and that of structuralism, even if one may be heir to the other, are not really of the same nature. The structuralist point of view refers humanism to an episteme of the past and therefore finds a compelling epistemological justification, whereas Heideggerian antihumanism remains metaphysical in nature. "He hypostasizes Being to all dimensions of history."[26] He produced a philosophy that, more than a conception of the end of history, was a conception of metahistory whose core was Being, a perspective that was not at all shared by structuralism in its diverse manifestations.

Foucault: "I Am Simply Nietzschean"

Foucault's ties to Nietzsche are obvious and overt: "I am simply Nietzschean."[27] Foucault wrote within a Nietzschean scope and even used the same metaphor of an erased figure of man at the end of *The Order of Things*; he deconstructed the subject in the same way as Nietzsche had and substituted the project of a genealogy: "Everything is already interpretation."[28] Like Nietzsche, Foucault scoured the lower depths and exhumed what history had forgotten, deciphering the advance of a disciplinary society lying behind the progress of the Lumières, occulted by the predominance of a liberating legal-political discourse. Madness was repressed in this way by the very development of Reason, of a Western culture that was vacillating in the mid-twentieth century. Foucault was a brilliant student of Nietzschean thinking, and adopted the dissolution of the figure of man, perceived as a simple fleeting passage between two modes of being of language: "More than the death of God, . . . what Nietzsche's thinking presages is the end of his murderer, the explosion of the face of man."[29] And from this death of men, he also concluded the primacy of philology and of an examination of discourse, already heralded by Nietzsche and readdressed by Mallarmé.

Hermeneutics became semiology when it infinitely interpreted interpretation, the sign having broken its moorings with the original signified. Humanism had been erected on false foundations of lack and inexistence and was a form of consolation; the principal issue then became knowing why and under what conditions man conceives something that will forever be situated outside of him.

For Foucault, Nietzsche represented the first uprooting of anthropology, whose collapse indicated "the imminent death of man."[30] Nietzsche's genealogy also inspired work rooted in the historical present rather than in an impossible search for origins, so Foucault did not try to understand the continuities that proclaim by bespeaking our world, but rather pointed out the discontinuities, the shifting of the epistemes. Historical knowledge had to its credit the fact that it problematized, that it broke the constants and the consolatory game of recognition.

During the course of his archaeology, Foucault was led to pay particular attention to archives, to the document understood as a monument that let him retrace the fault lines and point out the singularity of events freed from any teleological finality. The fact that Foucault carried on a dialogue with historians, more often than not shot through with mutual incomprehension, and even went so far as to work with historians such as Michelle Perrot and Arlette Farge, that he was, during the last months of his life counseled by Paul Veyne, is not at all fortuitous but corresponded to Foucault's genealogical approach. "The genealogist needs history in order to conjure away the chimera of the origin."[31] Highlighting heterogeneity, deconstructing history, and working toward giving the myriad of lost events a sense by making them once again into events—such are the orientations of a Foucault who transported Nietzscheism onto historical terrain.

To a lesser degree, we can also perceive Nietzsche's influence on Lévi-Strauss's work. Jean Duvignaud sees this particularly in *Tristes Tropiques* and in the "finale" of *The Naked Man*, where Lévi-Strauss's general vision bathes in a profound aestheticism that harks back to Nietzsche: "Aesthetics always emerges as soon as history is eliminated."[32] Thus, structuralism's circularity in Lévi-Strauss, based on which myths refer to each other in a magnificent construction of logic, would refer to Nietzsche's eternal return.

Citing Reason

Heidegger's influence is even more obvious and widespread for the various components of structuralism. Foucault declared that "Heidegger was always the essential philosopher for me."[33] Unlike Nietzsche, who was a constant reference, Heidegger's influence on Foucault was implicit, although Foucault quickly became familiar with the work of the German philosopher. Foucault's friend Maurice Pinguet describes his first encounter at Ulm with the young Michel Foucault, whom he heard intelligently holding forth in his metallic voice with some impassioned friends about notions of *Dasein* and being-for-death.[34] Nothing more ordinary for a young ENS student in 1950, when Heideggerianism was the *koine* of every philosopher. But Heidegger is present in the work itself of Michel Foucault.

In speaking of Kant in *The Order of Things*, Foucault employed the typically Heideggerian expression of the "analytics of finitude," according to which man discovers that he is "always already" in the work and that it is therefore vain to look for origins: "Removed from all origins, he is already there."[35] We also find Heidegger in *Madness and Civilization*, where "the entire theme of reason that only becomes reason by exclusion is typically Heideggerian."[36] *The Archaeology of Knowledge* is an implicit debate with Heidegger's *Letter on Humanism*. Similarly, the way of seeing a disciplinary society unfold behind the society of the Lumières in *Discipline and Punish* corresponds to Heidegger's inspection of reason and points to a fundamentally pessimistic vision of the fate of Western society. Of course, the lessons to be drawn from this diagnosis went unassimilated; very few similarities exist in terms of praxis between commitment in the sense of the resistance to power as Foucault understood it and Heidegger's "commitment"!

In Lévi-Strauss's case, Heidegger's influence was neither direct nor acknowledged, as it was for Foucault. And yet it is no less diffuse and present in Lévi-Strauss's profound skepticism with regard to modernity, in his critique of global technologization, and in his denunciation of its destructive—and potentially genocidal—character. Questioning planetary homogenization and the suppression of differences is also part of the same sensibility.

Lacan and Heidegger

Heidegger's influence on Lacan was also quite clear. As Élisabeth Roudinesco has pointed out, Lacan was fascinated by Heidegger's style, as indeed was the entire French postwar intelligentsia. The first meeting between the two took place in 1950, but it was above all thanks to Heidegger's French disciple, Jean Beaufret, who began an analysis with Lacan in 1946, that Lacan came to know Heidegger via the patient on his couch who became the very source of the diffusion of Heidegger in France. Indeed, Lacan and Jean Beaufret struck up a friendship, which made it easier for Heidegger's language to take root.

Lacan's first reference to Heidegger dates precisely from this period. In September 1946, at the Bonneval colloquium, Lacan gave his presentation "Regarding Psychic Causality." The allusion made it clear that Lacan had read *Plato and the Doctrine of Truth*, which Heidegger had published in 1941–42.[37] Later, Lacan visited Heidegger in Freiburg.[38] Shortly thereafter, he translated the article entitled "Logos," submitted it to Heidegger, and then published it in the first issue of his review *La Psychanalyse* in 1953. Lacan paid a resonant homage to Heidegger on this occasion: "With respect to the presence here of Monsieur Heidegger, for all those who know where the highest meditation in the world takes place, this presence alone guarantees that there is, at the very least, a manner of reading Freud that does not bear witness to a mind as cheap as one patent loyalist to phenomenology claims it to be."[39]

Despite his enthusiasm, Lacan did not translate more than four-fifths of the text, and he amputated the end in which Heidegger saw poetic writing as a means of escaping the drama of human existence. For Lacan, neither escape nor salvation were possible; he perceived no glimmering of Being. Élisabeth Roudinesco tells of Heidegger's first trip to France, which, in that August of 1955, looked quite picturesque. He came to participate in the interviews at Cerisy-la-Salle organized by Jean Beaufret and Kostas Axelos. Lacan organized a small meeting at Guitrancourt in honor of the illustrious guest.

> Heidegger stayed at the Prévôté, then visited the cathedral at Chartres. Lacan drove as fast as he ran his sessions. Sitting in the front seat, Heidegger did not budge or show any signs of nervousness, but his wife kept asking Lacan to drive more slowly. Sylvia explained her worries to Lacan, but to no avail: the master drove faster and faster. On the way back, Heidegger remained silent and his wife's protests got louder, while Lacan kept his foot down on the accelerator. The trip came to an end and everyone went home.[40]

Their relationship could have been warmer, obviously, but what counted was the conceptual borrowing beyond any direct communication, which was made difficult by the fact that Heidegger considered that there was only one true language—German—which Lacan was able to translate but could not speak.

Lacan took up Heidegger's notion of ek-sistence, the idea that man is separated from any form of essence, and took inspiration from the distancing of Being with respect to being. Each time Lacan quoted Heidegger, it was to use the notion of ek-sistence as well as being-for-death. The Lacanian idea that a real life is not a real life but a symbolic life "is an idea that is everywhere in Heidegger. It is even essential to his philosophy."[41]

Heidegger's influence on Lacan's paradigms is easily deciphered. Not only does one find there the fundamental pessimism of Heidegger, man's decentering, the deconstruction of the subject that is split and forever inaccessible to itself, the long path of loss, of the Forgetting of Being starting with the structuring experience of the Mirror Stage, but one can also find borrowings from Heidegger's vocabulary. Everything having to do with the relationship to Truth, to authenticity, to full and empty speech stems from a Heideggerian approach transposed onto psychoanalytic terrain. All the commentary on Greek philosophy, on *alétheia*, is common to both. In Lacan's "Seminar on the Purloined Letter," the letter's circularity recalls the structuralist model and is, at the same time, supported by a whole Heideggerian concern for a site in which truth is unveiled, which is the very site of the letter, a site where it is not in its place. Thus Lacan, in the early fifties, was truly fascinated with Heidegger, a fascination that went unreciprocated, for Heidegger was always indifferent to Lacan's work. It is therefore impossible to agree that "Lacan was never a Heideggerian,"[42] and to reduce what he borrowed to a simple matter of vocabulary, even if it is true that with respect to the problem of science, their positions were opposed. For what is most essential—that is, Heidegger's proposal of a philosophy as a common language for all the social sciences—there is a legacy that goes much further than Lacan and Lacanian thought.

Jacques Derrida and Heidegger

Heidegger's influence was clearer on Jacques Derrida, despite what he has said since the "Farías affair."[43] Derrida considered the epithet "Heideggerian," to be clumsy and he rejected it. At the same time, he claimed that Lévi-Strauss, Althusser, and Foucault were never influenced by Heidegger![44] And to support his thesis about the total absence of Heideggerian influence in France, Derrida recounted an anecdote going back to 1967–68. Driving with Foucault one day, he asked why he never spoke about Heidegger. Foucault answered that it was both too important and too difficult, that Heidegger was beyond his grasp.

But if we limit ourselves to Derrida's texts, Heidegger's omnipresence is not only obvious but explicit: "Nothing that I have tried to do would have been possible without the opening of Heideggerian questions, . . . without the attention to what Heidegger calls the difference between Being and being, the ontic-ontological difference such as it remains unthought in a certain fashion by philosophy."[45] Of course Derrida did not servilely adopt or claim Heidegger's thinking as his own, for his deconstruction also attacked the very knots of this thinking and, as with Lacan, sought to radicalize its theses.

For Derrida, the *Ereignis*, man as shepherd of Being, were vestiges in Heidegger of the debris of a humanism to be deconstructed. Derrida's starting point, however, still remained the privilege Heidegger granted language as the medium of Being, and the transition from a philosophy of consciousness to one of language. Commentary held a similar fascination for Derrida. While participating in the general orientation of structuralism, he distinguished himself by criticizing in turn Claude Lévi-Strauss in *On Grammatology*, Michel Foucault in *Writing and Differance*, and Jacques Lacan in *The Truth Factor*.[46] We will return to his criticisms, which introduce us to the main echos of French Nietzschean-Heideggerianism, which adopted structuralism as its emblem in order to deploy the particularly diverse research potentialities in the entire field of knowledge of the social sciences.

Thirty-eight

Growing Pains

To understand structuralism's success, we must do more than broadly paint its historical context and identify the philosophical positions to which the movement was heir. We must also describe the state and shape of the social sciences themselves during the period. For, contrary to what much reductive thinking might imply, the history of each discipline was generally independent of the others and to the history leading to its creation. As Gilles Gaston-Granger put it, the life of concepts at this level is autonomous. We can shed some light on the social conditions surrounding the appearance and transformation of a common theory like structuralism if we consider the interdisciplinary rubbing of shoulders among researchers and teachers, and more generally in the intellectual world.

The Intense Socialization of the Social Sciences

This period of flourishing structuralist activity was also one during which the social sciences, and particularly those fighting for their place in the sun, were expanding in a spectacular way. These new social sciences were in search of their legitimacy, but they also needed to win over a growing intellectual audience of the fifties and sixties. Their identity was forged around a rupture so that they could circumvent established, traditional positions. The structuralist break presented itself as a scientific revolution drawing numerous disciplines under its banner, and this intense socialization helped win the day.

The profoundly scientific and ideological aspects of the movement during this period cannot therefore be ignored, nor can the ideological aspects of its history, for this much-sought socialization led to an ideologization of structuralism's scientific discourse. The structural method does not sum up the history of structuralism. Indeed, we might even raise the question of whether "scientific revolutions are not, in fact, this intense socialization."[1]

In this respect, no science is protected against ideologization or socialization. As we know, physical observation implied purely ideological issues during the time of Copernicus and Galileo; the transition from a geocentric vision of the universe to a heliocentric one generated theological conflicts. Paul Rivet understood the necessity of socialization for the institutional success of French ethnology in its early years. Born during a period when colonial thinking had left its mark on this science, ethnology was steeped in ideology. Rivet saw that he could use the situation and reverse it to radically change the perception of cultural and social alterity, and he deliberately used ethnology as an ideological weapon and a major element in the intellectual debates of the thirties, thereby facilitating its institutionalization. Ethnology underwent a certain metamorphosis. From a conditioned discipline, it became a conditioning discipline, bearing with it an ethics and a policy of antiracism.

Intense socialization and ideologization therefore corresponded to a mode of being in these newly armed sciences. Conceptually forceful, however, they were nonetheless disarmed on the level of institutional legitimacy. What was true for ethnology during the thirties was even more dramatically so for the sciences of the sign during the fifties and sixties, for they could profit from the support of the media, which was playing an increasing role in the intellectual field.

The media were in fact taking over the debates of the sixties and placing the issues in the public arena. One could even hear the famous Picard/Barthes duel described as a new Dreyfus Affair. Some considered that the only tangible reality of structuralism was in fact this media hype and that once the media noise was eliminated, "structuralism no longer exists."[2] In the same way that the divergences and contradictions counted more among Descartes, Spinoza, Pascal, or Hobbes, the similarities among the structuralists stemmed from their contemporaneity, but their differences were more pertinent. Behind the facade of homogeneity, the conflicts and polemics that exercised all the researchers were particularly lively. But media amplification was sought out of a concern for making the phenomenon better known, for recognition, and in a quest for intellectual legitimacy.

Maurice Godelier embodied another attempt at dissociating a form of thinking opposing science and ideology,[3] by virtue of his radical distinction between the structural method, based on pertinent, rigorous, scientific analyses of kinship ties and mythic structures, for example, and structuralism, which belonged more to the realm of the ideological, to general speculative declarations about humanity, society, and the progress of thought. These were completely different for Godelier, even if researchers combined method and an ideological dimension. "My argument is that the structural analysis of myths, Claude Lévi-Strauss's method, does not at all imply his structuralism; he is the one who defined his method, not because his method is limited but because he wanted to define it for other reasons."[4] Science, ideology, socialization, mediatization—structuralism was all of these at once, like an entangled skein of yarn whose untangling depends on contextualizing certain moments, currents, issues, and their stakes.

Philosophers Respond to the Challenge of the Social Sciences

The taste for structuralism therefore corresponded to an intense socialization of the social sciences and to an explosion such that these became part of a veritable policy of development from the fifties onward. In 1958, for example, a new sociology *Licence* was created thanks to Raymond Aron's influence: sociology had made considerable progress in establishing itself institutionally. More generally, those actors in the social sciences in full swing "did not look to philosophers' recognition; on the contrary, they sought to differentiate themselves ostentatiously."[5] We can appreciate structuralism's success in this respect as a response from philosophers to the challenge raised by the social sciences, which for the most part had come from the same philosophical house. Philosophers were shaken up by the competition from disciplines with more scientific and pragmatic ambitions and that were able to articulate concepts and fieldwork. They reacted by appropriating the program in order to consolidate and strengthen their position on the intellectual playing field.

Philosophy witnessed the waning of two programs. Sartrean

existentialism, articulated around the notion of a constituent, transcendental, omnipotent, and completely abstract subject from which everything and all meaning proceeded, was in complete disarray in the sixties and ran up on the shoals of history against which it had foundered: "One of the last models of the idealism of the French university."[6] Structuralism, by virtue of the immobility of structures and the decentering, if not the extinction, of the subject, offered the means for reacting radically to those philosophers who wanted to mark their distance from this idealism. Sartre had inaugurated a new style of philosophy as a stake in a public debate, and this strongly contributed to his popularity during the postwar years and during the decade of the fifties. But he was the first victim of this new mode of relationship with a public that would elude him and be drawn to the structuralists, who turned against him the same weapons he had used to win preeminence for his philosophy. The economic situation, the end of the war in Algeria, the disengagement from political commitment, and a general disillusionment all contributed to the creation of a new style of intellectual. Sartre no longer incarnated this intellectual and he became the expiatory victim of the détente.

The second program on the wane was phenomenology, from which the structuralists also dissociated themselves. Of course structuralism did adopt some phenomenological approaches—for example, the priority of structures and of the search for meaning—so much so in fact that Jean Viet, the author of the first thesis on structuralism, saw phenomenology as a specific tendency of structuralism.[7] And yet, phenomenology remained a philosophy of consciousness and basically sought to describe phenomena. For Jacques Derrida, phenomenology remained enclosed in the "closure of representation," by maintaining the principle of the subject: "Deconstructions replaced descriptions."[8] The notion of deconstruction, which would orient all of structuralist thinking, was first introduced by Derrida when he translated Heidegger's *Destruktion*, a term with neither negative nor positive connotations. "Deconstruction seeks to propose a theory of philosophical discourse. Such a program is manifestly critical."[9]

Born of the protest against phenomenology, philosophical structuralism carried the critical paradigm to its zenith. It used phenomenology as a way of opening up or raiding the legacy of the field of investigation of the social sciences. Most structuralists were trained philosophers: Claude Lévi-Strauss, Pierre Bourdieu, Jacques Lacan, Louis Althusser, Jacques Derrida, Jean-Pierre Vernant. And yet, in search of something else, they had all broken with the traditional philosophy taught at the university. This was a philosophical generation intensely aware of the challenges of the social sciences and it broke with traditional university rhetoric. But in order to do so, it had to circumvent the traditional, legitimized institutional structures and directly address the intelligentsia. This meant choosing new philosophical objects with a specifically relevant and contemporary orientation, by articulating thinking with the social realm and institutions and acquiring a praxeological value.

Moreover, for these philosophers, structuralism helped renew a discourse that had become more scientific and that offered them a defense against the social sciences. Pierre Bourdieu baptized this the "logy-effect,"[10] when he observed the success of archaeology, grammatology, and semiology. "Logy" evoked the scientific aspirations of speculative structuralism, which borrowed as much from mathematical logic as it did from linguistics in order to establish itself as a scholarly pole in the history of science. Foucault described this fault line, which he emphasized and which transcended all other forms of opposition: "This is what separates a philosophy of experience, meaning, and the subject from a philosophy of knowledge, rationality, and the concept. On the one hand, there is the line of Sartre and Merleau-Ponty, and on the other, of Cavaillès, Bachelard, Koyré, and Canguilhem."[11]

The social sciences appropriated a whole series of questions, and even the privilege of reflection of a philosophical nature. The philosophical avant-garde thus spearheaded a successful counteroffensive under the structuralist banner. Philosophy—open, renewed, carried along by its growing public—would emerge revitalized by the contest and markedly stronger by its growing batallion of teachers: the number of high-school philosophy jobs rose from 905 in 1960 to 1,311 in 1965 and 1,673 in 1970.[12] The number of postsecondary teaching jobs rose from 124 in 1963 to 267 in 1967.

The gurus of structuralism wanted to assimilate the social sciences. They nonetheless criticized their model of positivity and crossed swords with them. Structuralist philosophers increased their virulent attacks on the scientistic pretensions of the social sciences: Lacan against psychology, Althusser against history, and Foucault against the methods of classification in the social sciences. A veritable barrage of fire was opened up against the ostensible imposture of the social sciences and their scientific certitudes. The structuralists unleashed an epistemological critique against them, fueled by the work of Gaston Bachelard and Georges Canguilhem.

Étienne Balibar described this successful turn quite well. The social sciences, purified by the structuralist critique, sought their positivity in the models and concepts that philosophers had developed. "Thus the text I contributed to *Reading Capital* (1965) seduced anthropologists and a few historians because I was constructing a concept of the mode of production and they found it operational."[13] Structuralism could maintain the primacy of this renovated philosophy—based on a "formula of compromise"[14] between a redefinition that added a dimension of dynamism, which was critical of humanism and led to radical rupture, and the preservation of the elevated status of the philosophical discipline, despite the frequent reference to the end of philosophy that seemed to mask the phenomenon—by privileging an essentially conceptual and theoretical discourse and by casting the borders and divisions among the rising social sciences into some degree of uncertainty and confusion. As Louis Pinto pointed out, this was the concern that made Foucault's use of the term "archaeology" able to satisfy the double requirement of proposing a historical discourse about the social sciences, but that would make it possible to consider them philosophically, which is to say, differently and better than they could conceive themselves on their own.[15]

In this respect, the philosophical avant-garde fully responded to the challenge of the social sciences and even favored their expansion during the sixties. At the same time, it preserved philosophy's prestigious place as the "crowning discipline" among the disciplines. Philosophy remained at the zenith of the high-school curriculum, and particularly in the institutions where the national elite was shaped: *khâgne* and the Écoles Normales Supérieures. Philosophy withstood the offensive rather well. Witness the assurance with that Louis Althusser rejected the "so-called social sciences" as an anathema that "cannot be explained without referring to their weakened institutional (and often intellectual) state in the fifties."[16] The battle of the humanities with respect to the social sciences at this level reiterated the joust between the ENS and the ENA in shaping the national elite, between a classical elite and the new, technocratic elite.

Emancipation from History

Structuralism did not limit itself to attacking academic philosophy. It also attacked history, that other ancient and well-ensconced canonical discipline certain of its positions and methods. This destablization not only of the university discipline but of historicity in general was another characteristic trait of structuralism. War was declared against historicism, the historical context, the search for origins, diachrony, teleology and the argument made in favor of permanent invariables, synchrony, and the hermetic text. The *Annales* school took up the challenge. In 1958, Fernand Braudel favored the *longue durée* and temporal tripartition as the common language of all the social sciences under history's baton. At the end of the sixties, the third generation of the *Annales* deconstructed a fractured and anthropologized history.[17] Structuralist literary criticism or semiology began to define itself by repudiating history. Of course it had to cut itself off from traditional, academic literary history of the man and the work, but in its concern for formalization, semiology went quite far in negating any historical elucidation, and thus cut itself off from any psychological or historical referent.

Historians, including those who were most open to dialogue with the other social sciences, could not help but feel challenged by structuralism. They reacted by attending to the study of socioeconomic structures, cycles, and repeated phenomena, which had already been part of their own program. But they could not call themselves structuralists for the antinomy would have been too marked. There was therefore a profound desire for emancipation with respect to history, pushed to the absurd negation of any historical foundation. Michelle Perrot, a professor at Paris VII who was at the very summit of modernism in history, gave a seminar at the time with colleagues in literature who turned the seminar into a dead end. Perrot thought that she was taking a step toward interdisciplinary progress, but the attacks against all reference to any kind of historical context whatsoever gave her "the feeling of being completely out of date." Indeed, for those partisans of new literary criticism, "the very word 'context' made them jump—it was spurned. We had to stay with the closed text, which made conversation very difficult."[18]

Antiacademicism

This determination to have it out with the canonized disciplines— traditional philosophy, history, psychology—was part of a larger context of antiacademic revolt. This was the only means for the philosophical avant-garde or for the young sciences of the sign to make a place for themselves within the institution. For most of the adherents of structuralism, their status was in fact precarious.

Innovation came essentially from those institutions considered marginal at the time, such as the Sixth Section of the EPHE, or even the Collège de France. While considered the high point of intellectual legitimation, these institutions were nonetheless at the margins of the university, the principal teaching and research structure.

The paths of the structuralists were, in this respect, significant because they essentially took place outside the university. This was true for Lévi-Strauss among others, as he freely admitted: "It was therefore an active university career whose most striking characteristic is doubtless that it always took place outside the university per se."[19] The same was true for Barthes, Greimas, Althusser, Dumézil, Todorov, and Lacan. Considering the courses given at the Sorbonne in 1967, one notices with no small surprise that the linguistics courses were given by linguistics professors who, with the exception of André Martinet, were entirely different from those who are well known today. "In 1967, there was not even any linguistics department at the Sorbonne, but only a simple Institut de Linguistique. . . . When I was a high-school teacher doing my thesis in linguistics, I was planning to be unemployed since what I was doing was absolutely useless."[20]

The weight of tradition and the recalcitrant conservatism of the venerable Sorbonne kept the French university system closed to new influences. Its immobility in turn helped to fan the revolt and the necessary rupture. In order to make a place for themselves, the sciences of the sign had to get beyond the institution and find massive and effective support. Structuralism made it possible to federate the avant-gardes of different disciplines and to transform the revolt into a revolution.

This was the context in which references to Nietzsche, Marx, and Saussure became operational as true arms of an antiacademic critique of those partisans of a university and mandarin orthodoxy. The structuralists in fact adopted an older program in order to make it relevant and current. They were determined to bring areas that obeyed specific rationalities into the realm of the sciences of man, an idea that went back to Auguste Comte.

Structuralism's other main paradigm held that the objective relationships between isolated elements are important rather than any particular elements without the interference of consciousness, the idea of a lag between behavior and consciousness; this view of things had already been clearly proclaimed by Durkheimians and Hegelians. What was new was that a program rather than its contents became a reality, as well as the speed with which this program was applied and produced tangible scientific results.

Linguistics: A Common Program

Structural linguistics provided a method and a common language for bringing about a scientific renewal of the social sciences. Linguistics appeared as the model for a whole series of sciences lacking in formalism, and it penetrated ever more deeply into anthropology, literary criticism, and psychoanalysis and profoundly changed the mode of philosophical questioning. And yet, a certain number of social sciences remained essentially removed from this dramatic change, or were simply only marginally affected by the debate; it did not shake their fundamental positivism. Psychology at this point was developing systems of modeling and scientific structures free of metaphysical problems, and the situation in economics was essentially the same.

Linguistic contagion had affected disciplines in precarious institutional positions or those in search of an identity because of the internal contradictions between pretensions to scientific positivity and a link with the political arena, as was the case with sociology. Finally, there were those disciplines, like literary studies or philosophy, that were fully caught up in a quarrel between the ancients and the moderns. These circumstances contributed to the weakening of disciplinary boundaries and structuralism appeared as the unifying project: "At the end of the sixties, it appeared necessary to unify the diverse attempts at renewing the human sciences into a single current or even into a single discipline that was more general than linguistics."[21] Roland Barthes and Umberto Eco expressed the temptation even more clearly by agreeing to propose a general semiology that could confederate the human sciences around the study of the sign.

Modernization was therefore joined with interdisciplinarity. It was necessary to violate the sacrosanct boundaries so that the linguistic model could penetrate the entire field of the social sciences. From the moment when everything has to do with language and we are all made of language in a world that is language, "everything becomes interchangeable, permutable, transformable, convertible, everything."[22] This interdisciplinarity, which put the brakes on Humboldt's model of a university in which each discipline had its place within strict limits, created a veritable taste for all the variants of formalism, for knowledge that was immanent to itself. The password of the period was communication. Beyond the review of the same name, the term conveyed this multidisciplinary euphoria.

A Unitary Science

Just after the war, Lévi-Strauss was the first to formulate this unifying program in the social sciences. Of course his constellation gravitated around social anthropology, which he represented, the sole discipline deemed capable of carrying out this totalizing undertaking. For Lévi-Strauss, anthropology's particular vocation came from its ability to position itself at the crossroads between the natural sciences and the social sciences. Consequently, anthropology "does not abandon the hope of one day awakening among the natural sciences, at the hour of the Last Judgment."[23]

To construct his anthropology, Lévi-Strauss drew inspiration and a certain number of logical-mathematical models or operational techniques from the natural and exact sciences. He aspired to erase the frontier between the natural sciences and the social sciences thanks to scientific rigor. Encouraged by his fruitful meeting during the war in the United States with Jakobson, Lévi-Strauss gave the linguistic model a certain pride of place in his anthropological approach. In his search for invariants, in his paradigmatic and syntagmatic deconstructions, he adopted the lessons of Jakobson's phonology: binary oppositions, differential divergence, and so on. Linguistics, thanks to Jakobson, further enriched a particularly rich area of knowledge. If, thanks to the priority given to language and to deciphering signs, Lévi-Strauss oriented anthropology toward culture, the aspiration of unity was by no means left along the wayside. His quest for *enceintes mentales* also implied biology, a discipline that was absolutely fundamental in structural anthropology even if it was not truly exploited. Structural analysis found that "its model is already present in the body, I have already mentioned . . . the exhaustive research that has been done on the mechanism of visual perception in various animals."[24] "Instead of opposing ideal and real, abstract and concrete, 'emic' and 'etic,' one will recognize that the immediate data of perception cannot be reduced to any of these terms but lies betwixt and between: that is, already encoded by the sense organs as well as by the brain, in the manner of a text."[25]

In aspiring to a totality, Lévi-Strauss was adopting Marcel Mauss's goal of constructing a "total social fact." He therefore sought to embrace the full scientific arena and finally to make structural anthropology *the* science of man, a discipline federating those sciences on the basis of logico-mathematical models, strengthened by the contribution of phonology and by a boundless realm of investigation that took in, in a single glance and over the face of the planet, societies without history or writing.

The anthropologist could therefore reach the unconscious dimension of social practices and could restore the complex combinations of rules operating in all human societies. We can understand how such aspirations could vex all those sciences that take man as their primary object, and how it provoked a number of reactions from other disciplines—competition from some and support to the dynamic conqueror from others, in order to win some degree of legitimacy for themselves. Defined this way, the goal was equivalent to the difficulty anthropology had encountered early on in positioning itself institutionally:

> Newly established sciences find difficulty in inserting themselves into traditional structures. It can never be sufficiently emphasized that anthropology is by far the youngest of these young sciences (the social sciences) and that the general solutions appropriate to its elders have what is, for it, an already traditional aspect. It has, as it were, its feet planted on the natural sciences, its back resting against the humanistic sciences and its eyes directed toward the social sciences.[26]

If anthropology did not manage to dig out the human sciences entirely on its own, structuralism took up the relay. It was in fact the common paradigm, for want of being a common school, for a whole series of disciplines all working toward the same end of establishing a total unified science.

A French Phenomenon

The structuralist blaze was essentially a French phenomenon that radiated outward from France. The Anglo-Saxon world grouped the many works that made the structuralist moment famous under the general category of French Criticism. Why, more than elsewhere, was France a better soil in which structuralism could take root and flourish? We can suggest a few answers. First of all, the weight of the humanities in France blocked the social sciences within the French university, contrary to the situation in American universities, where they were triumphing. The philosophical avant-garde in France reacted to the growth of the social sciences by appropriating the structuralist program, making it possible for the renovated humanities to triumph in the quarrel between tradition and modernity. What's more, the joust between the partisans of tradition and those of modernism was also a typically French phenomenon, which merely replayed the debates of the early century between the "new" and the "ancient" Sorbonne. The weight of the humanities also enabled the French intellectual to speak in the name of humanity and to be engaged as a spokesperson in a context that did not call on a specific expertise.

Another tradition existed that went back largely to the eighteenth century, but that was expanded during the nineteenth century with the Dreyfus Affair, and incarnated during the twentieth century by Jean-Paul Sartre. Even if structuralism took its distance from Sartre and the figure of the committed intellectual, it would amply use the practice of circumventing structures in order to directly address and persuade the readers and the public of its theses and short-circuit its peers. Conversely, in the United States, the university professor is evaluated in dollars and "has no particular right to speak in the name of humanity."[27] Similarly in Germany, few university professors were involved in a media network where it was possible to make a breakthrough, as was the case in Canada for Marshall McLuhan, although the university made him pay for it dearly.

In France, the university grip on its own autonomy was weakening because there were other possibilities of institutional consecration. Underlying the theoretical debates were issues of power represented by the new ambitions of the young social sciences facing the monopoly of the traditional humanities. We once again find the specifically French situation of a highly centralized and routinized university, an old Napoleonic legacy, unchanged during the fifties and sixties. The weight of the humanities is also revealed by the central position of an institution like the École Normale Supérieure on the rue d'Ulm in elaborating the structural paradigm; where the major reviews of the period—Les Cahiers pour l'analyse and the Cahiers marxistes-léninistes—were created and produced there. And Althusser, Derrida, and Lacan were at Ulm.

Another given of the period that went beyond the university was the relationship between French intellectuals and the history of their own country. Suddenly they became aware, in a decolonized and pacified France, that they no longer lived in the country that had presented itself as the guiding light of humanity since 1789. France was no longer a great power but simply a modest part of a plural Europe. As François Furet saw so clearly, the French intellectual, "despite the Gaullist rhetoric, no longer has the feeling of making human history. That France, the one that is expelled from history, accepts all the more easily the expulsion of history."[28] Jean Duvignaud confirmed this. He saw the French specificity of the success of structuralism as "a flight from history."[29] Coming together in France and speaking among themselves gave intellectuals the need to fortify an ideology able to create a reassuring cohesion and new aspirations. "There we have the search for an order, practically in the chivalrous, initiative meaning of the word."[30]

This would contribute to the radical destabilization of history and thus to the success of structuralism on French soil. In addition, and conversely, there was an element that pointed to the preeminence of the antimodern spiritualist tradition among French intellectuals, a tradition strengthened by the dominance of philosophy constructed, if not against science, then at least removed from it and subordinating it, "which amounts to this incredible thing where we see Althusser giving lessons in scientificity to scientists."[31] Marcel Gauchet found in the intellectual community's expression of antimodernism the old opposition between the spirit and industry, between art and the horrors of a civilization of the masses, an old, recurrent theme of French intellectual history.

Thomas Pavel offered other views on why France was the favored land for structuralism. He explained the phenomenon through the internal logic of the development of epistemology in France. The taste for structuralism, he claimed, resulted from France's considerable tardiness with respect to its European neighbors. France remained so removed from the debates on language of the early twentieth century and unaware of the Vienna school (Rudolf Carnap, Otto Neurath, Herbert Feigl, Karl Popper) in the thirties that at the moment when this school went into exile because of the rise of Nazism, the diaspora found refuge in the Anglo-Saxon countries, essentially the United States. France's epistemological removal was clear and even further underscored by the fact that it was ignored as a possible place of refuge. "The work of Claude Lévi-Strauss, of the early Barthes, and of Lacan in part represented a deferred—and all the more visible—explosion in France of the hidden debate on language and the epistemology of knowledge."[32] After Lévi-Strauss, who had assimilated linguistics as a model for building structural anthropology, the avant-garde philosophers, cut off from the analytic current, also hurried to adopt the linguistic model, but without any epistemological precaution, by appropriating a Saussurean linguistics that was already outmoded by the advances of analytical philosophy.

The intensity of Parisian life that made it possible to short-circuit the traditional university and institutional networks also assured a swift diffusion of the structuralist paradigm on the French cultural market. Its adherents were transformed into media stars, the new gurus of a public that had broadened thanks to the spectacular rise in the number of students in letters and social sciences during the sixties. It was thus beneath the tricolor flag of France, and of France alone, that structuralism would flourish and fascinate other countries. But it was always a specifically French product that we indulged in because of our need for exoticism.

Appendix: List of Interviewees

(Parisian universities are listed as Paris I through Paris X.)

Marc Abélès, anthropologist, researcher at the Laboratoire d'Anthropologie Sociale, EHESS.

Alfred Adler, anthropologist, researcher at the Laboratoire d'Anthropologie Sociale, EHESS.

Michel Aglietta, economist, professor of economy at Paris X.

Jean Allouch, psychoanalyst, director of the journal *Littoral*.

Pierre Ansart, sociology professor at Paris VII.

Michel Arrivé, linguistics professor at Paris X.

Marc Augé, anthropologist, director of studies at the EHESS, president of the EHESS.

Sylvain Auroux, philosopher and linguist, director of research at the CNRS.

Kostas Axelos, philosopher, former editor in chief of the journal *Arguments*, teaches at the Sorbonne.

Georges Balandier, anthropologist, professor at the Sorbonne, director of studies at the EHESS.

Étienne Balibar, philosopher, lecturer at Paris I.

Henri Bartoli, economist, professor at Paris I.

Michel Beaud, economist, professor at Paris VIII.

Daniel Becquemont, anthropologist and professor of English at the Université de Lille.

Jean-Marie Benoist, philosopher, assistant director to the History of Modern Civilization chair at the Collège de France, deceased in 1990.

Alain Boissinot, literature professor, teaches advanced classes at Louis-le-Grand High School.

Raymond Boudon, sociologist, professor at Paris IV, director of the Groupe d'Études des Méthodes de l'Analyse Sociologique (GEMAS).

Jacques Bouveresse, philosopher, professor at Paris I.

Claude Brémond, linguist, director of studies at the EHESS.

Hubert Brochier, economist, professor at Paris I.

Louis-Jean Calvet, linguist, professor at the Sorbonne.

Jean-Claude Chevalier, linguist, professor at Paris VII, general director of the journal *Langue française*.

Jean Clavreul, psychoanalyst.

Claude Conté, psychoanalyst, former head of the clinic at the Paris Medical School.

Jean-Claude Coquet, linguist, professor at Paris VIII.

Maria Daraki, historian, professor at Paris VIII.

Jean-Toussaint Desanti, philosopher, taught at Paris I and at the École Normale Supérieure in Saint-Cloud.

Philippe Descola, anthropologist, associate director of the Laboratoire d'Anthropologie Sociale.

Vincent Descombes, philosopher, professor at Johns Hopkins University.

Jean-Marie Domenach, philosopher, former director of the journal *Esprit*, founder of the CREA.

Joël Dor, psychoanalyst, director of the journal *Esquisses psychanalytiques*, professor at Paris VII.

Daniel Dory, geographer, researcher at the CNRS and at Paris I.

Roger-Pol Droit, philosopher, editorialist at *Le Monde*.

Jean Dubois, linguist, professor at Paris X, on the editorial board of the journal *Langages*.

Georges Duby, historian, professor at the Collège de France.

Oswald Ducrot, linguist, director of studies at the EHESS.

Claude Dumézil, psychoanalyst.

Jean Duvignaud, sociologist, professor at Paris VII.

Roger Establet, sociologist, member of the CERCOM (EHESS).

François Ewald, philosopher, president of the Association for the Michel Foucault Center.

Arlette Farge, historian, director of research at the EHESS.

Jean-Pierre Faye, philosopher, linguist, professor at the Université Philosophique Européenne.

Pierre Fougeyrollas, sociology professor at Paris VII.

Françoise Gadet, linguistics professor at Paris X.

Gilles Gaston-Granger, philosopher, professor at the Collège de France.

Marcel Gauchet, historian, editor in chief of the journal *Le Débat*.

Gérard Genette, linguist, semiologist, director of studies at the EHESS.

Jean-Christophe Goddard, philosopher, professor for Hautes Études Commerciales preparatory courses.

Maurice Godelier, anthropologist, scientific director at the CNRS, director of studies at the EHESS.

Wladimir Granoff, psychoanalyst, head physician at the medical-psychology center in Nanterre.

André Green, psychoanalyst, former head of the Institut de Psychanalyse in Paris.

Algirdas Julien Greimas, linguist, honorary director of studies at the EHESS.

Marc Guillaume, economist, professor at the Université Paris-Dauphine, lecturer at the École Polytechnique, director of the journal *IRIS*.

Claude Hagège, linguist, professor at the Collège de France.

Philippe Hamon, linguist, professor at Paris III.

André-Georges Haudricourt, anthropologist and linguist.

Louis Hay, literature professor, researcher at the CNRS.

Paul Henry, linguist, researcher at the CNRS.

Françoise Héritier-Augé, anthropologist, professor at the Collège de France, head of the Laboratoire d'Anthropologie Sociale.

Jacques Hoarau, philosopher, professor at the Centre de Formation des Professeurs in Molignon.

Michel Izard, anthropologist, director of research at the CNRS, co-director of the journal *Gradhiva*.

Jean-Luc Jamard, anthropologist, researcher at the CNRS.

Jean Jamin, anthropologist, researcher at the ethnology laboratory of the Musée de l'Homme, codirector of the journal *Gradhiva*.

Julia Kristeva, linguist, professor at Paris VII.

Bernard Laks, linguist, researcher at the CNRS.

Jérôme Lallement, economist, lecturer at Paris I.

Jean Laplanche, psychoanalyst, professor at Paris VII, director of the journal *Psychanalyse à l'Université*.

Francine Le Bret, philosopher, professor at Jacques Prévert High School in Boulougne-Billancourt.

Serge Leclaire, psychoanalyst.

Dominique Lecourt, philosophy professor at Paris VII.

Henri Lefebvre, philosopher, former professor in the Universities of Strasbourg, Nanterre, and Paris VIII.

Pierre Legendre, philosopher, professor at Paris I.

Gennie Lemoine, psychoanalyst.

Claude Lévi-Strauss, anthropologist, professor at the Collège de France.

Jacques Lévy, geographer, researcher at the CNRS, codirector of the journal *Espaces-Temps*.

Alain Lipietz, economist, associate researcher at the CNRS and at the CEPREMAP.

René Lourau, sociology professor at Paris VIII.

Pierre Macherey, philosopher, lecturer at Paris I.

René Major, psychoanalyst, teaches at the Collège International de Philosophie, director of *Cahiers Confrontations*.

Serge Martin, philosopher, professor at Pontoise High School.

André Martinet, linguist, emeritus professor at the Université René Descartes, and in the Fourth Section of the EPHE.

Claude Meillassoux, anthropologist, director of research at the CNRS.

Charles Melman, psychoanalyst, director of the journal *Discours psychanalytique*.

Gérard Mendel, psychoanalyst, former intern at the Hôpital Psychiatrique de la Seine.

Henri Mitterand, linguist, professor at the new Sorbonne.

Juan-David Nasio, psychoanalyst, leads the Séminaire de Psychanalyse de Paris.

André Nicolaï, economist, professor at Paris X.

Pierre Nora, historian, director of studies at the EHESS, director of the journal *Le Débat*, editor at Gallimard.

Claudine Normand, linguist, professor at Paris X.

Bertrand Ogilvie, philosopher, professor at the École Normale at Cergy-Pontoise (as of 1992, École Normale schools, which are teacher-training institutions, have become the Institut Universitaire de la Formation des Maîtres).

Michelle Perrot, historian, professor at Paris VII.

Marcelin Pleynet, writer, former secretary of the journal *Tel Quel*.

Jean Pouillon, philosopher and anthropologist, researcher at the Laboratoire d'Anthropologie Sociale, EHESS.

Joëlle Proust, philosopher, research group on cognition, CNRS.

Jacques Rancière, philosopher, teacher at Paris VIII.

Alain Renaut, philosopher, professor at the Université de Caen, founder of the Collège de Philosophie.

Olivier Revault d'Allonnes, philosopher, professor at Paris I.

Élisabeth Roudinesco, writer and psychoanalyst.

Nicolas Ruwet, linguist, professor at Paris VIII.

Moustafa Safouan, psychoanalyst.

Georges-Elia Sarfati, linguist, teacher at Paris III.

Bernard Sichère, philosopher, professor at the Université de Caen, former member of the team of *Tel Quel*.

Dan Sperber, anthropologist, researcher at the CNRS.

Joseph Sumpf, sociologist and linguist, professor at Paris VIII.

Emmanuel Terray, anthropologist, director of studies at the EHESS.

Tzvetan Todorov, linguist, semiologist, researcher at the CNRS.

Alain Touraine, sociologist, director of research at the EHESS.

Paul Valadier, philosopher, former editor in chief of the journal *Études*, professor at the Centre Sèvres in Paris.

Jean-Pierre Vernant, classicist, honorary professor at the Collège de France.

Marc Vernet, semiologist of cinema, professor at Paris III.

Serge Viderman, psychoanalyst, medical doctor.

Pierre Vilar, historian, honorary professor at the Sorbonne.

François Wahl, philosopher, editor at Seuil.

Marina Yaguello, linguistics professor at Paris VII.

Notes

One. The Eclipse of a Star: Jean-Paul Sartre

1. *Khâgne*, preceded by *hypokhâgne* (from the Latin for lazy), are the two arduous years of preparatory courses following but taking place in a high school. These are primarily humanities courses designed for selected students hoping to pass the entrance exams to the École Normale Supérieure (ENS).—*Trans.*

2. Pascal Ory and Jean-François Sirinelli, *Les Intellectuels en France, de l'affaire Dreyfus à nos jours*, p. 166.

3. Billancourt is a southwestern, largely working-class Parisian suburb where the Renault factories were located. For Sartre, it was important that the working class not imagine that it was being forgotten or ignored.—*Trans.*

4. *Les Temps modernes*, no. 89 (April 1953), "Le marxisme de Sartre," by Claude Lefort; "Réponse à Claude Lefort," by Jean-Paul Sartre.

5. Annie Cohen-Solal, *Sartre*, p. 447.

6. Régis Debray, *Le Nouvel Observateur*, April 21, 1980.

7. Normal Schools were established by the Third Republic to train teachers for the newly instituted secular schools. Normal Superior was reserved for the elite students, selected, as they are today, by arduous competitive examination. Students are admitted for four years of subsidized training, in exchange for which they are assigned to teach in French high schools. The ENS on the rue d'Ulm, located in the Parisian Latin Quarter, was reserved for men (the women's branch is located in Saint-Cloud, a southwestern suburb of Paris) and renowned for the intellectual quality of its teachers and students.—*Trans.*

8. The title of *agrégé* was created in 1808 when the imperial university was organized. At the time, it designated an associate high-school professor. An examination, aggregating several parts, was established in 1821 and was designed to recruit professors for high schools. It was only in 1883 that women were admitted to the *agrégation* exam. There are currently twelve subject matters in which one can be agrégé.—*Trans.*

9. Jean Pouillon, interview with the author.

10. *Les Temps modernes*, no. 126 (July 1956); reprinted in Jean Pouillon, *Fétiches sans fétichisme*, 1975.

11. Pouillon, *Fétiches sans fétichisme*, p. 301.

12. Ibid., p. 307.

13. Ibid., p. 312.

14. The École Pratique des Hautes Études was created by Victor Duruy during the Second Empire, as a rather experimental research institution that was not a diploma-granting institution. A number of sections were created according to themes. The Fifth Section was that of Religious Sciences and was created by Lévi-Strauss. The section that is most important for the history of structuralism was the Sixth Section with its theme of the social or human sciences. The first section president was the representative of the *Annales*, Lucien Febvre. The Sixth Section of the École Pratique became the École des Hautes Études en Sciences Sociales (EHESS) in 1977, at a time during which this institution, which was marginal until that point, was allowed to grant recognized diplomas. At this point, the margins converged toward the center, the Sorbonne.—*Trans.*

15. Jean Pouillon, *Séminaire de Michel Izard*, Laboratoire d'Anthropologie Sociale, November 24, 1988.

16. Jean Pouillon, interview with the author.

17. Pouillon, quoted by Cohen-Solal, *Sartre*, p. 502.

18. Pouillon, *Séminaire de Michel Izard*, Laboratoire d'Anthropologie Sociale, February 9, 1989.

19. Ibid.

20. Georges Balandier, interview with the author.

21. Georges Dumézil, *Entretiens avec Didier Éribon*, p. 204.

22. Ibid., p. 208.

23. Claude Lévi-Strauss, *De près et de loin*, p. 219.

Two. The Birth of a Hero: Claude Lévi-Strauss

1. Claude Lévi-Strauss, *De près et de loin*, p. 15.

2. Ibid., p. 19.

3. Claude Lévi-Strauss, *Le Monde*, interview with Jean-Marie Benoist, January 21, 1979.

4. Claude Lévi-Strauss, *Tristes Tropiques*, p. 18.

5. Lévi-Strauss, *De près et de loin*, p. 47.

6. Ibid., p. 64.

7. Ibid., p. 81.

8. Francine Le Bret, interview with the author.

9. Raymond Boudon, interview with the author.

10. Ibid.

11. Claude Lévi-Strauss, *Le Regard éloigné*; translated as *The View from Afar*, p. 103.

12. Émile Durkheim, "La prohibition de l'inceste," *L'Année sociologique*, vol. 1, 1848.

13. Lévi-Strauss, *Tristes Tropiques*, p. 57.

14. Ibid.

15. Claude Lévi-Strauss, *La Pensée sauvage*, p. 155; translated as *The Savage Mind*.

16. The forerunner of the French Socialist Party.

17. Philippe Descola, interview with the author.

18. Claude Lévi-Strauss, *Structural Anthropology*, p. 14.

19. A. R. Radcliffe-Brown, "The Study of Kinship Systems," *Journal of the Royal Anthropology Institute* (1941): p. 17.

20. Lévi-Strauss, *Tristes Tropiques*, p. 59.

21. Robert H. Lowie, "Exogamy and the Classificatory Systems of Relationship," *American Anthropologist*, vol. 17 (April–June 1915).

22. Lévi-Strauss, *De près et de loin*, p. 58.

23. Jean Jamin, interview with the author.

24. Claude Lévi-Strauss, "L'analyse structurale en linguistique et en anthropologie," *Word*, vol. 1, no. 2 (1945): pp. 1–21; reprinted as "Linguistique et anthropologie," *Supplement to the International Journal of American Linguistics*, vol. 19, no. 2 (April 1953); reprinted as "Linguistics and Anthropology" in *Structural Anthropology*.

Three. Where Nature and Culture Meet: Incest

1. Claude Lévi-Strauss, *La Vie familiale et sociale des Indiens Nambikwara* (Paris: Société des Américanistes, 1948); *The Elementary Structures of Kinship*, preface to the first edition, p. xxiii.
2. Marc Augé, interview with the author.
3. Olivier Revault d'Allonnes, interview with the author.
4. Emmanuel Terray, interview with the author.
5. Lévi-Strauss, *The Elementary Structures of Kinship*, preface to the first edition, p. ix.
6. Dan Sperber, *Qu'est-ce que le structuralisme? Le structuralisme en anthropologie*, p. 26.
7. Lévi-Strauss, *The Elementary Structures of Kinship*, p. 30.
8. Ibid., p. 14.
9. Jean-Marie Benoist, *La Révolution structurale*, p. 112.
10. Claude Lévi-Strauss, *Structural Anthropology*, pp. 31–32.
11. Claude Lévi-Strauss, *De près et de loin*, p. 63.
12. Lévi-Strauss, *Structural Anthropology*, p. 32.
13. Roman Jakobson, *Six leçons sur le son et le sens* (Paris: Minuit, 1976), preface by Claude Lévi-Strauss; reprinted in *Le Regard éloigné*, "Les leçons de la linguistique" (Paris: Plon, 1983).
14. Nicolai Trubetzkoy, "La phonologie actuelle," *Psychologie du langage* (Paris: 1933), p. 243; quoted by Lévi-Strauss in *Structural Anthropology*, p. 31 n. 8.
15. Yvan Simonis, *Lévi-Strauss ou la passion de l'inceste*, p. 19.
16. Lévi-Strauss, *Structural Anthropology*, p. 68.
17. Ibid., p. 82.
18. Ibid., p. 46.
19. Ibid., p. 62.
20. Jean Pouillon, interview with the author.
21. Raymond Boudon, interview with the author.
22. Jean Pouillon, interview with the author.
23. Simone de Beauvoir, *Les Temps modernes* (November 1949): p. 943.
24. Ibid., p. 949.
25. Claude Lefort, "L'échange et la lutte des hommes," *Les Temps modernes* (February 1951).
26. Jean Pouillon, "L'œuvre de Claude Lévi-Strauss," *Les Temps modernes*, no. 126 (July 1956); reprinted in Jean Pouillon, *Fétiches sans fétichisme*, p. 310.

Four. Ask for the Program: The Mauss

1. Claude Lévi-Strauss, "Introduction à l'œuvre de Marcel Mauss," in *Marcel Mauss, Sociologie et anthropologie*, 1968 (1950); translated as *Introduction to the Work of Marcel Mauss*.
2. Claude Lévi-Strauss, *De près et de loin*, p. 103.
3. Algirdas Julien Greimas, interview with the author.
4. Jean Jamin, interview with the author.

5. Ibid.

6. Robert Hertz, *Mélanges de sociologie religieuse et folklore*, 1928.

7. Jean Jamin, interview with the author. [The Collège de Sociologie was founded around 1933 by Georges Bataille and Roger Caillois to train sociologists. The major influences in the school's orientation included surrealists, Hegelianism through Kojève's work, Freud, and work being done in anthropology.—*Trans.*]

8. Lévi-Strauss, "Introduction à l'œuvre de Marcel Mauss"; *Introduction to the Work of Marcel Mauss*, p. 3.

9. Ibid., p. 10.

10. Claude Lévi-Strauss, "Le sorcier et sa magie," *Les Temps modernes*, no. 41 (March 1949).

11. Marcel Mauss, "Essai sur le don. Forme et raison de l'échange dans les sociétés archaïques," in *Année sociologique*, 1921; translated as *The Gift*.

12. Lévi-Strauss, *Introduction to the Work of Marcel Mauss*, p. 26.

13. Ibid., p. 8.

14. Ibid., p. 34.

15. Ibid., pp. 35–36.

16. Ibid., p. 37.

17. Vincent Descombes, *Le Même et l'autre*, p. 121.

18. Claude Lévi-Strauss, *The Elementary Structures of Kinship*, p. 51.

19. Ibid., p. 485.

20. Ibid., p. 481.

21. Vincent Descombes, interview with the author.

22. Lévi-Strauss, *Introduction to the Work of Marcel Mauss*, p. 53.

23. Claude Lefort, "L'échange et la lutte des hommes," *Les Temps modernes* (February 1951); reprinted in Claude Lefort, *Les Formes de l'histoire*, p. 17.

24. Lévi-Strauss, *Introduction to the Work of Marcel Mauss*, p. 35.

Five. Georges Dumézil: An Independent

1. The Académie Française was founded in 1635 by Cardinal Richelieu under Louis XIII to bring together the wise men of the country. Forty members, known as "immortals," were and continue to be elected by their peers to continue the work of writing and revising a dictionary of the French language.—*Trans.*

2. Georges Dumézil, *Mythe et Épopée*, Introduction.

3. Claude Lévi-Strauss, "Dumézil et les sciences humaines," *France-Culture*, October 2, 1978.

4. Georges Dumézil, *Entretiens avec Didier Éribon*, p. 64.

5. Franz Bopp, *Système de conjugaison de la langue sanscrite, comparé à celui des langues grecque, latine, persane et germanique* (1816); translated as *Analytical Comparison of the Sanskrit, Greek, Latin, and Teutonic Languages Showing the Original Identity of Their Grammatical Structure* (1974).

6. Claude Lévi-Strauss, "Réponse à Dumézil reçu à l'Académie Française," *Le Monde*, July 15, 1979.

7. Dumézil, *Entretiens avec Didier Éribon*, p. 174.

8. Claude Hagège, *Le Monde*, October 14, 1986.

Six. The Phenomenological Bridge

1. Maurice Merleau-Ponty, *La Structure du comportement*; *Phénoménologie de la perception*.

2. Vincent Descombes, interview with the author.

3. Maurice Merleau-Ponty, "Sur la phénoménologie du langage," lecture delivered to the First International Phenomenology Colloquium in Brussels, 1951; reprinted in *Signs*.

4. Ibid., p. 49.

5. Maurice Merleau-Ponty, *Cahiers internationaux de sociologie*, 10, pp. 55–69; reprinted in *Signs*, p. 98.

6. Claude Lévi-Strauss, *De près et de loin*, p. 88.

7. Merleau-Ponty, *Signs*, pp. 116, 118.

8. Vincent Descombes, interview with the author.

9. Merleau-Ponty, *Signs*, p. 122.

10. Vincent Descombes, interview with the author.

11. George W. Stocking, *Histoires de l'anthropologie: XVIe–XIXe siècles*, pp. 421–31.

12. Langues Orientales trains students in Eastern (Arabic) and Oriental (Asian) languages.—*Trans.*

13. Established by royal decree on February 22, 1821, the École des Chartes trained specialists in reading medieval documents (*chartes*). The school depends on the Ministry of National Education, and prepares paleographic archivists during the three years and nine months of studies.—*Trans.*

14. Jean Jamin, *Les Enjeux philosophiques des années cinquante*, p. 103.

15. Alfred Adler, *Séminaire de Michel Izard*, Laboratoire d'Anthropologie Sociale, November 17, 1988.

16. Michel Arrivé, interview with the author.

17. Algirdas Julien Greimas, interview with the author.

18. Jean-Marie Benoist, interview with the author.

19. Michel Foucault, "Structuralism and Post-Structuralism," *Telos*, vol. 16 (1983): pp. 195–211; interview with Georges Raulet.

20. Michel Foucault, *Les Mots et les choses*; translated as *The Order of Things: An Archaeology of the Human Sciences*.

21. Foucault, *The Order of Things*, p. 248.

Seven. The Saussurean Break

1. Vincent Descombes, *Le Même et l'autre*, p. 100.

2. Ferdinand de Saussure, *Cours de linguistique générale*.

3. Françoise Gadet, "Le signe et le sens," *DRLAV, Revue de linguistique*, no. 40 (1989).

4. Ibid., p. 4.

5. Algirdas Julien Greimas, interview with the author.

6. Gadet, "Le signe et le sens," p. 18.

7. Roland Barthes, "Saussure, le signe, la démocratie," *Le Discours social*, nos. 3–4 (April 1973); reprinted in Roland Barthes, *L'Aventure sémiologique*, p. 221.

8. See Tzvetan Todorov, *Théories du symbole*.

9. Claudine Normand, interview with the author.

10. Ibid.

11. Ibid.

12. Jean-Claude Coquet, interview with the author.

13. Sylvain Auroux, interview with the author.

14. André Martinet, interview with the author.

15. Ibid.

16. Ibid.

17. Saussure, *Cours de linguistique générale*, p. 126.
18. Ibid.
19. Oswald Ducrot and Tzvetan Todorov, *Dictionnaire encyclopédique du langage*, p. 133.
20. Louis-Jean Calvet, *Pour et contre Saussure*, pp. 82–83.
21. Saussure, *Cours de linguistique générale*, p. 33.
22. Sylvain Auroux, interview with the author.
23. Louis-Jean Calvet, interview with the author.
24. Calvet, *Pour et contre Saussure*.
25. Jean Starobinski, *Mercure de France*, February 1964; then *Les Mots sous les mots*, 1971.
26. Saussure, *Cours de linguistique générale*, p. 30.
27. Claude Hagège, *L'homme de parole*, p. 305.
28. Oswald Ducrot, interview with the author.

Eight. Roman Jakobson: The Man Who Could Do Everything

1. Roman Jakobson, final text of the Conference of Anthropologists and Linguists, held at Indiana University in 1952, *Essais de linguistique générale*.
2. Ibid., p. 42.
3. Ibid. (1957), p. 72.
4. Ibid. (1957), p. 74.
5. Roman Jakobson, interview with Tzvetan Todorov, *Poétique*, no. 57 (February 1984): p. 4.
6. Ibid., p. 12.
7. Roman Jakobson, interviewed by Jean-José Marchand on the television program *Archives du XX$_e$ siècle* (February 10, 1972; January 2, 1973; September 14, 1974), and rebroadcast on Channel 7 in October 1990.
8. *Poétique*, no. 57 (February 1984): p. 16.
9. Roman Jakobson, preface to Tzvetan Todorov, *Théorie de la littérature*, p. 9.
10. Marina Yaguello, interview with the author.
11. Jean-Pierre Faye, interview with the author.
12. Ibid.
13. J. Makarovsky, reprinted in *Change*, no. 3 (1971).
14. "1929 Theses," published by *Change* (1969): p. 31.
15. Jakobson, in *Archives du XXe siècle*.
16. Editorial, *Word*, no. 1 (1945).
17. Françoise Gadet, *DRLAV, Revue de linguistique*, no. 40 (1989): p. 8.
18. Jakobson, *Essais de linguistique générale*, pp. 35–36.
19. Roman Jakobson, "Les douze traits de sonorité," in "Phonologie et phonétique" (1956), in *Essais de linguistique générale*, pp. 128–29.
20. Roman Jakobson, "Deux aspects du langage et deux types d'aphasie," in *Essais de linguistique générale*, pp. 50–51.
21. Jean-Claude Chevalier, interview with the author.

Nine. A Pilot Science without a Plane: Linguistics

1. André Martinet, in "La création de revues dans les années soixante," interview with Jean-Claude Chevalier and Pierre Encrevé, *Langue française*, no. 63 (September 1984): p. 61.

2. Robert-Léon Wagner, foreword to his *Introduction to French Linguistics* (1947); quoted by Chevalier and Encrevé in ibid.

3. Bernard Quémada, in "La création de revues dans les années soixante," interview with Chevalier and Encrevé.

4. Michel Arrivé, interview with the author.

5. Bernard Pottier, in "La création de revues dans les années soixante," interview with Chevalier and Encrevé.

6. Chevalier and Encrevé, *Langue française*, no. 63 (September 1984).

7. Bernard Quémada, interview with Chevalier and Encrevé.

8. Jean-Claude Chevalier, interview with the author.

9. Philippe Hamon, "Littérature," in *Les Sciences du langage en France au XXe siècle*, p. 285.

10. Ibid., p. 284.

11. Gérard Genette, interview with the author.

12. Jean-Claude Chevalier, interview with the author.

13. André Martinet, interview with the author.

14. André-Georges Haudricout, interview with the author.

15. Ibid.

16. Ibid.

17. Ibid.

18. Ibid.

Ten. At Alexandria's Gates

1. Algirdas Julien Greimas, interview with the author.

2. Ibid.

3. Roland Barthes, *Michelet par lui-même*.

4. Algirdas Julien Greimas and Roland Barthes, quoted by Louis-Jean Calvet, *Roland Barthes*, p. 124.

5. Charles Singevin, quoted in ibid.

6. Algirdas Julien Greimas, preface to Louis Hjelmslev, *Prolegomena to a Theory of Language*.

7. Louis Hjelmslev, *Language: An Introduction*, p. 96.

8. Thomas Pavel, *Le Mirage linguistique*, p. 92.

9. Hjelmslev, *Prolegomena to a Theory of Language*, p. 23.

10. Jean-Claude Coquet, interview with the author.

11. Ibid.

12. André Martinet, interview with the author.

13. Ibid.

14. André Martinet, review of Hjelmslev's *Prolegomena to a Theory of Language* in the *Bulletin de la société de linguistique*, vol. 42 (1946): pp. 17–42.

15. Serge Martin, interview with the author.

16. Serge Martin, *Langage musical, sémiotique des systèmes*.

Eleven. The Mother Figure of Structuralism: Roland Barthes

1. Le Degré zéro de l'écriture.

2. Ibid., p. 10.

3. Maurice Nadeau, *Les Lettres nouvelles* (July 1953): p. 599.

4. Jean-Bertrand Pontalis, *Les Temps modernes* (November 1953): pp. 934–38.

5. Barthes, *Le Degré zéro de l'écriture*, p. 24.
6. Ibid., p. 45.
7. Ibid., p. 55.
8. Ibid., p. 65.
9. Roland Barthes, interviews with Jean-Marie Benoist and Bernard-Henri Lévy, *France-Culture*, February 1977, rerun December 1, 1988.
10. Roland Barthes, *Océaniques*, FR3, November 1970–May 1971, rerun on January 27, 1988.
11. The *Licence* is a university degree awarded after the third year of study, before a master's or a doctorate. With it one can teach in high schools but not in the university or any advanced school.—*Trans.*
12. The Collège de France is a teaching institution established in Paris in 1530 by François I as the Collège du Roi, through the initiative of Guillaume Budé, a classical scholar and humanist. The Collège elects its peers based on publications. A university diploma is not a prerequisite for election, which allowed "marginals" like Barthes to be recognized. For Barthes, the recognition by peers of his work legitimated him and salved the wound of having received no advanced university degree, which would have allowed him to teach as a regular faculty member.—*Trans.*
13. Louis-Jean Calvet, interview with the author.
14. Barthes, *Océaniques*, FR3.
15. Roland Barthes, *Mythologies*, p. 109.
16. Louis-Jean Calvet, *Roland Barthes*, p. 67.
17. Ibid.
18. Barthes, *Mythologies*, p. 229.
19. Ibid., p. 251.
20. Barthes could teach, therefore, without a university degree, having been recognized for the work he had published, even if he was not sanctioned by the official diploma-dispensing university.—*Trans.*
21. André Green, interview with the author.
22. Roland Barthes, "Mère courage aveugle," in *Essais critiques*, pp. 49–50.
23. Georges-Elia Sarfati, interview with the author.
24. Georges Mounin, *Introduction à la sémiologie*, p. 193.

Twelve. An Epistemic Exigency

1. Alexandre Koyré, *De la mystique à la science; cours, conférences et documents* (1922–62), p. 129.
2. Jean-Louis Fabiani, *Les Enjeux philosophiques des années cinquante*, p. 125.
3. Martial Guéroult, *Leçon inaugurale au Collège de France* (December 4, 1951), pp. 16–17.
4. Ibid., p. 43.
5. Gilles Gaston-Granger, interview with the author.
6. Marc Abélès, interview with the author.
7. Ibid.
8. Jean-Christophe Goddard, interview with the author.
9. Guéroult, *Leçon inaugurale au Collège de France*, p. 18.
10. Joëlle Proust, *Bulletin de la société française de philosophie* (July–September 1988): p. 81.
11. Martial Guéroult, *Descartes selon l'ordre des raisons*.
12. Ibid., p. 10.
13. Jean-Christophe Goddard, interview with the author.

14. Martial Guéroult, *Philosophie de l'histoire de la philosophie*, p. 243.

15. Jean Piaget, *Psychologie et épistémologie*, p. 10.

16. Jean Piaget, Éléments d'épistémologie génétique.

17. Vincent Descombes, interview with the author.

18. Jean Cavaillès, *Sur la logique et la théorie des sciences*.

19. Pierre Fougeyrollas, interview with the author.

20. Ibid.

21. Georges Canguilhem, interview with Jean-François Sirinelli, *Génération intellectuelle*, p. 597.

22. Ibid., p. 598.

23. Bertrand Saint-Sernin, *Revue de métaphysique et de morale* (January 1985): p. 86.

24. "Essai sur quelques problèmes concernant le normal et le pathologique."

25. Georges Canguilhem, *Le Normal et le pathologique*, p. 8.

26. Pierre Fougeyrollas, interview with the author.

27. Georges Canguilhem, "La décadence de l'idée de progrès," *Revue de métaphysique et de morale*, no. 4 (1987): p. 450.

28. Michel Foucault, *Revue de métaphysique et de morale* (January 1985): p. 3.

29. Ibid., p. 14.

30. Pierre Macherey, "La philosophie de la science de Canguilhem," *La Pensée*, no. 113 (January 1964).

31. Ibid., p. 74.

32. Georges Canguilhem, "Qu'est-ce que la psychologie?" Lecture given December 18, 1956, at Jean Wahl's Collège Philosophique and reprinted in *Revue de métaphysique et de morale* (1958): pp. 12–25, in *Les Cahiers pour l'analyse*, no. 2 (March 1966), and in Georges Canguilhem, *Études d'histoire et de philosophie des sciences*.

33. Vincent Descombes, *Les Enjeux philosophiques des années cinquante*, p. 159.

34. Michel Serres, *La Traduction*, p. 259.

35. Michel Serres, "Structure et importation: des mathématiques aux mythes" (November 1961); reprinted in *Hermès*, vol. 1, "La Communication" (Paris: Minuit, 1968).

36. Ibid., p. 26.

37. Ibid., p. 32.

38. Serres, "Structure et importation," p. 34.

Thirteen. A Rebel Named Jacques Lacan

1. Élisabeth Roudinesco, *Histoire de la psychanalyse en France*, p. 155.

2. Ibid., p. 154.

3. Ibid., p. 124.

4. Ibid., p. 129.

5. "De la psychose paranoïaque dans ses rapports avec la personnalité."

6. See *Boris Souvarine et "La Critique sociale,"* ed. Anne Roche.

7. Bertrand Ogilvie, *Lacan, le sujet*, pp. 20–21.

8. Jean Allouch, interview with the author.

9. This 1936 version was later revised and delivered at the sixteenth International Congress of Psychoanalysis in Zurich in 1949 and published in the *Revue française de psychanalyse*, no. 4 (October–December 1949). This final version was translated as *The Mirror Stage: Theory of a Structuring and Genetic Moment of the Constitution of Reality, Conceived in Relationship with the Experience of Psychoanalytic Doctrine*, and in *Écrits: A Selection*, as "The Mirror Stage as Formative of the Function of the I as Revealed in Psychoanalytic Experience," pp. 1–7.

10. Joël Dor, *Introduction à la lecture de Lacan*, p. 100.

11. Ibid., p. 101.

12. "Le stade du miroir comme formateur de la fonction du Je" ("The Mirror Stage as Formative of the Function of the I as Revealed in Psychoanalytic Experience").

13. Ogilvie, *Lacan, le sujet*, p. 107.

14. Anika Lemaire, *Lacan*, p. 27.

15. Ibid., p. 277.

16. Moustafa Safouan, interview with the author.

17. Jean Hyppolite, *La Psychanlayse*, vol. 1, pp. 29–39, with Lacan's response, reprinted in Jacques Lacan, *Écrits*, pp. 879–87.

18. Vincent Descombes, *Les Enjeux philosophiques des années cinquante*, p. 155.

19. Like the poetic notion of scansion, the Lacanian use of the term involves punctuation, but in this case the punctuation, and end, of a therapeutic session. Lacan, and others, ended a session on a word uttered by the patient in a way that left its greater significance muted. Ending the session on the term drew attention to it and shifted the weight of its meaning.—*Trans.*

20. Wladimir Granoff, interview with the author.

21. Gennie Lemoine, interview with the author.

22. Jean Laplanche, interview with the author.

23. Joël Dor, interview with the author.

24. Wladimir Granoff, interview with the author.

25. Ibid.

26. Jean Clavreul, interview with the author.

27. Roudinesco, *Histoire de la psychanalyse in France*, p. 294.

28. Jean Clavreul, interview with the author.

Fourteen. Rome Calls (1953): The Return to Freud

1. André Green, interview with the author.

2. Maurice Merleau-Ponty, *La Structure du comportement.*

3. André Green, interview with the author.

4. Claude Dumézil, interview with the author.

5. Ibid.

6. The French pun comes from the aural homology between *le nom du père, le non du père,* and *le non dupe erre.*—*Trans.*

7. Claude Demézil, interview with the author.

8. Ibid.

9. Élisabeth Roudinesco, interview with the author.

10. Wladimir Granoff, interview with the author.

11. Ibid.

12. Ibid.

13. Gérard Mendel, *Enquête par un psychanalyste sur lui-même*, p. 165.

14. Élisabeth Roudinesco, *Histoire de la psychanalyse en France*, vol. 2, p. 272.

15. Jacques Lacan, "Rapport de Rome," in *Écrits*, vol. 1 (1953) ("Report to the Rome Congress held at the Istituto di Psicologia della Università di Roma, 26 and 27 September, 1953," trans. Alan Sheridan, in *Écrits: A Selection*, p. 57).

16. Ibid., p. 40.

17. Ibid., p. 65.

18. Ibid., p. 66.

19. Ibid., p. 73.

20. Ibid., p.76.

21. René Major, interview with the author.

22. Lacan, "Report to the Rome Congress," p. 86.

23. Bernard Sichère, *Le Moment lacanien*, p. 59.

24. Charles Melman, interview with the author.

25. Psychiatry in France, as in America, is a medical field of specialization and therefore practiced by medical doctors. Psychoanalysis can also be practiced by doctors, but it is not a medical field. There is no single, formally recognized psychoanalytic training institute in France, but rather a proliferation of institutes and groups, which may or may not offer training programs. The situation appears chaotic and even dangerous in American eyes, particularly since a psychoanalyst can authorize himself or herself to practice, according to the Lacanian dictum. In terms of pathways to analysis, many practicing analysts are trained in philosophy, have themselves been in analysis, and are therefore close to the central, linguistic problematic around which French psychoanalysis has been focused, particularly since Lacan.—*Trans.*

26. Jacques Lacan, "L'instance de la lettre dans l'inconscient," in *Écrits*, vol. 1, p. 251; "The Agency of the Letter in the Unconscious or Reason since Freud," trans. Alan Sheridan, in *Écrits: A Selection*, p. 147.

27. Ibid., p. 149.

28. Ibid.

29. Ibid., p. 154.

30. Ibid., pp. 165–66.

31. Michel Arrivé, interview with the author.

32. Joël Dor, *Introduction à la lecture de Lacan*, pp. 55–56.

33. Jacques Lacan, "Séminaire sur la lettre volée," in *Écrits* , vol. 1, pp. 35, 40.

34. Dor, *Introduction à la lecture de Lacan*, pp. 59–60.

35. Ibid., p. 63.

36. Jacques Lacan, "La chose freudienne" (1956), in *Écrits*, vol. 1, p. 144; "The Freudian Thing," trans. Alan Sheridan, in *Écrits: A Selection*, p. 125.

37. Anika Lemaire, *Lacan*, p. 340.

38. Ibid., p. 347.

39. Georges Mounin, *Introduction à la sémiologie*, pp. 184–85.

40. Ibid., p. 188.

41. Lemaire, *Lacan*, p. 30.

Fifteen. The Unconscious: A Symbolic Universe

1. Claude Lévi-Strauss, *Introduction to the Work of Marcel Mauss*, trans. Felicity Baker, London: Routledge and Kegan Paul, 1987), p. xx.

2. Jacques Lacan, "Remarques sur le rapport de Daniel Lagache" (1958), in *Écrits*, p. 648.

3. Claude Lévi-Strauss, *De près et de loin*, p. 107.

4. Janson High School in Paris is well known as being one of the best high schools. Located in the rich west side of Paris, it is the high school for many French writers and intellectuals.—*Trans.*

5. Claude Lévi-Strauss, interview with the author.

6. Ibid.

7. *Le Totémisme aujourd'hui.*

8. Claude Lévi-Strauss, "Le sorcier et sa magie," *Les Temps modernes*, no. 41 (March 1949): pp. 3–24; "L'Efficace Symbolique," *Revue d'histoire des religions*, no. 1 (1949): pp. 5–27; reprinted in *Anthropologie Structurale*. See "The Sorcerer and His Magic" and "The Effectiveness of Symbols," in *Structural Anthropology*, trans. Claire

Jacobson and Brooke Grundfest Schoepf (New York: Anchor Books, 1967), pp. 161–80 and 181–201, respectively.

9. Lévi-Strauss, "Le sorcier et sa magie," p. 201; "The Sorcerer and His Magic," p. 177.

10. Lévi-Strauss, "L'Efficace symbolique," p. 224.

11. Ibid.

12. R. Georgin, *De Lévi-Strauss à Lacan*, p. 125.

13. Lévi-Strauss, *Introduction to the Work of Marcel Mauss*, p. 56.

14. E. R. de Ipola, "Le Structuralisme ou l'histoire en exil," p. 122.

15. Ibid., p. 126.

16. Claude Lévi-Strauss, *La Pensée sauvage*, p. 174; translated as *The Savage Mind*.

17. De Ipola, "Le Structuralisme ou l'histoire en exil," p. 244.

18. Claude Lévi-Strauss, interview with Raymond Bellour (1972), Paris: Idées-Gallimard, 1979), p. 205.

19. Lévi-Strauss, *De près et de loin*, p. 150.

20. Claude Lévi-Strauss, *La Potière jalouse*, p. 243; translated as *The Jealous Potter*, p. 185.

21. Ibid., p. 193.

22. André Green, *Séminaire de Michel Izard*, Laboratoire d'Anthropologie Sociale, December 8, 1988.

23. Gérard Mendel, *La Chasse structurale*, p. 262.

24. Gérard Mendel, interview with the author.

25. François Roustang, *Lacan*; see also Vincent Descombes, "L'équivoque du symbolique," *Confrontations*, no. 3 (1980): pp. 77–95.

26. Jacques Lacan, "Situation de la psychanalyse en 1956," in *Écrits*, vol. 2, p. 19.

27. Ibid.

28. Roustang, *Lacan*, pp. 36–37.

29. Jacques Lacan, *Le Séminaire III: Les Psychoses*, p. 208.

30. Joël Dor, interview with the author.

31. Claude Conté, interview with the author.

32. Jacques Lacan, *Séminaire XX, Encore (1973–1974)*, p. 45.

33. Charles Melman, interview with the author.

Sixteen. Real/Symbolic/Imaginary (RSI): The Heresy

1. Jean Allouch, interview with the author.

2. Ibid.

3. Moustafa Safouan, interview with the author.

4. The French original reads: "Tu t'y es mis un peu tard," and the acronym is "T.t.y.e.m.u.p.t."—*Trans.*

5. Jacques-Alain Miller, *Ornicar*, no. 24 (1981).

6. Ibid.

7. Claude Conté, interview with the author.

8. Pierre Fougeyrollas, *Contre Claude Lévi-Strauss, Lacan, Althusser* (Paris: Lavelli, 1976), p. 99.

9. François George, *L'Effet yau de poêle* (Paris: Hachette, 1979), p. 65. [The pun in French is on perversion, which becomes *père-version.—Trans.*]

10. Jacques Lacan, "Rapport de Rome," in *Écrits*, vol. 1 (1953), p. 168.

11. Information taken from Élisabeth Roudinesco, *Histoire de la psychanalyse en France*, vol. 2, p. 318.

12. Maurice Merleau-Ponty, 6ᵉ Colloque de Bonneval, in *L'Inconscient* (Paris: Desclée de Brouwer, 1966).

13. Serge Leclaire, "L'inconscient, une étude psychanalytique," in *L'Inconscient*, pp. 95–130, 170–77; reprinted in *Psychanalyser*, pp. 99 and 116.

14. Serge Leclaire, interview with the author.

15. Jean Laplanche, interview with the author.

16. Jean Laplanche, 6ᵉ Colloque de Bonneval, in *L'Inconscient*, p. 115.

17. Ibid., p. 121.

18. Jean Laplanche, interview with the author.

19. Jean Laplanche, *Psychanalyse à l'Université*, vol. 4, no. 15 (June 1979): pp. 523–28.

20. Ibid., p. 527.

21. Ibid.

22. Roudinesco, *Histoire de la psychanalyse en France*, vol. 2, p. 323.

23. Anika Lemaire, *Lacan*.

24. Jacques Lacan, "Position de l'inconscient," in *Écrits*, vol. 2, p. 196.

25. Ibid., p. 211. [The pun in French is between *homme* and *hommelette.*—Trans.]

26. Jacques Lacan, interview, Belgian Radio Television, December 14, 1966.

27. *Lettre* and *l'Être* ("Letter" and "Being") are homonyms punning on *lettre* (letter, language) and *l'être* (being).—Trans.

Seventeen. The Call of the Tropics

1. Serge Martin, interview with the author.

2. Claude Lévi-Strauss, "Race et histoire" (1952); reprinted in *Anthropologie structurale*, vol. 2, p. 399; translated as "Race and History."

3. Ibid.

4. Ibid., p. 415.

5. Bertrand Ogilvie, interview with the author.

6. Roger Caillois, "Illusions à rebours," *Nouvelle Revue française* (December 1, 1954): pp. 1010–21; (January 1, 1955): pp. 58–70.

7. Roger Caillois, "La réponse de R. Caillois," *Le Monde*, June 28, 1974.

8. Claude Lévi-Strauss, "Diogène couché," *Les Temps modernes*, no. 195 (1955): pp. 1187–1221.

9. Caillois, "Illusions à rebours," p. 1021.

10. Ibid., p. 1024.

11. Lévi-Strauss, "Diogène couché," p. 1187.

12. Ibid., p. 1202.

13. Ibid., p. 1214.

14. Claude Lévi-Strauss, *Tristes Tropiques*, trans. John and Doreen Weightman (New York: Atheneum, 1974).

15. Claude Lévi-Strauss, interview with Jean-José Marchand, *Arts* (December 25, 1955).

16. Claude Lévi-Strauss, *De près et de loin*, p. 76.

17. Lévi-Strauss, *Tristes Tropiques*, p. 408.

18. Ibid., p. 393.

19. Ibid., p. 413.

20. Claude Lévi-Strauss, "Le droit au voyage," *L'Express* (September 21, 1956).

21. Lévi-Strauss, *Tristes Tropiques*, p. 386.

22. Ibid., p. 411.

23. Ibid., p. 390.

24. Claude Lévi-Strauss, *Anthropologie structurale*, vol. 2, p. 51.
25. Ibid., pp. 46–47.
26. Claude Lévi-Strauss, "Des Indiens et leur ethnographe," excerpts from *"Tristes Tropiques* Soon to Be Published," *Les Temps modernes*, no. 116 (August 1955).
27. Raymond Aron, *Le Figaro*, December 24, 1955.
28. François-Régis Bastide, *Demain*, January 19, 1956.
29. Madeleine Chapsal, *L'Express*, February 24, 1956.
30. Jean Lacroix, *Le Monde*, October 13–14, 1957.
31. P. A. Renaud, *France-Observateur*, December 29, 1955.
32. J. Meyriat, *Revue française de science politique*, vol. 6, no. 2.
33. Claude Roy, *Libération*, November 16, 1955.
34. Georges Bataille, "Un livre humain, un grand livre," *Critique*, no. 115 (February 1956).
35. Alfred Métraux, *L'Ile de Pâques* (1956).
36. Bataille, "Un livre humain, un grand livre," p. 101.
37. René Etiemble, *Evidences* (April 1956): p. 32.
38. Ibid., p. 36.
39. Lévi-Strauss, *Tristes Tropiques*, p. 38.
40. *Le Figaro*, December 1, 1956.
41. Maxime Rodinson, "Racisme et civilisation," *Nouvelle Critique*, no. 66 (1955); no. 69 (November 1955); *La Pensée* (May–June 1957).
42. Rodinson, "Racisme et civilisation," p. 130.
43. Etiemble, *Évidences*, pp. 33–34.
44. Lévi-Strauss, *Anthropologie structurale*, vol. 2, p. 331–32.
45. Michel Izard, interview with the author.
46. Michel Izard, *Séminaire*, Laboratoire d'Anthropologie Sociale, June 1, 1989.
47. Michel Izard, interview with the author.
48. Ibid.
49. Ibid.
50. Izard, *Séminaire*.
51. Françoise Héritier-Augé, interview with the author.
52. Ibid.
53. Olivier Herrenschmidt, *Séminaire de Michel Izard*, Laboratoire d'Anthropologie Sociale, January 19, 1989.
54. Louis Dumont, quoted by Herrenschmidt in ibid.
55. Claude Lévi-Strauss, *Leroi-Gourhan ou les voies de l'homme*, pp. 205–6.
56. Hélène Balfet, *Séminaire de Michel Izard*, Laboratoire d'Anthropologie Sociale, 1989.

Eighteen. Reason Raves: Michel Foucault's Work

1. Pierre Nora, *Les Français d'Algérie*.
2. Jacques Rancière, interview with the author.
3. Edgar Morin, *L'Esprit du temps*, p. 149.
4. Didier Éribon, *Michel Foucault*, p. 21.
5. Bernard Sichère, interview with the author.
6. Daniel Defert, *France-Culture*, July 7, 1988.
7. Ibid.
8. *Libération* poll, June 30, 1984.
9. Michel Foucault, *Ethos* (fall 1983): p. 5.
10. *Histoire de la sexualité*.

11. Michel Foucault, interview with André Berten, Catholic University of Louvain, 1981; shown on FR3, January 13, 1988.
12. Michel Foucault, "Jean Hyppolite, 1907–1968," *Revue de métaphysique et de morale*, vol. 14, no. 2 (April–June 1969): p. 131.
13. "Genèse et structure de la phénoménologie de l'esprit."
14. *Surveiller et punir.*
15. Michel Foucault, quoted by Éribon, *Michel Foucault*, p. 35.
16. "Nietzsche, la généalogie, l'histoire."
17. Michel Foucault, *Hommage à Hyppolite.*
18. Jacques Proust, *Libération* poll, June 30, 1984.
19. *Maladie mentale et personnalité.*
20. Éribon, *Michel Foucault*, p. 49.
21. From the word for alligator, *caïman* designates the ENS professor assigned particularly to training students for the *agrégation* examination.—*Trans.*
22. Olivier Revault d'Allonnes, interview with the author.
23. Maurice Pinguet, *Le Débat*, no. 41 (September–November 1986): pp. 125–26.
24. Ibid., pp. 129–30.
25. Quoted by Éribon, *Michel Foucault*, p. 179.
26. Michel Foucault, quoted by Pinguet in *Le Débat*, p. 126.
27. Quoted by Éribon, *Michel Foucault*, p. 96.
28. Georges Dumézil, *Entretiens avec Didier Éribon*, p. 215.
29. Michel Foucault, *Folie et déraison* (Paris: Plon, 1961), Preface, p. x.
30. Michel Foucault, *Le Monde*, July 22, 1961.
31. Pierre Macherey, interview with the author.
32. Ibid.
33. Quoted by Éribon, *Michel Foucault*, p. 133.
34. Michel Foucault, "Vérité et pouvoir," interview with M. Fontana, *L'Arc*, no. 70, p. 16.
35. Michel Foucault, *Politique-Hebdo*, interview, March 4, 1976.
36. Ibid.
37. Foucault, *Folie et déraison*, pp. i–v.
38. Ibid.
39. Vincent Descombes, *Le Même et l'autre*, p. 138.
40. Pascal, *Pensées*, Éditions Brunschwicg, no. 414, quoted by Michel Foucault, *Histoire de la folie*, p. 47 (*Madness and Civilization*, trans. Richard Howard, Preface, p. ix).
41. Foucault, *Madness and Civilization*, p. 59.
42. *Histoire de la folie*, p. 147.
43. Ibid., p. 415.
44. Ibid., p. 523.
45. Éribon, *Michel Foucault*, p. 131.
46. *L'Enfant et la famille sous l'Ancien Régime.*
47. Philippe Ariès, *Un historien du dimanche*, p. 145.
48. Roland Barthes, "De part et d'autre," *Critique*, no. 17 (1961): pp. 915–22; reprinted in *Essais critiques*, p. 171.
49. Ibid., p. 168.
50. Maurice Blanchot, "L'oubli, la déraison," *Nouvelle Revue française* (October 1961): pp. 676–86; reprinted in *L'Entretien infini*, p. 292.
51. Robert Mandrou, "Trois clés pour comprendre l'histoire de la folie à l'époque classique," *Annales*, no. 4 (July–August 1962): pp. 761–71.
52. Michel Serres, "Géométrie de la folie," *Mercure de France*, no. 1188 (August

1962): pp. 683–96, and no. 1189 (September 1962): pp. 63–81; reprinted in *Hermès ou la communication*.

53. *Les Mots et les choses*.

54. Éribon, *Michel Foucault*, p. 147.

55. Robert Castel, "Les aventures de la pratique," *Le Débat*, no. 41 (September–November, 1986): p. 43.

56. Marcel Gauchet and Gladys Swain, *La Pratique de l'esprit humain: L'institution asilaire et la révolution démocratique*.

57. Luc Ferry and Alain Renaut, *La Pensée 68*, p. 131.

58. Ibid., p. 132.

Nineteen. Marxism in Crisis: A Thaw or the Deep Freeze Again?

1. Marcel Gauchet, interview with the author.

2. Alain Renaut, interview with the author.

3. Georges Balandier, interview with the author.

4. René Lourau, interview with the author.

5. Quoted by Pascal Ory and Jean-François Sirinelli, *Les Intellectuels en France, de l'affaire Dreyfus à nos jours*, p. 188.

6. Michel Foucault, *Océaniques*, FR3, January 13, 1988 (1977, at Vézelay, home of Maurice Clavel).

7. Pierre Fougeyrollas, interview with the author.

8. Gérard Genette, interview with the author.

9. Olivier Revault d'Allonnes, interview with the author.

10. Jean-Pierre Faye, interview with the author.

11. Alfred Adler, interview with the author.

12. Alfred Adler, *Séminaire de Michel Izard*, Laboratoire d'Anthropologie Sociale, November 17, 1988.

13. Ibid.

14. Ibid.

15. Ibid.

16. Ibid.

17. Ibid.

18. Cornelius Castoriadis, "Les divertisseurs," *Le Nouvel Observateur*, June 20, 1977; reprinted in *La Société française* (Paris: 10/18, 1979), p. 226.

19. Edgar Morin, *Le Vif du sujet* (Paris: Seuil, 1969).

20. Edgar Morin, "Arguments, trente ans après," interviews, *La Revue des revues*, no. 4 (fall 1987): p. 12.

21. Kostas Axelos, in ibid., p. 18.

22. Kostas Axelos, "Le jeu de l'autocritique," *Arguments*, nos. 27–28 (1962).

23. Morin, "Arguments, trente ans après," p. 19.

24. Daniel Becquemont, interview with the author.

25. Ibid.

Twenty. The French School of Economics Takes a Structural Path

1. André Nicolaï, interview with the author.

2. Michel Aglietta, interview with the author.

3. Ibid.

4. André Nicolaï, interview with the author.

5. Mario Dehove, *L'Etat des sciences sociales en France*, p. 252.

6. Robert Boyer, "La croissance française de l'après-guerre et les modèles macro-économiques," *La Revue économique*, vol. 27, no. 5 (1976).

7. François Perrroux, in *Sens et usages du terme de structure*, ed. Roger Bastide (Paris: Mouton, 1972 [1962]), p. 61.

8. Henri Bartoli, *Economie et création collective*, p. 315.

9. Karl Marx, *Le Capital*, book 2, vol. 3, p. 208.

10. René Clémens, "Prolégomènes d'une théorie de la structure," *Revue d'économie politique*, no. 6 (1952): p. 997.

11. Ernest Wagemann, *Introduction à la théorie du mouvement des affaires*, pp. 372–73; and *La Stratégie économique*, pp. 69–70.

12. François Perroux, *Comptes de la nation*, p. 126.

13. André Marchal, in Bastide, ed., *Sens et usages du terme de structure*.

14. André Marchal, *Méthode scientifique et science économique*.

15. André Marchal, *Systèmes et structures*.

16. André Nicolaï, *Comportement économique et structures sociales*.

17. André Nicolaï, interview with the author.

18. Bartoli, *Économie et création collective*, p. 344.

19. Henri Bartoli, interview with the author.

20. Bartoli, *Économie et création collective*, p. 345.

21. Gilles Gaston-Granger, *Pensée formelle et science de l'homme*, p. 53.

Twenty-one. Get a Load of That Structure!

1. Roger Bastide, ed., *Sens et usages du terme de structure*.

2. *Entretiens sur les notions de genèse et de structure*, colloquium at Cerisy, July–August 1959 (Paris: Mouton, 1965). There was also a colloquium in 1957, organized by the Centre International de Synthèse: *Notion de structure et structure de la connaissance* (Paris: Albin Michel, 1957).

3. Étienne Wolff, in Bastide, ed., *Sens et usages du terme de structure*, p. 23.

4. Nicolai Trubetzkoy, "La phonologie actuelle," in *Psychologie du langage* (Paris, 1933), p. 245.

5. Claude Lévi-Strauss, in Bastide, ed., *Sens et usages du terme de structure*, p. 44.

6. Daniel Lagache, in ibid., p. 81.

7. Raymond Aron, in ibid., p. 113.

8. Lucien Goldmann, in *Entretiens sur les notions de genèse et de structure*, p. 10.

9. Lucien Goldmann, *Le Dieu caché*.

10. Jean Piaget, in *Entretiens sur les notions de genèse et de structure*, p. 42.

11. Maurice de Gandillac, in ibid., p. 120.

12. Claude Lévi-Strauss, *Anthropologie structurale*, reprinted in *Histoire et ethnologie, Revue de métaphysique et de morale*, nos. 3–4 (1949): pp. 363–91 (*Structural Anthropology*, "History and Anthropology," pp. 1–28.)

13. Ibid., p. 13.

14. Ibid., p. 19.

15. Ibid., pp 23–24.

16. Ibid., p. 82.

17. Ibid., p. 95.

18. Ibid., p. 278.

19. Ibid.

20. Maurice Godelier, interview with the author.

21. Philippe Descola, interview with the author.

22. Claude Roy, "Claude Lévi-Strauss ou l'homme en question," *La Nef*, no. 28 (1959): p. 70.

23. Jean Duvignaud, *Les Lettres nouvelles*, no. 62 (1958).

24. Letter from Claude Lévi-Strauss, quoted by Jean Duvignaud in *Le Langage perdu*, p. 234.

25. Ibid., p. 251.

26. Georges Mounin, *Introduction à la sémiologie*, p. 202.

27. Ibid., p. 204.

28. Lévi-Strauss, *Structural Anthropology*, p. 60.

29. Ibid., p. 41.

30. Ibid., p. 90.

31. François Dosse, *L'Histoire en miettes*.

32. "La Méditerranée et le monde méditerranéen à l'époque de Philippe II."

33. "La Crise de l'économie française à la fin de l'Ancien Régime."

34. Ernest Labrousse, "La Crise de l'économie française à la fin de l'Ancien Régime et au début de la crise révolutionnaire," p. 170.

35. Ernest Labrousse, *Actes du congrès historique du centenaire de la révolution de 1848*, p. 20.

36. Pierre Vilar, *La Catalogne dans l'Espagne moderne. Recherches sur les fondements économiques des structures nationales*.

37. Pierre Vilar, interview with the author.

38. Michelle Perrot, *Essais d'ego-histoire*, p. 277.

39. Michelle Perrot, interview with the author.

40. Ibid. [The French title of Perrot's thesis is "Les Ouvriers en grève, France (1871–1890)."—*Trans.*]

41. Jean-Pierre Vernant, interview with the author.

42. Jean-Pierre Vernant, "Le mythe hésiodique des races: Essai d'analyse structurale," *Revue de l'histoire des religions* (1960): pp. 21–54.

43. Jean-Pierre Vernant, in *Entretiens sur les notions de genèse et de structure*.

44. Jean-Pierre Vernant, "Le mythe hésiodique des races" (1960), in *Mythe et pensée chez les Grecs*, p. 21.

45. Jean-Pierre Vernant, interview with the author.

46. Ibid.

47. Ibid.

48. Claude Lévi-Strauss, "Leçon inaugurale au Collège de France," January 5, 1960; reprinted in *Anthropologie structurale*, vol. 2, p. 20.

49. Ibid., p. 24.

50. Pierre Nora, interview with the author.

51. Lévi-Strauss, "Leçon inaugurale au Collège de France."

52. Claude Lévi-Strauss, *De près et de loin*, p. 96.

53. Claude Lévi-Strauss, in Georges Charbonnier, *Entretiens avec Claude Lévi-Strauss*, p. 181.

Twenty-two. Contesting the Sorbonne: The Quarrel of the Ancients and the Moderns

1. Alain Boissinot, interview with the author.

2. Ibid.

3. André Martinet, interview with the author.

4. Jean-Claude Chevalier, interview with the author.

5. Ibid.

6. Jean-Claude Chevalier, "La Notion de complément chez les grammairiens."
7. Jean-Claude Chevalier, interview with the author.
8. Ibid.
9. Tzvetan Todorov, interview with the author.
10. Ibid.
11. Ibid.
12. Marina Yaguello, interview with the author.
13. Françoise Gadet, interview with the author.
14. Ibid.
15. Philippe Hamon, interview with the author.
16. Élisabeth Roudinesco, interview with the author.
17. François Ewald, interview with the author.
18. Ibid.
19. Roger-Pol Droit, interview with the author.
20. Sylvain Auroux, interview with the author.
21. Gérard Genette, interview with the author.
22. Philippe Hamon, "Littérature," in *Les Sciences du langage in France au XXe siècle*, p. 289.
23. *Work in Linguistics and Literature.*
24. Louis Hay, interview with the author.
25. Ibid.
26. "Le Vocabulaire politique et social en France de 1849 à 1872."
27. Henri Mitterand, interview with the author.
28. Knud Togeby, *Les Structures immanentes de la langue française.*
29. Maurice Gross, in "La création de revues dans les années soixante," interview with Jean-Claude Chevalier and Pierre Encrevé, *Langue française*, no. 63 (September 1984): p. 91.
30. Jean Dubois, in ibid.
31. André-Georges Haudricourt, interview with the author.
32. Henri Mitterand, interview with the author.
33. Ibid.
34. Jean-Claude Chevalier and Pierre Encrevé, "La création de revues dans les années soixante," p. 97.
35. A *directeur d'études* can lecture without necessarily having an advanced university degree. Barthes's published work had justified his election at the EPHE.—*Trans.*
36. Hamon, "Littérature," p. 289.
37. Claude Lévi-Strauss, "La structure et la forme," *Cahiers de l'ISEA*, no. 99 (March 1960), series M; no. 7; reprinted in *Anthropologie structurale*, vol. 2.
38. Claude Lévi-Strauss and Roman Jakobson, *L'Homme*, II, no. 1 (January–April, 1962).
39. Jean Rousset, *Forme et signification: Essais sur les structures littéraires de Corneille à Claudel.*
40. Ibid., p. vii.
41. Ibid., p. xx.

Twenty-three. 1964: The Semiological Adventure Makes a Breakthrough

1. Joseph Sumpf, interview with the author.
2. Ibid.
3. Ibid.

4. Michel Foucault, "Le structuralisme et l'analyse littéraire," in *Mission culturelle française Information*, French embassy in Tunisia, April 10–May 10, 1987 (1965); unedited tapes of two lectures by Michel Foucault at the Club Tahar Haddad, p. 11 (Centre Michel-Foucault, Bibliothèque du Saluchoir).

5. Ibid.

6. Tzvetan Todorov, "La description de la signification en littérature," *Communications*, no. 4 (1964): p. 36.

7. Claude Brémond, "Le message narratif," p. 4.

8. Ibid., p. 31.

9. *Le Système de la mode.*

10. Roland Barthes, *Océaniques*, FR3, January 27, 1988 (interview, 1970).

11. Algirdas Julien Greimas, interview with the author.

12. Roland Barthes, *Le Système de la mode*, p. 9.

13. Barthes, "Les éléments de sémiologie," *Communications*, no. 4 (1964); reprinted in *L'Aventure sémiologique*, p. 28.

14. Ibid., p. 29.

15. Ibid., p. 51.

16. Ibid., p. 82.

17. Louis-Jean Calvet, *Roland Barthes*, p. 83.

18. Roland Barthes, "L'activité structuraliste," *Les Lettres nouvelles* (1963); reprinted in *Essais critiques*, p. 214.

19. Ibid., p. 215.

20. Roland Barthes, "L'imagination du signe," *Arguments* (1962); reprinted in *Essais critiques*, p. 207.

21. Ibid., p. 209.

22. Roland Barthes, interview with Georges Charbonnier, *France-Culture*, December 1967; rebroadcast November 21 and 22, 1988.

23. Ibid.

24. Ibid.

25. Ibid.

Twenty-four. The Golden Age of Formal Thinking

1. Algirdas Julien Greimas, interview with the author.

2. Ibid.

3. André Martinet, interview with the author.

4. Algirdas Julien Greimas, interview with the author.

5. Jean-Claude Coquet, "La sémiotique," in *Les Sciences du langage en France au XXᵉ siècle*, p. 175.

6. Algirdas Julien, Greimas, *Sémantique structurale*, p. 6.

7. Ibid., p. 8.

8. Algirdas Julien Greimas, interview with the author.

9. Greimas, *Sémantique structurale*, p. 31.

10. Ibid., p. 60.

11. Ibid., p. 223.

12. Thomas Pavel, *Le Mirage linguistique*, p. 151.

13. Claude Brémond, *Logique du récit*.

14. Claude Brémond, interview with the author.

15. Ibid.

16. Ibid.

17. Jacques Hoarau, interview with the author.

18. Marc Vernet, interview with the author.
19. Louis Hay, interview with the author.
20. Jean-Claude Coquet, interview with the author.
21. Ibid.
22. Ibid.
23. Claude Brémond, interview with the author.
24. Ibid.
25. André Martinet, interview with the author.
26. Algirdas Julien Greimas, interview with the author.
27. Ibid.
28. Roland Barthes, *Le Système de la mode*, p. 16.
29. Ibid., p. 17.
30. Ibid., p. 18.
31. Ibid., p. 38.
32. Ibid., p. 282.
33. Jean-François Revel, "Le rat et la mode," *L'Express*, May 22, 1967.
34. Raymond Bellour, "Entretien avec R. Barthes," *Les Lettres françaises*, no. 1172 (March 2, 1967).
35. Julia Kristeva, "Le sens et la mode," *Critique*, no. 247 (December 1967): p. 1008.
36. Roland Barthes, "De la science à la littérature," *Times Literary Supplement* (1967); reprinted in *Le Bruissement de la langue*, p. 17.
37. Roland Barthes, interviews with Georges Charbonnier, *France-Culture*, December 1967.
38. Ibid.
39. Jacques Hoarau, interview with the author.
40. Ibid.
41. *Les Idéalités mathématiques.*
42. Sylvain Auroux, interview with the author.
43. Jean Piaget, *Psychologie et épistémologie*, p. 145.
44. Oswald Ducrot, interview with the author.
45. Ibid.
46. Gottlob Frege, *Les Fondements de l'arithmétique*, p. 12.
47. Élisabeth Roudinesco, *Histoire de la psychanalyse en France*, vol. 2, p. 410.
48. Ibid., p. 413.
49. Joël Dor, interview with the author.
50. Gennie Lemoine, interview with the author.

Twenty-five. Great Confrontations

1. Roland Barthes, "Histoire et littérature: à propos de Racine," *Annales* (May–June 1960): pp. 524–37.
2. Ibid., in *Sur Racine*, p. 157.
3. Ibid., p. 146.
4. Ibid., p. 13.
5. Ibid., p. 14.
6. Ibid., p. 21.
7. Ibid., p. 60.
8. Raymond Picard, *Nouvelle Critique ou nouvelle imposture* (Paris: J.-J. Pauvert, 1965), pp. 30–34.
9. Ibid., p. 52.
10. Ibid., p. 66.

11. Roland Barthes, *Océaniques*, FR3, February 8, 1988 (November 1970–May 1971).

12. Jean Dubois, interview with the author.

13. Olivier Revault d'Allonnes, interview with the author.

14. Jacqueline Piatier, *Le Monde*, October 23, 1965; quoted by Louis-Jean Calvet, *Roland Barthes*, p. 187.

15. Ibid., p. 188.

16. Ibid.

17. Roland Barthes, *Critique et vérité* (Paris: Seuil, 1966), p. 13.

18. Ibid., p. 35.

19. Ibid., p. 56.

20. Ibid., p. 57.

21. Ibid., p. 71.

22. René Pommier, *Assez décodé* (Paris: Éditions Roblot, 1978), and *R. Barthes, Ras le bol!* (Paris: Éditions Roblot, 1987), in which he attacks Barthes and the "jobarthians." He writes, among other things: "The idiocies of a R. Barthes are, for me, an insult to human intelligence" (p. 40); "When I read him, I never say to myself that R. Barthes is too intelligent; I constantly say to myself, with an ever-present surprise: how can you be such an ass?" (p. 27). The tone is noteworthy.

23. Georges Gurvitch, "Le concept de structure sociale," *Cahiers internationaux de sociologie*, no. 19 (1955).

24. Ibid., p. 31.

25. Claude Lévi-Strauss, *Structural Anthropology*, p. 322.

26. Gilles Gaston-Granger, "Événement et structure dans les sciences de l'homme," *Cahiers de l'ISEA* (December 1959).

27. Ibid., p. 168.

28. Ibid., p. 174.

29. Ibid., p. 175.

30. Gilles Gaston-Granger, interview with the author.

31. Ibid.

32. Roger Establet, interview with the author.

33. Ibid.

34. Pierre Ansart, interview with the author.

35. Ibid.

36. Jean Duvignaud, interview with the author.

37. Jean Duvignaud, *Le Langage perdu*, p. 215.

38. Claude Lévi-Strauss, *The Savage Mind*, p. 268.

39. Ibid., p. 1.

40. Claude Lévi-Strauss, *Le Totémisme aujourd'hui*, p. 25.

41. Ibid., p. 128.

42. Lévi-Strauss, *The Savage Mind*, p. 104.

43. Claude Roy, "Un grand livre civilisé: *La Pensée sauvage*," *Libération*, June 19, 1962.

44. Edmond Ortigues, *Critique*, no. 189 (February 1963): p. 143.

45. Jean Lacroix, *Le Monde*, November 27, 1962.

46. Robert Kanters, *Le Figaro littéraire*, June 3–23, 1962.

47. Roland Barthes, "Sociologie et socio-logique," *Informations sur les sciences sociales*, no. 4 (December 1962): p. 242.

48. Lévi-Strauss, *The Savage Mind*, p. 254.

49. Ibid., p. 257.

50. Ibid., p. 258.

51. Ibid., p. 261.
52. Ibid., p. 262.
53. Pierre Verstraeten, "Claude Lévi-Strauss ou la tentation du néant," *Les Temps modernes*, no. 206 (July 1963): p. 83.
54. Claude Lévi-Strauss, remarks quoted by Jean-Marie Domenach, interview with the author.
55. Jean-Marie Domenach, interview with the author.
56. Paul Ricoeur, *Esprit* (November 1963): p. 605.
57. Ibid., p. 644.
58. Ibid., p. 618.
59. Claude Lévi-Strauss, in ibid., p. 637.
60. André Green, "La psychanalyse devant l'opposition de l'histoire et de la structure," *Critique*, no. 194 (July 1963).
61. Ibid., p. 661.

Twenty-six. Signifying Chains

1. Jean Laplanche, "Une révolution sans cesse occultée," Communication aux journées scientifiques de l'Association Internationale d'Histoire de la Psychanalyse, April 23–24, 1988.
2. Jacques Lacan, "L'excommunication," *Ornicar?* (1977).
3. See Élisabeth Roudinesco, *Histoire de la psychanalyse en France*, vol. 2, pp. 399–403.
4. Ibid., p. 383.
5. Jacques Lacan, *Écrits*, p. 805.
6. Marcel Arrivé, *Linguistique et psychanalyse*, p. 12.
7. Jean Allouch, *Littoral*, nos. 23–24 (October 1987): p. 5.
8. "Objet petit a": "The 'a' in questions stands for '*autre*' (other), the concept having been developed out of the Freudian 'object' and Lacan's own exploitation of 'otherness.' The '*petit a*' (small 'a') differentiates the object from (while relating it to) the '*Autre*' or '*grand Autre*' (the capitalized 'Other'). However, Lacan refuses to comment on either term here, leaving the reader to develop an appreciation of the concepts in the course of their use. Furthermore, Lacan insists that '*objet petit a*' should remain untranslated, thus acquiring, as it were, the status of an algebraic sign" (*Écrits: A Selection*, p. xi).—*Trans.*
9. Jean-David Nasio, *Les Sept Concepts cruciaux de la psychanalyse*.
10. Martin Heidegger, *Poetry, Language, Thought*, trans. A. Hofstadter (New York: Harper and Row, 1971 [1975]).
11. Alain Juranville, *Lacan et la philosophie*, p. 167.
12. Serge Leclaire, interview with the author.
13. Jacques-Alain Miller, *Ornicar?* no. 24 (1981): p. 43.
14. Lacan, *Écrits*, p. 863.
15. Juranville, *Lacan et la philosophie*, p. 175.
16. Ibid., p. 195.
17. Ibid., p. 286.
18. Gennie Lemoine, interview with the author.
19. Serge Leclaire, "L'objet a dans la cure," *Rompre les charmes*, p. 174.
20. Jean Clavreul, interview with the author.
21. Joël Dor, interview with the author.
22. Jean Laplanche, interview with the author.
23. André Green, "Le bon plaisir," *France-Culture*, February 25, 1989.

24. Ibid.

25. André Green, interview with the author.

26. André Green, "Le langage dans la psychanalyse," in *Langages, Les Rencontres psychanalytiques d'Aix en Provence*.

27. Lacan, *Écrits*, p. 873.

28. André Green, "Le langage dans la psychanalyse," p. 231.

29. Jean-Marie Benoist, interview with the author.

30. Gérard Mendel, interview with the author.

31. Bernard Sichère, interview with the author.

32. Ibid.

33. Jacques Lacan, "Subversion of the Subject and Dialectic of Desire," in *Écrits: A Selection*, p. 297.

34. André Green, *L'Affect*.

35. André Green, interview with the author.

36. Ibid.

37. Charles Bally, *Le Langage et la vie*.

38. Serge Viderman, interview with the author.

39. Wladimir Granoff, interview with the author.

40. François Roustang, *Lacan*, p. 58.

41. Jean Clavreul, interview with the author.

42. Serge Leclaire, interview with the author.

43. Jean Laplanche, interview with the author.

44. Claude Dumézil, interview with the author.

Twenty-seven. Mythology's Earth Is Round

1. Claude Lévi-Strauss, *The Raw and the Cooked: Introduction to a Science of Mythology*, vol. 1, p. 3.

2. Claude Lévi-Strauss, *The Naked Man: Introduction to a Science of Mythology*, vol. 4, p. 639.

3. Lévi-Strauss, *The Raw and the Cooked*, p. 245.

4. Claude Lévi-Strauss, *From Honey to Ashes: Introduction to a Science of Mythology*, vol. 2, p. 472.

5. Claude Lévi-Strauss, *Paroles données*, p. 14.

6. Claude Lévi-Strauss, "The Structural Study of Myths" (1955); reprinted in *Structural Anthropology*, pp. 202–28.

7. Ibid., pp. 207-8.

8. Claude Lévi-Strauss, *The Savage Mind*, p. 130.

9. Lévi-Strauss, *Structural Anthropology*, p. 220.

10. Lévi Strauss, *The Savage Mind*, p. 17.

11. Jean-Marie Benoist, *La Révolution structurale*, p. 32.

12. Lévi-Strauss, *The Raw and the Cooked*, p. 18.

13. Lévi-Strauss, "L'avenir de ethnologie, 1959–1960," in *Paroles données*, p. 34.

14. Lévi-Strauss, *The Raw and the Cooked*, p. 341.

15. Lévi-Strauss, *From Honey to Ashes*, p. 303.

16. Ibid., p. 256.

17. Claude Lévi-Strauss, interview with Raymond Bellour, *Les Lettres françaises*, no. 1165 (January 12, 1967); reprinted in *Le Livre des autres*, p. 38.

18. Ibid., p. 38.

19. Lévi-Strauss, *From Honey to Ashes*, p. 356.

20. Jean Pouillon, *La Quinzaine littéraire*, August 1–31, 1968, p. 21.

21. Claude Lévi-Strauss, interview with Raymond Bellour, *Le Monde*, November 5, 1971.

22. Claude Lévi-Strauss, *The Naked Man*, p. 598.

23. Ibid., pp. 621–22.

24. Ibid., p. 629.

25. Catherine Backès-Clément, in *Le Magazine littéraire* (November 1971), points out that this analogy works with a single exception.

26. Lévi-Strauss, *The Naked Man*, p. 649.

27. Ibid., p. 653.

28. Ibid., p. 687.

29. Ibid.

30. Claude Lévi-Strauss, *Le Magazine littéraire* (November 1971).

31. Jean Duvignaud, *Le Langage perdu*, p. 243.

32. Lévi-Strauss, *The Raw and the Cooked*, p. 341.

33. Ibid., p. 240.

34. Thomas Pavel, *Le Mirage linguistique*, p. 48.

35. Lévi-Strauss, *The Raw and the Cooked*, p. 135.

36. Manfred Frank, *Qu'est-ce que le néo-structuralisme?* p. 56.

37. Lévi-Strauss, *The Raw and the Cooked*, p. 16.

38. Lévi-Strauss, From *Honey to Ashes*, p. 475.

39. Lévi-Strauss, *The Naked Man*, p. 322.

40. Ibid., p. 607.

41. Ibid.; quote taken from Marcel Proust, *Le Temps retrouvé*, vol. 2 (Paris: Gallimard, 1954), p. 15.

42. Benoist, *La Révolution structurale*, p. 275.

43. Lévi-Strauss, *The Naked Man*, p. 694.

44. Jean-Marie Domenach, "Le requiem structuraliste," in *Le Sauvage et l'ordinateur*, p. 81.

45. Ibid., p. 85.

46. Jean-Marie Domenach, interview with the author.

Twenty-eight. Africa: The Continental Divide of Structuralism

1. Georges Balandier, interview with the author.

2. Ibid.

3. Claude Lévi-Strauss, *The Savage Mind*, pp. 234–35 n.

4. Georges Balandier, interview with the author.

5. Ibid.

6. Ibid.

7. Georges Balandier, *Histoire d'autres*, p. 187.

8. Ibid., p. 183.

9. Georges Balandier, *Anthropologie politique*.

10. Ibid., p. 22.

11. Meyer Fortes and E. E. Evans-Pritchard, eds., *African Political Systems*, 1940.

12. Balandier, *Anthropologie politique*, p. 27.

13. *Lundis de l'histoire*, France-Culture, March 11, 1968.

14. Marc Augé, interview with the author.

15. Ibid.

16. Ibid.

17. Dan Sperber, interview with the author.

18. In the French university system, the first two years of training, the first cycle, cul-

minate in a DEUG (Diplôme d'études universitaires générales), the third year is the second cycle and leads to a *Licence*, and, during the third cycle, one prepares a *maîtrise*, after which a doctoral thesis. The first part of this cycle is the DEA or Diplôme d'études approfondies, which is crowned, in its turn, by a doctoral thesis.—*Trans.*

19. Dan Sperber, interview with the author.

20. Ibid.

21. Ibid.

22. Claude Meillassoux, interview with the author.

23. Ibid.

24. Ibid.

25. Jean Duvignaud, interview with the author.

26. Jean Duvignaud, *Chebika* (1991).

27. *Remparts d'argile.*

28. Jean Duvignaud, "Après le fonctionalisme et le structuralisme, quoi?" in *Une anthropologie des turbulences. Hommage à G. Balandier*, p. 151.

29. Ibid., p. 152.

30. A research group created by Lévi-Strauss within the institutional framework of the Collège de France. Izard therefore belonged to two different research institutions, the one at the Collège and the other at the EHESS.

31. Michel Izard, interview with the author.

32. Jean Pouillon, interview with the author.

Twenty-nine. Reviews

1. *La Psychanalyse*, no. 1 (1956): p. iv.

2. *La Linguistique*, no. 1 (1966); director: André Martinet; general secretary, Georges Mounin.

3. *Langages*, no. 1 (March 1966), Larousse; editorial board: Roland Barthes, Jean Dubois, Algirdas Julien Greimas, Bernard Pottier, Bernard Quémada, Nicolas Ruwet.

4. Ibid., Introduction.

5. Jean-Claude Chevalier, Pierre Encrevé, *Langue française*, no. 63 (September 1984): p. 95.

6. Algirdas Julien Greimas, *Langages*, no. 1 (March 1966): p. 96.

7. Jean Dubois, interview with the author.

8. *Communications*, no. 1 (Paris: Seuil, 1961), Introduction: pp. 1–2.

9. *Communications*, editorial board: Roland Barthes, Claude Brémond, Georges Friedmann, Edgar Morin, Violette Morin.

10. Contributors to *Communications*, no. 8, were Roland Barthes, Algirdas Julien Greimas, Claude Brémond, Umberto Eco, Jules Gritti, Violette Morin, Christian Metz, Tzvetan Todorov, and Gérard Genette.

11. *Tel Quel*, secretary-general and director: Jean-Edern Hallier, editorial board: Boisrouvray, Jacques Coudol, Jean-Edern Hallier, Jean-René Huguenin, Renaud Matignon, Philippe Sollers.

12. Jean-Pierre Faye, interview with the author.

13. *Tel Quel*, no. 1 (1960, Seuil), quote of Nietzsche.

14. Ibid., p. 3.

15. Marcelin Pleynet, interview with the author.

16. Ibid.

17. Ibid.

18. Ibid.

19. Ibid.

20. *Tel Quel*, no. 47 (fall 1971): p. 142.

21. Ibid.

22. Claude Brémond, interview with the author.

23. Roland Barthes, *Océaniques*, FR3 (1970–71), January 27, 1988.

24. Julia Kristeva, "Le bon plaisir," *France-Culture*, December 10, 1988.

25. Jean-Pierre Faye, interview with the author.

26. Frédérique Matonti, "Entre Argenteuil et les barricades: *La Nouvelle Critique* et les sciences sociales," *Cahiers de l'Institut d'histoire du temps présent*, no. 11 (April 1989): p. 102.

27. Louis Althusser, "Freud et Lacan," *La Nouvelle Critique*, nos. 161–62 (1964).

28. Jacques Milhau, "Les débats philosophiques des années soixante," *La Nouvelle Critique*, no. 130 (1980): pp. 50–51.

29. "*Tel Quel* répond; présentation," *La Nouvelle Critique* (November–December 1967): p. 50.

30. Matonit, "Entre Argenteuil et les barricades," p. 18.

31. Pierre Vilar, "Les mots et les choses dans la pensée économique," *La Nouvelle Critique*, no. 5 (1967); Jeannette Colombel, "Les mots de Foucault et les choses," *La Nouvelle Critique*, no. 5 (1967); Georges Mounin, "Linguistique, structuralisme et marxisme," *La Nouvelle Critique*, no. 7 (1967); Lucien Sève, "Marxisme et sciences de l'homme," *La Nouvelle Critique*, no. 2 (1967).

32. Robert Linhart, quoted by Hervé Hamon and Philippe Rotman, *Génération*, vol. 1, p. 313.

33. Dominique Lecourt, interview with the author.

34. Ibid.

35. Ibid.

36. Ibid.

37. *Les Cahiers pour l'analyse*, reprinted in *Société du Graphe*, nos. 1–2 (Paris: Seuil, 1969).

Thirty. Ulm or Saint-Cloud: Althusser or Touki?

1. Jean-Toussaint Desanti, *Un destin philosophique*, p. 129.

2. Sylvain Auroux, interview with the author.

3. Jean-Toussaint Desanti, interview with the author.

4. Ibid.

5. Jean-Toussaint Desanti, *Autrement*, no. 102 (November 1988): p. 116.

6. Jean-Toussaint Desanti, interview with the author.

7. Ibid.

8. Sylvain Auroux, interview with the author.

9. Ibid.

10. Ibid.

11. Jacques Bouveresse, interview with the author.

12. Ibid.

13. Ibid.

14. Louis Althusser, *Manifestes philosophiques de Feuerbach*.

15. Pierre Macherey, interview with the author.

16. Ibid.

17. Roger Establet, interview with the author.

18. Ibid.

19. Élisabeth Roudinesco, *Histoire de la psychanalyse en France*, vol. 2, p. 386.
20. Pierre Macherey, interview with the author.
21. Ibid.
22. Jacques Rancière, interview with the author.
23. Ibid.
24. Ibid.
25. Ibid.
26. Ibid.
27. Ibid.
28. Roudinesco, *Histoire de la psychanalyse en France*, vol. 2, p. 387.

Thirty-one. The Althusserian Explosion

1. Vincent Descombes, *Le Même et l'autre*, p. 147.
2. Letter from Althusser to Jean Guitton, July 1972, in *Lire*, no. 148 (January 1988): p. 85.
3. Jean Guitton, in ibid., p. 89.
4. Vincent Descombes, interview with the author.
5. Ibid.
6. Étienne Balibar, interview with the author.
7. "Ouverture d'un débat: marxisme et humanisme," *La Nouvelle Critique*, no. 164 (March 1965): p. 1.
8. Michel Simon, *La Nouvelle Critique*, no. 165 (April 1965): p. 127.
9. Pierre Macherey, "Marxisme et humanisme," *La Nouvelle Critique*, no. 166 (May 1965): p. 132.
10. Michel Verret, *La Nouvelle Critique*, no. 168 (July–August 1965): p. 96.
11. Roger Garaudy, quoted by Jeannine Verdès-Leroux in *Le Réveil des somnambules*, p. 296; full text of the meeting of philosophers at Choisy in January 1966, pp. 125–48.
12. Daniel Lindenberg, *Le Marxisme introuvable*, p. 38.
13. Interview 64, in Verdès-Leroux, *Le Réveil des somnambules*, p. 197.
14. Central committee of the PCF, March 11–13, 1966, *Cahiers du communisme* (May-June 1966), quoted in ibid., pp. 119–20.
15. Roger-Pol Droit, interview with the author.
16. Jacques Bouveresse, interview with the author.
17. Dominique Lecourt, interview with the author.
18. Pierre Macherey, interview with the author.
19. J. Verdès-Leroux, *Le Réveil des somnambules*, p. 295.
20. Louis Althusser, *Lire Le Capital*, vol. 1, p. 16.
21. Ibid., p. 20.
22. Daniel Becquemont, interview with the author.
23. Althusser, *Lire Le Capital*, vol. 1, p. 26.
24. Dominique Lecourt, interview with the author.
25. Louis Althusser, *Pour Marx*, p. 27.
26. Ibid., p. 39.
27. Ibid., p. 171.
28. Ibid., p. 108.
29. Ibid., p. 196.
30. Pierre Vilar, interview with the author.
31. Paul Valadier, interview with the author.
32. Althusser, *Pour Marx*, p. 248.

33. Althusser, *Lire Le Capital*, vol. 2, p. 59.

34. Ibid., p. 47.

35. K. Naïr, "Marxisme ou structuralisme?" in *Contre Althusser* (Paris: 10/18, 1974), p. 192.

36. Althusser, *Lire Le Capital*, vol. 2, p. 171.

37. Jean-Marie Vincent, "Le théoricisme et sa rectification," in *Contre Althusser*, p. 226.

38. Vincent Descombes, interview with the author.

39. Althusser, *Pour Marx*, p. 212 n. 48.

40. Jean-Marie Benoist, *La Révolution structurale*, p. 85.

41. Althusser, *Pour Marx*, p. 236.

42. Étienne Balibar, interview with the author.

43. Étienne Balibar, *Lire Le Capital*, vol. 2, p. 204.

44. Ibid., p. 205.

45. Ibid., p. 249.

46. Althusser, *Lire Le Capital*, vol. 1, p. 170.

Thirty-two. Marxism's Second Wind

1. Alain Badiou, "Le (re)commencement du matérialisme dialectique," *Critique* (May 1967).

2. Pierre Macherey, interview with the author.

3. Badiou, "Le (re)commencement du matérialisme dialectique," p. 441.

4. Joëlle Proust, interview with the author.

5. Paul Henry, interview with the author.

6. Ibid.

7. Thomas Herbert, "Réflexions sur la situation théorique des sciences sociales, spécialement de la psychologie sociale," *Les Cahiers pour l'analyse*, no. 2 (March–April 1966); Thomas Herbert, "Remarques pour une théorie générale des idéologies," *Les Cahiers pour l'analyse*, no. 9 (summer 1968): pp. 74–92.

8. Michel Pêcheux, *L'Analyse automatique du discours*.

9. Paul Henry, "Épistémologie de *L'Analyse automatique du discours* de Michel Pêcheux," in *Introduction to the Translation of M. Pêcheux's Analyse automatique du discours* (text given by Paul Henry).

10. Ibid.

11. Ibid.

12. Emmanuel Terray, interview with the author.

13. Emmanuel Terray, *Le Marxisme devant les sociétés primitives*.

14. Emmanuel Terray, interview with the author.

15. Marc Augé, interview with the author.

16. Marc Augé, *Le Rivage Alladian*.

17. Marc Augé, interview with the author.

18. *La Monnaie chez Marx*.

19. Charles Bettelheim, *Calcul économique et formes de propriété*.

20. Robert Linhart, *Lénine, les paysans, Taylor*.

21. Louis Althusser, "Freud et Lacan," *La Nouvelle Critique*, nos. 161–62 (December 1964–January 1965).

22. Ibid.; reprinted in *Positions* (Paris: Éditions sociales, 1976), p. 16.

23. Ibid., p. 15.

24. Ibid., p. 26.

Thirty-three. 1966: Annum mirabile (I): A Watershed Year for Structuralism

1. Gilles Lapouge, "Encore un effort et j'aurai épousé mon temps," *La Quinzaine littéraire*, no. 459 (March 16–30, 1986): p. 30.

2. Roland Barthes, *Essais critiques* (Paris: Points-Seuil, 1981), "Avant-Propos: 1971," p. 7.

3. Philippe Hamon, interview with the author.

4. Renaud Matignon, *L'Express*, May 2, 1966.

5. Algirdas Julien Greimas, quoted by Jean-Claude Chevalier and Pierre Encrevé, *Langue française*, p. 97.

6. Jean Pouillon, interview with the author.

7. François Wahl, interview with the author.

8. *Le Nouvel Observateur*, no. 91 (August 10, 1966); quoted by Anne-Sophie Perriaux, "Le structuralisme en France," DEA thesis directed by Jacques Julliard, September 1987, p. 34.

9. Information provided by Pierre Nora.

10. Pierre Nora, interview with the author.

11. *Masse et puissance.*

12. *Ethnologie et langage.*

13. *Les Étapes de la pensée sociologique.*

14. Pierre Nora, interview with the author.

15. *La Religion romaine archaïque.*

16. Georges Dumézil, interview with Jean-Pierre Salgas, *La Quinzaine littéraire*, no. 459 (March 16, 1986).

17. *L'Amour de l'art.*

18. *Pour une théorie de la production littéraire.*

19. *Le Normal et le pathologique.*

20. *Les Paysans de Languedoc.*

21. *Louis XIV et vingt millions de Français.*

22. *La Méditerranée et le monde métiterranéen à l'époque de Philippe II.*

23. *Pensée formelle et science de l'homme.*

24. Philippe Hamon, interview with the author.

25. *Forme et signification.*

26. Jacques Lacan, *Les Cahiers pour l'analyse*, no. 3 (May 1966): pp. 5–13.

27. Algirdas Julien Greimas, "L'analyse structurale du récit," *Communications*, no. 8 (1966); reprinted by Points-Seuil (1981), p. 34.

28. Claude Brémond, interview with the author.

29. Ibid.

30. Claude Lévi-Strauss, "La structure et la forme," *Cahiers de l'Institut de science économique appliquée*, no. 9 (March 1960), M series, no. 7: pp. 3–36.

31. Lévi-Strauss, in ibid.; reprinted in *Anthropologie structurale*, vol. 2, p. 159.

32. Vladimir Propp, in the Appendix to *Morphologia della fiaba*.

33. Vladimir Propp, *Les Racines historiques du conte* (*Theory and History of Folklore*).

34. Claude Brémond, interview with the author.

35. Umberto Eco, *Communications*, no. 8 (1966); reprinted by Points-Seuil, 1981, p. 98.

36. Tzvetan Todorov, in ibid., p. 131.

37. "Problèmes du structuralisme," *Les Temps modernes*, no. 246 (November 1966);

contributors: Jean Pouillon, Marc Barbut, Algirdas Julien Greimas, Maurice Godelier, Pierre Bourdieu, Pierre Macherey, Jacques Ehrmann.
38. Jean Pouillon, in ibid., p. 769.
39. Ibid., p. 772.
40. Algirdas Julien Greimas, in ibid.; reprinted in *Du sens*, p. 106.
41. Ibid., p. 107.
42. Maurice Godelier, "Système, structure et contradiction dans *Le Capital*," *Les Temps modernes*, no. 246 (November 1966): p. 832.
43. Ibid., p. 829.
44. Pierre Bourdieu, "Champ intellectuel et projet créateur," in ibid., p. 866.
45. Roland Barthes, interview in *Aléthéia* (February 1966): p. 218.
46. "Structuralismes, idéologies et méthodes," *Esprit*, no. 360 (May 1967); articles by Jean-Marie Domenach, Mikel Dufrenne, Paul Ricoeur, Jean Ladrière, Jean Cuisenier, Pierre Burgelin, Yves Bertherat, and Jean Cornilh.
47. Jean-Marie Domenach, "Le système et la personne," *Esprit*, no. 360 (May 1967): pp. 771–80.
48. Mikel Dufrenne, "La philosophie du néo-positivisme," in ibid., pp. 781–800.
49. Paul Ricoeur, "La structure, le mot, l'événement," in ibid., pp. 801–21.
50. *L'Arc*, no. 30 (fourth quarter 1966).
51. Bernard Pingaud, in ibid., p. 1.
52. Jean-Paul Sartre, in ibid., pp. 87–88.
53. Ibid., p. 89.
54. Ibid., pp. 91–92.
55. Ibid., p. 93.
56. Ibid., p. 94.
57. Jacques Lacan, *Le Figaro littéraire*, December 29, 1966, p. 4.
58. Ibid.
59. Jean-François Revel, "Sartre en ballottage," *L'Express*, no. 802 (November 7–13, 1966).
60. *Les Chemins actuels de la critique*, Cerisy proceedings.
61. See Élisabeth Roudinesco, *Histoire de la psychanalyse en France*, vol. 2, p. 414.
62. Jacques Derrida, "De la grammatologie," *Critique*, no. 223–24 (December 1965).
63. *The Structuralist Controversy: The Languages of Criticism and the Sciences of Man*, ed. Richard Marksey and Eugenio Donato (Baltimore and London: Johns Hopkins University Press, 1970 and 1972).
64. Jean-Pierre Vernant, interview with the author.
65. Ibid.

Thirty-four. 1966: Annum mirabile (II): Foucault Sells like Hotcakes

1. Michel Foucault, *The Order of Things*, p. 208.
2. Michel Foucault, *Lectures pour tous* (1966), INA document, shown on *Océaniques*, FR3, January 13, 1988.
3. Ibid.
4. Ibid.
5. Ibid.
6. Jean Lacroix, "La fin de l'humanisme," *Le Monde*, June 9, 1966.
7. Robert Kanters, "Tu causes, tu causes, c'est tout ce que tu sais faire," *Le Figaro*, June 23, 1966.
8. François Chatelet, "L'homme, ce Narcisse incertain," *La Quinzaine littéraire*, April 1, 1966.

9. Madeleine Chapsal, *L'Express*, no. 779 (May 23–29, 1966): pp. 119–21.

10. Gilles Deleuze, "L'homme, une existence douteuse," *Le Nouvel Observateur*, June 1, 1966.

11. Michel Foucault, interview, *La Quinzaine littéraire*, no. 5 (May 15, 1966).

12. *Crise de la conscience européenne*.

13. Raymond Bellour, *Les Lettres françaises*, no. 1125 (March 31, 1966); reprinted in *Le Livre des autres*, p. 14.

14. Didier Éribon, *Michel Foucault*, p. 189.

15. Jean Piaget, *Le Structuralisme*, p. 108.

16. François Ewald, interview with the author.

17. Foucault, *The Order of Things*, p. xxiii.

18. Jean-Marie Benoist, *La Révolution structurale*, p. 202.

19. Michel Foucault, *France-Culture*, rebroadcast, June 1984.

20. Benoist, *La Révolution structurale*, p. 27.

21. Claude Lévi-Strauss, *Tristes Tropiques*, p. 413.

22. Michel Foucault, *The Order of Things*, p. 379.

23. Ibid.

24. Benoist, *La Révolution structurale*, p. 38.

25. Foucault, *The Order of Things*, p. 369.

26. Ibid., p. 327.

27. Ibid., pp. 368–69.

28. Ibid., p. 208.

29. Ibid., p. 332.

30. Pierre Ansart, interview with the author.

31. Foucault, *The Order of Things*, p. xxii.

32. Ibid., p. 17.

33. Ibid., p. 30.

34. Ibid., p. 47–48.

35. Ibid., p. 61.

36. Ibid., p. 136.

37. Ibid., p. 226.

38. Ibid., p. 284.

39. Ibid., p. 370.

40. Michel Foucault, *France-Culture*, July 10, 1969.

41. Hubert Dreyfus and Paul Rabinov, *Foucault, un parcours philosophique*, p. 71.

42. Foucault, *The Order of Things*, pp. 261–62.

43. Étienne Balibar, interview with the author.

Thirty-five. 1966: Annum mirabile (III): Julia Comes to Paris

1. Philippe Sollers, "Le bon plaisir de J. Kristeva," *France-Culture*, December 10, 1988.

2. Philippe Sollers, "Littérature et totalité" (1966), in *L'Écriture et l'expérience des limites*, p. 73.

3. Stéphane Mallarmé, quoted by Sollers, in ibid., p. 87.

4. Jean Dubois, interview with the author.

5. *Pour une théorie de la production littéraire*.

6. Ibid., p. 165.

7. Ibid., p. 167.

8. Ibid., p. 174.

9. Gérard Genette, "Structuralisme et critique littéraire, " *L'Arc*, no. 26; reprinted in *Figures*, vol. 1, p. 161.

10. Ibid., p. 156.

11. Macherey, *Pour une théorie de la production littéraire*, p. 88.

12. Antoinette Fouque, "Le bon plaisir," *France-Culture*, June 1989.

13. Jacques Lacan, "La science et la vérité," *Les Cahiers pour l'analyse*, no. 1 (1966); reprinted in *Écrits*, vol. 2, p. 226.

14. Ibid.

15. Lacan, *Écrits*, vol. 1, p. 80.

16. *Rationalité et irrationalité en économie*.

17. Maurice Godelier, interview with the author.

18. Godelier, *Rationalité et irrationalité en économie*, p. 95.

19. Maurice Godelier, interview with the author.

Thirty-six. The Postmodern Hour Sounds

1. Carl Schorske, *Fin de siècle Vienna*.

2. Félix Torrès, *Déjà vu*, p. 142.

3. See Jean-Luc Marion, "Une modernité sans avenir," *Le Débat*, no. 4 (September 1980): pp. 54–60.

4. Michel Foucault, *The Order of Things*, p. 208.

5. Paul Valadier, interview with the author.

6. Jean Jamin, interview with the author.

7. Jean-François Lyotard, *Le Magazine littéraire*, no. 225 (December 1985): p. 43.

8. Michel Foucault, interview with K. Boesers, "Die Folter, das ist die Vernunft," *Literaturmagazin*, no. 8 (Reibek: Rowohlt, 1977).

9. Michel Foucault, remarks made at Maurice Clavel's in Vézelay in 1977, *Océaniques*, January 13, 1988.

10. Maurice Godelier, interview with the author.

11. Daniel Dory, interview with the author.

12. Marcel Gauchet, interview with the author.

13. Jean Antoine de Condorcet, *Esquisse d'un tableau historique des progrès de l'esprit humain* (1793).

14. Régis Debray, *Critique de la raison politique*, p. 290.

15. Ibid., p. 299.

16. Ibid., p. 52.

17. Jean Chesneaux, *De la modernité*, p. 50.

18. François Furet, "Les intellectuels français et le structuralisme," *Preuves*, no. 92 (February 1967); reprinted in *L'Atelier de l'histoire*.

19. Michel Foucault, *Arts*, June 15, 1966.

20. Gilles Deleuze, *Le Nouvel Observateur*, April 5, 1967; reprinted in Lucien Sève, *Structuralisme et dialectique*.

21. Pierre Nora, *Les Lieux de mémoire, La République*, p. xviii.

22. Gilles Lipovetsky, *L'Ère du vide: Essais sur l'individualisme contemporain*, p. 11.

23. Jean-François Lyotard, *La Condition post-moderne* (Paris: Minuit, 1979), p. 11 (*The Postmodern Condition: A Report on Knowledge*, p. 3).

24. Ibid., p. 39.

25. Ibid., p. 41.

26. Claude Lévi-Strauss, interview with Jean-Marie Benoist, *Le Monde*, January 21, 1979.

27. Claude Lévi-Strauss, *Anthropologie structurale*, vol. 2, p. 65.

28. Claude Lévi-Strauss, *The Naked Man*, p. 694.
29. Michel Foucault, interview with Bernard-Henri Lévy, *Le Nouvel Observateur*, March 12, 1977; republished on June 29, 1984.
30. Pierre Daix, *Structuralisme et révolution culturelle*, p. 29.
31. Paul Valadier, interview with the author.

Thirty-seven. Nietzschean-Heideggerian Roots

1. Martin Heidegger, *Questions*, vol. 1, p. 188.
2. Pierre Fougeyrollas, interview with the author.
3. Friedrich Nietzsche, *Human, all too human*, vol. 1, paragraph 248, pp. 117–18.
4. Ibid., vol. 2, paragraph 463, p. 169.
5. Jürgen Habermas, *The Philosophical Discourse of Modernity: 12 Lectures*.
6. Friedrich Nietzsche, *Considérations inactuelles*, vol. 2, p. 327.
7. Friedrich Nietzsche, *Untimely Meditations*, p. 62.
8. Nietzsche, *Human, all too human*, vol. 2, paragraph 239, p. 114.
9. Ibid., paragraph 473, p. 173.
10. Ibid.
11. Gianni Vattimo, *La Fin de la modernité*, p. 11.
12. Luc Ferry and Alain Renaut, *Heidegger et les modernes*, p. 82.
13. Martin Heidegger, "Le discours du rectorat" (May 27, 1933), *Le Débat*, no. 27 (November 1983): p. 97.
14. Georges Steiner, *Martin Heidegger*, p. 87.
15. Nietzsche, *Human, all too human*, vol. 1, p. 52.
16. Ibid., vol. 1, paragraph 107, p. 57 (Hollingdale).
17. Martin Heidegger, *An Introduction to Metaphysics*.
18. Jean-Paul Sartre, *Existentialism Is a Humanism*.
19. Martin Heidegger, *Lettre sur l'humanisme*, p. 107.
20. Habermas, *The Philosophical Discourse of Modernity*.
21. Friedrich Nietzsche, *The Gay Science*, p. 336.
22. Rey, "La philosophie du monde scientifique et industriel," in *Histoire de la philosophie*, pp. 151–87.
23. Michel Foucault, *Hommage à Hyppolite*, p. 168.
24. Friedrich Nietzsche, *La Volonté de puissance*, vol. 1, pp. 79 and 141.
25. Luc Ferry and Alain Renaut, *La Pensée 68*, pp. 28–36.
26. Georges-Elia Sarfati, interview with the author.
27. Michel Foucault, *Les Nouvelles littéraires*, June 28, 1984.
28. Michel Foucault, *Actes du Colloque de Royaumont: Nietzsche, Freud, Marx* (Paris: Minuit, 1967 [1964]), p. 189.
29. Michel Foucault, *The Order of Things*, pp. 384–85.
30. Ibid., p. 353.
31. Foucault, *Hommage à Hyppolite*, p. 150.
32. Jean Duvignaud, *Le Langage perdu*, p. 225.
33. Foucault, *Les Nouvelles littéraires*, June 28, 1984.
34. Maurice Pinguet, *Le Débat*, no. 41 (September–November 1986).
35. Foucault, *The Order of Things*, p. 343.
36. Marcel Gauchet, interview with the author.
37. Élisabeth Roudinesco, *Les Enjeux philosophiques des années cinquante*, p. 93.
38. Élisabeth Roudinesco, *Histoire de la psychanalyse en France*, vol. 2, p. 309.
39. Jacques Lacan, *La Psychanalyse*, vol. 1, p. 6.
40. Roudinesco, *Histoire de la psychanalyse en France*, vol. 2, pp. 309–10.

41. Bertrand Ogilvie, interview with the author.
42. Élisabeth Roudinesco, interview with the author.
43. Victor Farías, *Heidegger and Nazism*, ed. Joseph Margolis and Tom Rockmore (Philadelphia: Temple University Press, 1989). Born in Chile, Farías teaches in Berlin and was a student of Heidegger. In his book, he argued that Heidegger had been a voluntary Nazi, his position based on lifelong convictions. This thesis created a controversy in France over the relationship between philosophy and politics.—*Trans.*
44. Jacques Derrida, *France-Culture*, March 21, 1988.
45. Jacques Derrida, *Positions*, p. 18.
46. *Le Facteur de la vérité.*

Thirty-eight. Growing Pains

1. Jean Jamin, interview with the author.
2. Bernard Ogilvie, interview with the author.
3. Maurice Godelier, interview with the author.
4. Ibid.
5. Jean-Louis Fabiani, *Les Enjeux philosophiques des années cinquante*, p. 125.
6. Paul Valadier, interview with the author.
7. Jean Viet, *Les Méthodes structuralistes*, p. 11.
8. Vincent Descombes, *Le Même et l'autre*, p. 96.
9. Ibid., p. 98.
10. Pierre Bourdieu, *Choses dites*, p. 16.
11. Michel Foucault (1977), *Revue de métaphysique et de morale*, no. 1 (January–March 1985): p. 4.
12. Louis Pinto, *Les Philosophes entre le lycée et l'avant-garde*, p. 68.
13. Étienne Balibar, interview with the author.
14. Pinto, *Les Philosophes entre le lycée et l'avant-garde*, p. 78.
15. Ibid., p. 96.
16. Fabiani, *Les Enjeux philosophiques des années cinquante*, p. 116.
17. François Dosse, *L'Histoire en miettes*.
18. Michelle Perrot, interview with the author.
19. Claude Lévi-Strauss, interview, *Libération*, June 2, 1983.
20. Louis-Jean Calvet, interview with the author.
21. Thomas Pavel, *Le Mirage linguistique*, p. 61.
22. Georges Balandier, interview with the author.
23. Claude Lévi-Strauss, "Leçon inaugurale au Collège de France," January 5, 1960, in *Anthropologie structurale* vol. 2, p. 27.
24. Claude Lévi-Strauss, *The Naked Man*, p. 692.
25. Claude Lévi-Strauss, *The View from Afar*, p. 118.
26. Claude Lévi-Strauss, "The Place of Anthropology in the Social Sciences," in *Structural Anthropology*, p. 359.
27. Maurice Godelier, interview with the author.
28. François Furet, "Les intellectuels français et le structuralisme," *Preuves*, no. 92 (February 1967): p. 6; reprinted in *L'Atelier de l'histoire*, p. 42.
29. Jean Duvignaud, interview with the author.
30. Ibid.
31. Marcel Gauchet, interview with the author.
32. Pavel, *Le Mirage linguistique*, p. 188.

Bibliography

Adler, Alfred. *Séminaire de Michel Izard*. Laboratoire d'Anthropologie Sociale, November 17, 1988.

Allouch, Jean. *Littoral*, nos. 23–24 (October 1987).

Althusser, Louis. "Freud et Lacan." *La Nouvelle Critique*, nos. 161–62 (December 1964–January 1965); reprinted in *Positions* (Paris: Éditions sociales, 1976).

———. *Lire Le Capital*. Vol. 1. Paris: Petite Collection Maspero, 1971 (1965).

———. *Manifestes philosophiques de Feuerbach*. Paris: PUF, 1960.

———. *Pour Marx*. Paris: Maspero, 1965.

Ariès, Philippe. *Un historien du dimanche*. Paris: Le Seuil, 1982.

Aron, Raymond. *Les Étapes de la pensée sociologique*. Paris: Gallimard, 1967.

Arrivé, Marcel. *Linguistique et psychanalyse*. Paris: Klincksieck, 1987.

Augé, Marc. *Le Rivage Alladian*. Paris: ORSTOM, 1969.

Badiou, Alain. "Le (re)commencement du matérialisme dialectique." *Critique* (May 1967).

Balandier, Georges. *Anthropologie politique*. Paris: PUF, 1967.

———. *Histoire d'autres*. Paris: Stock, 1977.

Balibar, Étienne. *Lire Le Capital*. Vol. 2. Paris: Maspero, 1967 (1965).

Bally, Charles. *Le Langage et la vie*. Paris: Droz, 1965 (1913).

Barthes, Roland. *L'Aventure sémiologique*. Paris: Seuil, 1985. (*The Semiotic Challenge*. Trans. Richard Howard [New York: Hill and Wang, 1988].)

———. *Critique et vérité*. Paris: Seuil, 1966.

———. "De la science à la littérature." *Times Literary Supplement* (1967); reprinted in *Le Bruissement de la langue* (Paris: Seuil, 1984).

———. "De part et d'autre." *Critique*, no. 17 (1961): pp. 915–22; reprinted in *Essais critiques* (Paris: Seuil, 1971).

———. *Le Degré zéro de l'écriture*. Paris: Points-Seuil, 1972 (1953).

———. "Les éléments de sémiologie." *Communications*, no. 4 (1964); reprinted in *L'Aventure sémiologique*.

———. *Essais critiques*. Paris: Points-Seuil, 1971 (1964).

———. "Histoire et littérature: à propos de Racine." *Annales* (May–June 1960).

————. Interview with Georges Charbonnier. *France-Culture*, December 1967.

————. *Michelet par lui-même.*

————. *Mythologies.* 1957. Paris: Seuil.

————. "Saussure, le signe, la démocratie." *Le Discours social,* nos. 3–4 (April 1973); reprinted in *L'Aventure sémiologique* (Paris: Seuil, 1985).

————. "Sociologie et socio-logique." *Informations sur les sciences sociales,* no. 4 (December 1962).

————. *Sur Racine.* Paris: Points-Seuil, 1979 (1963).

————. *Le Système de la mode.* Paris: Seuil, Points-Seuil, 1983 (1967).

Bartoli, Henri. *Économie et création collective.* Paris: Economica, 1977.

Bastide, Roger, ed. *Sens et usages du terme de structure.* Colloquium, January 10–12, 1959. Paris: Mouton, 1972 (1962).

Bataille, Georges. "Un livre humain, un grand livre." *Critique,* no. 115 (February 1956).

Bellour, Raymond. "Entretien avec R. Barthes." *Les Lettres françaises,* no. 1172 (March 2, 1967).

————. *Les Lettres françaises,* no. 1125 (March 31, 1966); reprinted in *Le Livre des autres* (Paris: 10/18, 1978).

Benoist, Jean-Marie. *La Révolution structurale.* Paris: Denoël, 1980.

Bettelheim, Charles. *Calcul économique et formes de propriété.* Paris: Seuil-Maspero, 1970.

Blanchot, Maurice. "L'oubli, la déraison." *Nouvelle Revue française* (October 1961): pp. 676–86; reprinted in *L'Entretien infini* (Paris: Gallimard, 1969).

Bopp, Franz. *Système de conjugaison de la langue sanscrite, comparé à celui des langues grecque, latine, persane et germanique.* Frankfurt am Main, 1816. (*Analytical Comparison of the Sanskrit, Greek, Latin, and Teutonic Languages Showing the Original Identity of Their Grammatical Structure* [Amsterdam: Amsterdam Studies in the Theory and History of Linguistic Science, 1974].)

Boris Souvarine et "La Critique sociale." Ed. Anne Roche. Paris: La Découverte, 1990.

Bourdieu, Pierre. *Choses dites.* Paris: Minuit, 1987.

Boyer, Robert. "La croissance française de l'après-guerre et les modèles macro-économiques." *La Revue économique,* vol. 27, no. 5 (1976).

Brémond, Claude. *Logique du récit.* Paris: Seuil, 1972.

————. "Le message narratif." *Communications,* no. 4. Paris: Seuil, 1964.

de Brunhoff, Suzanne. *Marx on Money.* Trans. Maurice J. Goldbloom. New York: Urizen Books, 1976.

Caillois, Roger. "Illusions à rebours." *Nouvelle Revue française* (December 1, 1954; January 1, 1955).

————. "La réponse de R. Caillois." *Le Monde,* June 28, 1974.

Calvet, Louis-Jean. *Pour et contre Saussure.* Paris: Payot, 1975.

————. *Roland Barthes.* Paris: Flammarion, 1990.

Canetti, Élias. *Masse et puissance.* Paris: Gallimard, 1966.

Canguilhem, Georges. "La décadence de l'idée de progrès." *Revue de métaphysique et de morale,* no. 4 (1987).

————. *Le Normal et le pathologique.* Paris: PUF, 1975 (1966).

————. "Qu'est-ce que la psychologie?" *Revue de métaphysique et de morale* (1958), pp. 12–25, and in *Les Cahiers pour l'analyse,* no. 2 (March 1966), and in Georges Canguilhem, *Études d'histoire et de philosophie des sciences.* Paris: Vrin, 1968.

Castel, Robert. "Les aventures de la pratique." *Le Débat,* no. 41 (September–November 1986).

Castoriadis, Cornelius. "Les divertisseurs." *Le Nouvel Observateur*, June 20, 1977; reprinted in *La Sociéte française* (Paris: 10/18, 1979).

Cavaillès, Jean. *Sur la logique et la théorie des sciences*. Paris: PUF, 1947.

Charbonnier, Georges. *Entretiens avec Claude Lévi-Strauss*. Paris: 10/18, 1969 (1961). (*Conversations with Claude Lévi-Strauss*. Trans. John and Doreen Weightman [London: Jonathan Cape, 1969].)

Châtelet, François. "L'homme, ce Narcisse incertain." *La Quinzaine littéraire*, April 1, 1966.

Chesneaux, Jean. *De la modernité*. Paris: Maspero, 1973.

Chevalier, Jean-Claude. "La Notion de complément chez les grammairiens." Paris: Droz, 1968.

Chevalier, Jean-Claude, and Pierre Encrevé. "La création de revues dans les années soixante." *Langue française*, no. 63 (September 1984).

Clémens, René. "Prolégomènes d'une théorie de la structure." *Revue d'économie politique*, no. 6 (1952).

Cohen-Solal, Annie. *Sartre*. Paris: Gallimard, 1985.

Condorcet, Jean Antoine de. *Esquisse d'un tableau historique des progrès des l'esprit humain* (1793).

Coquet, Jean-Claude. "La sémiotique." In *Les Sciences du langage en France au XXe siècle*, ed. Bernard Pottier. Paris: SELAF, 1980.

Daix, Pierre. *Structuralisme et révolution culturelle*. Paris: Casterman, 1971.

Debray, Régis. *Critique de la raison politique*. Paris: Gallimard, 1981.

de Gandillac, Maurice. In *Entretiens sur la notion de genèse et de structure*. Colloquium at Cerisy, July–August 1959. Paris: Mouton, 1965.

Dehove, Mario. *L'État des sciences sociales en France*. Paris: La Découverte, 1986.

de Ipola, D. R. "Le Structuralisme ou l'histoire en exil." Thesis, 1969.

Deleuze, Gilles. "L'homme, une existence douteuse." *Le Nouvel Observateur*, June 1, 1966.

Derrida, Jacques. "De la grammatologie." *Critique*, no. 223–24 (December 1965).

———. *Positions*. Paris: Minuit, 1972.

Desanti, Jean-Toussaint. *Autrement*, no. 102 (November 1988).

———. *Un destin philosophique*. Paris: Grasset, 1982.

Descombes, Vincent. *Les Enjeux philosophiques des années cinquante*. Paris: Éditions du Centre Georges Pompidou, 1989.

———. "L'équivoque du symbolique." *Confrontations*, no. 3 (1980).

———. *Le Même et l'autre*. Paris: Minuit, 1979.

Domenach, Jean-Marie. "Le requiem structuraliste." In *Le Sauvage et l'ordinateur*. Paris: Seuil, 1976.

———. "Le système et la personne." *Esprit*, no. 360 (May 1967).

Domenach, Jean-Marie, Mikel Dufrenne, Paul Ricoeur, Jean Ladrière, Jean Cuisenier, Pierre Burgelin, Yves Bertherat, and Jean Cornilh. "Structuralismes, idéologies et méthodes." *Esprit*, no. 360 (May 1967).

Dor, Joël. *Introduction à la lecture de Lacan*. Paris: Denoël, 1985.

Dosse, François. *L'Histoire en miettes*. Paris: La Découverte, 1987.

Dreyfus, Hubert L., and Paul Rabinow. *Foucault, un parcours philosophique*. Paris: Gallimard, 1984.

Dubois, Jean. *Le Vocabulaire politique et social en France de 1849 à 1872*. Paris: Larousse, 1962.

Ducrot, Oswald, and Tzvetan Todorov. *Dictionnaire encyclopédique du langage*. Paris: Seuil, 1972.

Dumézil, Georges. *Entretiens avec Didier Éribon*. Paris: Gallimard, 1987.
———. *Mythe et Épopée*. "Introduction." Paris: Gallimard, 1973.
———. *La Religion romaine archaïque*. Paris: Payot, 1966.
Durkheim, Émile. "La prohibition de l'inceste." *L'Année sociologique*, vol. 1 (1898).
Duvignaud, Jean. "Après le fonctionalisme et le structuralisme, quoi?" In *Une anthropologie des turbulences. Hommage à G. Balandier*. 1985.
———. *Chebika*. Paris: Gallimard, 1968; reprinted by Plon (1991).
———. *Le Langage perdu*. Paris: PUF, 1973.
———. *Les Lettres nouvelles*, no. 62 (1958).
Entretiens sur les notions de genèse et de structure. Colloquium at Cerisy, July–August 1959. Paris: Mouton, 1965.
Éribon, Didier. *Michel Foucault*. Paris: Flammarion, 1989.
Etiemble, René. *Évidences* (April 1956).
Fabiani, Jean-Louis. *Les Enjeux philosophiques des années cinquante*. Paris: Éditions du Centre Georges Pompidou, 1989.
Ferry, Luc, and Alain Renaut. *Heidegger et les modernes*. Paris: Grasset, 1988. (*Heidegger and Modernity*. Trans. Franklin Philip [Chicago: University of Chicago Press, 1990].)
———. *La Pensée 68*. Paris: Gallimard, 1985.
Fortes, Meyer, and E. E. Evans-Pritchard, eds. *African Political Systems*. London: Oxford University Press, 1940.
Foucault, Michel. *Actes du Colloque de Royaumont: Nietzsche, Freud, Marx*. Paris: Minuit 1967 (1964).
———. *The Archaeology of Knowledge*. Trans. Alan Sheridan Smith. New York: Pantheon Books, 1972.
———. *Discipline and Punish: The Birth of the Prison*. Trans. Alan Sheridan. New York: Pantheon Books, 1977.
———. *Ethos* (fall 1983). Interview.
———. *Folie et déraison*. Paris: Plon, 1961. (*Madness and Civilization: A History of Insanity in the Age of Reason*. Trans. Richard Howard. New York: Pantheon, 1965].)
———. *The History of Sexuality*. 3 vols. Trans. Robert Hurley. New York: Vintage Books, 1990.
———. *Hommage à Hyppolite*. Paris: PUF, 1969.
———. Interview in *Politique-Hebdo*, March 4, 1976.
———. "Jean Hyppolite, 1907–1968." *Revue de métaphysique et de morale*, vol. 14, no. 2 (April–June 1969).
———. *Lectures pour tous* (1966). INA document, shown on *Océaniques*, FR3, January 13, 1988.
———. *Les Mots et les choses*. Paris: Gallimard, 1966. (*The Order of Things: An Archaeology of the Human Sciences*. New York: Vintage Books, 1973].)
———. *Les Nouvelles littéraires*, June 28, 1984.
———. "Structuralism and Post-Structuralism." *Telos*, vol. 16 (1983); interview with Georges Raulet.
———. "Le structuralisme et l'analyse littéraire." in *Mission culturelle française Information*, French embassy in Tunisia, April 10–May 10, 1987 (1965); unedited tapes of two lectures by Michel Foucault at the Club Tahar Haddad. Centre Michel-Foucault, Bibliothèque du Saluchoir.
———. "Vérité et pouvoir." Interview with M. Fontana, *L'Arc*, no. 70.
Fougeyrollas, Pierre. *Contre Claude Lévi-Strauss, Lacan, Althusser*. Paris: Lavelli, 1976.

Frank, Manfred. *Qu'est-ce que le néo-structuralisme?* Paris: Cerf, 1989. (*What Is Neostructuralism?* Trans. Sabine Wilke and Richard Gray [Minneapolis: University of Minnesota Press, 1989].)

Frege, Gottlob. *Les Fondements de l'arithmétique.* Paris: Seuil, 1969.

Furet, François. "Les intellectuels français et le structuralisme." *Preuves,* no. 92 (February 1967); reprinted in *L'Atelier de l'histoire* (Paris: Flammarion, 1982).

Gadet, Françoise. "Le signe et le sens." *DRLAV, Revue de linguistique,* no. 40 (1989).

Gaston-Granger, Gilles. "Événement et structure dans les sciences de l'homme." *Cahiers de l'ISEA* (December 1959).

———. *Pensée formelle et science de l'homme.* Paris: Aubier, 1960.

Gauchet, Marcel, and Gladys Swain. *La Pratique de l'esprit humain: L'institution asilaire et la révolution démocratique.* Paris: Gallimard, 1980.

Genette, Gérard. "Structuralisme et critique littéraire." *L'Arc,* no. 26; reprinted in *Figures,* vol. 1 (Paris: Seuil, 1966; Points-Seuil, 1976).

George, François. *L'Effet yau de poêle.* Paris: Hachette, 1979.

Georgin, R. *De Lévi-Strauss à Lacan.* 1983.

Godelier, Maurice. *Rationalité et irrationalité en économie.* Paris: Maspero, 1966.

———. "Système, structure et contradiction dans *Le Capital.*" *Les Temps modernes,* no. 246 (November 1966).

Goldmann, Lucien. *Le Dieu caché.* Paris: Gallimard, 1956.

———. In *Entretiens sur les notions de genèse et de structure.* Colloquium at Cerisy, July–August 1959. Paris: Mouton, 1965.

Goubert, Pierre. *Louis XIV et vingt millions de Français.* Paris: Fayard, 1966.

Green, André. *L'Affect.* Paris: PUF, 1970.

———. "Le bon plaisir." *France-Culture,* February 25, 1989.

———. "Le langage dans la psychanalyse." In *Langages: Les Rencontres psychanalytiques d'Aix-en-Provence* (1983). Paris: Les Belles Lettres, 1984.

———. La psychanalyse devant l'opposition de l'histoire et de la structure." *Critique,* no. 194 (July 1963).

———. *Séminaire de Michel Izard.* Laboratoire d'Anthropologie Sociale, 1988.

Greimas, Algirdas Julien. *Du sens.* Paris: Seuil, 1970.

———. "L'actualité du saussurisme." *Le Français moderne,* no. 3 (1956).

———. "L'analyse structurale du récit." *Communications,* no. 8 (1966); reprinted by Points-Seuil, 1981.

———. Preface to Gottlob Frege, *Les Fondements de l'arithmétique* (Paris: Seuil, 1969).

———. *Sémantique structurale.* Paris: Larousse, 1966.

Gross, Maurice. "La création de revues dans les années soixante." *Langue française,* no. 63 (September 1984).

Guéroult, Martia. *Descartes selon l'ordre des raisons.* Paris: Aubier, 1953.

———. *Leçon inaugurale au Collège de France* (December 4, 1951).

———. *Philosophie de l'histoire de la philosophie.* Paris: Aubier, 1979.

Gurvitch, Georges. "Le concept de structure sociale." *Cahiers internationaux de sociologie,* no. 19 (1955).

Habermas, Jürgen. *The Philosophical Discourse of Modernity: 12 Lectures.* Trans. Fredrick Laurence. Cambridge: MIT Press, 1987.

Hagège, Claude. *L'homme de parole.* Paris: Gallimard, Folio, 1985.

Hamon, Hervé, and Philippe Rotman. *Génération.* Vol. 1. Paris: Seuil, 1987.

Hamon, Philippe. "Littérature." In *Les Sciences du langage en France au XXᵉ siècle,* ed. Bernard Pottier. Paris: SELAF, 1980.

Heidegger, Martin. "Le discours du rectorat" (May 27, 1933). *Le Débat*, no. 27 (November 1983).

———. *An Introduction to Metaphysics*. Trans. Ralph Mannheim. New Haven: Yale University Press, 1959.

———. *Lettre sur l'humanisme*. Paris: Aubier, 1983 (1946).

———. *Poetry, Language, Thought*. Trans. A. Hofstadter. New York: Harper and Row, 1971 (1975).

———. *Questions*. Vol. 1. Paris: Gallimard, n.d.

Henry, Paul. "Épistémologie de *L'Analyse automatique du discours* de Michel Pêcheux." In *Introduction to the Translation of M. Pêcheux's Analyse automatique du discours*.

Herbert, Thomas [Michel Pêcheux]. "Reflexions sur la situation théorique des sciences sociales, spécialement de la psychologie sociale." *Les Cahiers pour l'analyse*, no. 2 (March–April 1966); reprinted 1–2.

———. "Remarques pour une théorie générale des idéologies." *Les Cahiers pour l'analyse*, no. 9 (summer 1968).

Hertz, Robert. *Mélanges de sociologie religieuse et folklore*. 1928.

Hjelmslev, Louis. *Language: An Introduction*. Trans. Francis J. Whitfield. Madison: University of Wisconsin Press, 1970.

———. *Prolegomena to a Theory of Language*. Trans. Francis J. Whitfield. Madison: University of Wisconsin Press, 1961.

Hyppolite, Jean. *La Psychanlayse*, vol. 1. Paris: PUF, 1956; with Lacan's response, reprinted in Jacques Lacan, *Écrits* (Paris: Éditions du Seuil, 1966).

Izard, Michel. *Séminaire*. Laboratoire d'Anthropologie Sociale. June 1, 1989.

Jakobson, Roman. "Deux aspects du langage et deux types d'aphasie." In *Essais de linguistique générale*. Paris: Points-Seuil, 1970.

———. *Essais de linguistique générale*. 2 vols. Paris: Points-Seuil, 1970.

———. "Les douze traits de sonorité." In "Phonologie et phonétique" (1956). In *Essais de linguistique générale*.

———. Preface to Tzvetan Todorov, *Théorie de la littérature*. Paris: Seuil, 1965.

———. *Six leçons sur le son et le sens*. Paris: Minuit, 1976; preface by Claude Lévi-Strauss ("Les leçons de la linguistique"), reprinted in *Le Regard éloigné* (Paris: Plon, 1983).

Jamin, Jean. *Les Enjeux philosophiques des années cinquante*. Paris: Éditions Centre Georges Pompidou, 1989.

Juranville, Alain. *Lacan et la philosophie*. Paris: PUF, 1988 (1984).

Kanters, Robert. "Tu causes, tu causes, c'est tout ce que tu sais faire." *Le Figaro*, June 23, 1966.

Koyré, Alexandre. *De la mystique à la science; cours, conférences et documents* (1922–62). Ed. Pietro Redondi. Paris: Éditions de l'École des Hautes Études en Sciences Sociales, 1986.

Kristeva, Julia. "Le sens et la mode." *Critique*, no. 247 (December 1967).

Labrousse, Ernest. *Actes du congrès historique du centenaire de la révolution de 1848*. Paris: PUF, 1948.

———. "La Crise de l'économie française à la fin de l'Ancien Régime et au début de la crise révolutionnaire" (1944).

Lacan, Jacques. "La chose freudienne" (1956). In *Écrits*, vol. 1. ("The Freudian Thing." Trans. Alan Sheridan, in *Écrits: A Selection*.)

———. *Écrits*. Paris: Seuil, 1966.

———. *Écrits: A Selection*. Trans. Alan Sheridan. New York: W. W. Norton, 1977.

———. "L'excommunication." *Ornicar?* (1977).

———. "L'instance de la lettre dans l'inconscient." In *Écrits*, vol. 1. ("The Agency of the Letter in the Unconscious or Reason since Freud." Trans. Alan Sheridan. In *Écrits: A Selection*.)

———. "Position de l'inconscient." *Écrits*, vol. 2.

———. *La Psychanalyse*. Vol. 1. Paris: PUF, 1956.

———. "De la psychose paranoïaque dans ses rapports avec la personnalité." Thesis for medical degree, 1932.

———. "Rapport de Rome" (1953). In *Écrits*, vol. 1. "Report to the Rome Congress Held at the Istituto di Psicologia della Università di Roma, 26 and 27 September, 1953." Trans. Alan Sheridan, in *Écrits: A Selection*.)

———. "Remarques sur le rapport de Daniel Lagache" (1958). In *Écrits*.

———. *Le Séminaire*. Vol. 3: *Les Psychoses* (1955–56). Paris: Seuil, 1981.

———. *Séminaire XX, Encore (1973–1974)*. Paris: Seuil, 1975.

———. "Séminaire sur la lettre volée." In *Écrits*, vol. 1. ("Seminar on the *Purloined Letter*." Trans. Alan Sheridan. In *Écrits: A Selection*.)

———. "Situation de la psychanalyse en 1956." In *Écrits*, vol. 2. Paris: Points-Seuil, 1971.

———. "Le stade du miroir." *Écrits*, vol. 1. ("The Mirror Stage as Formative of the Function of the Ego as Revealed in Psychoanalytic Experience." Trans. Alan Sheridan. In *Écrits: A Selection*.)

———. "Subversion of the Subject and Dialectic of Desire." In *Écrits*, vol. 1.

Lacroix, Jean. "La fin de l'humanisme." *Le Monde*, June 9, 1966.

Laplanche, Jean. *Psychanalyse à l'Université*. Vol. 4, no. 15 (June 1979).

———. "Une révolution sans cesse occultée." Communication aux journées scientifiques de l'Association internationale d'histoire de la psychanalyse, April 23–24, 1988.

Lapouge, Gilles. "Encore un effort et j'aurai épousé mon temps." *La Quinzaine littéraire*, no. 459 (March 16–30, 1986).

Leclaire, Serge. "L'inconscient, une étude psychanalytique." In *L'Inconscient*. Paris: Desclée de Brouwer, 1966; reprinted in *Psychanalyser* (Paris: Points-Seuil, 1968).

———. "L'objet a dans la cure." In *Rompre les charmes*. Paris: InterEditions, 1981 (1971).

Lefort, Claude. "L'échange et la lutte des hommes." *Les Temps modernes*, February 1951; reprinted in Claude Lefort, *Les Formes de l'histoire* (Paris: Gallimard, 1978).

Lemaire, Anika, *Lacan*. Paris: Mardaga, 1977.

Le Roy Ladurie, Emmanuel. *Les Paysans de Languedoc*. Paris: Annales, 1966. (*The Peasants of Languedoc*. Trans. John Day [Urbana: University of Illinois Press, 1974].)

Lévi-Strauss, Claude. "L'analyse structurale en linguistique et en anthropologie." *Word*, vol. 1, no. 2 (1945); reprinted in *Anthropologie structurale*.

———. *Anthropologie structurale*. 2 vols. Paris: Plon, 1958. (*Structural Anthropology*. Trans. Claire Jacobson and Brooke Grundfest Schoepf [New York: Anchor Books, 1967].)

———. *Le Cru et le cuit*. Paris: Plon, 1964. (*The Raw and the Cooked: Introduction to a Science of Mythology*. Vol. 1. Trans. John and Doreen Weightman [New York and Evanston, Ill.: Harper Torchbooks, Harper and Row, 1969].)

———. *De près et de loin*. Paris: Odile Jacob, 1988.

———. "Diogène couché." *Les Temps modernes*, no. 195 (1955).

———. "Le droit au voyage." *L'Express*, September 21, 1956.

———. "Dumézil et les sciences humaines." *France-Culture*, October 2, 1978.

———. *Du miel aux cendres*. Paris: Plon, 1964. (*From Honey to Ashes: Introduction to a Science of Mythology.* Vol. 2. Trans. John and Doreen Weightman [London: Jonathan Cape and Harper and Row, 1973].)

———. "L'Efficace Symbolique." *Revue d'histoire des religions,* no. 1 (1949). ("The Effectiveness of Symbols." Reprinted in *Structural Anthropology,* trans. Claire Jacobson and Brooke Grundfest Schoepf [New York: Anchor Books, 1967].)

———. "History and Anthropology." In *Structural Anthropology.*

———. *L'Homme Nu.* Paris: Plon, 1971. (*The Naked Man: Introduction to a Science of Mythology.* Vol. 4. Trans. John and Doreen Weightman [New York and Evanston, Ill.: Harper Torchbooks, Harper and Row, 1981].)

———. "Des Indiens et leur ethnographe." Excerpts from "*Tristes Tropiques* Soon to Be Published." *Les Temps modernes,* no. 116 (August 1955).

———. Interview with Jean-José Marchand. *Arts* (December 28, 1955).

———. Interview with Raymond Bellour. *Le Monde,* November 5, 1971.

———. "Introduction à l'œuvre de Marcel Mauss." In *Marcel Mauss, Sociologie et anthropologie.* Paris: PUF, 1968 (1950). (*Introduction to the Work of Marcel Mauss.* Trans. Felicity Baker [London: Routledge and Kegan Paul, 1987].)

———. "Leçon inaugurale au Collège de France," January 5, 1960. Reprinted in *Anthropologie structurale,* vol. 2 (Paris: Plon, 1973).

———. *Leroi-Gourhan ou les voies de l'homme.* Paris: Albin Michel, 1988.

———. "Linguistics and Anthropology." In *Supplement to the International Journal of American Linguistics,* vol. 19, no. 2 (April 1953); reprinted in *Structural Anthropology,* trans. Claire Jacobson and Brooke Grundfest Schoepf (New York: Anchor Books, 1967).

———. *The Origin of Table Manners,* trans. John and Doreen Weightman (New York: Harper and Row, 1978).

———. *Paroles données.* Paris: Plon, 1984.

———. *La Pensée sauvage.* Paris: Plon, 1962. (*The Savage Mind* [Chicago: University of Chicago Press, 1966].)

———. *La Potière jalouse.* Paris: Plon, 1985. (*The Jealous Potter.* Trans. Bénédicte Choriet [Chicago: University of Chicago Press, 1988].)

———. "Race et histoire" (1952). Reprinted in *Anthropologie structurale,* vol. 2 (Paris: Plon, 1958).

———. *Le Regard éloigné.* (*The View from Afar.* Trans. Joachim Neugroschel and Phoebe Hoss. New York: Basic Books, 1984].)

———. "Réponse à Dumézil reçu à l'Académie Française." *Le Monde,* July 15, 1979.

———. "Le sorcier et sa magie." *Les Temps modernes,* no. 41 (March 1949); reprinted in *Anthropologie structurale.* Translated as "The Sorcerer and His Magic."

———. *Structural Anthropology.* Trans. Claire Jacobson and Brooke Grundfest Schoepf. New York: Anchor Books, 1967.

———. "La structure et la forme." *Cahiers de l'ISEA,* no. 99 (March 1960), series M, no. 7; reprinted in *Anthropologie structurale,* vol. 2.

———. *Les Structures élémentaires de la parenté.* Paris: PUF, 1949. (*The Elementary Structures of Kinship.* Trans. James Harle Bell, John Richard von Sturmer, and Rodney Needham [London: Eyre and Spottiswoode, 1969].)

———. *Le Totémisme aujourd'hui.* Paris: Plon, 1962.

———. *Tristes Tropiques.* Trans. John and Doreen Weightman. New York: Atheneum, 1974.

———. *La Vie familiale et sociale des Indiens Nambikwara.* Paris: Société des américanistes, 1948.

Lévi-Strauss, Claude, and Roman Jakobson. *L'Homme, II*, no. 1, Mouton (January–April 1962).

———. Interview with Raymond Bellour. *Les Lettres françaises*, no. 1165 (January 12, 1967); reprinted in *Le Livre des autres* (Paris: 10/18, 1978).

Lindenberg, Daniel. *Le Marxisme introuvable*. Paris: 10/18, 1979 (reprint).

Linhart, Robert. *Lénine, les paysans, Taylor*. Paris: Seuil, 1976.

Lipovetsky, Gilles. *L'Ere du vide: Essais sur l'individualisme contemporain*. Paris: Gallimard, 1983.

Lowie, Robert H. "Exogamy and the Classificatory Systems of Relationship." *American Anthropologist*, vol. 17 (April–June 1915).

Lyotard, Jean-François. *La Condition post-moderne*. Paris: Minuit, 1979. (*The Postmodern Condition: A Report on Knowledge*. Trans. Geoff Bennington and Brian Massumi [Minneapolis: University of Minnesota Press, 1984].)

Macherey, Pierre. "La philosophie de la science de Canguilhem." *La Pensée*, no. 113 (January 1964).

———. *Pour une théorie de la production littéraire*. Paris: Maspero, 1966.

Mandrou, Robert. "Trois clés pour comprendre l'histoire de la folie à l'époque classique." *Annales*, no. 4 (July–August 1962).

Marchal, André. *Méthode scientifique et science économique*. Paris: Éditions de Médicis, 1955.

———. In *Sens et usages du terme de structure*. Ed. Roger Bastide. Paris: Mouton, 1972 (1962).

———. *Systèmes et structures*. Paris: PUF, 1959.

Marion, Jean-Luc. "Une modernité sans avenir." *Le Débat*, no. 4 (September 1980).

Marksey, Richard, and Eugenio Donato, eds. *The Structuralist Controversy: The Languages of Criticism and the Sciences of Man*. Baltimore and London: Johns Hopkins University Press, 1970 and 1972.

Martin, Serge. *Langage musical, sémiotique des systèmes*. Paris: Klincksieck, 1978.

Marx, Karl. *Le Capital*. Paris: Éditions sociales, 1960.

Matonti, Frédérique. "Entre Argenteuil et les barricades: *La Nouvelle Critique* et les sciences sociales." *Cahiers de l'Institut d'histoire du temps présent*, no. 11 (April 1989).

Mauss, Marcel. "Essai sur le don. Forme et raison de l'échange dans les sociétés archaïques." In *L'Année sociologique* (1921). (*The Gift*. Trans. I. Cunnison [London: Cohen and West, 1954].)

Mendel, Gérard. *La Chasse structurale*. Paris: Payot, 1977.

———. *Enquête par un psychanalyste sur lui-même*. Paris: Stock, 1981.

Merleau-Ponty, Maurice. *Phénoménologie de la perception*. Paris: Gallimard, 1945.

———. *Signes*. Paris: Gallimard, 1960.

———. *La Structure du comportement*. Paris: PUF, 1942.

———. "Sur la phénoménologie du langage." Lecture delivered to the First International Phenomenology Colloquium in Brussels, 1951. Reprinted in *Signes*. (*Signs*. Trans. Richard McCleary [Evanston, Ill.: Northwestern University Press, n.d.].)

Merleau-Ponty, Maurice, et al. 6ᵉ Colloque de Bonneval. *L'Inconscient*. Paris: Desclée de Brouwer, 1966.

Métraux, Alfred. *L'Ile de Pâques*. Paris: Gallimard, 1941; 2d ed., 1956.

Miller, Jacques-Alain. *Ornicar?* no. 24 (1981).

Morin, Edgar. "Arguments, trente ans après." Interviews. *La Revue des revues*, no. 4 (fall 1987).

———. *L'Esprit du temps*. Paris: Grasset, 1962.

———. *Le Vif du sujet*. Paris: Seuil, 1969.

Mounin, Georges. *Introduction à la sémiologie*. Paris: Minuit, 1970.

Nadeau, Maurice. *Les Lettres nouvelles* (July 1953).

Naïr, K. "Marxisme ou structuralisme?" In *Contre Althusser*. Paris: 10/18, 1974.

Nasio, Jean-David. *Les Sept Concepts cruciaux de la psychanalyse*. Paris: Éditions Rivages, 1988.

Nicolaï, André. *Comportement économique et structures sociales*. Paris: PUF, 1960.

Nietzsche, Friedrich. *The Gay Science*. Trans. Walter Kaufman. New York: Vintage Books, 1974.

———. *Human, all too human*. Trans. R. J. Hollingdale. Cambridge: Cambridge University Press, 1986.

———. *Human, all too human*. Trans. Walter Kaufman. New York: Portable Nietzsche, Viking Portable Library, 1968.

———. *Untimely Meditations*. Trans. R. J. Hollingdale. Cambridge: Cambridge University Press, 1983.

———. *La Volonté de puissance*. 2 vols. Paris: Gallimard, n.d.

Nora, Pierre. *Les Français d'Algérie*. Paris: Julliard, 1961.

———. *Les Lieux de mémoire, La République*. Paris: Gallimard, 1984.

Ogilvie, Bertrand. *Lacan, le sujet*. Paris: PUF, 1987.

Ortigues, Edmond. *Critique*, no. 189 (February 1963).

Ory, Pascal, and Jean-François Sirinelli. *Les Intellectuels en France, de l'affaire Dreyfus à nos jours*. Paris: Armand Colin, 1986.

Pavel, Thomas. *Le Mirage linguistique*. Paris: Minuit, 1988.

Pêcheux, Michel. *L'Analyse automatique du discours*. Paris: Dunod, 1969.

Perrot, Michelle. *Essais d'ego-histoire*. Paris: Gallimard, 1987.

Perroux, François. *Comptes de la nation*. Paris: PUF, 1949.

———. In *Sens et usages du terme de structure*. Ed. Roger Bastide. Paris: Mouton, 1972 (1962).

Piaget, Jean. *Éléments d'épistémologie génétique*. Paris: PUF, 1950.

———. In *Entretiens sur les notions de genèse et de structure*. Colloquium at Cerisy, July–August 1959. Paris: Mouton, 1965.

———. *Psychologie et épistémologie*. Paris: PUF, 1970 (1947, Amsterdam).

———. In *Le Structuralisme*. Collection "Que sais-je?" Paris: PUF, n.d.

Picard, Raymond. *Nouvelle Critique ou nouvelle imposture*. Paris: J.-J. Pauvert, 1965.

Pinguet, Maurice. *Le Débat*, no. 41 (September–November 1986).

Pinto, Louis. *Les Philosophes entre le lycée et l'avant-garde*. Paris: L'Harmattan, 1987.

Pommier, René. *Assez décodé*. Paris: Éditions Roblot, 1978.

———. *R. Barthes, Ras le bol!* Paris: Éditions Roblot, 1987.

Pouillon, Jean. "L'œuvre de Claude Lévi-Strauss." *Les Temps modernes*, no. 126 (July 1956); reprinted in Jean Pouillon, *Fétiches sans fétichisme* (Paris: Maspero, 1975).

———. *Séminaire de Michel Izard*. Laboratoire d'Anthropologie Sociale, November 24, 1988.

Pouillon, Jean, Marc Barbut, Algirdas Julien Greimas, Maurice Godelier, Pierre Bourdieu, Pierre Macherey, and J. Ehrmann. "Problèmes du structuralisme." *Les Temps modernes*, no. 246 (November 1966).

Propp, Vladimir. *Morphologia della fiaba*. Turin: Einaudi, 1966 (*Morphology of the Folktale* [Austin: University of Texas Press, 1968].)

———. *Les Racines historiques du conte*. Paris: Gallimard, 1983. (*Theory and History of Folkore*. Trans. Ariadna Y. Martin and Richard P. Martin [Minneapolis: University of Minnesota Press, 1984].)

Radcliffe-Brown, A. R. "The Study of Kinship Systems." *Journal of the Royal Anthropology Institute*, 1941.
Revel, Jean-François. "Le rat et la mode." *L'Express*, May 22, 1967.
———. "Sartre en ballottage." *L'Express*, no. 802 (November 7–13, 1966).
Rey, Jean-Michel. "La philosophie du monde scientifique et industriel." In *Histoire de la philosophie*, ed. François Châtelet. Paris: Hachette, 1973.
Rodinson, Maxime. "Racisme et civilisation." *Nouvelle Critique*, no. 66 (1955).
Roudinesco, Élisabeth. *Les Enjeux philosophiques des années cinquante*. Paris: Éditions du Centre Georges Pompidou, 1989.
———. *Histoire de la psychanalyse en France*. Paris: Seuil, 1986.
Rousset, Jean. *Forme et signification: Essais sur les structures littéraires de Corneille à Claudel*. Paris: José Corti, 1962.
Roustang, François. *Lacan*. Paris: Minuit, 1986.
———. *Sémantique structurale*. Paris: Larousse, 1966.
Roy, Claude. "Claude Lévi-Strauss ou l'homme en question." *La Nef*, no. 28 (1959).
———. "Un grand livre civilisé: *La Pensée sauvage*." *Libération*, June 19, 1962.
Saint-Sernin, Bertrand. *Revue de métaphysique et de morale* (January 1985).
Saussure, Ferdinand de. *Cours de linguistique générale*. Paris: Payot, 1965 (1915).
Sartre, Jean-Paul. *Existentialism Is a Humanism*. Trans. and intro. Philip Mairet. Brooklyn: Haskell House, 1977.
Schorske, Carl. *Fin de siècle Vienna*. New York: Alfred A. Knopf, 1979.
Serres, Michel. "Géométrie de la folie." *Mercure de France*, no. 1188 (August 1962): pp. 683–96, and no. 1189 (September 1962): pp. 63–81. Reprinted in *Hermès ou la communication* (Paris: Minuit, 1968).
———. "Structure et importation: des mathématiques aux mythes" (November 1961). Reprinted in *Hermès ou la communication* (Paris: Minuit, 1968).
———. *La Traduction*. Paris: Minuit, 1974.
Sève, Lucien. *Structuralisme et dialectique*. Paris: Messidor, 1984.
Sheridan, Alan. *Écrits: A Selection*. New York: W. W. Norton, 1977.
Sichère, Bernard. *Le Moment lacanien*. Paris: Grasset, 1983.
Simonis, Yvan. *Lévi-Strauss ou la passion de l'inceste*. Paris: Champs-Flammarion, 1990 (1968).
Sirinelli, Jean-François. *Génération intellectuelle*. Paris: Fayard, 1988.
Sollers, Philippe. "Le bon plaisir de J. Kristeva." *France-Culture*, December 10, 1988.
———. "Littérature et totalité" (1966). In *L'Ecriture et l'expérience des limites*. Paris: Point-Seuil, 1968.
Sperber, Dan. *Qu'est-ce que le structuralisme? Le structuralisme en anthropologie*. Paris: Points-Seuil, 1968.
Starobinski, Jean. "Les anagrammes de Ferdinand Saussure." *Mercure de France*, February 1964.
———. *Les Mots sous les mots*. Paris: Gallimard, 1971.
Steiner, Georges. *Martin Heidegger*. Paris: Flammarion, 1981.
Stocking, George W. *Histoires de l'anthropologie: XVIe–XIXe siècles*. Paris: Klincksieck, 1984.
Terray, Emmanuel. *Le Marxisme devant les sociétés primitives*. Paris: Maspero, 1969.
Todorov, Tzvetan. "La description de la signification en littérature." *Communciations*, no. 4. Paris: Seuil, 1964.
———. *Théories du symbole*. Paris: Le Seuil, 1977. (*Theories of the Symbol*. Trans. Catharine Porter [Ithaca, N.Y.: Cornell University Press, 1982].)
Torrès, Félix. *Déjà vu*. 1986.

Trubetzkoy, Nicolai. "La phonologie actuelle." In *Psychologie du langage* (1933).

Vattimo, Gianni. *La Fin de la modernité*. Paris: Seuil, 1987 (1985).

Verdès-Leroux, Jeannine. *Le Réveil des somnambules*. Paris: Fayard, 1987.

Vernant, Jean-Pierre. In *Entretiens sur les notions de genèse et de structure*. Colloquium at Cerisy, July–August 1959. Paris: Mouton, 1965.

———. "Le mythe hésiodique des races" (1960). In *Mythe et pensée chez les Grecs*. Vol. 1. Paris: Maspero, 1970.

———. "Le mythe hésiodique des races: Essai d'analyse structurale." *Revue de l'histoire des religions* (1960).

Verstraeten, Pierre. "Claude Lévi-Strauss ou la tentation du néant." *Les Temps modernes*, no. 206 (July 1963).

Viet, Jean. *Les Méthodes structuralistes*. Paris: Mouton, 1965.

Vilar, Pierre. *La Catalogne dans l'Espagne moderne: Recherches sur les fondements économiques des structures nationales*. Paris: SEVPEN, 1962.

Vincent, Jean-Marie. "Le théoricisme et sa rectification." In *Contre Althusser*. Paris: 10/18, 1974.

Wagemann, Ernst. *Introduction à la théorie du mouvement des affaires*. Paris: Payot, 1932.

———. *La Stratégie économique*. Paris: Payot, 1938.

Wagner, Robert Léon. Foreword to his *Introduction to French Linguistics* (1947). Quoted by Jean-Claude Chevalier and Pierre Encrevé.

Index

Compiled by Hassan Melehy

François Dosse received his degree in history from the University of Paris-Vincennes in 1972, and passed the prestigious agregation exam the following year. In 1974, he began teaching at Pontoise High School, and five years later began working on his doctorate, under Jean Chesneaux, on the Annales School and the media since 1968, which became the basis for his first best-selling book, *L'histoire en miettes: Des "Annales" à la "nouvelle histoire"* (1987) (published in translation as *New History in France: The Triumph of the Annales* [1994]). Today, Dosse teaches at the University of Paris-Nanterre and at the Political Science Institution in Paris, and is a guest lecturer at the University of Lausanne, where he lectures on historiography, methodology, historical epistemology, and the relationship between history and the social sciences. He is the author of a rapidly growing list of publications, the most recent of which is *L'Empire du Sens, l'humanisation des sciences humaines* (forthcoming in translation from the University of Minnesota Press). He is also on the editorial board of *EspaceTemps*, and is currently working on an intellectual biography of Paul Ricoeur.

Deborah Glassman received a Ph.D. in French from Yale University in 1982. She is the author of *Marguerite Duras: Fascinating Vision and Narrative Cure* (1990), among other shorter works, and directed the Paris Center for Critical Studies from 1988 to 1992. She is working on a guide to ethnic eating in Paris, where she has lived and worked since 1988.